JUVENILE DELINQUENCY AND JUVENILE JUSTICE

ROY LOTZ
John Jay College of Criminal Justice

ERIC D. POOLE
Auburn University

ROBERT M. REGOLI
University of Colorado, Boulder

WITH A FOREWORD BY JAMES F. SHORT, JR.

RANDOM HOUSE, INC. NEW YORK

First Edition
987654321

Library of Congress Cataloging in Publication Data
Lotz, Roy, 1943–
Juvenile delinquency and juvenile justice.
Includes bibliographies and index.
1. Juvenile delinquency—United States.
2. Juvenile justice, Administration of—United States.
I. Poole, Eric D., 1950– II. Regoli, Robert M.
III. Title.
HV9104.L67 1985 364.3′6′0973 84-17874
ISBN 0-394-33037-4

Manufactured in the United States of America
Cover design by Dana Kasarsky Design
Cover photo by Leonard Speier

Chapter Opener Photo Credits

Page 1: Michael Hanulak/Photo Researchers; *page 32*: Joel Gordon; *page 56*: Paul Conklin; *page 88*: Jim Anderson/ Woodfin Camp & Associates; *page 118*: Donald Patterson/Stock, Boston; *page 146*: Paolo Koch/Photo Researchers; *page 168*: Arthur Tress; *page 196*: Michael D. Sullivan; *page 228*: Historical Pictures Service; *page 252*: Sylvia Johnson/Woodfin Camp & Associates; *page 304*: Nancy J. Pierce/Photo Researchers; *page 332*: Dani Carpenter/The Picture Cube; *page 370*: Bill Powers/Criminal Justice Photos.

Dedicated to my son Travis.
RL

To my mother and father who made it all possible.
To my spouse Zoë and my daughter Heather
who make it all worthwhile.
EDP

For Andrea, Adam, and John D. Lillywhite—
an inspirational teacher.
RMR

Foreword

Writers of good textbooks rarely receive the credit their labors deserve. The world of academia places its highest value on research and theoretical work which produces knowledge, rather than on communication of knowledge to those outside the academic community.

While I subscribe to the values represented by these priorities, I believe we slight the importance of high quality writing for the classroom and for public consumption in general. We often complain about failures to understand what we have to say, on the part of policy makers, professionals in law enforcement, corrections, and the judiciary, and the public. We complain, too, of inadequate mass media coverage of our research. Yet most of us write primarily for specialists in our own disciplines—often within rather esoteric corners of those disciplines—and we make little effort to communicate effectively to these audiences.

A strong case can be made, I believe, for raising substantially the value placed on all forms of communication outside the professional journals and books in which we publish primarily for other social scientists. It is no longer necessary to make the case for the importance of applied work in the basic social science disciplines. That case has been made many times, effectively and eloquently (see, e.g., Rossi, 1981; Whyte, 1982; Freeman et al., 1983) and that battle has been won. But most of that effort has been devoted to working with social policy makers and those who implement policy. Equally important—more so in the long run—is effective communication with those who will constitute the policy makers and implementers, and the voters, in the future. It is they who must make decisions concerning what to do about crime and delinquency, and the many other hazards confronted by communities, states, nations—indeed throughout the world. We must hope they will do so guided by wisdom born of understanding. Toward that end, communication of the realities, including the complexities, of such problems as crime and delinquency is a vital component.

Juvenile Delinquency and Juvenile Justice is a lucid and comprehensive treatment of these realities. Without slighting the complexities, it presents clearly what is known about juvenile delinquency, what has been and is being done about it. By focusing on public perceptions, it addresses directly the sorts of problems of understanding with which students are faced outside the classroom.

The authors come well prepared to their task. Each is a contributing scholar to the base of knowledge about juvenile delinquency and juvenile justice. They have "paid their dues." It is a pleasure to recommend this book to those who will have the pleasure of learning from it.

James F. Short, Jr.
Washington State University

REFERENCES

ROSSI, PETER H.
1980 "The challenge and opportunities of applied social research." *American Sociological Review* 45(December):889–904.

WHYTE, WILLIAM FOOTE
1982 "Social inventions for solving human problems." *American Sociological Review* 47(February):1–13.

FREEMAN, HOWARD; RUSSELL H. DYNES; PETER H. ROSSI; AND WILLIAM FOOTE WHYTE (EDS.)
1983 *Applied Sociology.* San Francisco: Jossey-Boss.

Preface

Juvenile Delinquency and Juvenile Justice is a book intended to provide broad coverage, so that both students and professors will be able to explore those parts of the field which they find of particular interest or importance. In contrast to other delinquency texts, which tend to either deemphasize sociological criminology or criminal justice, we have tried to include material that will be of interest to both aspects of the discipline. Specifically, the first half of the book is slanted more toward sociology, the latter half toward criminal justice.

In addition to extensive coverage, we also focus on a few issues that are sometimes given short shrift. These are dealt with in the first two chapters. First, we look at the basic questions that continue to inspire disagreement among criminologists: (1) How serious is the problem of crime and delinquency? (2) Who is largely responsible for the present level of crime and delinquency? and (3) How can crime and delinquency be controlled and reduced? Second, we take a long look at public perceptions. Attitudes and opinions of the general public, we argue, are a fundamental part of the juvenile and criminal justice systems, but these attitudes and opinions have often been misunderstood, thus giving rise to questionable official policies.

Organizationally, we have chosen to focus on institutions. This means, quite simply, that there is one chapter on the family and delinquency. By taking this kind of institutional approach, we can present a broader view of each institution, then delve into the possible links each has with delinquency. The family and delinquency, for example, is a large topic which has over the years included issues such as father's absence, mother's employment, black matriarchy, emotional closeness between parents and children, supervision, punitiveness, and so on. Presenting all of this material in the same chapter provides more unity and clarity than is possible in books that include references to these topics in eight or ten chapters on delinquency theory.

Finally, we have included six ethnographic accounts of delinquency and seven excerpts describing delinquency in other cultures and societies (for example, China, Costa Rica, Cuba, Japan, and the Soviet Union). The ethnographic accounts give a feel for or inside look into everyday life as experienced by people involved in delinquency or its control. How these are interpreted and analyzed depends on the reader. The accounts from other cultures are intended to stimulate readers to the realization that delinquency and its control are not everywhere the same; in some ways, each culture's delinquency problem is unique.

Many people have contributed to the successful completion of this work. Bert Lummus, Lisa Moore, and Mary Shuford of Random House have proded and guided us along the way. Professors Lois B. DeFleur (Washington State University), Travis Hirschi (University of Arizona), James F. Short, Jr. (Washington State University), and Charles Thomas (University of Florida) have taught and encouraged us. Others, too, however, have been helpful in the preparation of this work. Paul Melevin (Washington State University) proofread each chapter, and Professors John D. Hewitt (Ball State University), Andrew W. Miracle, Jr. (Texas Christian University), and Ralph Weisheit (Illinois State University) read and commented on segments of the work. We also gratefully acknowledge the thoughtful comments of our colleagues whom Random House asked to review our work and who brought alternative interpretations to our attention. We extend our thanks to Roy L. Austin (Pennsylvania State University), William Sims Bainbridge (Harvard University), Abraham S. Blumberg (University of Missouri-Kansas City), Donald R. Cressey (University of California-Santa Barbara), Nanette J. Davis (Portland State University), Robert C. Evans (Louisiana State University), Frederick Galt (Dutchess College), Forrest J. Harris (University of Minnesota), Vincent J. Hoffman (Michigan State University), Lloyd W. Klemke (Oregon State University), Edward Latessa (University of Cincinnati), and Joseph Waldron (Youngstown State University). Gloria Portas of the Department of Sociology and Marilyn Sena of the Institute of Behavioral Sciences both at the University of Colorado are gratefully acknowledged for their typing and editorial assistance. And, while it sometimes goes without saying, our spouses and friends provided us with invaluable support. Each one made the task easier than it otherwise would have been.

Juvenile Delinquency and Juvenile Justice reflects our joint efforts. Some wrote more words; conceived of more ideas; managed to "keep the boat afloat" and steer the project toward a successful completion; and some provided much needed emotional support. In the end, however, *Juvenile Delinquency and Juvenile Justice* reflects our collective efforts and approach to the topic. Together, we assume responsiblity for its content.

Roy Lotz
Eric D. Poole
Robert M. Regoli

Contents

Foreword vii

Preface ix

1 THE NATURE OF CRIME AND DELINQUENCY 3

Introduction 3
Definitions 3
Concern About Delinquency 5

Two Opposing Views 7

The Problem 8
The Alarmist View 8
The Reassuring View 9
Research on the Problem of Crime and Delinquency 10
Europe's Dead-End Kids 14

The Blame 17
The Alarmist View 17
The Reassuring View 18
Research on Who Is Responsible 18

The Solution 22
The Reassuring View 22
The Alarmist View 24
Evaluating the Proposed Solutions 25

Summary 26

Discussion Questions 28

References 28

2 PUBLIC PERCEPTIONS OF CRIME AND DELINQUENCY 33

Introduction 33

The Importance of Public Perceptions 34
Police Need Cooperation 34
Citizens in the System 34
Cooperation Reflects Attitudes 35
Courts Need Citizen Support 35
Prisons Need Support 36
Legislators Need Public Support 36
Stirring Up the Public 36
Public Tolerance Matters 37
Public Perceptions Misunderstood 37

The Problem 38

The Blame 42

The Solution 44

Media Influences 47

Summary 50

Discussion Questions 51

References 52

3 FAMILY AND DELINQUENCY 57

Introduction 57

The Family in Transiton 58
Research Findings 63

Parenting Skills 68
Costa Rica 70

Parental Attachment 71

Social Class 72

Summary 75

Discussion Questions 77
Assault With A Deadly Weapon 78

References 84

4 SCHOOLS AND DELINQUENCY 89

Introduction 89

Schools in Decline 90
Misbehavior and Fear 90
Transience 91
Scholarship 91
Teacher Inadequacies 94
Urban Schools 95

Schools and Delinquency: Four Theories 96
Loss of Teacher Authority 96
Regimentation and Revenge 98
Israel 99
Tracking 100
IQ and Delinquency 102

Research 103

Summary 107

Discussion Questions 108
To Become Somebody 109

References 115

5 ADOLESCENCE, PEERS, AND DELINQUENCY 119

Adolescence 119

Peer Groups 121
A Youthquake in Russia 125
Research 127

Peers and Male Delinquency 131

Peers and Female Delinquency 135
Konopka's Theory 135
Adler's Theory 137
Simon's Theory 138
Are Girls Catching Up? 138

Summary 139

Discussion Questions 140

References 141

6 BIOLOGICAL AND PSYCHOLOGICAL THEORIES 147

What Theories Are 147

Some Early Explanations 149

Biological Theories 150
Lombroso and Positivism 150
Physique, Temperament, and Behavior 152
Genetics and Crime 152
Chromosomal Abnormalities 154
Blood Chemistry and Deviance 154

Psychological Theories 156
Intelligence 156

Psychopathy 157
Fearlessness 158
Hyperactivity 159
Runaway Delinquents 160
Theories of Aggression 160

Summary 163

Discussion Questions 164

References 165

7 SOCIOLOGICAL THEORIES: THE CHICAGO SCHOOL AND ANOMIE 169

The Chicago School 169
Clifford Shaw and Henry McKay 170

Social Control and Deviance in Cuba 174

Edwin Sutherland 177
Walter Miller 179

Anomie Theories 181
Robert K. Merton 182
Albert Cohen 183
Richard Cloward and Lloyd Ohlin 186

Broken Earth 187

Summary 189

Discussion Questions 190
Crime as Work 191

References 194

8 SOCIOLOGICAL THEORIES: CONTROL AND LABELING 197

Introduction 197

Control Theory 198
Stake in Conformity 198
Internal, Direct, and Indirect Controls 200
Drifting into Delinquency 201
Bond to Society 203

Research on Control Theory 205

Labeling Theory 208
The Dramatization of Evil 208
Primary and Secondary Deviation 210
Moral Entrepreneurs 211
Radical Nonintervention 213

Research on Labeling Theory 215

Summary 216
Why Freddy Got His Gun 219

Discussion Questions 218

References 226

9 ORIGINS OF THE JUVENILE COURT 229

The Early History of Institutional Control 231

Contemporary History 239

Recent Developments 246

Summary 247

Discussion Questions 248

References 249

10 THE CONTEMPORARY JUVENILE COURT 253

Juvenile Justice Processing: An Overview 253
The Police 254
Court Intake 255
Court Hearings 256

Juvenile Court Jurisdiction 257

Waiver of Juvenile Court Jurisdiction 259
The Impact of Kent *v.* United States *261*
*Post-*Kent *Developments 263*

Detention 264
Screening Procedures 264
Detention Criteria 265
Time Limitations 267
Secure Detention: Children in Jail 268
The Nature of Jails and Their Effect on Youth 269
Alternatives to Secure Detention 271

Court Intake 273

Juvenile Court Dispositions 274
Institutionalization 276
Probation 278
Fines and Restitution 279
Duration of Dispositional Orders 280
Revocation of Probation and Changes in Dispositional Orders 280
Aftercare 281

Public Access to Juvenile Court Proceedings and Records 282
The Right to Public Trial 282
Confidentiality of Juvenile Court Records 283
Media Involvement 283
Destruction of Records 284

Summary 285

Discussion Questions 286
The Child Savers 287

References 299

11 JUVENILE DIVERSION 305

Questions About Juvenile Diversion 305
What Is Diversion? 306
Who Should Be Diverted? 307
When Should Youth Be Diverted? 307
Where Should Youth Be Diverted? 308

The Role of the Police in Diversion 309
Police Discretion 309
Rationales for Police Diversion 310

Japan as Number One 311

Types of Police Diversion 313

Some Warnings 316

Court Diversion Alternatives 316
Informal Adjustment 316
Mediation 317
Youth Service Bureaus 319
Community Youth Boards 319

Issues in Program Evaluation 320

The Impact of Diversion on the Juvenile Justice System 323
Increased Efficiency 324
Increased Effectiveness 325

Summary 327

Discussion Questions 328

References 329

12 JUVENILE CORRECTIONS 333

Introduction 333

Conceptual Models 335

Inmate Adaptations 338
The Deprivation Perspective 338
The Importation Perspective 339
The Contextual Perspective 340

Correctional Evaluation 343
The Focus of Evaluation Research 343
Recidivism as an Evaluative Criterion 345
A View from the Inside 347
Reviews of Evaluation Research 347

An Alternative Corrections Strategy 349
Community Involvement 350
The Integration of Youth 352

Summary 354

Discussion Questions 355
Manchild in the Promised Land 356

References 366

13 CRITICAL ISSUES IN JUVENILE JUSTICE 371

A Legacy of Failure 371
Ideology and Policy 373

Contemporary Concerns and Points of Departure 375
Age of Accountability 376
The Status Offense Controversy 378

Children's Rights 382

Conclusion 385

Discussion Questions 387

References 388

GLOSSARY 391

INDEX 397

JUVENILE DELINQUENCY AND JUVENILE JUSTICE

SCREAMING EAGLES

1 The Nature of Crime and Delinquency

INTRODUCTION

Definitions

People are expected to obey society's rules—and most of them do most of the time, which makes social life fairly regular and predictable. This also makes the social sciences possible, since they depend on generalizations about the main patterns around which everyday life is organized. But when we look at the world around us, it is apparent that conformity is not complete. Rules are violated, and if we do not observe this fact personally, it is brought forcefully to our attention by the news media and the fictional dramas in movies, television shows, and books. People rape, rob, and assault. They join exotic cults, experience psychotic episodes, smoke pot, place bets with bookies, and commit suicide. A student of society needs to understand deviance as well as conformity in order to make sense of life in the modern United States.

Social scientists looking into deviance have traditionally focused on six major types: suicide, drug use, alcoholism, mental disorders, sexual deviance (principally prostitution and homosexuality), and crime and delinquency (Akers, 1977). In other societies the list of major kinds of deviance might well be quite different; even within the United States, there are disputes and challenges to these six areas. For example, there are current movements to portray homosexuality and drug use as elements of an acceptable "alternative lifestyle." Similarly, with the modern movements advocating health and physical fitness, a clean environment, and the end of racism and discrimination, new attempts are aimed at defining as deviant such behaviors as telling ethnic jokes, appearing overweight in public, smoking cigarettes in taxis and restaurants, and being a "male chauvinist" (Baker, 1980).

One might expect that crime and delinquency would be the least debatable variety of the six kinds of deviance—the one that no pressure group could redefine as permissible behavior. This expectation is partly true; crime continues to retain its traditional meaning (activity that the criminal law declares punishable), and it has few apologists. The scope of delinquency, however, is in transition, with its traditional definition under attack in recent years. Beginning at about the turn of the century, delinquency was defined broadly because officials and commentators were so optimistic that they could treat and cure it. States generally included three categories in their delinquency laws in those early years: (1) *crimes*—specific offenses that are punishable whether committed by adults or by juveniles, (2) *status offenses*—specific offenses (such as truancy, incorrigibility, curfew violations, and running away from home) that juveniles can be punished for but adults cannot, and (3) violations of the *omnibus clause,* a clause some states included in their delinquency laws that was meant to cover anything the more specific statutes inadvertently left out. One example of the omnibus or "catch-all" clause is "deports self so as to injure self or others"; another one is "in an occupation or situation dangerous to self or others" (Levin and Sarri, 1974). Such phrasing made the omnibus clauses so vague that almost any behavior or condition could be construed as delinquent.

In the 1970s and 1980s, delinquency laws changed in some states, a change stimulated by the U.S. Supreme Court decision in the 1967 case *In re Gault,* which criticized traditional juvenile court procedures and juvenile delinquency laws. Some states responded by dropping their omnibus clauses; critics had claimed that such clauses were hopelessly imprecise (and thus contrary to legal ideals, according to which laws should be specific) and gave undue authority to officials, allowing them to arrest and confine juveniles almost at whim. Some states also removed status offenses from the books, so that these are no longer considered forms of delinquency. Reformers contended that these activities were too trivial to warrant intervention by the courts or police. But after striking status offenses from the category of juvenile delinquency, many states have brought them back under another name, such as PINS (persons in need of supervision), MINS (minors in need of supervision), or CHINS (children in need of supervision). In a purely technical sense, then, the scope of juvenile delinquency is becoming more limited to crime. But juveniles are still being arrested and detained for the same status offenses as they were many years ago.

Delinquency is almost invariably defined legally. It is behavior that delinquency laws mention. On the other hand, the term *delinquent* need not be defined legally. Long ago, scholars of a legalistic bent would define a juvenile delinquent as a person who has been declared delinquent in a juvenile court hearing. But sociologically, our interest lies in people who commit delinquent acts and why they do so; when this is our focus, it is not important whether the person was caught, arrested, turned over to the court, and found to be officially delinquent. This process tells us more about the juvenile justice system than about the individual juvenile. Thus, the juvenile delinquent is a person who is a juvenile and who has committed any activities that are violations of law. This is a nonlegal definition, and it is the definition scholars use when they conduct studies of unofficial delinquency. Throughout this book we will be citing the results of many such studies.

Concern about Delinquency

There is a great deal of interest in juvenile delinquency. There are 3,000 courts that handle delinquency cases. Police departments in most large and some medium size cities have special bureaus devoted to handling juveniles. Numerous treatment programs have been developed to rehabilitate juvenile offenders. At colleges and universities, nearly all sociology and criminal justice departments offer a delinquency course, although these departments almost never teach a course that deals with the many other aspects of adolescent life. And the delinquency of other age groups is entirely ignored; there are, for example, no schools with a course devoted wholly to the delinquency of the middle-aged or of senior citizens. Thus, when juveniles are studied, their delinquency is emphasized; and if any age group's delinquencies are studied, it is juveniles'.

There is no law that juvenile delinquency has to receive such lavish attention; one textbook on developmental psychology allots it no more space than anorexia nervosa—one page (Berger, 1980). Conceivably, the whole society could be equally as blasé and assign the subject of delinquency very little importance. But in fact delinquency has typically attracted considerable attention. Perhaps this emphasis on juvenile delinquency is an outgrowth of America's preoccupations with the related topics of law, youth, and social problems.

Americans have a special interest in law because it provides an official seal of approval for particular norms. The United States lacks the universal traditions and beliefs that older European, Asian, and African societies have. Citizens represent diverse backgrounds and ancestries, so they often disagree about which norms are right, which beliefs are true, which values are sacred. Therefore, some Americans turn to the law (courts and legislatures) to show that their norms are the officially accepted ones, the ones approved by society as a whole. Law thus fills the void created when people cannot agree on norms (Diamond, 1971). In some of these cases, people try to impose their morality on other groups in the society, turning what they see as sins or immorality into crime. Prohibition is the most famous example from the past; the current controversies over abortion, busing, legalization of marijuana, and school prayer reflect more contemporary ones. Even aside from these issues of morality, the United States would still be a very litigious society. It has more than 700,000 lawyers—a figure predicted to reach 1 million by the mid-1990s (Naisbitt, 1984)—who use the courts to settle disputes over land, taxes, contracts, and other economic issues. Finally, people make innumerable demands on government to assist them, including those people who consistently complain about government regulation and red tape. "There ought to be a law" represents the broad, activist view that law should be used to set policies and attain goals—not ritualistically follow age-old precedents (Schlossman, 1977).

America is also said to be child-centered, a trait not found much in the distant past or in certain other societies. DeMause (1974) claims that children throughout the world received worse treatment the farther back in time one goes. Infanticide was common until the fourth century A. D.; indeed "London Bridge is falling down" refers to child sacrifice to the river gods. Abandonment was common from the fourth to the thirteenth centuries, and many children died before the age of five because they received so little attention. In colonial New England, children began to get more attention, a change fostered by religion. Strict Christians (Evangelicals) believed they needed to break a child's will so he or she could follow the will of God (Greven, 1977). They thought children were born in sin and thus had to be disciplined, purified, and converted if they were ever to go to heaven. This emphasis on discipline meant two things: children began to receive plenty of attention, but it involved criticism and scolding. Much later, in the late nineteenth century, religion had lost much of its influence in America, and booming cities offered new temptations to youths, while families exerted less control over them. These developments disturbed Progressives, a group of reformers who vowed to make society raise children more sensibly. Their child-centeredness led them to propose laws to institute compulsory schooling, to reduce child labor, and to establish juvenile courts, among others. Finally, after World War II child-centeredness emerged in full force with the baby boom (1946–1964). Many families moved to the suburbs to give their children more room to play; parents chauffeured them to piano lessons and Little League practice; television arrived and provided children's shows (*Howdy Doody*, *Leave It to Beaver*, and so on); communities built new schools and colleges to accommodate these children; and Dr. Benjamin Spock, the eminent baby doctor, predicted that the postwar babies would be America's best and brightest generation (Jones, 1980).

In addition to their interest in law and youth, Americans have shown a fascination with social problems. These are conditions widely regarded as undesirable but subject to improvement through practical intervention. In

America, these issues rise and fall with remarkable speed. About a dozen years ago, the environment was regarded as a serious problem, a preoccupation that emerged at the same time that the problem of civil rights was slipping into the background. The problem of drug use and abuse was defined as ominous in the 1970s; then concern fell to lower levels. In the area of discrimination, there has been a shifting in concern; in the 1960s, racism was defined as the problem, then sexism began to be emphasized, and finally both were deemphasized as ageism became the most prominent social problem. Americans have traditionally been eager to control the world about them—first the physical world and later the social world. Barzini (1981) contends that it is a uniquely American characteristic to believe that all problems can be solved with money and hard work. This can-do optimism about solving social problems reached its peak during the presidency of Lyndon Johnson (1963–1969), when there was talk about achieving a "Great Society" (via the War on Poverty).

Juvenile delinquency has captured American attention partly because it combines these three national preoccupations: law, youth, and social problems. First there is a desire that youth conform to societal norms. Second, youths are identified as a social problem because they fail to live up to the wishes of their elders; Rice (1978) says adults typically regard the young as irreverent, immoral, irresponsible, and rebellious. Third, Americans have sometimes responded by turning to the law. Early nineteenth-century leaders created reformatories called Houses of Refuge. In the late nineteenth century, the Progressives pushed legislatures to pass laws that cut down on child labor, forced children to attend school, and established juvenile courts. None of this was inevitable. America could have followed the example of more traditional societies that revere the aged instead of the young, accept undesirable conditions as inevitable and unchangeable, and cling to ancient customs rather than pass new laws.

TWO OPPOSING VIEWS

Experts and commentators generally agree that juvenile delinquency and crime are important matters. Beyond this, however, disagreements arise, even on the most fundamental questions. This is not to say that they look at different questions. Quite often the questions are the same; it is the answers that are so different. The basic questions are obvious: how serious is the problem of juvenile delinquency and crime, who is largely responsible for the crime and delinquency rates being as high as they are, and what are the most sensible ways to reduce these rates?

To make matters simple, we have chosen to emphasize two diametrically opposed approaches to these issues; we call them the *alarmist view* and the *reassuring view*. This chapter will present these views in some detail to show

how some experts and commentators fight over the basic questions. In Chapter 2, we will deal with some of the same questions but will focus on the opinions of the American public instead of the commentators'. In both chapters, we will often look at crime and juvenile delinquency as a single entity; their similarities will be emphasized rather than their differences. Why? Because that is the common practice of many commentators and the lay public. In subsequent chapters, we will focus on juvenile delinquency exclusively.

Walter Miller (1974) has presented the most thorough analysis of opposing views of crime and delinquency. His discussion differs from ours on two counts: he contrasts political ideologies (left versus right) and he identifies ten different positions along this left-right spectrum. He cites such commentators as Spiro Agnew, William Buckley, and George Wallace on the right and Abbie Hoffman, Benjamin Spock, and Tom Wicker from the left. Those on the right talked about the need for law and order and toughness; they complained about leniency, permissiveness, and favoring the rights of lawbreakers. Leftists complained that the legal system makes too many activities illegal, puts too many people behind bars, and discriminates against minorities. In the years since Miller wrote his article, however, the partisan political nature of arguments over crime and delinquency has died down (Bayer, 1981). Thus, we will not use the right-left distinction here. Nor will we set forth ten positions on each issue. We will mention only two, since our purpose is to highlight the basic issues, not to present all the nuances and shadings of the positions.

THE PROBLEM

In general, the alarmist and reassuring views confront the same issues but offer different answers to them, and it is interesting to see which side students align themselves with. The issues simply stated are: (1) How bad is the problem of crime and delinquency? (2) Who is primarily responsible for crime and delinquency? and (3) What is the best way to reduce crime and delinquency? One might expect criminologists to have answered such basic questions long ago and then moved on to studying more advanced issues. Indeed, they have moved on, but they never achieved a consensus on the basic questions. Thus, we shall look at the issues they cannot agree on.

The Alarmist View

The alarmist argument is well publicized nowadays, having seeped into even the most respected newspapers and newsmagazines. The following excerpt from *Time* gives a sense of the tone that often pervades crime and delinquency stories.

> The curse of violent crime is rampant, not just in the ghettos of depressed cities, where it has always been a malignant force to contend with, but everywhere. . . . More significantly, the crimes are becoming more brutal, more irrational, more random—and therefore all the more frightening (Magnuson, 1981:16).

Take away all the purple prose, and the alarmist position on the crime problem can be summarized as follows:

1. There has been a drastic increase in the incidence of crime and delinquency. The data that show rapidly increasing crime rates are real and valid, not just the result of better reporting or some other kind of measurement error. There is a crime wave now, and it is truly a new crisis. According to James Q. Wilson (1975:4), "Crime soared. It did not just increase a little; it rose at a faster rate and to higher levels than at any time since the 1930s. . . ."
2. The crime problem is now widespread, and large numbers of people are being victimized. For example, Wilson claims

   > If the murder rate holds constant at today's level, then a child born in 1974 in Detroit and living there all his life has a one in thirty-five chance of being murdered. And if the murder rate continues to increase at its present pace, his chances of meeting a felonious end increase to one *in fourteen* (1975:19).

3. Not all crimes have an equal impact on the surrounding community. White-collar crimes and crimes by big business ("crime in the suites") have little effect on the average citizen, while street crimes or "predatory" crimes are very serious. The latter inevitably destroy property, harm people physically, and undermine community ties.
4. Crime has no redeeming virtues, no silver linings. Its most serious effect is to undermine relationships among people living near each other. According to Wilson (1975:23):

   > by disrupting the delicate nexus of ties . . . by which we are linked with our neighbors, crime atomizes society and makes its members mere individual calculators estimating their own . . . chances for survival. . . .

The Reassuring View

Each of these claims is countered by the reassurers. In disputing them, the reassuring view attempts to calm the public's fears and anxieties. First of all, the reassurers declare that media accounts of crime and delinquency are inflammatory and exaggerated; therefore they should not be believed. If the rate of crime and delinquency falls, the media will not publicize the fact (or at least not emphasize it), because it does not fit their notion of what is newsworthy. According to the reassuring view:

1. There have always been strident and irresponsible claims about the skyrocketing crime rate (Cook, 1971). "Crime waves are not new; they have existed throughout history" (Conklin, 1975:3). Despite the present surge of publicity about new and higher rates of crime, crime is probably no higher now than it was in the past.
2. The average person's chances of becoming a victim in any particular year are actually very small, even minusclule. Everyday mishaps, such as slipping in the bathtub, are more likely to cause physical injury than crime is. Some years ago, the President's Commission on Law Enforcement and Administration of Justice placed the odds of being a victim of violent crime during an average year at only 1 in 550. It added that the risk of injury serious enough to require hospitalization was only 1 in 3,000 (1968).
3. From a purely economic standpoint, street crime is not a critical problem. It pales in importance when compared with the losses caused by white-collar crime. Fraud, for instance, accounts for a greater loss each year than all the robberies, burglaries, larcenies, and motor-vehicle thefts combined, according to the President's Commission (1968).
4. Some criminologists even claim that crime and delinquency have some desirable consequences ("positive functions"). Daniel Bell (1960), for instance, says that organized crime provides goods and services sought by ordinary citizens but forbidden by law (such as drugs and gambling) and provides social mobility for some immigrants and their offspring. More relevant here is Emile Durkheim's (1938) argument that crime is functional because it arouses people of the community, who band together in response to it, offer each other moral support, and take out their indignation on the offenders. This unites the community more than if there were no crime.

Fragments of the reassuring view of the problem of crime and delinquency are scattered throughout the professional literature in books and articles not likely to be read by the average citizen. By contrast, the alarmist view is readily accessible. Television and the tabloids serve it up daily.

The alarmist and reassuring views can be considered ideologies, to be accepted on faith. But they might also be considered testable hypotheses, to be examined by referring to the most appropriate data. We prefer to think of them in the latter fashion. Thus, in the following discussion, the claims of each view will be looked at in light of existing research findings.

Research on the Problem of Crime and Delinquency

First, is the rate of crime and delinquency rapidly increasing? People who believe it is usually cite official data such as the FBI's Uniform Crime Reports (UCR). These are annual summaries of data on offenses and arrests recorded

TABLE 1–1
Rate Changes For Index Crimes

	Rate Increases 1960–1970	Rate Increases 1970–1980
Murder	55%	29%
Forcible rape	95%	95%
Robbery	186%	42%
Aggravated assault	91%	76%
Burglary	113%	54%
Larceny-theft	101%	52%
Motor-vehicle theft	149%	8%

Source: Webster, 1983.

by thousands of local police departments. The number of arrests is compiled for many different kinds of offenses, but the number of offenses is compiled for only those serious crimes included in the Crime Index: murder, forcible rape, aggravated assault, robbery, burglary, larceny-theft, and motor-vehicle theft (arson was added in 1977). Thus, any estimate of a change in the official crime rate will be limited to these few Crime Index offenses. During the 1960s, these seven index offenses appeared to increase dramatically. Some rates went up more than 100 percent. But in the period from 1970 to 1980, the rates increased by smaller amounts (see Table 1–1). European countries also experienced increased crime in these decades, a fact sometimes construed as support for the UCR claim that crime rose in the United States (Radzinowicz and King, 1977; Gurr, 1980).

The increasing rates of aggravated assaults and rapes during the 1970s tend to support the alarmist view that crime is on a rapid upswing. But many critics question the validity of UCR data. To begin with, they point to the *dark figure of crime* (Biderman and Reiss, 1967), a term that refers to the gap between the number of offenses that occur and the number that find their way into official police records. Some offenses go unrecorded because there are no witnesses. Others are witnessed but not reported to the police. Sometimes witnesses do not come forward because they are afraid; more often, they think the police cannot do anything about the offense. A third group of offenses are witnessed and reported to the police but not recorded. The Philadelphia and Milwaukee police are notorious for underrecording (Skogan, 1976). Police have *discretion* in what to call an incident; if they choose not to file an offense report, they save themselves time and paperwork.

One of the original reasons for introducing the Uniform Crime Reports in the 1930s was to ensure professionalism and objectivity and thus put an end to reckless claims about crime waves. Under J. Edgar Hoover's long reign, however, the FBI manipulated and misinterpreted data to scare the public (Mauss, 1975; Ryan, 1976; Turner, 1970). Since Hoover's death in 1972, the FBI rhetoric has been more subdued, but some criminologists still maintain that FBI data are biased and inadequate for measuring crime trends. Because so many offenses go unrecorded, even a very small increase in reporting or recording habits can have an extreme impact on crime rates, making it appear that crime is rising dramatically (Biderman et al., 1967; Sparks, 1976).

Because UCR data may be unreliable, some criminologists have chosen to measure the amount of crime and delinquency with *victimization surveys*. Ennis (1967) reports on interviews with 33,000 persons in 10,000 households across the country. In each household, a knowledgeable member was asked about any offenses in which a person in the household was a victim in the preceding twelve months. And the Census Bureau now conducts surveys on more than 60,000 households annually, which permits us to view the crime rate over time. Between 1975 and 1983, the number of offenses in the entire country was estimated to increase slightly from 23.4 million to 23.6 million. Crime rates, however, declined because the crime rate is defined as the number of crimes per 100 households. In 1983, there were many more households than in 1975. In 1975, there was a 32 percent chance that one's household would be victimized; by 1983, the chance had dropped to 27 percent (U.S. Department of Justice, 1981; *New York Times*, May 14, 1984).

By and large, the victimization data are more credible than the UCR data as measures of trends in crime rates. But not all the UCR data should be discarded; many observers believe that UCR estimates of murders and motor-vehicle thefts are reasonably accurate (since police vigorously pursue possible murder cases and motor-vehicle thefts must be reported to the police in order for victims to receive insurance compensation). Between 1970 and 1980, UCR figures show that the murder rate went up 29 percent and the motor-vehicle theft rate increased by 8 percent. The Census Bureau victimization survey includes seven offenses: rape, robbery, assault, personal larceny, burglary, household larceny, and motor-vehicle theft. If we combine the two UCR crimes (which increased slightly from 1970 to 1980) with the seven victimization survey crimes (which dropped an average of 16 percent from 1975 to 1983—a rate of 27 is a 16 percent drop from a rate of 32), then on the whole we cannot conclude that the crime rate has skyrocketed in recent years. We cannot even conclude that it has risen at all, unless we compare the present time with 1960. If we compare the present with 1970, crime seems to have stabilized or perhaps declined slightly. On this question, then, the reassuring view seems to be more accurate.

Second, is the crime problem in America widespread? There are different ways to answer this; one method is to compare crime and delinquency levels in the United States with levels elsewhere. Few countries have very reliable statistics, however, so cross-cultural comparisons are limited to places such as Canada, Japan, and Western Europe (Brantingham and Brantingham,

1984). None of these has a crime problem that matches ours. Radzinowicz and King (1977:6) report that there is more crime in the United States and it is more violent:

> There are as many murders in Manhattan each year as in the whole of England and Wales; and Houston is even worse. Detroit, with much the same population as Northern Ireland, has even in these grim days five times the murders.

The authors then point out that Philadelphia has fourty-four times as many homicides as Vienna, Chicago more burglaries than all of Japan, and Los Angeles more drug addiction than the whole of Western Europe. Cross-cultural comparisons are notoriously unreliable. But even so, we seem safe in concluding that there is more crime and delinquency in the United States than in other industrialized Western nations.

If we look only at the United States, the best way to measure the prevalence of crime is the victimization survey. These surveys use uniform measurement techniques, unlike the UCR, which must rely on the not-so-uniform procedures of 40,000 different police departments. Victimization surveys also are better able to handle the problem of nonreporting, a problem that seriously undermines UCR efforts to estimate the amount of crime. Victimization surveys are not error-free, however. They suffer from two deficiencies: memory decay and ignorance. Memory decay occurs when the person being interviewed forgets an incident in which a household member was victimized. Ignorance occurs when the person being interviewed was never informed by the victim that an incident took place and thus cannot pass along that information to the interviewer. Both kinds of error lead to an underestimate of the actual amount of crime and delinquency.

Despite this underestimation, victim surveys lead us to conclude that crime and delinquency are pervasive. As already noted, between 27 and 32 percent of households are victimized annually, and some experience multiple victimizations. An Associated Press report breaks down the figures by offense for the year 1980:

> Rape, robbery or assault touched 6 percent of all households. Another 14 percent had their purses snatched, their pockets picked, or experienced theft with no contact away from home. Burglaries and household theft hit . . . 17 percent of all American families. An additional 2 percent had cars stolen. Black and white respondents were hit almost equally—32 percent and 30 percent respectively in 1980 (*New York Post*, April 9, 1981:7).

In short, alarmists appear to be right that crime in America is widespread.

Third, which is more harmful—violent crime or white-collar crime? Different crimes cause different kinds of damages, and these damages cannot all be translated into dollars and cents. What kind of price tag can be assigned to a loss of life? Or to fear? Or loss of trust? Economists dealing with such

EUROPE'S DEAD-END KIDS

The "monster myth" applies mainly to the United States, but occasional press reports from other countries indicate that youths there also appear monstrous, with no aims or ideals. What they do have is considerable anger, which they take out on others, as in the vicious attacks on Pakistanis in England.

They are young and restless—with a bent for violence. Their rebellion began in the free-and-easy streets of Amsterdam, where homeless young dropouts "cracked" their way into abandoned apartment buildings and pitched camp on a few square feet of crumbling floor space. Now, in cities all over Western Europe, aimless young people are creating a separate culture—or perhaps anti-culture—that defies the control and understanding of the older generation. They routinely tangle with police and fling rocks through shopwindows, convinced that mayhem is the best way to communicate with "Them." "We started with housing," says a Dutch squatter named Jared, 24. "But we soon saw that all society is rotten."

Unlike the hopeful young Europeans who paraded for peace and love in the 1960s, Europe's dead-end kids have lost faith in the future. They share no political commitment, no heroes, no ideology—and, often, no enthusiasm for solutions. Their ranks are diverse, including street people in Zurich, runaways in West Berlin, racebaiters in Britain. But their philosophy is strikingly similar; "Self, not society," as the graffiti in West Berlin put it. Activists who oppose nuclear power or support the revolutionaries in El Salvador tend to be lonely crusaders on the fringes of what the Swiss call *die Bewegung*—the movement. For most of the new breed, changing the world just is not on the agenda.

The principal target of youthful anger is the welfare state's smug preoccupation with cleanliness, order and prosperity. "Everything is perfect," one crash-helmeted protester told a reporter recently as he heaved a rock through a shop window in Zurich. "It's all too rich. It makes me want to throw up." In the past ten months, Zurich police have arrested 1,590 demonstrators and have shot 70,000 rubber bullets at rioters who caused nearly $5 million worth of property damage. "Zurich is on fire," crowed a recent youth pamphlet. "People are asking, 'Why Zurich—clean, quiet Zurich?' We don't have an answer, except that is's high time this happened."

War Zone: In Berlin, rampaging young people have turned the elegant shop-

questions use the term *opportunity costs,* which refer to the consequences of fear of crime—for example, avoiding parks and other public places, refusing to work at a night job, paying more to use taxis instead of buses or subways.

ping street, the Kurfürstendamm, into a war zone. The sidewalks of other German cities—Bremen, Hanover, Nuremberg—are often covered with broken glass. Picturesque Amsterdam frequently is the scene of pitched battles between kids and cops. Last spring, after the coronation of Queen Beatrix, rampaging anti-royalists caused $2.5 million worth of damage. The Dutch movement is so well-organized that if demonstrators are needed for a march, word is broadcast on an unlicensed "pirate" radio station called The Free Kaiser or passed by bike-riding couriers. Others are alerted by phone. Within a few hours, 30,000 people are ready to pound the pavement.

Dissent in Great Britain has a more vicious character. White youths, many of them poor and unemployed, have focused their wrath on the country's minority groups—West Indians, Pakistanis and other Asians. Indiscriminate beatings of the non-whites—known as "Paki-bashing"—have become common. At soccer games, beer-swilling ruffians sporting leather jackets and "skinhead" haircuts shout "Zimbabwe" and grunt like apes when black players take the field. Young thugs are flocking to neo-Nazi organizations, such as the National Front. This spring the well-dressed roughneck is wearing heavy black boots and swastika armbands. Explains National Front member John Merritt, 19: "No government ever asked the people if they wanted a multiracial society."

Recession: Much youthful frustration is linked to the shrinking job market. During the past twenty years, unemployment among European teen-agers has soared. Currently, 40 per cent of the jobless people in the Common Market are less than 25 years of age. When economic recession compels employers to make work-force reductions, unions often urge them to do it through attrition, so that vacancies caused by resignation or retirement are left unfilled. As a result, young people never get a chance at a job. One British father, Ken Millward, recently placed a newspaper advertisement offering a $4,500 reward to any firm that would hire his boy as an electrician's apprentice. "It was terrible to watch a youngster who was so keen to work getting knocked back time after time," says Millward. In many West European cities, the housing market is just as discouraging. In Amsterdam, 60,000 people are on waiting lists for affordable apartments, and an estimated 50,000 others haven't even bothered to submit their names.

Angry young people say that chaos is not only the most appropriate expression of their frustration, but one that the establishment understands best. "We live in a violent society and, unfortunately, we must sometimes use that language to be heard," says Klaus G., a young West German troublemaker.

Source: Fred Bruning, "Europe's Dead-End Kids," *Newsweek* 97 (April 27, 1981): 52.

Several attempts have been made to estimate the direct economic costs of various crimes. Perhaps most interesting is the one by Wright (1973), who divides the offenses into two types, which he calls white-collar crimes and

TABLE 1–2
Economic Cost of Crime (1965)

White-Collar Crimes		Crimes of the Poor	
Embezzlement	$200 million	Robbery	$27 million
Fraud	$1,350 million	Burglary	$251 million
Tax fraud	$100 million	Auto theft	$140 million
Forgery	$80 million	Larceny ($50+)	$190 million

Source: Wright, 1973:29.

crimes of the poor (we prefer to use the term "street crimes" for the latter type). Wright's figures, presented in Table 1–2, indicate that white-collar crime, especially fraud, is much more costly than street crime. Conklin (1981) provides another estimate of the economic costs; he claims that white-collar crime costs the country $44 billion a year, while the figure for property crime or street crime is only $4 billion. On this issue, if we focus on the economic costs, the reassuring view is more accurate than the alarmist view.

Finally, is crime only destructive and corrosive, or does it have positive effects? Is Durkheim right in claiming that crime is an integral part of all healthy societies because it arouses community passions against the offenders and binds the rest of the people together for social support? Alarmists don't think so; they reject this idea and claim that crime has no positive consequences. If anything, it undermines and destroys community solidarity.

It is difficult to determine which view of the link between crime and community solidarity is more accurate, perhaps because community solidarity is so hard to measure or perhaps because so few researchers have examined this relationship. One criminologist who has shown an interest in this subject is John Conklin (1975), who mentions several relevant cases. One concerns Kitty Genovese, a young woman murdered in Queens, New York, early one morning while thirty-eight witnesses looked on and did not intervene.

> The murder occurred in a middle-class neighborhood with a relatively low crime rate. As Miss Genovese was returning home from work at three o'clock in the morning, an assailant attacked her with a knife. She screamed. Lights went on in nearby apartments, and people looked out their windows. One witness to the violence shouted at the assailant to leave the woman alone. He left the scene but soon returned. Again lights went on, and again he left. He returned a third time and this time killed the woman. The three attacks took place over a period of thirty-five minutes, and at least thirty-eight witnesses knew of the violence. Only after the assaults were over did one man call the police, and he did that from a neighbor's apartment in order to avoid personal involvement (1975:215).

People who are unresponsive bystanders like the thirty-eight above could conceivably band together later in some kind of response to crime. With this possibility in mind, Conklin brings up another case, this one involving a small town in Kansas, where a prominent family was killed. (This case achieved notoriety because it gave rise to Truman Capote's 1965 book *In Cold Blood.*) The grisly murder did not bring people together.

> Most people reacted by trying to provide greater security for themselves, their families, and their homes; there were few collective efforts to protect the community. The proprietor of a local hardware store said that "locks and bolts are the fastest-going item. Folks ain't particular what brand they buy; they just want them to hold" (Conklin, 1975:57).

If the reassuring view is correct, people should react to crime with *collective mobilizations* such as neighbors agreeing to watch each other's houses when they go away, or belonging to a local crime-watch group. The alarmist view predicts that people will react with *individual mobilizations* (purchasing items such as alarms and weapons) or *avoidance* techniques (locking one's doors, keeping lights on, and staying home a lot). Avoidance techniques are the most widely used responses; about 85 percent of citizens interviewed say they lock the doors at night and always identify people before letting them in (Gallup, 1981; Friedberg, 1980). Individual mobilizations are fairly common; as a response to crime, 20 percent say they have a trained dog, 16 percent own guns, and 11 percent carry a weapon. Collective mobilization, on the other hand, is quite rare; only 5 percent of respondents say they belong to a local crime-watch group.

THE BLAME

The Alarmist View

If crime is widespread, how much of it can be blamed on teenagers? Do they contribute more than their share? Do they dominate crime? Or do they play a less conspicuous role? The alarmist view of these issues argues:

1. Young people are greatly overrepresented in criminal activity. *Newsweek* suggests that this is the one undeniable fact about crime. "It is a young man's game. . . . The best explanation of the crime surge that began in the 1960s is demographic: the baby boom that filled the nation's schools also filled its jails" (March 23, 1981:50).
2. Young people pose a great danger in American society, because they are particularly overrepresented in the crimes of violence. According to *Time*, "young people commit most of the violent crime in America" (Magnuson,

1981:20). This is a particularly strong statement, since young people do not comprise a majority of the population.

3. Violent young offenders not only are numerous but also lack human feelings. Silberman is typical of those writers who are disturbed by the "new viciousness" of the young offenders.

> A lawyer who was a public defender noted for her devotion to her clients' interests . . . speaks of "a terrifying generation of kids" that emerged during the late 1960s and early '70s. When she began practicing, she told me, adolescents and young men charged with robbery had, at worst, pushed or shoved a pedestrian or storekeeper to steal money or merchandise; members of the new generation kill, maim, and injure without reason or remorse (1978:4–5).

Thus, alarmists single out youths as mainly responsible for crime. According to the alarmists' "monster myth," about 5 or 10 percent of young people routinely terrorize communities and commit especially vicious, violent, and pointless crimes.

The Reassuring View

The alarmists' effectiveness in establishing their view is indicated by the fact that it is almost impossible to find an opposing opinion. Hints of a reassuring view of responsibility are both rare and timid. The following list is an attempt to assemble these few bits and pieces.

1. There are several categories of age—not just two. The age groups most overrepresented in crime are older adolescents and young adults (Quinney, 1975). Teenagers do commit more than their share of offenses, but adults too must be included.
2. Youths are not the brutal marauders that *Time* and other media accuse them of being. They actually account for a rather modest proportion of violent crime. Sheley says youngsters do not dominate violent crime; instead, "older persons have higher percentages of 'crimes of passion' and dispute crimes (homicide and aggravated assault)" (1979:65).
3. The "monster myth" is simply a myth. Most cities do not have a very large percentage of youths roaming the streets and repeatedly committing extremely violent and vicious offenses.

Research on Who Is Responsible

First, what proportion of the crime problem can actually be attributed to youth? This depends on how we define "youth" and which offenses we examine. Dividing lines between youth and adulthood often vary, depending on the situation: there may be one age for drinking alcohol, another for driving a car, and a third for seeing X- and R-rated movies. But the most

TABLE 1–3
Age of Arrestees for Common Offenses

	Number of Arrests for All Ages (in thousands)	Percent Who Are under 18
Driving under the influence	1,613	2%
Larceny-theft	1,169	32
Drunkenness	977	3
Disorderly conduct	679	14
Drug-abuse violations	617	12
Other assaults	482	16
Burglary	416	38
Liquor laws	427	27
Fraud	262	8
Aggravated assault	261	13

Source: Webster, 1984:179.

appropriate boundary is the age when a person is legally an adult to the courts. In most states, that age is 18. Persons under 18 are routinely sent to juvenile court; those 18 and over go to criminal court.

To determine whether youths are overrepresented in crime, it is first necessary to determine what percent of the population is made up of youths. In the United States, this percentage is about 30; thus, for youths to be overrepresented in crime they must commit more than 30 percent of all offenses. To examine this claim, we can consult the Uniform Crime Reports for a breakdown on which age groups commit the most common offenses. From the data in Table 1–3 it appears that youths generally are *not* overrepresented among persons arrested for these offenses. In fact, they account for only about 12 percent of such arrests—far *less* than their share of the population. Of course, youth may appear to commit less than its share simply because this age category includes not only teenagers but also the very young, who obviously commit very few crimes and produce very few arrests. One could thus argue that Table 1–3 offers an unfair comparison between the young and the old because it lumps babies and small children in with teenagers. But one could also argue that it is unfair to group senior citizens in the same category as young adults. Like infants and small children, senior citizens account for very few arrests.

Therefore, we need an age breakdown with finer categories. Figure 1–1 compares the population of each age group with its number of arrests. From this we can draw several conclusions:

1. Some age groups are particularly underrepresented in crime—namely people 12 and under and those 65 and older, or the very young and the very old.

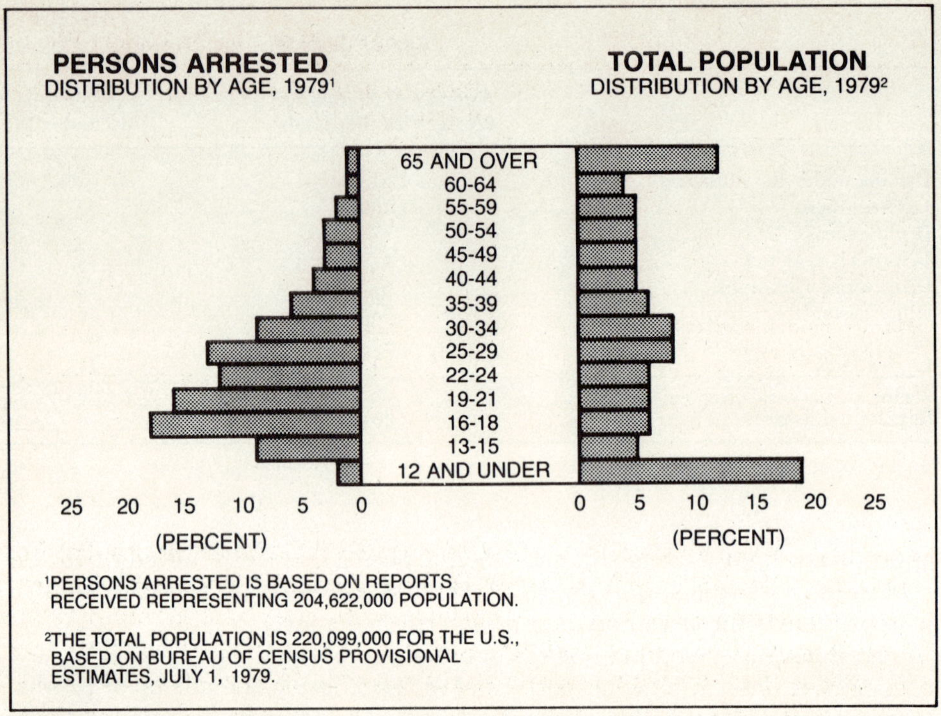

FIGURE 1–1
Age and Population Arrest Data, 1979
Source: Webster, 1980:187.

2. Some age categories are overrepresented in these data—namely, people in late youth (16–18) and those in early adulthood (19–21).
3. Between the ages of 16 and 49, there is a tendency for arrest rates to decrease as people get older. Matza (1964) and others call this *maturational reform.*

These data provide more support for the reassuring view than for the alarmist position.

Second, are youths overrepresented in violent crimes? This can be checked against UCR data on arrests for different age groups. Table 1–4 lists the kinds of violent crime. People under age 18 do not account for more than 30 percent of the arrests for any of these crimes. Apparently, then, young people do not dominate arrests for violence. Indeed, for the most serious crime of all—murder—93 percent of those arrested are adults. Thus, neither the most

TABLE 1–4
Age of Arrestees for Violent Offenses

	Number of Arrests for All Ages (in thousands)	Percent Who Are under 18
Other assaults	482	16%
Aggravated assault	261	13
Weapons offenses	161	14
Robbery	134	26
Offenses against family	46	3
Forcible rape	30	15
Murder and nonnegligent manslaughter	18	7

Source: Webster, 1984:179.

common nor the most serious crimes are strictly youthful activities. The UCR monitors 29 kinds of offenses altogether; of these, youths account for more than half of the arrests for only (1) curfew and loitering and (2) running away. According to UCR data, no adults were arrested for these two offenses, thus indicating that they are juvenile status offenses. Of the offenses for which adults and juveniles can both be arrested, youths never dominate, never account for more than half the arrests.

Do 5–10 percent of young people repeatedly commit violent crimes? Dinitz and Conrad (1980) tested this hypothesis by studying 811 boys and girls who were born in Columbus, Ohio, between 1956 and 1958 and who were arrested at least for one violent offense before age 18. These youngsters represented less than 2 percent of the 50,000 people in that age group in Columbus, a minuscule proportion. In addition, among these 2 percent, most of the youths were not arrested for violence very often. Of these 811 arrestees, a whopping 87 percent were arrested for a violent offense only once; 13 percent had two or more arrests for violence. If the focus is on more serious crimes—aggravated crimes of violence—only twenty-two youngsters could be considered "monsters" who were arrested at least twice for these. Twenty-two monsters out of 50,000 youths is only .05 percent, far short of the alarmist claim of 5–10 percent. Of course, one could argue that Columbus, Ohio, is an unsuitable location for estimating the percentage of youths involved in careers of violence. It is not noted as a hotbed of delinquency. Dinitz and Conrad concede that it does not resemble the bleak urban landscape of North Philadelphia or the South Bronx. They add, however, that Columbus is more typical; there are many more cities with populations between 500,000 and 1 million than there are very large cities.

THE SOLUTION

Predictably enough, claims about the scope of the problem are followed by proposals on how best to deal with it. Alarmists want a stern and vigorous response by the legal system. They oppose the tender-hearted approach favored by the reassurers. They particularly dislike the softness of the original juvenile court philosophy, which emerged at about the turn of the century as part of the Progressive program. The Progressives were determined to root out political corruption and "Old World" vices such as drunkenness and prostitution, and replace them with hard work and moral uprightness. Several reforms focused on children, especially children of immigrants, because (1) these children were very numerous and (2) their parents (and poor people generally) were thought by reformers to be not knowledgeable enough to raise children properly.

The Reassuring View

The Progressives did not regard juvenile offenders as criminals who deserved punishment. They felt that penalties should be administered only if they could be justified as promoting positive results—most notably, rehabilitation. Rehabilitation involved focusing on the child as a person, not on the offense he or she had committed. It also meant that the child would receive some kind of treatment in hopes that the child's delinquent tendencies would be cured. Finally, rehabilitation meant an emphasis on the individual; before the specialists (psychologists or psychiatrists) could help a child, they had to diagnose what his or her special problem was, and special problems might require a special cure, one suited only to that particular child. Clearly, the juvenile court philosophy did not have some kind of assembly-line justice in mind.

The Progressives' second emphasis was on keeping children out of adult or criminal courts. Progressives regarded children as persons who were still growing up, still in the process of character formation. Hard-line justice would be inappropriate for them at so early a stage of growth; a more understanding approach better fitted their tender years. Subjecting them to criminal trials and criminal institutions might very easily propel them into full-blown criminal careers. This emphasis on the innocence and immaturity of youth was partly a reflection of new theories of adolescence and partly a reflection of Progressives' liberalism. Progressive reformers thought that as innocents, children deserved to be shielded and protected from the vices surrounding them in the city.

Serious or intractable youthful offenders would still be sent to institutions, as they had been since the early part of the nineteenth century (Fox, 1970). But the great majority of youths who appeared before the juvenile court and were pronounced delinquent would receive probation, which was a relatively new idea at the turn of the century. They would be assigned a trained social worker with whom they could talk periodically. They would remain home, not be institutionalized; and the social worker would ensure that their home life improved. Progressives believed lower-class and immigrant families needed to be taught how to raise their children. According to one of the first spokesmen for the juvenile court philosophy, a Judge Tuthill:

> the probation officer can go into the home and demand to know the cause of the dependency or delinquency of a child. . . . He becomes practically a member of the family and teaches them lessons of cleanliness and decency, of truth and integrity (Rothman, 1980:219).

Thus, the Progressives combined their willingness to help with an air of moral superiority and paternalism.

In 1899, Illinois became the first state to have a juvenile court. According to the juvenile court philosophy, many children needed help if they were to become healthy, striving members of society. In rapidly growing cities like Chicago, children of immigrants needed particular help, it was argued, because urban vices were very tempting and immigrant parents were frequently unable to control or guide their offspring.

The juvenile court, supporters promised, would help in several ways. Children who seemed headed toward delinquency would be brought before the court, where a probation officer or child psychologist would conduct an in-depth analysis to see what made the child tick. The psychologist would pay little attention to the child's offenses (if there were any). All parties in the court would be on the same side, trying to do what they thought was in the child's *best interests*. There would be no adversary system—that is, no fight between prosecuting and defense attorneys. Legal formalities would be replaced by informal discussions between the juvenile and the judge (who was supposed to be like a kindly father).

The juvenile court philosophy (which remains the reassurers' view of the proper solution to the delinquency problem) thus focuses on four points:

1. The only justification for legal punishment is that it will bring about rehabilitation.
2. Because young people are innocent and immature, they should not be treated as adult offenders, lest they become such.
3. Youths who are declared delinquent should usually receive probation, not be confined in a reformatory.
4. Youths should be sent to a special court, one which specializes in handling juveniles' problems.

Because these are such optimistic beliefs, it seems appropriate to consider the juvenile court philosophy as exemplifying the reassuring view.

The Alarmist View

The alarmist view of the solution is more tough-minded. First, alarmists reject rehabilitation as a justification for punishment. They oppose rehabilitation on ideological grounds, saying offenders need to be penalized rather than treated. They also oppose it on empirical grounds, saying that programs that attempt to rehabilitate offenders are almost invariably failures. In this regard, they point to the work of Robert Martinson, who evaluated hundreds of reports on programs that treated offenders. He concluded: "With few and isolated exceptions, the rehabilitative efforts that have been reported have had no appreciable effect on recidivism" (1974:355). Alarmists respond to these findings by saying that punishment should continue but with a justification other than rehabilitation. Several options exist:

1. *General deterrence.* According to this idea, punishment of offenders will strike fear in the hearts of other people, which will make them less likely to commit offenses.
2. *Special deterrence.* This idea proposes that punishment of offenders will strike fear in *their* hearts and thus make *them* less likely to offend again.
3. *Incapacitation.* This is the simplest justification. It claims that while people are locked up in an institution, they cannot commit offenses against people in the outside world.
4. *Retribution.* This justification does not propose that anything good or useful will follow from punishing offenders. It is based on the idea that offenders should be punished because they deserve it; a punishment is morally right and just in light of the harm and damage caused by the offense.

Alarmists tend to embrace all of these justifications, but they are probably most deeply committed to retribution.

Second, alarmists would like to change the rules about age. Most offenders under 18 are now handled by the juvenile court. Alarmists would like to reduce the age limit so that young persons who are accused of serious offenses can be sent to criminal court. This is already an option; juvenile courts can waive jurisdiction and send the youth on to the criminal courts. Alarmists, however, want this procedure to be more automatic and less discretionary. One state that has moved in this direction is New York. In 1976, that state's legislature passed the Juvenile Justice Reform Act and created a set of offenses known as "designated felonies." Under this law, 14- and 15-year-old children charged with murder, kidnapping, arson, manslaughter, assault, rape and a few other offenses

> would be tried in a special court (with a locked door) which was enjoined to keep the need for the protection of the community in mind, as well as the needs and best interests of the respondent. If one of these older children was found to have committed such an act, he could be incarcerated for a period extending to five years. . . . The increased severity seems to have accomplished what its framers and their constituents intended. In July 1978, the director of the State Division of Youth . . . reported that the Designated Felony Courts had achieved an 85 percent rate of conviction—a higher rate than can be achieved in the adult courts (Prescott, 1981:29–30).

These changes are possible because of the alarmist belief that young males are not innocent or immature. Rather, alarmists see them as mature, calculating, dangerous offenders who will take advantage of the fact that they will be treated as juveniles by the court system and commit heinous crimes.

Third, alarmists propose that every serious offense detected should result in punishment. This is clearly a reflection of the policy of retribution that we have suggested is a key element in alarmist thinking. Boland and Wilson suggest that punishment can take several different forms. It

> could involve victim restitution [paying back the victim for damages caused by the offense], community service, or a weekend or two in jail, or more severe punishment in some cases. The object would be to heighten the credibility of the justice system and of the legal and moral code it is charged with enforcing, by establishing early in the prospective criminal career that some penalty (not "probation" . . .) follows any detected serious offense (1978:32–33).

Thus, alarmists ask that probation—the favored response of the reassurers to delinquency—be completely eliminated from the list of sentencing options.

Finally, the alarmists' most extreme proposal is to abolish the juvenile court. They argue that age and behavior are not related in the way suggested by the traditional juvenile court philosophy. Juvenile offenders are not innocent, naive, or merely wayward; they are at least as committed to serious crime as adults (Boland and Wilson, 1978). Alarmists therefore propose dismantling the present two-track system of one court for juveniles and another for adults. They advocate a single track for all offenders. But if two tracks must remain, they say, one should be for lesser and infrequent offenders while the other should concentrate on serious, repeat offenders. In this new system only the seriousness of the offense would matter in the decision about where to send the suspect. Young people would be just as likely as adults to land in the criminal court.

Evaluating the Proposed Solutions

Since both the alarmist and reassuring solutions are essentially mere proposals about what should be done, we cannot point to a set of data that show one side to be more valid than the other. But we can at least comment on both proposed solutions. In large part, the alarmists and reassurers each offer a consistent package; their suggested solutions tend to follow quite predictably from their ideas about the seriousness of the problem and who is responsible for it. People do not propose harsh or drastic solutions unless they think there is a very serious problem. Nor would people apply such strong measures to young people unless they thought young people were largely to blame for the problem. Alarmists, of course, think that the problem of crime and delinquency has reached crisis proportions, that young people commit most crime, and that young people are particularly drawn to vicious and violent crimes. But the available data do not support these claims. Alarmists are right in some of their claims (how widespread crime is and the effect of crime on the community's solidarity), but on the crucial questions their claims are very dubious. And since their solutions are a direct outgrowth of the hypotheses about the problem and the blame, we must at least question how sound their proposed solutions are. This is particularly important in view of alarmists' strong influence on public policy. For instance, in President Reagan's task force report on crime and delinquency in 1981,

> Participants unanimously agreed that violent juvenile repeaters should be sent to prison, that juvenile recidivists should be treated as career criminals, that violent juveniles accused of serious crime should be prosecuted in adult court. . . (Chambers, 1981:117–118).

When it comes to solutions, alarmists are being heard.

SUMMARY

Most people obey most of society's rules most of the time, but rules do get violated on occasion. Major forms of deviance focused on by sociologists have traditionally included suicide, drug use, alcoholism, mental disorders, sexual deviance, and most prominently crime and delinquency. Crime has long been defined as activity that the criminal law declares punishable. The definition of delinquency has not been so stable. Traditionally, it included three categories: crimes, status offenses, and violations of the omnibus clause. In the 1970s and 1980s, however, several states dropped their omnibus clauses, whose vagueness had allowed courts to confine juveniles for almost any activity. Some states also took status offenses out of the category of delinquency. The new definition that states are moving toward is thus very close to the standard definition of crime, except that the label of "delinquent" is applied to juveniles only.

A great deal of interest in delinquency has existed in America for perhaps 150 years. This interest seems to be an outgrowth of interest in three related subjects: law, youth, and social problems. Law has long interested Americans, because, as people from many different backgrounds and ancestries, we cannot always agree on what the norms should be. Law helps to fill this void. American interest in youth has gone through three phases. Colonial New England Evangelicals watched children closely because they thought a child's will had to be broken before the child would accept God's will. Progressive child-centeredness focused on legislation: child-labor laws, compulsory-schooling laws, and the juvenile court. The arrival of the baby boom after World War II brought a new emphasis on family life organized around the interests and needs of children. The American preoccupation with social problems means a readiness to declare that certain conditions are deplorable but curable.

Once a concern about delinquency and crime developed, Americans turned to experts for analysis and solutions. But the experts and commentators have been unable to agree on even the most basic issues. Alarmists believe that crime and delinquency rates have been rising drastically in recent years, that present rates are very high, that the most harmful offenses are street crimes, and that crime undermines community solidarity. Reassurers, on the other hand, claim that crime is not increasing, that an individual's risk of victimization is quite minuscule, that other crimes are more harmful than street crime, and that crime helps to unite communities. The research available seems to support alarmists on the issues of the prevalence of crime and its effect on communities. Data support reassurers on the questions of increasing crime rates and which crimes are most damaging.

Alarmists blame crime mostly on young people, especially crimes of violence, and they add that 5–10 percent of youths are "monsters" who repeatedly commit especially violent and vicious crimes. Reassurers rarely deal with these issues, but when they do they point out that older teenagers and young adults are both overrepresented in crime, that young people do not commit more than their share of violent crimes, and that the "monster myth" is a gross overstatement. By and large, the data seem to support the reassuring view on these issues, though the alarmist view is much more widely publicized and believed.

Finally, alarmists propose that retribution replace rehabilitation as the justification for punishment, that the age limits for being sent to criminal court be lowered, that every serious offense result in some punishment, and that, if possible, the juvenile court be abolished. The reassuring view, however, carries on the original juvenile court philosophy, which says that rehabilitation or therapy is the only acceptable justification for punishment, that children are naive and innocent and should be treated as such, that most delinquents should be placed on probation, and that juveniles should be sent to a juvenile court designed especially for them. There is no way to determine whose solution is better; they are both proposals and so are untestable. But since the solutions grow out of hypotheses about the problem and the blame, the alarmists' solution seems to be on somewhat shaky ground.

DISCUSSION QUESTIONS

1. Why does juvenile delinquency receive so much attention in America?
2. What types of behavior have delinquency laws traditionally included under juvenile court jurisdiction? Define each.
3. What is the alarmist position on the problem of crime?
4. What is the reassuring view of the crime problem?
5. According to the available data, is crime rapidly increasing or not?
6. What are the major weaknesses of victimization surveys?
7. What evidence supports or refutes the "monster myth"?
8. What elements comprise the juvenile court philosophy?
9. What major proposals have alarmists offered to deal with the delinquency problem?
10. Why do alarmists reject rehabilitation as a justification for punishment?

REFERENCES

AKERS, RONALD L.
1977 *Deviant Behavior.* Belmont, Calif.: Wadsworth.

BAKER, RUSSELL
1980 *So This Is Depravity.* New York: Washington Square Press.

BARZINI, LUIGI
1981 The Americans. *Harper's* 263 (December):29–36, 83–85.

BAYER, RONALD
1981 Crime, punishment, and the decline of liberal optimism. *Crime and Delinquency* 27 (April):169–190.

BELL, DANIEL
1960 *The End of Ideology.* New York: Free Press.

BERGER, KATHLEEN STASSEN
1980 *The Developing Person.* New York: Worth.

BIDERMAN, ALBERT D., ET AL.
1967 *Report on a Pilot Study in the District of Columbia on Victimization and Attitudes toward Law Enforcement.* Washington: U.S. Government Printing Office.

BIDERMAN, ALBERT D., AND ALBERT J. REISS, JR.
1967 On exploring the "dark figure" of criminality. *Annals of the American Academy of Political and Social Science* 374 (November):1–15.

BOLAND, BARBARA, AND JAMES Q. WILSON
1978 Age, crime, and punishment. *The Public Interest* 51 (Spring):22–34.

BRANTINGHAM, PAUL, AND PATRICIA BRANTINGHAM
1984 *Patterns in Crime.* New York: Macmillan.

CAPOTE, TRUMAN
1965 *In Cold Blood.* New York: Random House.

CHAMBERS, MARILYN
1981 How the police target young offenders. *New York Times Magazine* (September 20):116–124.

CONKLIN, JOHN E.
1981 *Criminology.* New York: Macmillan.
1975 *The Impact of Crime.* New York: Macmillan.

COOK, FRED J.
1971 There's always a crime wave. Pp. 23–37 in Donald R. Cressey (ed.), *Crime and Criminal Justice.* Chicago: Quadrangle.

DeMAUSE, LLOYD
1974 *The History of Childhood.* New York: Psychohistory Press.

DIAMOND, STANLEY
1971 The rule of law versus the order of custom. *Social Research* 38 (Spring):42–72.

DINITZ, SIMON, AND JOHN P. CONRAD
1980 The dangerous two percent. Pp. 139–155 in David Shichor and Delos H. Kelly (eds.), *Critical Issues in Juvenile Delinquency.* Lexington, Mass.: Lexington Books.

DURKHEIM, EMILE
1938 *The Rules of the Sociological Method.* New York: Free Press.

ENNIS, PHILIP H.
1967 *Criminal Victimization in the United States.* Washington: U.S. Government Printing Office.

FOX, SANFORD
1970 Juvenile justice reform: A historical perspective. *Stanford Law Review* 22 (June):1187–1239.

FRIEDBERG, ARDY
1980 *America Afraid.* New York: New American Library.

GALLUP, GEORGE H.
1981 Americans see surge of crime. *The Gallup Report* No. 187 (April):4–19.

GREVEN, PHILIP
1977 *The Protestant Temperament.* New York: Knopf.

GURR, TED ROBERT
1980 On the history of violent crime in Europe and America. Pp. 411–432 in Egon Bittner and Sheldon L. Messinger (eds.), *Criminology Review Yearbook.* Beverly Hills, Calif.: Sage.

JONES, LANDON
1980 *Great Expectations.* New York: Coward, McCann & Geoghegan.

LEVIN, MARK M., AND ROSEMARY C. SARRI
1974 *Juvenile Delinquency: A Study of Juvenile Codes in the U.S.* Ann Arbor, Mich.: University of Michigan Press.

MAGNUSON, ED.
1981 The curse of violent crime. *Time* 117 (March 23):16–21.

MARTINSON, ROBERT
1974 What works?—Questions and answers about prison reform. *The Public Interest* 35 (Spring):22–54.

MATZA, DAVID
1964 *Delinquency and Drift.* New York: Wiley

MAUSS, ARMAND L.
1975 *Social Problems as Social Movements.* Philadelphia: Lippincott.
MILLER, WALTER
1974 Ideology and criminal justice policy. *Journal of Criminal Law and Criminology* 64 (June):141–162.
NAISBITT, JOHN
1984 *Megatrends.* New York: Warner.
NEWSWEEK
1981 The plague of violent crime. 97 (March 23):46–54.
PRESCOTT, PETER S.
1981 *The Child Savers.* New York: Knopf.
PRESIDENT'S COMMISSION ON LAW ENFORCEMENT AND ADMINISTRATION OF JUSTICE
1968 *The Challenge of Crime in a Free Society.* New York: Avon.
QUINNEY, RICHARD
1975 *Criminology.* Boston: Little, Brown.
RADZINOWICZ, SIR LEON, AND JOAN KING
1977 *The Growth of Crime.* New York: Basic.
RICE, F. PHILIP
1978 *The Adolescent.* Boston: Allyn & Bacon.
ROTHMAN, DAVID J.
1980 *Conscience and Convenience.* Boston: Little, Brown.
RYAN, WILLIAM
1976 *Blaming the Victim.* New York: Random House.
SCHLOSSMAN, STEVEN L.
1977 *Love and the American Delinquent.* Chicago: University of Chicago Press.
SHELEY, JOSEPH F.
1979 *Understanding Crime.* Belmont, Calif.: Wadsworth.
SILBERMAN, CHARLES E.
1978 *Criminal Violence, Criminal Justice.* New York: Random House.
SKOGAN, WESLEY G.
1976 *Sample Surveys of the Victims of Crime.* Cambridge, Mass.: Ballinger.
SPARKS, RICHARD F.
1976 Crimes and victims in London. Pp. 43–71 in Wesley G. Skogan (ed.), *Sample Surveys of the Victims of Crime.* Cambridge, Mass.: Ballinger.
TURNER, WILLIAM W.
1970 *Hoover's FBI.* New York: Dell.
U.S. DEPARTMENT OF JUSTICE
1981 *The Prevalence of Crime.* Washington: U.S. Government Printing Office.
WEBSTER, WILLIAM
1984 *Crime in the U.S.* Washington: U.S. Government Printing Office.
1983 *Crime in the U.S.* Washington: U.S. Government Printing Office.
1980 *Crime in the U.S.* Washington: U.S. Government Printing Office.
WILSON, JAMES Q.
1975 *Thinking About Crime.* New York: Basic.
WRIGHT, ERIK OLIN
1973 *The Politics of Punishment.* New York: Harper & Row.

Public Perceptions of Crime and Delinquency 2

INTRODUCTION

In Chapter 1, we looked at the views of various experts and commentators on crime and delinquency. In this chapter, we focus upon public perceptions of these problems. Most delinquency and criminology books do not cover public opinion in great detail; indeed, the usual practice is to ignore the subject altogether. We think that that is a mistake and that public perceptions are sufficiently important to warrant an entire chapter. Our reasons for this are several:

1. By themselves, police usually cannot capture offenders or make arrests. They need public cooperation to accomplish these tasks.
2. The public is actually a part of the juvenile and criminal justice systems, as are the police, courts, and corrections.
3. The degree to which citizens cooperate with the police depends, in part, on citizens' attitudes toward and perceptions of crime.
4. Courts also require assistance from the public; this includes attitudinal support of court decisions.
5. Prisons and other correctional institutions need public support. If resistance in a community is fierce, the institution probably will not be built there. Furthermore, prisons rely on local people to staff them.

6. Legislators need public support if they are to pass bills dealing with crime and delinquency.
7. Controlling crime and delinquency competes with other issues for public funding. The concern of people about their safety will affect these economic decisions.
8. The degree to which people tolerate crime and delinquency affects how much crime and delinquency they will experience in their society.
9. Typically, public perceptions regarding crime and delinquency are poorly understood, and speculation about "what the public wants" is largely based on nothing more substantial than guesses.

After going into some detail on each of these nine items, we will look at public perceptions of the issues covered in Chapter 1: the problem, the blame, and the solution. This will enable us to determine how closely public opinion parallels either the alarmist or the reassuring views. We will conclude the chapter by examining how or whether the mass media influence the public's understanding of crime and delinquency.

THE IMPORTANCE OF PUBLIC PERCEPTIONS

Police Need Cooperation

In the United States, there are almost 750,000 police officers (there were no forces 150 years ago). In addition, modern police are better trained, more educated, more conscientious, and less corrupt than police in earlier eras (Lane, 1980; Fogelson, 1977). But in spite of the increased numbers and improved quality, police do not apprehend many suspects without help (Phillips and DeFleur, 1982). When Black and Reiss (1970) observed routine police patrolling in Chicago, Boston, and Washington, D.C., they found that 72 percent of police-juvenile encounters resulted from citizen mobilizations. That is, a citizen observed juveniles involved in a mischievous act and phoned the police department; then, the police dispatcher sent a patrol car to investigate. The other 28 percent of police-juvenile encounters were initiated by police on patrol.

> Hence it would seem that the moral standards of the citizenry have more to do with the definition of juvenile deviance than do the standards of policemen on patrol (Black and Reiss, 1970:66).

Citizens in the System

If the police are so dependent upon the public to bring suspects to their attention, then perhaps we need to broaden our conception of the juvenile and criminal justice systems to include the general public. At one time, the role of the public was obvious. From the mid 1700s, vigilantes were a continuing presence in America; the forces of law and order were weak in the frontier regions, so pioneers took the law in their own hands (Brown, 1969). Even today, citizens are a crucial element in social control. After they have called the police station, citizens continue to play an influential role in police-juvenile encounters. As witnesses or complainants, they may tell the officer what to do with the youth. Police do not have to comply with these wishes, but they often do.

> In not one instance did the police arrest a juvenile when the complainant lobbied for leniency. When a complainant explicitly expresses a preference for an arrest . . . the tendency of the police to comply is also quite strong (Black and Reiss, 1970:70).

Cooperation Reflects Attitudes

People will report incidents to the police only if they think such incidents are important enough to deserve official intervention, if they think police will respond to the call, and if they think police will be able to provide some useful service once they arrive on the scene. Surveys show that Americans have positive images of the police; people regard the police more favorably than they view most other organizations and institutions, including the Supreme Court, Congress, the press, and the American Medical Association (Peek et al., 1978). At the same time, some citizens question police effectiveness. Often people who have been victimized do not report the fact to the police. When asked why, most of them reply that nothing could be done, so calling the police would be useless, and some of the other nonreporters said they simply did not want to get involved (Biderman et al., 1967).

Courts Need Citizen Support

Citizens make important contributions to the courts by serving as jurors and witnesses. Beyond these services, the public pressures the courts to get tougher in the handling of suspects and defendants. Public opinion of the courts has turned more critical in recent years. In 1965, the Gallup Poll found that only 45 percent of respondents indicated that the courts were too lenient with offenders; by 1973, the figure had jumped to 74 percent (Wattenberg, 1976) and has risen a bit higher since then. Courts are criticized not only for handing out lenient sentences but for dismissing cases on legal technicalities. In a study of Washington state citizens, Lotz (1976) found that 84 percent agreed that "instead of worrying about legal technicalities, courts should just try to find out whether the defendant did what he is accused of doing." Thus, courts are attacked for focusing on legal guilt instead of actual guilt. One result of all this criticism is that judges (many of whom are elected) appear to have gotten tougher. This is suggested by the fact that the adult prison population has been rising steeply. From less than 230,000 in 1974, it grew to about 440,000 in 1983, thus almost doubling in less than ten years (U.S. Department of Justice, 1984).

Prisons Need Support

There must be public support for prisons to be built (prison construction is a booming industry now), staffed, and allowed into certain areas or communities.The last issue is often a contested one; most people are in favor of building new prisons (Gallup, 1982), reformatories, halfway houses, and detention centers. Indeed, it is generally conceded that the present population boom in prisons is traceable primarily to public opinion (Gardner, 1982; Blumstein, 1983). But people typically do not want them built in their own community, where loitering or escaped offenders could harass local citizens or commit more offenses. It seems that most people favor prisons only if they exist somewhere far away—not in their own backyard. Such thinking echoes the conservative view of Ernest van den Haag (1975), who favors bringing back banishment and exile of prisoners to small, remote, and uninhabited islands. Clearly, van den Haag and the public want convicts far away; they do not want to be responsible for reintegrating them back into society.

Legislators Need Public Support

Sociologists and legal theorists have long argued about how laws emerge. Consensus theorists such as Durkheim (1964), Sumner (1906), and Bohannon (1965) argue that laws are generally based on customs and norms already existing in the society. Conflict theorists dispute this, claiming that laws are not based on the will of the people at all but are instead designed to reflect the interests of the ruling class (Thomas and Hepburn, 1983). Whichever view is more correct, we will suggest that there are *some* issues involving crime and delinquency that elicit strong opinions from many citizens. On these issues, many, if not most, legislators tend to listen to their constituents and vote the way their constituents want. Thus, as support for capital punishment has achieved new heights among the general public in recent years, more and more states have passed laws establishing the death penalty. Determinate sentencing laws (laws that require judges to sentence offenders for a specific number of years) are another instance in which the legislature thinks it is giving the public what it wants.

Stirring Up the Public

Sometimes the public must be manipulated into believing that a problem has gotten out of hand. Certainly, the American public has been subjected to many such attempts. Sometimes these carefully orchestrated manipulations have centered around drug use. The Narcotics Division of the Treasury Department was particularly active in trying to change public conceptions of drug addiction. Once, addiction was regarded by most people as a sickness, more to be pitied than condemned. After the Harrison Act was passed in 1914, the Narcotics Division (charged with enforcing it) flooded the media with the message that drug addicts are moral degenerates and violent criminals who seek to convince others to become users (Mauss, 1975). In recent times, the Nixon administration is said to have conducted an even more extensive campaign against drugs by convincing network chiefs to slip this message into television dramas. The plan was to stir up drug hysteria so that a massive organization could be created to fight drugs and other "evils" the administration opposed (Epstein, 1977).

Public Tolerance Matters

How much deviance a society experiences depends largely on how much its citizens will tolerate. A number of social scientists have pointed out just how crucial informal social control can be; intimidation occurs (or fails to occur)

> at the level of the neighborhood, the community, and the reference group. Men and women often pay more attention to the opinions of their peers and neighbors than they do to the attitudes or potential actions of their rulers (McClosky and Brill, 1983:15).

The intolerance of deviance and the effectiveness of informal social control may not be obvious in America; but it is evident elsewhere, as Adler (1983) has shown in her study of countries with low crime rates (Switzerland, Ireland, Bulgaria, East Germany, Costa Rica, Peru, Algeria, Saudi Arabia, Japan, and Nepal). These countries are very different from one another politically and economically; their systems of justice also are different. But they have in common tree things that keep the crime and delinquency rates low: strong family ties, shared values, and "communal surrogates for the vanishing clan" (Adler, 1983:13) such as the Japanese factory, the Bulgarian commune, and the Nepalese village council *(panchayat)*, all of which emphasize the common good rather than personal interest.

Public Perceptions Misunderstood

Finally, we should note that officials and commentators frequently assume that they know what the public thinks, wants, or feels about an issue. This assumption often turns out to be based on a foundation no firmer than intuition or "gut feelings" and as such is notoriously unreliable. On all questions of public perceptions, we need to be able to point to research findings if we are to have any confidence in our conclusions.

Berk and Rossi (1977), for example, have surveyed opinions of high-ranking officials in the corrections system of three states. In each state, these officials generally held liberal or reformist views of how prisons should be run; but they assumed each other to be less liberal and the public to be downright punitive and hostile to prison reform. Berk and Rossi (1977:83) note:

> Without independent measures of actual public opinion in the three states, it is difficult to assess whether the elites were more or less accurately reporting on this matter or simply expressing a stereotyped view of the public as generally unenlightened.

Shortly after this research was conducted (but before it was published), a survey of public opinion was carried out in one of the three states (Washington). It found the public to be surprisingly liberal on several issues (Rose, 1975).

1. Seventy-four percent gave a high priority to the goal of rehabilitation in prison; only 36–47 percent gave high priority to incapacitation, general deterrence, or retribution.
2. Only 18 percent favored greater use of solitary confinement.
3. Most were in favor of permitting visits by prisoners' spouses for sexual purposes.
4. Most favored increased opportunities for probation and parole.
5. Most favored allowing prisoner participation in prison government.
6. Most favored greater use of community-based corrections centers.
7. Only 7 percent wanted greater use of physical punishment in prison.

As these findings indicate, it is hazardous to guess what public attitudes will be.

THE PROBLEM

Having explained at length why the study of public perceptions is important, we now turn to some of the issues covered in Chapter 1. Researchers have looked at public views of the problem of crime and delinquency for quite a few years. For a long time, these phenomena were regarded as fairly minor problems by the public. Around 1950, for instance, the public viewed the following as the nation's top five problems:

1. Poor housing and slums
2. Transportation
3. Unsanitary conditions

TABLE 2–1
Public Perceptions of Crime Rate

"Is there more crime in this area than there was a year ago, or less?"

Year	More	Less	Same	No Opinion
1983	37%	17%	36%	10%
1982	47	17	28	8
1981	54	8	29	9
1977	43	17	32	8
1975	50	12	29	9
1972	51	10	27	12

Source: Shriver, 1983:9.

4. High taxes
5. Corrupt politics

But beginning in the 1960s, crime and delinquency assumed greater perceived importance. The issue

> that in the last ten years or so has bugged Americans more deeply than any other is *crime* and its related phenomena: violence, disruption, drugs. Civil rights was the number-one problem for several years. Then Vietnam was the number-one issue for a few years. But crime—since the mid-'60s—rolls on endlessly, bothering, irking, scaring and arousing Americans, always hovering near the top of the scale of issues (Wattenberg, 1976:274).

Almost no one thinks the rate of crime and delinquency is decreasing; some think it is about the same as the previous year, but most people believe it has risen noticeably. On this question, public opinion leans toward the alarmist position (see Table 2–1).

In looking at public anxiety about crime and delinquency, Furstenberg (1971) makes an important distinction between fear and concern. In one part of his research, people were asked to choose from a list of ten problems the one they considered most serious—that is, the one government ought to do something about. If the one that people chose was "crime and lawlessness," then, by Furstenberg's definition, those people were high on *concern* about crime. Oddly, he found that people high on concern were a bit more likely to live in the city's *low*-crime areas. This does not mean that people in high-crime neighborhoods were oblivious to or unaware of crime. Rather, it appears that they felt they were faced with other problems that were even more pressing than crime—problems such as unemployment or discrimination (Furstenberg, 1971).

If crime in one's own neighborhood does not actually cause concern, what does? Furstenberg's data show that concern is highest among people who oppose social change. People who say that old moral values are dying out and that too much emphasis is given to economic equality and minority rights are likely to be high on concern (that is, to rank crime or lawlessness as society's top problem). Concern is thus relative; people compare crime to other social problems and decide it is the most serious one. It also is more closely associated with attitudes toward social change than with the local crime rate. *Fear* (which Furstenberg defines as believing that one is likely to be victimized), however, is not based on comparisons with other social problems, it is unrelated to attitudes toward social change, and it is high where crime is high. Research from the West Coast reports similar findings (Lotz, 1976).

More recent research suggests that not only must we distinguish between fear and concern but between two kinds of fear as well. One study calls these *formless fear* and *concrete fear.* Formless fear is a diffuse feeling that one is somehow not safe in one's environment (Friedberg, 1983). This is the kind of fear pollsters study most. Gallup, for instance, routinely asks, "Is there any area around here—that is, within a mile—where you would be afraid to walk alone at night?" The percentage of people saying yes to this has risen from 34 in 1965 to 48 in 1982. Friedberg (1983:49) says of formless fear:

> The threat is located near home, in your everyday environment, and the level of fear isn't as high as in concrete fear. The reality of formless fear results in double-locked doors and burglar alarms.

Not all categories of people are equally subject to formless fear. Friedberg found the highest levels among residents of large cities; he also found females more fearful than males and low-income people more fearful than people with comfortable incomes. Thus, urbanization, sex, and income may help to cause fear.

Friedberg did not pursue the issue of how fear might be linked to victimization, though common sense suggests that being victimized would have a powerful impact on one's level of fear. Hindelang et al. (1978), however, have looked at the relationship and, surprisingly, find no correlation between the two. Actually, this nonrelationship hides a more complicated reality. All other things being equal, if a person is victimized, he or she is likely to become more afraid of crime and delinquency. But there are countervailing forces at work. Females and older persons are in the odd position of being both less victimized than other groups (Clemente and Kleiman, 1977; Conklin, 1981; Hindelang et al., 1978) and more afraid than other groups. There are at least two possible explanations for this. The *protective reaction* hypothesis states that females and the elderly are more afraid to begin with, so they stay away from high-crime areas such as parks and alleys and avoid going out alone or at night—all of which leads them to have lower victimization rates. The *vulnerability hypothesis* depicts women and oldsters as less able to escape attackers, fight back, and withstand assault, so this leads them to become more afraid of becoming victimized and badly hurt.

While formless fear has been studied by many survey researchers, little is known about concrete fear. This is fear of becoming the victim of a specific crime such as murder, rape, or armed robbery. Since concrete fears refer to specific offenses, it is reasonable to ask which offense inspires the most fear. Traditionally robbery has been considered to hold this distinction (Wilson, 1975; President's Commission, 1968); but recent findings cast doubt on this notion. A CBS/*New York Times* poll found robbery to be rather low on the list; more people said they worried about forcible rape, corporate cheating, and burglary (Flanagan et al., 1980).

Because of various studies showing that fear and concern over crime and delinquency are somewhat widespread, some writers suggest that America is developing a fortress mentality.

> It isn't just the criminal offensive that affects our lives, it is our own growing defensive. When we learn to turn on the alarm, put the jewelry in the refrigerator, push down the buttons in the car, think twice about walking down a street, our lives are diminished (Goodman, 1981:39).

What these writers fail to mention are the psychological defenses people now use to calm their fears and worries. For instance, there are two kinds of *distancing beliefs* people employ. One is to claim that crime and delinquency are worse "elsewhere." In a study of white urbanites, for example, only 6 percent said their neighborhood was more dangerous than most others in the city (Hindelang et al., 1978). About ten times as many said their neighborhood was less dangerous. Even people living in high-crime areas maintain such attitudes (Biderman et al., 1967).

Researchers offer various explanations to account for this phenomenon. Perhaps people imagine "elsewhere" is a place with no well-defined features except that most crimes covered by the news media seem to occur there. Or perhaps people have in mind a particular "worst place" to which they assign a large number of crimes and other miseries. People living in locations such as San Diego or Seattle, for instance, may feel quite fortunate when comparing their cities to New York. But even in New York, widely mentioned as a "worst place" for criminal victimization, the same process occurs. Many people in Manhattan would not consider taking the subway to Brooklyn. Some Brooklyn residents in turn point to the Bronx as the real crime-ridden borough. And in the Bronx, people insist that crime is really not so bad as the stereotypes suggest.

The second distancing technique is to blame "outsiders" for crimes that occur in one's neighborhood. This allows people to continue living in their community and to continue thinking of their neighbors as trustworthy. Of course, it also may foster an intense distrust of strangers, as criminologists in the 1960s and 1970s often noted. They asserted that the public believed most crime was committed by

> the stranger, the unknown person who commits an unpredictable and violent attack on a vulnerable and innocent citizen who is merely going about his regular business. The stranger is seen as intending harm and as indiscriminate in his selection of a victim, making it difficult for the victim to avoid him (Conklin, 1975:7).

The public is thus somewhat alarmist: some people are quite fearful, and most people think that crime is on the increase, but there also are distancing beliefs that allow people to think well of their neighborhoods and the people living in them. People rarely move away from their neighborhood simply to get away from the crime and delinquency.

THE BLAME

Whom do people single out as the main cause of crime and delinquency? Polls by the Gallup organization find that several explanations are offered for the alleged increase in crime. These have been grouped into two types: economic and moral reasons. The economic causes include unemployment, inflation, and poverty; moral causes include drugs, permissiveness, and parental failure. About half the nation blames the economy for crime, while the other half cites moral factors.

Some of the moral reasons seem to focus particularly on youths. "Lack of parental guidance," for example, implies that persons committing the offenses are minors. "Permissiveness" also implies that youths are the offenders, though on rare occasions the term may be intended to include adults as well. Drugs, too, are often linked to teenagers, at least in the public mind. This link has probably been prominent since the rise of the Counterculture in the 1960s. Although these Gallup data do not conclusively show that most people attribute crime to youths, they strongly hint in that direction.

Another study (Lotz, 1979) asked the question differently and found somewhat stronger evidence that many people attribute crime to the young. Respondents were asked why a person turns to crime, and they could choose among several answers:

1. Person is born criminal.
2. Person learned crime from friends and associates.

3. Society never gave person a chance to succeed except through crime.
4. Person was not given enough discipline when young.
5. Person got too little attention and friendship from parents and associates.
6. Person chooses crime of his own free will.

A majority selected answers 4 and 5; since these include the phrases "when they were young" and "from their parents," both responses imply that the offenders are youths. These two answers were chosen by almost two-thirds of the respondents, a clear sign that the public thinks youngsters are the main culprits or at least most offenders begin their careers when young.

Other surveys have focused on people's reaction to youngsters. Young people, especially when they congregate in groups, arouse fear, even though they may be doing nothing threatening or illegal.

> Susan Estrich, of the Harvard Law School, has recently gathered together a number of surveys on the sources of public fear. One, done in Portland, Oregon, indicated that three-fourths of the adults interviewed cross to the other side of a street when they see a gang of teenagers; another survey, in Baltimore, discovered that nearly half would cross the street to avoid even a single strange youth. When an interviewer asked people in a housing project where the most dangerous spot was, they mentioned a place where young persons gathered to drink and play music, despite the fact that not a single crime had occurred there (Wilson and Kelling, 1982).

More evidence that youths are feared comes from the literature on danger signs and cues. Skolnick (1966), who focused on police perceptions, has written the best-known work in this area. He notes that the police generally think of themselves as specialists who are uniquely skilled at detecting unusual or suspicious circumstances. They are particularly alert for *symbolic assailants*—people whose gestures, speech, or dress are tipoffs that they could suddenly become violent. "A young man may suggest the threat of violence . . . by his manner of walking or strutting, the insolence in the demeanor being registered as a possible preamble to later attack" (Skolnick, 1966:46). Why are youths so feared? An interview of elderly men found that the young are believed to be irrational and unpredictable. Asked if they were afraid of youths, the elderly men answered:

> not afraid exactly, but leery, extremely leery of young people, that you never know what's on a young person's mind. Then one of them said that a lot of young people he knows, some of the things they do are just to be mean, just to be ornery, it serves no purpose, it's really senseless (Skogan and Maxfield, 1981:93).

Thus, again there is a tendency for the public to take an alarmist stance—in this case, to blame crime on the young and to fear them, and in the last item quoted even to verge on a "monster myth" hypothesis.

THE SOLUTION

As we noted in Chapter 1, ideas about the problem, the blame, and the solution generally fit together into a fairly neat and coherent pattern. Thus, if people think that the crime problem is serious and frightening and that youths are largely responsible for it, then we also would expect them to favor a strong, punitive response, including tougher police, tougher courts, retribution, capital punishment, and treating young and adult offenders alike. Indeed, it is frequently assumed that the majority of Americans wholeheartedly endorse such policies. A number of surveys have investigated how valid these assumptions are.

Survey researchers often ask whether people approve of their local police and how well the police are performing their duties. Similar questions are asked about the courts and judges. Typically, people rate the police quite favorably but give courts far less flattering judgments. This may seem surprising, especially since the occupational prestige of judges is much higher than that of police (Treiman, 1977; Hodge et al., 1964). Certainly it surprised researchers in the late 1960s, when police were routinely being reviled as brutal, racist, and reactionary. For example, Biderman et al. (1967:145) expressed surprise at "the generally high regard for police among all groups." Later studies produced similar findings (Peek et al., 1978; Erskine, 1975).

Surveys and polls show that the courts receive far less approval and public support than police get. Few people believe that the courts are doing a good job. Judges are criticized for dismissing too many cases and giving out too many lenient sentences. Prosecutors are taken to task for plea bargaining, defense attorneys for delaying tactics and technical defenses that allow factually guilty defendants to go free. Favorable public responses to the police and unfavorable views of the courts may be partly due to the relative visibility of their errors (Wheeler et al., 1968). In other words, the police are more likely to receive publicity when they are too tough (for brutality, arresting the wrong person, coercing a confession, or harassing innocent people). Courts, however, are more likely to receive publicity when they are too lenient (for dismissing a case on a technicality or for giving a mild sentence to a serious offender).

The approval of the police exists partly because they are seen as tough; the disapproval of the courts exists partly because they are seen as not tough enough. We know that many citizens are in favor of toughness in the abstract, but what happens when ordinary citizens have the power to decide actual cases? Are they still as hard-nosed in their decisions? If they are, juries should be much more prosecution-minded than judges. And if this were the case, then no defendant would request a jury trial. In fact, quite a few trials are jury trials, and their outcomes seem to be very similar to the outcomes of trials in which judges make the decisions (Kalven and Zeisel, 1966). Thus, when confronted with the full set of facts in a case, the general citizenry reacts in a fairly pragmatic fashion; people do not seem to be especially prosecution-minded when they sit on juries.

What correctional philosophy do citizens embrace? Are they in favor of rehabilitation, or do they prefer retribution or some other justification for punishment? Some rehabilitation programs focus on individual therapy, some on group therapy, some on milieu therapy (in which the whole institution is devoted to being therapeutic), some on education or training. The Martinson (1974) report demonstrated that none of these consistently succeed in convincing inmates not to return to offending after they are released. Alarmists say this study shows that rehabilitation does not work, so other justifications, such as retribution, ought to be emphasized.

To see if the public has soured on the rehabilitative ideal, Rose (1975) asked people whether they supported the following approaches to running prisons:

1. Protecting the public by putting most offenders behind bars.
2. Preventing crime by making examples of offenders.
3. Making most offenders pay their debt to society by punishing them.
4. Rehabilitating offenders so that they "go straight."

She found that rehabilitation was by far the most popular of these policies; 75 percent of respondents thought it should be emphasized. Incapacitation (1) and retribution (3) got 45 percent support and general deterrence (2) only 36 percent. More recent data by the Harris Poll organization produces similar results: 44 percent say prisons should emphasize rehabilitation, while only 19 percent favor retribution (Flanagan and McLeod, 1983). These results are not as clear-cut as they seem, however, because researchers tend to define rehabilitation as the curing of an offender so that he will go free and commit no more crimes or delinquencies. With this definition, the idea is bound to receive public endorsement. But a more appropriate definition of rehabilitation is that it is a kind of therapy or treatment program aimed at changing the offender. The degree to which the public approves of this we do not really know. As for retribution, surveys show generally that the public approves of it when it is stated in terms of the punishment fitting the crime, and generally disapproves of it when it is stated as providing punishment without any useful purpose.

One key issue in any study of public opinion about punishment and correctional policy is capital punishment. This is one of those rare topics on which almost everybody has an opinion. If we look at the standard questions on capital punishment in the Gallup polls, we find support is high: about 72 percent favored it in 1982 for persons convicted of murder. This finding is ambiguous, however, since it could mean such a punishment for some or for all such offenders. Would all of these 72 percent vote for the death penalty if they were sitting on a jury? Jurow (1971) looked at this question, presenting mock jurors with a case involving a defendant convicted of a capital crime. They could choose to give the defendant a death sentence, life imprisonment, or some lesser penalty. Before the experiment, 45 percent said they were for capital punishment and another 20 percent were neutral. But when faced with an actual case, only 8 percent chose capital punishment. Thus, a general disposition to favor capital punishment rarely leads people to choose it when they have a realistic case before them.

Why people support the idea of capital punishment has been the subject of considerable research and discussion (Thomas and Foster, 1975; Vidmar and Ellsworth, 1975). In a more recent study, Lotz and Regoli (1980) looked at a series of items to see if they were related to support for capital punishment. Several items that were expected to be related to such support were not, at least not strongly—fear of crime and being victimized by crime, for example. Other items, which were not expected to be related to capital punishment, turned out to be the best predictors of it.

1. (Oppose) granting weekend leaves for inmates to visit relatives or search for future employment.
2. Prosecutors should try to convict the offender of the crime committed, not reduce the charge.
3. (Oppose) letting inmates make formal complaints to the courts about prison conditions.
4. Using solitary confinement for disobedient inmates.
5. If we let the police get tough, the crime problem in this country will be solved.
6. One reason we have so much crime is that the courts are too lenient with youngsters who commit their first crime.
7. Defense attorneys cause too many delays in court.

These items reflect hostility toward suspects, defendants, and inmates. But perhaps the best tipoff comes from another question: which problem is the most serious one now facing people in the United States? Common sense dictates capital punishment support would be most strongly related to the answer "crime and delinquency." But in fact the answer "demands being made by various groups" was the one especially likely to be chosen by capital punishment supporters. (Of course, it was not spelled out just who these groups were, but presumably respondents had in mind minorities, plus perhaps women or unions.) Thus, people advocating capital punishment are typically not the fearful, the victimized, or those especially concerned about crime; instead, they are more likely the people who are hostile to certain minority groups and particularly hostile to offenders.

Finally, there is the question of how the public thinks juvenile offenders should be handled. Alarmists want youths and adults to be treated alike, while reassurers (embracing the juvenile court philosophy) want juveniles handled separately and treated kindly. A CBS/*New York Times* poll (Parisi et al., 1979) presents the issues. It shows that almost everybody (86 percent) wants juveniles sent to separate institutions. But the public is more evenly split on (1) whether juveniles and adults should be tried in the same courts and (2) whether juveniles and adults should receive identical sentences. Thus, the public is at least willing to consider the alarmist view. The reassuring view may have lost some of its popularity in recent years with respect to separation of juveniles and adults. More generally, the public views on the solution are not wholly reassuring or alarmist. On the contrary, they are complex and sociologically interesting. It will require years of research to make them understandable.

MEDIA INFLUENCES

"One hundred years ago there was no radio, no television, no movies; newspapers were little more than political organs, and magazines and books were the products of limited industries" (Rivers et al., 1980:14). But the mass media have blossomed since then, especially television. In 1946, less than 1 percent of homes had a television set; by 1967, the figure had reached 98 percent (Jones, 1980), and many homes had several sets. Now there is one television for every 1.7 persons in the country (Strathern, 1978). And the other media also have expanded rapidly in this century.

Newspapers have existed for a couple of centuries, but they take a very different form now than they once had. In the 1820s, for example, when most Americans were crowded along the Eastern seaboard, the typical daily newspaper was only four pages long, with the first and last pages devoted exclusively to advertising. Even the middle two were not all general news; they contained editorial columns, details of ship arrivals and their cargoes. These newspapers were expensive, so circulation was confined to business and government circles—hence the emphasis on commerce and politics in these papers (Schudson, 1978).

In the 1830s, however, the penny press was created. Prices of daily newspapers were slashed, and circulation rose, spreading to new segments of the population such as the poor and the barely literate. Cutting costs alone did not bring in all the new readers; other techniques were needed—notably, adding spice and sensationalism in the form of larger headlines, pictures, and scandals. For the first time, newspaper owners also hired reporters to cover particular "beats," including the police and courts.

In some instances, reporters created their own crime waves, as Lincoln Steffens reveals in his autobiography (1931). His post was a police station/jail, where both police officers and inmates often told stories of criminal activity (with the understanding that these would be off the record). Steffens wrote up one of these for his paper, the *New York Post.* Then Jacob Riis, a reporter for a competing paper, was asked by his editor why he failed to report the story. That afternoon, Riis got his revenge on Steffens by writing up another jailhouse story; then it was Steffens's turn to get chewed out by an editor. Soon the other New York papers joined in this competition, finding new crimes and rewriting the ones already reported on by Riis and Steffens. They grouped all these stories to show that there was a crime wave. Police commissioner Theodore Roosevelt was alarmed to find crime rising so fast in his new and honest administration. Later, one of his assistants consulted the records and found there was no increase in crimes at all. Although the crimes reported in the papers were true incidents, the impression that there was a wave of crime was purely an invention of the media.

As in earlier eras, modern newspapers rely on the police for much of their crime news. Reporters now depend on the police to send them data over the teletype. These accounts usually contain only the barest of details about the victims and offenders. (For an exception, though, see Karmen [1978] on media description of looters.) The offenses that police are most likely to include in their news summaries are street crimes such as armed robberies, burglaries, shootings, and muggings. In part, police decide what information to include in these summaries by first deciding what the press wants. The police-supplied incidents lead the media to support the belief that real crime is "crime on the streets, crime occurring between strangers, crime which brutalizes the weak and defenseless, and crime perpetrated by vicious youths" (Fishman, 1978:540).

People may be less gullible now than in Theodore Roosevelt's day, but many commentators assume that the media have a powerful impact on public perceptions of crime and delinquency—that newspapers and television make puppets of us all. Cohen and Young (1973:9), for instance, claim that the mass media "provide the guiding myths that shape our conception of the world." But they offer no evidence to back up this claim. In their book, the only pertinent data are supplied by Roshier, who found essentially no correlation "between the overall bias of the newpapers studied and the views of their readers" (1973:37).

Roshier's findings deal with England, so it could be argued that they do not apply to the United States. The best-known American study, by F. James Davis, is often cited as proof that the media have a strong impact on public perceptions of the nature and extent of crime (see, for example, Quinney, 1970; Becker, 1975). Actually, a close reading of the Davis article shows nothing of the sort, because he admits that "some of the evidence is inconclusive and some seems contrary to the hypothesis" (1952:330). Therefore, on the basis of his article, we cannot say anything conclusive about the effects of newspapers on public perceptions of crime. More recent studies must be consulted.

Graber (1980) studied the *Chicago Tribune* and its readers to see how closely they agreed on who the main offenders are and why they turn to crime. She found that the *Tribune* does not always mention the suspect's race, age, sex, or occupation—but it does some of the time. On those occasions, the *Tribune* data refer to criminals usually as white, male, over 25, and businessmen or professionals. *Tribune* readers offer a quite different view: they believe the typical offender is black, male, under 25, and unemployed. If we can generalize from the *Tribune*, newspapers tend to focus on the most-favored segment of society—older white men in the more prestigious occupations. The public, nevertheless, thinks of criminals more stereotypically as young black males.

When the *causes* of crime are addressed, the newspaper and its readers again disagree. Readers point to social conditions such as poverty and economic distress as the most important sources of crime and delinquency. On those rare occasions when they discuss causes, newspapers blame the justice system for being too lenient (Graber, 1980). Although newspapers probably devote an excessive amount of space to crime news and most people learn about such incidents from the media, most people are not necessarily dependent on the media for *understanding* crime. The media rarely provide analysis or interpretations of the incidents they report, so readers and viewers must form their own conclusions; in doing so, they sometimes rely on stereotypes, and sometimes they employ more original thinking.

We have thus far looked only at newspapers. But television too is often said to have important effects upon public perceptions. George Gerbner and his associates (1978; 1980) have been particularly strong advocates of this view. They argue that television is a primary source of enculturation in American society.

> The massive flow of stories showing what things are, how things work, and what to do about them has become the common socializer of our times. These stories form a coherent if "mythical" world in every home. Television dominates the symbolic environment of modern life (Gerbner et al., 1980:10).

Gerbner says heavy viewers (those who watch four or more hours per day) come to believe that what they see on television is quite true to life. They note that heavy viewing leads people to see more television violence; this in turn leads them to become more alienated, less trusting, more fearful, and to take more precautions against violence than other people do. Critics have raised doubts about Gerbner's research, however (Hughes, 1980; Hirsch, 1980). Hughes, for instance, claims that there are many questionable procedures used in Gerbner's work. He also claims that after controlling for other important variables such as age, sex, and city size, the relationship between television viewing and fear of being out alone at night completely vanishes. Sacco (1982) also tested this hypothesis, and although he found a relationship between television viewing and fear, it was very weak.

Why don't the media have a bigger impact on public perceptions? Rivers et al. (1980:27) offer some clues:

> People come to the media, as to other messages, seeking what they want, not what the media intend them to have. . . . They still have their defenses up; they still defend their strongly held positions. Because of their distance from the media . . . they tend to put great reliance on their own social groups and their own advisers. Interpersonal channels of communication are functioning side by side with mass media channels and these interpersonal channels are exerting much of the influence on society.

People thus take the media with a grain of salt or quickly forget their message and rely on other sources for their attitudes and opinions—including friends and associates.

SUMMARY

Several considerations make public perceptions of crime and delinquency significant:

1. By themselves, police usually cannot capture offenders or make arrests. They must rely on ordinary citizens to help them.
2. The public plays a role in the juvenile and criminal justice systems; citizens are not merely bystanders.
3. The degree to which people cooperate with the police is affected at least partly by their attitudes and opinions about crime and delinquency and the social control system.
4. Courts also need the cooperation of the public as witnesses, jurors, or perhaps supporters or critics.
5. Prisons need public support—both to staff them and to allow them to be built in certain communities.
6. Legislators need public support if they are to pass bills dealing with crime and delinquency.
7. Controlling crime and delinquency competes with other issues for money and attention. How much funding it gets may depend on how aroused citizens are.
8. How tolerant or intolerant people are of crime and delinquency affects how much deviance will occur in the society.
9. Public perceptions are widely speculated about but poorly understood because there is too little research and because existing research is too rarely read.

The public does not think crime and delinquency are declining. Furstenberg found that crime rates were not a good predictor of concern about crime, which instead tends to reflect opposition to social change. Fear, on the other hand, does seem to be related to crime rates. But Friedberg says it is necessary to distinguish between two types: formless and concrete. Formless fear is highest among urbanites, females, and the poor. Interestingly, this kind of fear is unrelated to the experience of being victimized, partly because women and the elderly are both more afraid of crime and less victimized by it. Most people are not paralyzed by fear. Instead, they develop distancing beliefs that allow them to go on thinking their neighborhood is reasonably safe and their neighbors trustworthy.

Several sources suggest the public singles out youths as the main cause of crime and delinquency. Gallup polls show that many people blame crime on lack of morality, meaning permissiveness, drugs, and parental failure, all three of which are linked in the public mind with youngsters. A West Coast study found most people believe that individuals turn to crime because they were not given enough discipline when young or too little attention from parents—again the focus is obviously on youths and childhood influences. Other studies have demonstrated that older people are afraid of groups of youths, even if they are not doing anything illegal or threatening.

When asked about punishment, the public takes many sides, perhaps because there are so many issues. They generally approve of the police and disapprove of the courts, possibly due to a phenomenon known as the visibility of errors. The philosophy of rehabilitation may be in disfavor with experts, but it is still popular with the general citizenry, perhaps because it is often misrepresented to them as being a cure for criminality.

The influence of the mass media on public perceptions of crime and delinquency remains questionable. Today's newspaper readers seem to be less naive and gullible than their nineteenth-century counterparts. Graber's research on *Chicago Tribune* readers suggests that their views about who typically commits crimes and why they do it are distinctly different from the information presented in the paper's crime stories—an example of the important lesson that assumptions about public perceptions turn out to be quite wrong embarrassingly often.

DISCUSSION QUESTIONS

1. How does the public affect social control in the United States?
2. What does the public perceive to be the causes of crime?
3. Why are certain youths perceived as symbolic assailants?
4. How is fear of victimization related to concern about crime?

5. What are the differences between formless fear and concrete fear?
6. What are some psychological defenses people use to calm their fears about crime?
7. Why do the police generally enjoy public approval and support while the courts do not?
8. How does the public view retribution and rehabilitation as correctional goals?
9. How do the mass media affect public perceptions of crime?
10. How do public perceptions of the characteristics of criminals and the causes of crime differ from newspaper accounts of crime?

REFERENCES

ADLER, FREDA
1983 *Nations Not Obsessed with Crime.* Littleton, Colo.: Rothman.

BECKER, HOWARD S.
1975 *Outsiders: Studies in the Sociology of Deviance.* New York: Free Press.

BERK, RICHARD A., AND PETER H. ROSSI
1977 *Prison Reform and State Elites.* Cambridge, Mass.: Ballinger.

BIDERMAN, ALBERT D., ET AL.
1967 *Report on a Pilot Study in the District of Columbia on Victimization and Attitudes toward Law Enforcement.* Washington: U.S. Government Printing Office.

BLACK, DONALD J., AND ALBERT J. REISS, JR.
1970 Police control of juveniles. *American Sociological Review* 35 (February):63–77.

BLUMSTEIN, ALFRED
1983 Prisons: Population, capacity, and alternatives. Pp. 229–250 in James Q. Wilson (ed.), *Crime and Public Policy.* San Francisco: Institute for Contemporary Studies.

BOHANNON, PAUL
1965 The differing realms of the law. *American Anthropologist* 67 (December):33–42.

BROWN, RICHARD MAXWELL
1969 The American vigilante tradition. Pp. 45–84 in Hugh Davis Graham and Ted Robert Gurr (eds.), *The History of Violence in America.* New York: Bantam.

CLEMENTE, FRANK, AND MICHAEL B. KLEIMAN
1977 Fear of crime in the United States. *Social Forces* 56 (December):519–531.

COHEN, STANLEY, AND JOCK YOUNG
1973 *The Manufacture of News.* London: Constable.

CONKLIN, JOHN
1981 *Criminology.* New York: Macmillan.
1975 *The Impact of Crime.* New York: Macmillan

DAVIS, F. JAMES
1952 Crime news in Colorado newspapers. *American Journal of Sociology* 57 (January):325–330.

DURKHEIM, EMILE
1964 *The Division of Labor in Society.* New York: Free Press.
EPSTEIN, EDWARD JAY
1977 *Agency of Fear.* New York: Putnam.
ERSKINE, HAZEL
1975 The polls. *Public Opinion Quarterly* 38 (Winter):623–634.
FISHMAN, MARK
1978 Crime waves as ideology. *Social Problems* 25 (June):531–543.
FLANAGAN, TIMOTHY J., AND MAUREEN McLEOD
1983 *Sourcebook of Criminal Justice Statistics.* Washington: U.S. Department of Justice.
FLANAGAN, TIMOTHY J., ET AL.
1980 *Sourcebook of Criminal Justice Statistics.* Washington: U.S. Department of Justice.
FOGELSON, ROBERT M.
1977 *Big-City Police.* Cambridge, Mass.: Harvard University Press.
FRIEDBERG, ARDY
1983 *America Afraid.* New York: New American Library.
FURSTENBERG, FRANK F., JR.
1971 Public reaction to crime in the streets. *The American Scholar* 40 (Autumn):601–610.
GALLUP, GEORGE H.
1982 Public Backs Wholesale Prison Reform, *Gallup Report* No. 200 (May) pp. 3–16.
GARDNER, RALPH, JR.
1982 Prison population jumps to 369,725. *Corrections Magazine* 8 (June):6–14, 46.
GERBNER, GEORGE, ET AL.
1980 The "mainstreaming" of America: Violence profile no. 11. *Journal of Communication* 30 (Summer):10–29.
1978 Cultural indicators: Violence profile No. 9. *Journal of Communication* 28 (Summer):176–207.
GOODMAN, ELLEN
1981 *At Large.* New York: Fawcett-Crest.
GRABER, DORIS A.
1980 *Crime News and the Public.* New York: Praeger.
HINDELANG, MICHAEL J., ET AL.
1978 *Victims of Personal Crime.* Cambridge, Mass.: Ballinger.
HIRSCH, PAUL M.
1980 The "scary world" of the nonviewer and other anomalies. *Communication Research* 7 (October):403–456.
HODGE, ROBERT W., ET AL.
1964 Occupational prestige in the United States, 1925–1963. *American Journal of Sociology* 70 (November):286–302.
HUGHES, MICHAEL
1980 The fruits of cultivation analysis. *Public Opinion Quarterly* 44 (Fall):287–302.
JONES, LANDON Y.
1980 *Great Expectations.* New York: Coward, McCann & Geoghegan.
JUROW, GEORGE L.
1971 New data on the effect of a "death qualified" jury on the guilt determination process. *Harvard Law Review* 84 (January):567–611.

KALVEN, HARRY, JR., AND HANS ZEISEL
1966 *The American Jury.* Boston: Little, Brown.
KARMEN, ANDREW
1978 How much heat, how much light. Pp. 179–200 in Charles Winick (ed.), *Deviance and Mass Media.* Beverly Hills, Calif.: Sage.
LANE, ROGER
1980 Urban police and crime in nineteenth-century America. Pp. 1–43 in Norval Morris and Michael Tonry (eds.), *Crime and Justice.* Chicago: University of Chicago Press.
LOTZ, ROY
1979 Public anxiety about crime. *Pacific Sociological Review* 22 (April):241–254.
1976 Criminal Justice in Washington State: What Are Your Views? Unpublished codebook.
LOTZ, ROY, AND ROBERT M. REGOLI
1980 Public support for the death penalty. *Criminal Justice Review* 5 (Spring):55–66.
MARTINSON, ROBERT
1974 What works?—Questions and answers about prison reform. *The Public Interest* 35 (Spring):22–54.
MAUSS, ARMAND L.
1975 *Social Problems as Social Movements.* Philadelphia: Lippincott.
McCLOSKY, HERBERT, AND ALIDA BRILL
1983 *Dimensions of Tolerance.* New York: Russell Sage Foundation.
PARISI, NICOLETTE, ET AL.
1979 *Sourcebook of Criminal Justice Statistics.* Washington: U.S. Department of Justice.
PEEK, CHARLES W., ET AL.
1978 Comparative evaluation of the local police. *Public Opinion Quarterly* 42 (Fall):370–379.
PHILLIPS, DRETHA M., AND LOIS B. DeFLEUR
1982 Gender ascription and the stereotyping of deviants. *Criminology* 20 (November):431–438.
PRESIDENT'S COMMISSION ON LAW ENFORCEMENT AND ADMINISTRATION OF JUSTICE
1968 *The Challenge of Crime in a Free Society.* New York: Avon.
QUINNEY, RICHARD
1970 *The Social Reality of Crime.* Boston: Little, Brown.
RIVERS, WILLIAM L., ET AL.
1980 *Responsibility in Mass Communications.* New York: Harper & Row.
ROSE, VICKI
1975 Prison and Correctional Policies and Reform. Unpublished codebook.
ROSHIER, BOB
1973 The selection of crime news by the press. Pp. 28–39 in Stanley Cohen and Jock Young (eds.), *The Manufacture of News.* London: Constable.
SACCO, VINCENT F.
1982 The effects of mass media on perceptions of crime. *Pacific Sociological Review* 25 (October):475–493.
SCHUDSON, MICHAEL
1978 *Discovering the News.* New York: Basic.
SHRIVER, JAMES
1983 One in four households hit by crime. *Gallup Report* No. 210 (March):3–9.
SKOGAN, WESLEY, AND MICHAEL G. MAXFIELD
1981 *Coping with Crime.* Beverly Hills, Calif.: Sage.

SKOLNICK, JEROME
1966 *Justice without Trial.* New York: Wiley.

STEFFENS, LINCOLN
1931 *The Autobiography of Lincoln Steffens.* New York: Harcourt, Brace & World.

STRATHERN, PAUL
1978 *The Book of Numbers.* New York: A & W.

SUMNER, WILLIAM GRAHAM
1906 *Folkways.* Boston: Ginn.

THOMAS, CHARLES W., AND SAMUEL C. FOSTER
1975 A sociological perspective on public support for capital punishment. *American Journal of Orthopsychiatry* 45 (July):641–657.

THOMAS, CHARLES W., AND JOHN R. HEPBURN
1983 *Crime, Criminal Law, and Criminology.* Dubuque, Iowa: Wm. C. Brown.

TREIMAN, DONALD J.
1977 *Occupational Prestige in Comparative Perspective.* New York: Academic Press.

U.S. DEPARTMENT OF JUSTICE
1984 *Prisoners in 1983.* Washington: Bureau of Justice Statistics.

VAN DEN HAAG, ERNEST
1975 *Punishing Criminals.* New York: Basic.

VIDMAR, NEIL, AND PHOEBE C. ELLSWORTH
1975 Public opinion on the death penalty. Pp. 125–151 in Hugo Adam Bedau and Charles M. Pierce (eds.), *Capital Punishment in the United States.* New York: AMS Press.

WATTENBERG, BEN J.
1976 *In Search of the Real America.* New York: Berkeley.

WHEELER, STANTON, ET AL.
1968 Agents of delinquency control. Pp. 31–60 in Stanton Wheeler (ed.), *Controlling Delinquents.* New York: Wiley.

WILSON, JAMES Q.
1975 *Thinking about Crime.* New York: Basic.

WILSON, JAMES Q., AND GEORGE L. KELLING
1982 Broken windows. *The Atlantic* 249 (March):29–38.

Family and Delinquency 3

INTRODUCTION

Delinquency takes many forms. It may be committed alone or in groups; it may be serious or trivial; it may be an uncharacteristic act or part of a long career. Thus, the heading of delinquency covers many activities that are quite different in meaning. It is the more serious, more careerist delinquents that interest social scientists, the media, and the public. One such individual is Peewee Brown, who was the subject of a long article in the *New York Times*.

> Over a four year period, from the age of 11 to 15, Peewee was arrested 15 times on charges ranging from sodomy to assault. . . . He now admits that those arrests were for only a small number of his crimes. For example, he said when he was 13 he shot and killed a man on a deserted street corner in Brooklyn, but was never caught. He added that he seriously wounded at least six others and committed countless other robberies (Kleiman, 1982:44).

Why do some youths, like Peewee Brown, commit serious crimes while countless others are immersed in baseball or video games? This question has inspired a number of explanatory theories; these will be covered in Chapters 6, 7, and 8. In this and the following two chapters we will be more concerned with some of the main factors that the theories are based on.

The article on Peewee Brown made no concerted effort to pinpoint the reasons why he committed his offenses. It did give some hints, however, such as bad eyesight, inability to read, and short stature, each of which might have made him turn to toughness as a way of proving himself. His family background is another possible factor:

> Harold (Peewee) Brown was born on Sept. 24, 1961, the son of an unemployed alcoholic who left his wife when Peewee was 7 months old and who died when the boy was 14. Peewee's mother, Louise, an articulate woman with a high school education, always worked to support herself and her three sons. She had to be at her job by 8 A.M. so she left them at home alone at 7 A.M. and did not return until 5 P.M. Often, she conceded, she did not know what they were doing while she was gone (Kleiman, 1982:44).

Even this description might lead one to ask what family characteristic prompted Peewee to embark on a delinquent career. Was it the (1) absent father, (2) working mother, (3) lack of adult supervision, or (4) parents' inability to handle him? These possibilities all imply that Peewee's parents, or at least the mother, wanted him to be nondelinquent and tried to teach him nondelinquent values. But some commentators would say that children become delinquent partly because parents actively encourage delinquent behavior; the best examples of this are families engaged in organized crime, in which the oldest son may be expected to follow in his father's footsteps. Most commentators, though, focus on families who are simply not strong enough to guide their children into a nondelinquent way of life. They are not strong enough, the argument goes, because the family structure has weakened in recent years. And delinquency is a direct result of this breakdown. Since this line of thinking has won many adherents, we will discuss it more fully in the following section.

THE FAMILY IN TRANSITION

How serious is the condition of the modern family in America? The neotraditionalists (Berger and Berger, 1983), whose view we will be presenting here, say it is very serious indeed. This view has filtered down to the general public, who widely accept it: the family is in critical condition and is getting progressively worse. When Caplow et al. interviewed people in a small Midwestern city, they discovered that

> Nearly everybody in Middletown knows about the crisis of the modern family and deplores it. Over and over again, they hear from politicians, educators, and neighbors down the street how serious the situation is. . . . Any intelligent housewife in Middletown can tick off the degenerative symptoms. . . . (1982:322).

The list of these degenerative symptoms cited by commentators typically include the following:

1. Marriage is something fewer and fewer people want.

If, as the commentators suggest, the family is in decline, the reason may be that people increasingly do not want to get married. At one time, people who remained unmarried were considered deviant.

> By the 1950s and '60s psychiatry had developed a massive weight of theory establishing that marriage—and, within that, the breadwinner role—was the only normal state for the adult male. Outside lay only a range of diagnoses, all unflattering (Ehrenreich, 1984:15).

Women were sometimes called "spinsters" or "old maids." As recently as 1957 an overwhelming majority of people (80 percent) agreed with the statement "For a woman to remain unmarried, she must be 'sick,' 'neurotic,' or 'immoral' " (Yankelovich, 1981:93). By the late 1970s, though, very few people thought this way; indeed, most respondents said it was acceptable not only to remain single but to stay single and have children, too (1981).

In addition to attitudes, actual behavior has changed, according to recent census reports. For instance, the number of single men—those who have their own residence and who have never married—more than doubled between 1970 and 1980. Similarly, the number of divorced and separated men living alone also doubled during this brief period. In all, the number of households increased by 16 million during this period, but married couples accounted for only 22 percent of the increase. Hacker attributes this to a reluctance to put up with the frustrations marriage entails:

> Far fewer people are willing to accept the constraints and obligations required for family ties, such as the duty to stay together, even when a marriage proves less than ideal (1982:37).

2. Being a homemaker is something that fewer and fewer women want.

Critics insist homemaking is a demeaning and mindless routine. In *The Feminine Mystique,* Betty Friedan said it takes little brainpower to dump clothes into a washing machine; indeed, most housework could be capably handled by the feeble-minded or by 8-year-olds (1963). If a woman does not want to marry and "homemake," then presumably she will seek satisfaction and fulfillment elsewhere. Working for a living may seem a normal alternative today, but it was once frowned on. In 1938, for instance, three out of four Americans thought that a woman should not earn money if she had a husband who could support her, an attitude that had persisted since the nineteenth century. Similarly, if a turn-of-the-century woman wore expensive clothes with ruffles, bustles, and numerous petticoats that made work impossible for her, she brought credit to her husband, for it showed that he was such a capable breadwinner he could afford a wife who was completely dependent upon him (Veblen, 1899). More generally, according to the nineteenth-century cult of domesticity, women were held responsible for the comfort and tranquility of the home, while men were supposed to work outside the home, make money, and raise the family status. Men and women thus occupied two distinct spheres (Degler, 1980).

Today, though, sex role behavior and ideology have changed significantly. World War II seems to have been one important factor in this shift; the manpower shortage it created in American factories led to the hiring of many women and lent respectability to the working wife. By 1978, only a quarter of the American public felt that a woman should not earn money if she has a husband who can support her. The economy also played a role in this transition. Today, half of working Americans have white-collar jobs, jobs that require an ability to read, write, and perform clerical tasks. These jobs seem to be well suited to women, so many have been hired to fill them; only one in five married women worked in 1950, but by 1980 this ratio jumped to one in two. And among women with school-age children, the percentage was even higher. Earlier in this century, almost all working women were single or poor; working was thought to be socially undesirable and only engaged in by the poor, while leisure was admired. Now many women work because it is important to them and because they need the income.

3. Fewer and fewer people want a large number of children.

As recently as 1945, half the adults in America said they would want to have four or more children. This attitude dominated for about two decades.

> At that time all the single women interviewed in the study assumed that they would marry and have children. All those already married who did not have children stated they planned to have them; most wanted three or four or more. . . . [Several mothers] admitted they had become pregnant without intending to, but no one felt comfortable saying outright that she did not want to have a child. It would not have been respectable to say so—or even think so (Yankelovich, 1981:92).

As a result, there was a baby boom between 1946 and 1964. Nearly all married couples had two to four children.

Now, however, the picture is quite different. The birth rate has declined greatly and since 1976 has hovered around 1.8 children per couple. One important reason for this change is that more and more parents are unwilling to have more than two children. In the 1950s, mothers who unintentionally got pregnant usually had the extra child; many families felt prosperous enough to take on a new member (Jones, 1980). By the 1970s, potential parents were far less willing to accept an unexpected child. Hence, abortions rose (and so did political sensitivity to them). The Alan Guttmacher Institute estimates there were 1.41 million abortions in 1978 and 1.54 million in 1979; there were 3.49 million births in 1979, so there were about 440 abortions for every 1,000 live births (Hacker, 1983).

4. Sacrifice and self-denial are things that fewer and fewer people are willing to practice.

Sacrifice and self-denial used to be grounded in the Protestant ethic, which urged believers to work hard and earn as much money as possible but discouraged them from spending it on any self-indulgences. This ethic eventually lost its significance as church doctrine and became known by psychologists as "deferral of gratification." It was still considered a very positive trait and a sign of maturity and future success. Parents who lived through the Depression of the 1930s also spoke glowingly of sacrifice as a virtue and a character builder. Yankelovich carries on this same theme: that sacrifice is a virtue that can contribute to future success.

> Both parents [in the traditional family] were expected to sacrifice for their children. It was assumed that successful family life required such sacrifices—the wife subordinating her own desires to the needs of husband and children, the man willingly accepting the frustrations of the workplace as long as the job paid well. . . . Husband and wife functioned as a unit, he on the job, she at home, to acquire the products and services that made life more secure and comfortable. If . . . one's standard of living failed to improve year by year, one could at least work hard to insure that the children would receive a good education so that they could attain a higher plateau of material well-being than their parents (1981:113).

In the United States, the Protestant ethic has been losing force. In 1970, more than one out of three Americans said work was at the center of their lives. By 1978, this figure had slipped to 13 percent. Affluence had some effect upon this decline: fewer and fewer people had to worry about falling into a life of dire poverty. And higher levels of education persuaded many people that there are other, loftier goals than material prosperity and "keeping up with the Joneses."

5. Hedonism and self-fulfillment are things that more and more people are pursuing.

If sacrifice, hard work, and frugality—the virtues celebrated by the Protestant ethic—are on the way out, they are being replaced, the neotraditionalists say, by hedonism and self-fulfillment. The pitfalls of these new concerns are suggested in the following anecdote, which involves a female patient who is complaining about her hectic life:

> too many big weekends, too many discos, too many late hours, too much talk, too much wine, too much love-making.
>
> "Why don't you stop?" asked the therapist mildly. Her patient stared blankly for a moment and then her face lit up, dazzled by an illumination.
>
> "You mean I really don't have to do what I want to do?" she burst out with amazement (Yankelovich, 1981:85–86).

As this comment suggests, modern norms encourage people to seek sensual pleasure and gratification rather than to maintain self-control. More people actively seek a life filled with new thrills and pleasure instead of order, predictability, and the tedium of work. Many of these new norms came from humanistic psychology, which asserted

> that people's impulses are basically good, that the human potential for creativity is vast, that spontaneity is preferable to stagnation and that, contrary to Freud, life is an "adventure" and not a tragedy (Ehrenreich, 1984:89).

Neotraditionalists fear that the rise in hedonism and the number of working women, plus the decline in the Protestant ethic and marriage and birth rates, will seriously endanger future generations. These critics argue that:

1. These five trends mean that the family is weakening.
2. The family is the one institution that holds society together.
3. If the family loses its influence, children will not get the guidance they need.
4. So children will grow up wild, unsocialized, and disruptive.

Neotraditionalists say the family should revert to the traditional form: it should have a resident father and an ever-present mother who instruct their children in values and morals; they should also provide role models, authority, and supervision. Otherwise, children might turn to drugs, sexual experimentation, or serious delinquency.

Neotraditionalists were not the first to complain about a decline in the American family. They were preceded by a group of social scientists in the 1960s who expressed concern about the changing nature of black families. The most famous work by this group, the Moynihan Report (prepared in 1965 by Daniel Patrick Moynihan, then President Johnson's undersecretary of labor) was written to alarm Johnson about the living conditions of some poor black families. In order to accomplish this goal, Moynihan deliberately expressed some of his ideas in dramatic, sometimes not very objective language. He hoped his report would cause the government to step in and correct some of the economic inequities that were hurting these families. He argued that the American economy and welfare policy were destructive, undermining black males' role in the family and causing many black families to be run by women. Moynihan thought this situation led to an unstable home life, which in turn contributed to black children's poorer performance in school. This would lead, he argued, to their difficulty in landing a high-paying job. In some cases, the result of this vicious cycle was delinquency.

Research Findings

We will begin this section by looking at studies of what happens when homes become broken by separation or divorce. First, we consider some general effects, then focus on the specific effect broken homes have on delinquency. Hetherington and her associates (1977; 1979; 1981) have published several studies comparing families of divorce with families that have remained intact. They report that after the first year of divorce, children in single-parent families are more likely to be disturbed psychologically, but in the long run they cope more successfully than children who are in intact families where the parents do not get along well.

There are three major effects of divorce on children, according to Hetherington. First, single mothers face the problem of task overload: they have two full-time jobs, working in the labor force and rearing children. Second, these women usually find themselves in financial straits; female-headed households earn less than half the income of male-headed families. Third, social isolation is common, with the mother having fewer people to provide social and emotional support. Her children are available, of course, but they often produce more frustration than joy. Boys, in particular, make mothers feel anxious, incompetent, and depressed, leading them to become less effective parents and thus prompting their sons to become even more difficult to manage.

Wallerstein and Kelly (1980) also studied broken families when they were in the early stages of breaking up, after eighteen months apart, and after five years. In the first period, both parents typically felt the pinch of a lower standard of living and were depressed and lonely. Mothers also were overburdened by having to juggle breadwinning and homemaking roles and had to stay up late to do so. Children were often upset and thoroughly opposed to the divorce. Younger children felt vulnerable and fearful—many wondered if they would have to go hungry. Some older children felt hurt because they began to receive less attention. In general, children became more angry, aggressive, and unruly during this initial stage of the breakup, due partly to their deteriorating relationship with their mother. Many mothers

> were unable to say no to demanding children or enforce unwelcome rules for fear the children would reject them in favor of the other parent. . . . As the fatigued parent felt increasingly helpless, the anxious children raised their demands and

> the stridency of their voices. . . . Many women felt severely threatened by their children's rebelliousness and were reduced to tears, nagging, or screeching (Wallerstein and Kelly, 1980:111–112).

Eighteen months later, some mothers were still depressed, but parent-child relations were healing, and children themselves improved. Fewer felt deprived or lonely. Girls improved more than boys by the end of this second stage. Many preadolescent boys were still troubled by the divorce and distressed that their fathers did not visit them often enough. At the five-year point, conditions were slightly worse than at eighteen months. Among children, there was increased evidence of anger and depression. In part, how the child progressed depended on the relationship with the same-sex parent. Boys' good adjustment was often linked to a strong father-son tie, a finding that may seem odd, given that the father had been long gone from the home. In many cases, a stepfather was introduced into the boy's life, but often older children did not accept him; in any case, the stepfather usually did not completely take over the role of the natural father.

One problem with Wallerstein and Kelly's research is that they had no intact families to compare the broken families with. This same defect plagues some early delinquency research. Breckenridge and Abbott (1912) studied youths who were brought before the first juvenile court (in Illinois). Their report fueled alarmist fires by claiming that 44 percent of youths referred to the court came from broken homes. When Healy (1915) conducted research in the same court several years later and produced the same results, the conclusion was firm: broken homes disrupt family life so much that delinquency ensues soon afterward. But this conclusion was unjustified because there were no comparison groups of youths from intact homes, which conceivably could produce even higher rates of delinquency.

Later studies corrected the problem of comparison groups, but they still relied on official data. That is, they defined delinquency as either arrest, court referral, or institutional placement. But in deciding whom to arrest, refer, or place, officials frequently take family status into account. Quite often, they assume that a broken home does not offer the kind of upbringing a child needs. Given this official bias against children from broken homes, it seems only appropriate to turn to other data.

Thus, most contemporary studies of broken homes and delinquency rely on self-report data. One such study was conducted in six Arizona high schools where Wilkinson (1980) looked at males and females, Anglo-Americans and Mexican-Americans, Catholics and Protestants, and rural and urban youths. She consistently found that children from broken homes were more delinquent than those from intact homes, but the relationships were usually weak (see Table 3–1).

Two observations about Table 3-1 are noteworthy. First, the strongest relationships (indicated by the higher gammas) occur for truancy and run-

TABLE 3–1
Father-Absence and Delinquency/Percent Admitting Offense

	Boys			Girls		
	Intact Home	Father Absent	GAMMA	Intact Home	Father Absent	GAMMA
Vandalism	32%	44%	.23	11%	13%	.09
Assault	24	27	.07	9	12	.20
Shoplifting	43	45	.05	29	38	.22
Auto theft	13	17	.12	7	9	.17
Marijuana use	42	51	.17	40	50	.20
Drinking	74	81	.19	69	78	.23
Truancy	53	66	.26	48	67	.37
Running away	9	16	.30	10	16	.27
Number of cases	1,125	298		1,105	339	

Source: Wilkinson, 1980:27.

ning away, both of them trivial status offenses. Second, there is a slight tendency for girls to be affected more by broken homes than boys are. Others also have found this link between broken homes and such minor matters as truancy and running away (Nye, 1958; Rankin, 1983), just as others have found broken homes more conducive to girls' delinquency than boys' (Nye, 1958; Gold, 1970; Austin, 1978; Datesman and Scarpitti, 1975; Chilton and Markle, 1972).

The stronger link between delinquency and broken homes for girls contradicts most predictions. Neotraditionalists warn against boys' having no father present. They argue that the loss of this male role model deals a major blow to the boy's chances of maturing. This could be true, but in fact very little is known about whom children choose as role models and which of these models' qualities they choose to emulate. It appears that children do a good deal of selecting and interpreting; they are not so impressionable that they accept and emulate whatever some adult would like them to (Skolnick, 1981).

The next issue is the connection between delinquent children and working mothers. One modern social scientist who has looked at this relationship is Urie Bronfenbrenner, who for years has worried about children who come home to empty houses ("latchkey children"):

> If there's any reliable predictor of trouble, it probably begins with children coming home to an empty house. . . . What happens? The kids find other kids who are coming home to empty houses. They create a peer-group culture, and it's likely to be an ugly culture—a culture of destroy, of break, of acting-out. . . . (Byrne, 1977:40)

Researchers have found one definite effect of mothers being in the labor force—they have less time to spend with their children. But Hill and Stafford (1979) report that college-educated working mothers try hard to compensate: they cut down on the time they spend on sleep and leisure more than they cut down on the time they spend with their children. The same authors also note that by the time children reach adolescence, parents in general spend only an hour or two per week in nurturing them, and under these circumstances there is little difference between working and nonworking mothers in the time they give.

Generally, the recent studies devoted to discovering the effects of mothers' employment on children and their development find very little if anything.

> Existing research offers no evidence that maternal employment by itself is either good or bad for children, or indeed has any distinctive effect (Hayes and Kamerman, 1983:vii).

> There is very little evidence that the employment of mothers per se has any pervasive effect—positive or negative—on the educational, family, or career paths of their sons or daughters (D'Amico et al., 1983:167).

Despite much rhetoric about the dire effects of maternal employment on juvenile delinquency, there is remarkably little research on the topic. The Gluecks (1957), in their study of lower-class families, found that regularly employed mothers were no more likely than other mothers to have delinquent sons. In a more recent investigation, Hirschi (1969) compared sons of housewives, women who worked part-time, and women who worked full-time. He found that 20 percent of sons of full-time working mothers, 17 percent of sons of part-time workers, and 16 percent of sons of housewives were delinquent. With differences this small, we can safely say there is no relationship. Similarly, Brown (1970), Riege (1972), and Roy (1963) found that delinquency and mother's employment status were unrelated. Thus, neither broken homes nor working mothers play an important role in children's delinquency. These variables are almost completely ignored by modern delinquency theorists.

Having looked at structural variables among families in general, we shall now focus specifically on black families. How valid is Moynihan's argument? This is not an easy question, because the Moynihan Report contains a series of hypotheses, not just one. First there is the claim that black families are structurally in decline. Judged solely on the basis of divorce rates, this would be true. Between 1970 and 1980, the rates climbed steeply for whites and even more so for blacks. The number of divorced white men per 1,000 jumped from 32 to 74; for black men, the figure went from 62 to 151. Partly as a result, the number of American children that live with only one parent doubled (*New York Times*, August 9, 1982); about half of black children now live with only one parent (Caudle, 1983).

What effects does the rising divorce rate have on black youths? Moynihan assumed that as divorces increased, the number of black youths completing high school would decrease considerably. The actual figures overwhelmingly refute Moynihan's prediction. In the years when divorce rates climbed, the percentage of blacks graduating from high school kept going higher and higher. "In 1960, only 20 percent [of all blacks] had finished high school and in 1970, 34 percent had. By 1980, 50.6 percent were high school graduates" (*New York Times*, April 20, 1982:B6).

Moynihan also argued that divorce would lead to an unstable family life and would undermine black youths' aspirations and goals. There are many studies that look at occupational or educational achievement. Most of these studies concern whites, but some include blacks as well. They show that blacks as a group do *not* have low aspirations, low self-esteem, or low expectations (Gordon, 1964; Coleman et al., 1966; Rosenberg and Simmons, 1971; Jencks, 1972).

> In sum, the oft-reported finding that blacks reach equal or higher educational levels than whites within categories of socioeconomic level and mental ability can be explained by the fact that blacks outperform whites academically, receive greater encouragement from significant others, and have higher self-esteem and educational aspirations than whites of similar parental status and ability (Portes and Wilson, 1976:423).

Thus, if a white child and a black child have the same social class background and the same IQ, the black child will tend to perform as well or better in school. If anything, these findings present blacks as "overachievers," contrary to the Moynihan Report.

How can it be that black youths have high aspirations and achievements when so many of them have no father present in the home? Among white males, status attainment is *strongly* influenced by the father's achievement. But this relationship does not hold true for black males. "The relationship between father's education and [son's] ambition, even for those black boys who are living with their fathers, is effectively zero" (Kerckoff and Campbell, 1977:711). In contrast, the mother "is a strong source of influence in goal setting among black boys, even in families where the father is present" (1977:711). In short, mothers are very influential in black families; fathers are not. These data do not really indicate whether black families tend to be matriarchal or not. But either way, several writers say that black families are noteworthy for their strengths (Billingsley, 1968; Hill, 1972; Stack, 1974). Hill, for instance, refers to

> (1) the large-scale incorporation of minor children, elders, and subfamilies into one's family structure. . . ; (2) the greater likelihood for black children rather than white children, born of unwed mothers, to remain within the family of procreation rather than to be adopted outside the family. . . (Blackwell, 1975:50).

Certainly, there is not much support for the claim that female-run households breed delinquency among lower-class blacks (Berger and Simon, 1974).

PARENTING SKILLS

Broken homes and working mothers have been convenient scapegoats, but their impact on delinquency appears to be quite minor. Therefore, we will now consider other aspects of the family. The first of these is what might be called parenting skills. A standard assumption in American society is that married adults automatically know how to be effective parents due to some universal common sense transmitted from one generation to the next. Patterson (1980) found otherwise: not only do parents of chronic delinquents not know how to parent effectively, but many of them do not care—they have almost no affection for their children.

Patterson found that the type of deviance that children tend to engage in most is the type parents tend to tolerate most. In the case of children who steal, for example:

> Many of the parents maintained that since they had never actually seen their child steal, they could not prove that their child had stolen, and therefore could not punish the child. In numerous instances, someone else had actually *seen* the child steal, but the child's "story" would be accepted by the parents, who would then rise to the child's defense and accuse others of picking on the child. As the parents used the word "steal," it could be used as a label only if it could be *proven*, which was usually impossible; ergo the child did not really steal, ergo no punishment could be applied (1980:82).

Patterson then compared parents of different kinds of children: normals, social aggressors, stealers, and abused children. Parents of children who steal stood out as the least punitive, especially the fathers. And when these parents did punish the child, punishment often backfired because the child became more disobedient. Patterson contends that the reason for this failure was that when stealers' parents made threats, they failed to follow them up with actual punishments. They would yell and scream but nothing more, except on occasion when they lost their patience and assaulted the child. Parents of normal children, in contrast, usually backed up their threats with punishment—and those punishments were withdrawal of privileges or imposition of additional work, not physical beatings.

At the Oregon Social Learning Center, Patterson and his colleagues try to teach parents how to raise their children more successfully. They teach the following seven rules of parenting (1980:81):

1. Notice what the child is doing.
2. Monitor it over long periods.
3. Model social skill behavior.
4. Clearly state house rules.
5. Consistently provide sane punishments for transgressions.
6. Provide reinforcement for conformity.
7. Negotiate disagreements so that conflicts and crises do not escalate.

The last three of these require some elaboration. Sane punishment for transgressions means that a child who does something forbidden (say, hitting her sister on the head with a shoe) should be responded to with negative punishment (taking away something the child likes) or positive punishment (providing something the child dislikes). Most behaviorists advocate non-physical punishments such as sending the child to his or her room, taking away television privileges, or assigning extra chores; they roundly criticize spanking, slapping, and so on.

Providing reinforcement for conformity is the basis of operant (instrumental) conditioning. Human beings are likely to repeat any given behavior if, in the past, it has been followed by rewards or social reinforcers such as attention and expressions of approval. This elementary principle of behaviorism may seem obvious, but parents violate it frequently. For example, many will give a child candy or loving attention right after the child has begun a temper tantrum. The child stops the tantrum, but it becomes more likely that the child will resort to tantrums in the future. Rewarded behavior gets repeated.

Negotiating disagreements is one way to forestall violence against the child. Centuries ago, violence and other forms of child abuse were not considered a social problem; in fact, they were widely accepted. In ancient Rome, for example, fathers had the right to do whatever they wished with their children; the law explicitly included the rights to sell, sacrifice, mutilate, or kill them (Bybee, 1979). Gradually, these practices were curtailed, but abuse still occurs in many families (Gelles and Straus, 1979). Patterson notes that parental violence often erupts at the end of a chain of events that began with a trivial incident. To avoid such violence, parents need to learn to break the chain. They must learn techniques of negotiating a settlement before minor matters get out of hand.

Does it do any good to teach these seven rules to parents of problem children? Patterson trained parents of children who steal, then checked up daily to see if the training had any impact. Parents reported stealing declined from an average of .83 incidents per week to only .07. These results still held when investigators rechecked six months later. This seems to indicate that some parents need to be taught parenting skills, that parenting skills can be taught, and that they have an effect on delinquency.

COSTA RICA

Historians point out that abandonment of children was common from the fourth to the thirteenth centuries in Europe, when parents were largely indifferent and uncaring. In underdeveloped countries, poverty and the headlong rush into cities have brought abandonment back into prominence, with various results, including delinquency.

There are several factors that might cause children to get into trouble. They are of an economic, social, environmental, educational, political, or other nature. However, we think the main factor underlying such problems in Costa Rica is the economic one: poverty, underdevelopment. Their economic status compels many parents to take their children out of school and to find them a job. As a result, these children lose the opportunity to receive an education or training necessary to earn a better living. That is, underdevelopment limits the opportunities, but family shortages of resources further reduce the quality of the manpower.

As in other Latin American countries, problems arise due to the concentration of the population in urban areas. Forty percent of the national population live and work in the capital city. Migration from the countryside to the city in search of better living conditions is continuing, and this gives rise to the expansion of slum areas. This, of course, is one of the main causes of social and economic problems, hindering the sound and normal development of young persons.

[In a survey of the problems of young people in a fringe area of the capital city] it has been found that many children in these areas are likely to be abandoned, which leads to delinquency. The term *child abandonment* refers to a child not attended to by his parents for different reasons: the mother is a prostitute, the father is an alcoholic, or the child is not recognized because he was born out of wedlock. . . .

Due to the increase in population, industrialization, and the move of people to urban areas, the problems of children and young people have become serious. During the decade of the 1980s, [Costa Rica] must solve not only child abandonment problems, but also those related to drugs, solvent inhalation, delinquency, and mental retardation and physical handicaps.

Source: Jorge A. Montero and Sonia Navarro, "Costa Rica," pp. 43–44. Reprinted by permission of New York University Press from *Justice and Troubled Children Around the World,* volume IV, edited by V. Lorne Stewart.

TABLE 3–2
Relationship Between Parental Approval and Youth's Type of Sexual Involvement

"My sexual behavior is pretty much the way my parents would want it to be."

	True	False
Inexperienced	46%	13%
Beginners	29	17
Monogamists	15	44
Adventurers	10	26
	100%	100%

Source: Sorensen, 1973:393.

PARENTAL ATTACHMENT

Neotraditionalists concerned about the family and its impact on delinquency focus on parental absence, leniency, and inadequte supervision. There are other ways parents may influence children, however, including emotional closeness. In other words, children who like their parents very much will respect their parents' wishes and stay out of trouble. Likewise, parental love may reduce delinquency because it is something children do not want to lose.

A very different line of thinking, however, says parents (not just children) sometimes have deviant impulses that they may act on. If this is true, then parents may pass on delinquent values and practices to their children. Presumably, this is more likely to occur if the behavior is a status offense rather than some more serious kind of activity. Sexual behavior would seem to be an appropriate area to examine to test the validity of this line of thinking.

Robert Sorensen (1973) conducted a large survey of teenagers that covers the relationship between sexual activity and many other factors. He divided youths into four groups according to their level of sexual activity. He called the first level Inexperienced; the sexual activity of these youths has not gone beyond kissing. Next are those teenagers whom Sorensen labeled Beginners. They also are virgins, but they have proceeded farther, perhaps as far as "heavy petting." The third stage is called Serial Monogamy. Youngsters in this category have had sexual intercourse, but they pursue only one relationship at a time. Finally, Sorensen identified a fourth group as Sexual Adventurers. These youths also have had intercourse, but they seek many different partners and have no interest in a continuous relationship with only one person.

To what extent were the sexual experiences of these youths consistent with their parents' beliefs and values? Consider the data presented in Table 3–2. Youths who agreed with their parents' sexual standards were quite likely to be Inexperienced (46 percent). Those who say their behavior does *not* conform to what their parents would like were likely to be Monogamists (44 percent) or Adventurers (26 percent). This finding suggests that perhaps children do not learn deviant or delinquent values from their parents.

Next we consider the effect of (1) parents' liking their children and (2) children's liking their parents. Which of these two factors has a bigger effect is a question self-report researchers rarely raise. Sorensen's data in Table 3–3 suggest it is the second (how much children like or dislike their parents). Youths who said they felt little affection for their parents became the most sexually active; 43 percent of them became Adventurers. Contrast this with the youths who felt strong affection for their parents; only 14 percent of those youths became Adventurers. These relationships show that closeness to parents is an extremely powerful predictor of behavior.

SOCIAL CLASS

The single aspect of families that delinquency specialists have studied most is social class. For many years, delinquency and crime were assumed to be heavily concentrated in the lower class. Indeed, people used to call this class the "dangerous class" or the "criminal class." In nineteenth-century urban America, fear was focused on immigrants more than on natives, and politicians and the middle class encouraged the police to clamp down on the poor, criminal, and riotous in any way possible. Police quickly learned that they were expected to deal with society's low-status groups—the young, the poor, and the heavy drinkers (Lane, 1980). Police activity in the big cities was like trawling, and most of the "fish" who were caught were lower-class adult males doing nothing worse than getting drunk (Friedman and Percival, 1981).

Even the Progressive "child savers" (Platt, 1969) who helped launch the juvenile court movement accepted the connection between delinquency and low social status. Charles Loring Brace, for example, expressed the conventional thinking when he referred to the "foreign childhood that floats along the streets and docks of the city—vagabondish, thievish, familiar with the vicious ways and places of the town" (1880:49). This idea that crime and delinquency were dominated by the lower class was eventually tested by Shaw and McKay (1942). These researchers, who were trained in sociology at the University of Chicago, divided the city of Chicago into 150 square-mile tracts and plotted the official rates of delinquency for each square mile. Then they produced data on other characteristics of each area. Of those measures, the one that had the highest correlation with delinquency was the percentage of families on relief (welfare). Thus, areas with high rates of delinquency also had many families on relief. Delinquency theories thereafter took it for granted that poverty was a powerful factor that pushes people into delinquency.

TABLE 3–3
Relationship Between Affection Toward Parents and Youth's Type of Sexual Involvement

"I don't feel any strong affection for my parents."

	True	False
Inexperienced	16%	32%
Beginners	21	23
Monogamists	21	30
Adventurers	43	14
	101%	99%

Source: Sorensen, 1973:385.

But relationships among variables at the neighborhood level do not mean that those variables also are related at the individual level (Robinson, 1950). To be sure, slums or lower-class areas have higher delinquency rates than do suburbs or middle-class areas. But one cannot conclude that lower-class *persons* are more delinquent than those in the middle class. There are several ways that class and delinquency could be related on the neighborhood level and not at the individual level: (1) police could be biased, arresting people for behaviors in lower-class areas that they might ignore in middle-class areas (for example, gambling), (2) people could leave their middle-class homes and go to lower-class areas to commit offenses (such as prostitution and drug sales), or (3) a small number of people might be committing a great majority of the offenses in the lower-class areas.

For such reasons, criminologists in recent decades have focused more on delinquency among individuals, and they have relied upon self-reports instead of official data. The most important early study to examine the link between social class and delinquency was by Nye et al. (1958). They sampled high-school students in several communities in the West and Midwest. Social class was measured by the occupational prestige of the students' fathers; a number of different items were used to measure delinquency. In comparing youths from the various social classes, Nye et al. found lower-class youths commit some delinquent activities more often (truancy, heterosexual relations, car theft) and upper-class youths commit a few offenses more often (destroying property and, surprisingly, gang fights). The middle class, for all intents and purposes, did not commit any offenses especially frequently. Nye et al. thus concluded that social class and delinquency are unrelated.

To say the least, these findings sparked controversy. Many criminologists simply scoffed at and ignored them. Other criminologists, though, were sufficiently intrigued to conduct their own research into the matter, using other samples to see if they would generate the same results as had Nye et al. For

TABLE 3–4
Correlations Between Social Class and Delinquency Using Official and Self-Report Data

Period	Official	Self-Report
Before 1950	−.73	—
1950s	−.43	−.04
1960s	−.22	−.11
1970s	+.04	−.03

Source: Tittle et al., 1978:649.

the most part, the results were the same: delinquency proved to be as common among middle-class children as among their lower-class counterparts (for example, Dentler and Monroe, 1961; Akers, 1964; Empey and Erickson, 1966).

In recent years, criminologists have looked back at the many studies of delinquency and social class and tried to summarize and clarify the wealth of findings. Tittle et al. (1978) concluded that the relationship between class and delinquency depends upon two factors: when and how the research was conducted. That is, the relationship varies from decade to decade, and self-report data yield results that are different from official data. According to Tittle et al., the relationship for official data was once very strong, but it weakened progressively in later decades; after a high of −.73 in the 1940s, it fell to practically zero in the 1970s. But for self-report studies, the average relationship between class and delinquency was never high; before 1950, there were no self-report studies of this relationship, and afterward the correlation remained weak, as shown in Table 3–4.

These findings lend themselves to several interpretations. Perhaps the official data of the 1940s and 1950s were invalid and should not be accepted. Or the official data may all be quite accurate, and the lower class used to monopolize delinquency but the middle class has now caught up to it. Tittle et al. reject both of these hypotheses and argue instead that self-report data are probably correct in showing that (1) the class/delinquency relationship has not changed essentially over the years, and (2) lower-class persons are only slightly more likely than other people to engage in delinquency. The authors suggest that official data were biased: police and courts discriminated against lower-class youths, arresting and referring them to court more often, particularly in the 1940s and 1950s. In later years, thanks to the civil rights movement, this bias subsided.

Not everyone agrees with Tittle et al. Hindelang et al. (1979), for instance, claim that there really is a relationship between class and delinquency—for serious offenses. But it is difficult to test this hypothesis because self-reports almost invariably concentrate on minor offenses such as truancy and petty theft; the really serious offenses such as rape and robbery are too rare to include in a survey of the general population of youngsters. One study of class and delinquency, however, has used such a large sample that it could include serious offenses. Elliott and Ageton (1980) were able to sample more than 5,000 respondents and ask them about a variety of offenses, including some serious ones.

1. Predatory crimes against persons (sexual assault, aggravated assault, simple assault, robbery).
2. Predatory crimes against property (vandalism, burglary, auto theft, larceny, stolen goods, fraud, joyriding).
3. Illegal service crimes (prostitution, selling drugs, buying or providing liquor for minors).
4. Public disorder crimes (carrying a concealed weapon, hitchhiking, disorderly conduct, drunkenness, panhandling, making obscene phone calls, marijuana use).
5. Status crimes (runaway, sexual intercourse, alcohol use, truancy).
6. Hard drug use (amphetamines, barbiturates, hallucinogens, heroin, cocaine).

The sample was divided into lower-class youths, middle-class youths and an intermediate category Elliott and Ageton labeled "working class." Then the researchers computed the average number of offenses committed by persons in each social class. They found that the classes were very similar to each other on all types of offenses except one: predatory crimes against persons. On this type, the differences were substantial. For every such crime committed by a middle-class youth, there were 2.5 such crimes committed by working-class youths and 3.5 by lower-class youths. Thus, Elliott and Ageton lead us to conclude that the lower class is similar to other classes on the common, run-of-the-mill offenses but more delinquent when it comes to the really serious offenses, supporting the Hindelang et al. hypothesis.

SUMMARY

Neotraditionalists argue that the family is in decline, which has aggravated the problem of delinquency. Yankelovich in particular points to the following changes:

1. Marriage is something that fewer and fewer people want.
2. Being a homemaker is something that fewer and fewer women want.

3. Fewer and fewer people want a large number of children.
4. Sacrifice and self-denial are things that fewer and fewer people are willing to practice.
5. Hedonism and self-fulfillment are things that more and more people are pursuing.

Neotraditionalists believe these changes are weakening the family, society's key institution; with the family wielding less influence, children lack the guidance they need and many will become wild and disruptive. The Moynihan Report expressed similar fears about lower-class black families: that the socioeconomic system produces an unstable family system (matriarchy), which leads to high rates of school failure, dropout, and delinquency among black youths.

Research on delinquency and broken homes has been conducted for many years, but much of the early work suffered from bias and error. More recent and less biased data from Wilkinson's research show that the relationship between broken homes and delinquency is weak; it is strongest for girls and for trivial offenses. These findings suggest that absent fathers have little effect on boys, contrary to conventional wisdom. Similarly, the little research that exists on the relationship between mothers' working outside the home and their children's delinquency also shows it to be negligible.

Research on family structure and delinquency among blacks casts doubt on Moynihan's claims. Although there is a continued structural decline among black families—the rates of divorce, illegitimacy, and single-parent families have reached very high levels in the 1980s—black children do not appear to have suffered as a result. There has been a steep rise in the number of black youths graduating from high school. And performance of black students in school does not seem to be affected by their fathers—even if they are present. Finally, Berger and Simon report that broken homes have no effect on delinquency among lower-class blacks.

Although family structure variables are relatively unimportant in causing delinquency, parenting skills can have a considerable effect, as shown by Patterson. His techniques for making children more obedient include reinforcing conformity and providing sane punishment for transgressions. Reinforcement alone is not enough, Patterson discovered, particularly with very problematic children. Research shows that parents can be taught to be more effective and that their children's misbehavior declines as a result.

Parental attachment is another family factor thought to have an effect on delinquency. Research by Sorensen (1973), for example, found the level of sexual activity to be quite closely linked to parental attachment.

Adventurers have weak or negative relations with their parents in many cases, while the Inexperienced tend to be quite close to their parents, suggesting that attachment to parents inhibits delinquency.

For years it was assumed that delinquency was primarily a lower-class activity, and early research largely upheld this assumption. But self-report studies of individuals, beginning with Nye et al., found *no* relationship between class and delinquency. Many subsequent research efforts were conducted to see who was right on this basic issue, but the answer still is not known.

Tittle et al. tried to sum up all the previous results and claimed that the class and delinquency findings vary, depending on the time of the study and whether self-report or official data were used. Tittle et al. concluded that people in the lower class were actually no more delinquent than middle-class people. This thesis was called into question by Hindelang et al., who found that minor delinquency is not related to social class but serious delinquency is more common in the lower class. One study, by Elliott and Ageton, provides tentative support for the Hindelang et al. hypothesis.

DISCUSSION QUESTIONS

1. What trends are believed to indicate a decline in the influence of the family?
2. What controversial issues concerning family life were raised in the Moynihan Report?
3. What short- and long-term effects of broken homes on family members were revealed in the Wallerstein and Kelly study?
4. What are the problems involved in using official data to study the relationship between broken homes and delinquency?
5. What recent evidence has called into question several views of the black family presented in the Moynihan Report?
6. What parenting skills appear to be instrumental in discouraging deviant behavior among children?
7. What is the relationship between parental attachment and the sexual activity of youths?
8. What may account for the decline over the past thirty years in the correlation between social class and delinquency based on official data?
9. What is the importance of the delinquency and social class study by Elliott and Ageton?
10. What are the effects of divorce on children? Explain your answer.

ASSAULT WITH A DEADLY WEAPON

Crime may be endemic in a family without the parents accepting it or knowing about it, as in the case of John Allen's mother. Of particular interest is John's reaction to the thought that his youngest brother might consider following John's example and pursue a career in delinquency.

It seems to me that the kind of neighborhood you come up in may make all the difference in which way you go and where you end up. There was a lot of people in my neighborhood that didn't do much work and there was a lot of people who did, but the majority didn't. Hustling was their thing: number running, bootlegging, selling narcotics, selling stolen goods, prostitution. There's so many things that go on—it's a whole system that operates inside itself. Say I was to take you by it. You want some junk, then I would take you to the dude that handles drugs. You want some clothes, I could take you somewhere that handles that. You want some liquor, I could take you someplace other than a liquor store. Of course, it's all outside the law.

That's how it was. Somebody was always doing something in each family. If it wasn't the adults, say the mother or father, then it was the son or daughter. I was sticking up; one of my brothers was stealing; one of my sisters was bootlegging; one of my uncles wrote numbers; one of my grandmothers occasionally wrote numbers; and my grandfather bootlegged.

My grandfather, though, worked on the same job for about thirty years, and I couldn't dig that at all. His main money came from bootlegging, but I think he had the job because he thought long-range. He knew they don't give you no pension for stickups, but I was too involved to see that. Like me, most people in our neighborhood lived in the present, turning that day. There was only a few who looked ahead and came out ahead, maybe got a little store and stopped everything. I even know a few people who got that store and haven't stopped. They're still doing things on the side. But the store or the laundromat, that was their goal.

In my early years, I was raised up in Southwest D.C. I think my mother was about sixteen when I was born, and most of my young life we lived with her parents, which are my grandparents. I remember them shuffling me around when I was about five because my grandfather's house would get raided, with all the gambling, bootlegging, and everything that used to go down. They'd wake me up with flashlights in my face. There was a lot of noise, a lot of flashlights being shined, people trying to run and hide. I would be shuffled through the window and told to go to my other grandmother's house, which was a few blocks away. The first time it happened was the first time that I had went from one house to the other in the dark. I was afraid and cold. I got over the back fence and I don't think I ever stopped running until I got there.

A few of the kids in my neighborhood had fathers at home, but most had broken families just like myself. The father was either in jail or just not there. Just deserted their mother or came every now and then. In my younger days I seldom saw my father. In fact, I remember one time that I hadn't seen him in so long that I didn't even recognize him, and that's the truth. That's the way it was with me, and so I would always stay with my grandfather. Perhaps that's why everybody say I'm like him.

My grandparents ran things like they supposed to be ran. My grandfather's about eighty now, real sick and very weak, but he used to run things with an iron hand, and I understood that. So I tried to stay on the good side of him. Some things I did that was wrong, he used to condone—like fighting. He used to love for me to be in a fight. But that's 'cause the whole environment was like that. The Southwest thing was pretty wild. The kids, we ran wild, and the adults were wild. It would be nothing for us to be on the front steps playing hide-and-seek and all of a sudden you hear bang, bang, bang, and people are shooting at each other in the street. And everybody ducking and hiding. This was normal. Eventually you'd be taking all this in. It's just a way of survival.

In Southwest everybody did the same thing, and it was a struggle just to get along. Some had a little bit more than others, some a little bit less. It was a close neighborhood, though—most people had been there for a long time. Everybody knew everybody's kid, everybody's dog. There was quite a few people who had come up from the South, but most had been born in Washington, like my parents and grandparents.

We lived the longest in Southwest on G Street. The houses were right on the sidewalk with no front yards but a lot of big old overgrown trees sitting right by the curb. We did have a large backyard, and behind it was a horse stable. Then there was a little frame house, which was almost like part of the stable only people lived there. There were three houses with airways between them next to that and then a big gray apartment building on the corner.

On the other side of the street was a place we used to call the barracks. Evidently it was an old army barracks that had been converted into a living area; people lived all through it. We used to walk up and down the wooden steps and look over the railings and play cowboy there. Then there was an alley. All our alleys had hip names—Brown's Court, Dixon's Court, Smoke Alley. But wouldn't nobody go through the alleys at night because of the rats. You could even see them in the daytime. They function just like people did, and I used to chase them, throwing rocks and then running away from them.

On the corner was a little Japanese store. You could take a book there—what you call a store book—get what you want, and the man would write it down in the book. Then at the end of the week he would get his money. Most people paid on time like they supposed to. I guess it was just a little pact they had formed among themselves in the neighborhood, 'cause at the end of the week everybody went there, bought the rest of their groceries, and paid their bill.

Now, I had a thing where I used to cop the store book and go over there and cop me some candy. Then my mother say, "Where did this extra twenty-five cents come from?" She always knew about her money all the way to the penny. Even though the man in the store knew what I'd be doing, he'd always ask,

"Your mother know that you're getting this?" And I say, "Uh-hum." He knew, but it was an extra quarter for him.

In Southwest, when I was ten or eleven, there were stores on just about every corner—Jew stores, Chinese stores, Japanese stores, black stores. Most of the owners lived over their stores, so robbery didn't keep them from doing business. On Fridays and Saturdays everybody be paying their bills, and of course, the store owners were extra careful on those days. A lot of them had particular kinds of reputations—people used to recognize them just like they recognize my family for being the bootleggers of the block. The store owner was the man you could go to during the week when you didn't have any cash and get grub on the store book. People respected that. In the event that they was robbed or stuck up, most of the people in the neighborhood would be sympathetic to them. Very seldom anybody in the neighborhood would rob a store that was in the neighborhood, because store owners knew everybody and everybody's children.

The numbers writers, the bootleggers, the gamblers, the pimps, and the prostitutes—in that neighborhood, I knew them all and they knew me. I used to go to the store to pick up little things that the prostitutes wanted. There was a big numbers man named James, and for a long time I dug his cool. I dug his manner, his nonchalant way of dealing with people. I always felt like he was a real big shot. He was about the biggest because everybody respected him, he always had plenty of money, he always dressed nice, and everybody always done what he wanted them to do. I dug the respect that he gave and that he got, and the orders that he gave were immediately carried out.

Another dude, Sherman, was nice-looking—a typical pimp. Dark-skinned, well-groomed, well-dressed, tone sharp as a razor when it come to saying something to a woman. It impressed me the way all the women went for him, because Sherman was the type of pimp that didn't have to go solicit broads. They came to him, and this was an advantage he always had. James and Sherman, these were the people that got a lot of respect in the neighborhood.

As for white people, I never had much contact with them at all, except the insurance man. My grandfather was a great believer in insurance. No doubt he had life insurance on just about all of us. The white insurance man gave me fifty cents one day, when I was four or five, and that's when somebody first said something about black and white. And I didn't understand. As far as whites living in the neighborhood or coming in regular, that didn't happen. I seen white people sometimes when my mother took me downtown to buy shoes or clothes, but I saw very few white people otherwise. Not at school, not on the playground, nowhere.

When I was in kindergarten or first grade, I went to Smallwood School around the corner. On the next block was another school—S.J. Bourne. Originally S.J. Bourne was an all-white school, 'cause during that time, integration wasn't in. Must have been in '48 they moved all the white kids out and moved us in, and they condemned Smallwood. We used to play in it, though, even after they boarded it up.

There was a library several blocks away that would show little movies, cartoons, and always there used to be somebody reading stories. That person would always be white. So I thought that white people was real smart, 'cause eveybody sitting down there listening and they reading. Can't nobody else read but them, and they was telling some hip stories. So I put them ahead of myself mentally because it seemed white people had accomplished more. They knew more. Occasionally when I ran into somebody white around my age, I always found that they could read better, spell better, and everything else, and I resented that. When I was seven or eight, I began to be more aware of words, and that's when prejudice started seeping in. Whites calling blacks "nigger" and blacks calling whites "redneck." That's how you begin to break people down into this category or that.

My family has always been close. I've got five sisters and three brothers, but I'm the oldest. So most of my younger days either they were real small or weren't even born. My sister Cookie comes next in age to me. Coming up together when we were kids, I really didn't like Cookie. Not at all. I used to do a lot of unkind things to her, but I'm glad that she growed up and didn't remember or didn't choose to hold it against me, because now I really love her.

My father never lived at home, but my mother, well, me and her were really tight. My whole family life was good to me as far as feeling for one another—like, I love my mother, I love my grandmother and grandfather, my sisters and brothers. I always felt that they felt the same way about me. They have shown me in many ways just how much they have cared, because I wasn't exactly what you'd call the best son on the block, you know.

My grandmother and my grandfather—my mother's parents—they were kind of brought up on the hustling life—they've been into all different things, but my mother was always kind of square—she never really did anything. Still, I think she understood why I was kind of wild. I never disrespect her. That's one of the things that kind of bothers me now when sometimes one of my younger brothers or sisters will say something to my mother. I never did say nothing smart to her, out of respect and sometimes out of fear that she would get right on my case.

The main thing with my mother was worrying about me. Like, by the time I was ten, I used to stay away from home maybe two or three days—all night—and she not knowing what I was doing. Usually she just assumed that wherever I was or whatever I was doing, it was wrong, and so she worried quite a bit. But Moms never really got on me too much about any of the things I did. She always told me, "My son, whatever you do, you're my son." When I was younger, she used to threaten me with "Just keep on getting in trouble, boy. I'm not going down there to get you out." Then as soon as I got busted, here she come. I kind of knew it, and I think I used to take advantage of her a lot because I knew she would come.

Most of the time when I was coming up my mother had different little jobs. Exactly what she was doing, I knew it wasn't nothing professional. She'd do housecleaning or what they'd call day's work, going to different people's houses on different days—in another neighborhood, of course—and cleaning their house for them and getting paid. Similar to the old thing about black folk working in the kitchen. I remember her working in a restaurant as a waitress, and I remember her working at a college in the cafeteria. I guess I must have been around ten or eleven during that time, and I stayed on the streets so much that I never really had a whole lot of time for her. But she always was around if something happened. If I got picked up by the police or thrown out of school, she always would be on the scene.

Mostly I think my mother wanted me to have some hopes that I would be something other than what I ended up being. She was always thinking about us kids and doing without. I recall an occasion when I told her it would be all right if she didn't get me something for Christmas or Easter. I didn't present her with a lot of problems as far as buying things for me, because I usually got things for myself. On a lot of occasions, I got things not only for myself but for her and my younger sisters and brothers as well.

I never did talk to my family too much about what I was doing in school or on the streets. My mother would sometimes make mention of how was I doing in school and how I better stay out of trouble. So would my grandfather, but I wouldn't talk much because a lot of the time I hadn't been to school in a week or so. She never would know, and I'd make up some kind of lie.

I never really knew my father until I got older, but I think he kind of swept Moms off her feet at a young age, 'cause he was a flashy dude, a hustler, a musician. He played quite a few instruments, but his main instrument was bongos. He could also play the guitar, piano, and saxophone. From what my mother and them told me, he had the reputation at one time of being the best dancer in Washington, D.C.

I was like so many of my children—a love child. In later years, after I got a little older, him and I really grew kind of close. We got real tight. Just about the time he died, when I was twenty-three, we was really doing a lot of things together. I never disliked him even though he never really done anything for me as a child or later on, like helping me, buying clothes or shoes, stuff like that. It was Moms's job. He never did, at no time. He went his own way and Moms went hers, but I always respected him as my father.

My brother Leonard is probably the most like me in the family. His nickname is Nicey, but I calls him Nut. After a while he was beginning to do most of the things I had done. I would never try to discourage him, because I don't feel like preaching to what people feel they want to do. Knowing my brother and knowing how much he was like me, it wouldn't have done any good anyway. The few times I did try to discourage him, he would say, "Man, when you was such and such an age, you did such and such a thing." What could I say? Because I had.

Stickup—armed robbery— was my thing, and I could do that very well. After Nut got a certain age, he begin to start sticking up people. I said, "This is what you want to do, this is what you're gonna do, then you might as well know the right way." So he did a few things with me in later years, since around '69. I guess he's about seven years younger than me, a real quiet dude but very dangerous, and I knew it 'cause I used to be kind of quiet myself for a long time. One time if I had to set a dude straight, there wouldn't be no words. I'd just hit him in the mouth and set him straight. And that's the way Nut is—real quiet. Whatever I was telling him, he was listening, especially if it was something about sticking up somebody. He learned pretty well while he was in that particular bag. When I started getting into drugs, he was at the Youth Center. By the time he came out, I was rolling kind of big, so I made him one of my lieutenants immediately.

Now another relative, Henry, he was a different story from my brother Nut and me. Everybody who know us always said, "Johnny and Nicey, something wrong with them, they're crazy. But Henry, he's such a good boy." But people don't know that Henry was using heroin before me and Nicey ever was. But it lasted only a short while. Then he turned to the church, and it worked out pretty good. I haven't been to church lately, but they tell me he preach a pretty good sermon.

I asked him about going to the church, 'cause I was really curious. I said, "Man, like what happened? What made you get out of this bag?" This was before I found out that he actually used drugs. And he said, "Man, I couldn't afford it. You and Nicey been in jail enough for everybody in the family. So I know I didn't need to go. I just didn't have no income. You know I ain't gonna take no pistol and stick nobody up. I can't steal, so I turned to the Lord." So I say, "Solid."

Well, he got himself together, and I was glad of that. He always in church. He just try to do everything within the system as much as possible. But he still a lot of fun to be around. When he's with me, we smoke and drink wine—he just a regular dude. But he knew that with a heroin habit, he'd eventually have to do the sticking up and robbing things, and he also knew he didn't know how to do them correctly. He knew that he would jeopardize himself as far as going to jail, and that was what he really didn't want to do—go to jail. So he just stopped. And I was kind of glad, kind of proud.

My youngest brother, Mo, during the time I was coming up was pretty young or even unborn—he's only sixteen now, so I'm twice as old. Out of all of us Mo is the tallest and also the darkest. He's pretty witty in his own way, even at the age of sixteen. Right now he helps me quite a bit around the house when I can catch up with him. They tell me that he's a pretty good athlete—football and basketball. I'm glad of that. One of his problems is he go to school, but he don't try hard enough. Another one of his problems is that he thinks being a tough guy really means something. Mo being my baby brother, I told him about the affection I have for him and the love that I have for him. But I also told him in a very nice way that if he ever got in any trouble or caused Moms as much trouble as Nicey or I caused her, that he would have to deal with me. He would find that even though I'm confined to a wheelchair, I am still the man that I've always been, and I plan to always be the man that I've always been. In simple words I told him, "Don't get into any trouble. I wouldn't like it at all. If you get into any trouble, then I will personally put my foot in your ass."

What I really want for Mo is for him to continue with sports and maybe get a scholarship and try to be something other than what his brother is: ex-convict criminal type confined to two jails—one the District jail and the other a wheelchair jail. I don't want any of my brothers or sisters or kids to go through what I went through.

Source: From *Assault with a Deadly Weapon: The Autobiography of a Street Criminal* by John Allen, Philip Heymann, and Diane Hall Kelly, pp. 1–10.

REFERENCES

AKERS, RONALD L.

1964 Socio-economic status and delinquent behavior. *Journal of Research in Crime and Delinquency* 1 (January):38–46.

AUSTIN, ROY L.

1978 Race, father-absence, and female delinquency. *Criminology* 15 (February):487–504.

BERGER, ALAN S., AND WILLIAM S. SIMON

1974 Black families and the Moynihan report. *Social Problems* 22 (December):145–161.

BERGER, BRIGITTE, AND PETER L. BERGER

1983 *The War Over the Family.* New York: Doubleday.

BILLINGSLEY, ANDREW

1968 *Black Families in White America.* Englewood Cliffs, N.J.: Prentice-Hall.

BLACKWELL, JAMES E.

1975 *The Black Community.* New York: Harper & Row.

BRACE, CHARLES LORING

1880 *The Dangerous Classes of New York and Twenty Years Among Them.* New York: Wynkoop and Hellenbeck.

BRECKENRIDGE, SOPHONISBA P., AND EDITH ABBOTT

1912 *The Delinquent Child and the Home.* New York: Russell Sage Foundation.

BROWN, S. W.

1970 A comparative study of maternal employment and non-employment. Doctoral dissertation, Mississippi State University.

BYBEE, ROGER

1979 Violence toward youth. *Journal of Social Issues* 35 (Spring):1–14.

BYRNE, SUSAN

1977 Nobody home: The erosion of the American family. *Psychology Today* 10 (May):40–47.

CAPLOW, THEODORE, ET AL.

1982 *Middletown Families.* Minneapolis: University of Minnesota Press.

CAUDLE, SHEILA

1983 Poverty haunts USA's children. *USA Today* (June 10):8A.

CHILTON, ROLAND, AND GERALD MARKLE

1972 Family disruption, delinquent conduct, and the effect of subclassification. *American Sociological Review* 37 (February):93–99.

COLEMAN, JAMES S., ET AL.

1966 *Equality of Educational Opportunity.* Washington: U.S. Government Printing Office.

D'AMICO, RONALD J., ET AL.

1983 The effects of mothers' employment on adolescent and early adult outcomes of young men and women. Pp. 130–219 in Cheryl D. Hayes and Sheila B. Kamerman (eds.), *Children of Working Parents.* Washington: National Academy Press.

DATESMAN, SUSAN, AND FRANK SCARPITTI

1975 Female delinquency and broken homes. *Criminology* 13 (May):33–55.

DEGLER, CARL N.

1980 *At Odds.* New York: Oxford University Press.

DENTLER, ROBERT A., AND LAWRENCE J. MONROE

1961 Social correlates of early adolescent theft. *American Sociological Review* 26 (October):733–743.

EHRENREICH, BARBARA
1984 *The Hearts of Men.* New York: Doubleday.
ELLIOTT, DELBERT S., AND SUZANNE S. AGETON
1980 Reconciling race and sex differences in self-reported and official estimates of delinquency. *American Sociological Review* 45 (February):95–110.
EMPEY, LAMAR T., AND MAYNARD L. ERICKSON
1966 Hidden delinquency and social status. *Social Forces* 44 (June):546–554.
FRIEDAN, BETTY
1963 *The Feminine Mystique.* New York: Norton.
FRIEDMAN, LAWRENCE M., AND ROBERT V. PERCIVAL
1981 *The Roots of Justice.* Chapel Hill, N.C.: University of North Carolina Press.
GELLES, RICHARD J., AND MURRAY A. STRAUS
1979 Violence in the American family. *Journal of Social Issues* 35 (Spring):15–39.
GLUECK, SHELDON, AND ELEANOR GLUECK
1957 Working mothers and delinquency. *Mental Hygiene* 41 (June):327–352.
GOLD, MARTIN
1970 *Delinquent Behavior in an American City.* Belmont, Calif.: Brooks/Cole.
GORDON, MILTON M.
1964 *Assimilation in American Life.* New York: Oxford University Press.
HACKER, ANDREW
1983 *U/S: A Statistical Portrait of the American People.* New York: Viking.
1982 Farewell to the family? *The New York Review of Books* 29 (March 18):37–44.
HAYES, CHERYL D., AND SHEILA B. KAMERMAN (EDS.)
1983 *Children of Working Parents.* Washington: National Academy Press.
HEALY, WILLIAM
1915 *The Individual Delinquent.* Boston: Little, Brown.
HETHERINGTON, E. MAVIS
1977 *Review of Child Development Research.* New York: Russell Sage Foundation.
HETHERINGTON, E. MAVIS, AND ROSS D. PARKE
1981 *Contemporary Readings in Social Psychology.* New York: McGraw-Hill.
1979 *Child Psychology: A Contemporary Viewpoint.* New York: McGraw-Hill.
HILL, C. RUSSELL, AND FRANK P. STAFFORD
1979 Parental care of children. *Journal of Human Resources* 15 (Spring):219–239.
HILL, ROBERT
1972 *The Strengths of Black Families.* New York: Emerson-Hall.
HINDELANG, MICHAEL J., ET AL.
1979 Correlates of delinquency. *American Sociological Review* 44 (December):995–1014.
HIRSCHI, TRAVIS
1969 *Causes of Delinquency.* Berkeley: University of California Press.
JENCKS, CHRISTOPHER
1972 *Inequality.* New York: Basic.
JONES, LANDON Y.
1980 *Great Expectations.* New York: Ballantine.
KERCKOFF, ALAN C., AND RICHARD T. CAMPBELL
1977 Race and social status differences in the explanation of educational ambition. *Social Forces* 55 (March):701–714.

KLEIMAN, DENA

1982 At 15, truant ends a trail of crime with a slaying. *New York Times* (February 28):1, 44.

LANE, ROGER

1980 Urban police and crime in nineteenth-century America. Pp. 1–43 in Norval Morris and Michael Tonry (eds.), *Crime and Justice.* Chicago: University of Chicago Press.

MOYNIHAN, DANIEL P.

1965 *The Negro Family.* Washington: U.S. Department of Labor.

NEW YORK TIMES

1982 U.S. reports 20% of children reside with only one parent. (August 9):B10.

1982 Census data show gains in housing and education. (April 20):Al, B6.

NYE, F. IVAN

1958 *Family Relationships and Delinquent Behavior.* New York: Wiley.

NYE, F. IVAN, ET AL.

1958 Socioeconomic status and delinquent behavior. *American Journal of Sociology* 63 (January):381–389.

PATTERSON, GERALD R.

1980 Children who steal. Pp. 73–90 in Travis Hirschi and Michael Gottfredson (eds.), *Understanding Crime.* Beverly Hills, Calif.: Sage.

PLATT, ANTHONY M.

1969 *The Child Savers.* Chicago: University of Chicago Press.

PORTES, ALEJANDRO, AND KENNETH L. WILSON

1976 Black-white differences in educational attainment. *American Sociological Review* 41 (June):414–431.

RANKIN, JOSEPH H.

1983 The family context of delinquency. *Social Problems* 30 (April):466–479.

RIEGE, MARY GRAY

1972 Parental affection and juvenile delinquency in girls. *British Journal of Criminology* 12 (January):55–73.

ROBINSON, WILLIAM S.

1950 Ecological correlations and the behavior of individuals. *American Sociological Review* 15 (June):351–357.

ROSENBERG, MORRIS, AND ROBERTA G. SIMMONS

1971 *Black and White Self-Esteem.* Washington: American Sociological Association.

ROY, PRODIPTO

1963 Adolescent roles: Rural-urban differences. Pp.165–181 in F. Ivan Nye and Lois Wladis Hoffman (eds.), *The Employed Mother in America.* Chicago: Rand McNally.

SHAW, CLIFFORD R., AND HENRY D. McKAY

1942 *Juvenile Delinquency and Urban Areas.* Chicago: University of Chicago Press.

SKOLNICK, ARLENE

1981 The family and its discontents. *Society* 18 (January/February):42–47.

SORENSEN, ROBERT C.

1973 *Adolescent Sexuality in Contemporary America.* New York: World.

STACK, CAROL B.

1974 *All Our Kin.* New York: Harper & Row.

TITTLE, CHARLES R., ET AL.

1978 The myth of social class and criminality. *American Sociological Review* 43 (October):643–656.

VEBLEN, THORSTEIN
1899 *The Theory of the Leisure Class.* New York: Macmillan.

WALLERSTEIN, JUDITH S., AND JOAN BERLIN KELLY
1980 *Surviving the Breakup.* New York: Basic.

WILKINSON, KAREN
1980 The broken home and delinquent behavior. Pp. 21–42 in Travis Hirschi and Michael Gottfredson (eds.), *Understanding Crime.* Beverly Hills, Calif.: Sage.

YANKELOVICH, DANIEL
1981 *New Rules.* New York: Random House.

Schools and Delinquency 4

INTRODUCTION

American schools have historically been a source of pride. Visitors from other countries have admired the United States for making mass education a success, and Americans admired their own educational system and had high hopes for what it would accomplish. The Progressives, for instance, claimed that education would promote democracy, social mobility, equality, and expert leadership (Robertson, 1980). This belief continued into the 1960s, when President Johnson declared, "The answer for all our problems comes in a single word. That word is education" (quoted in Johnson, 1983:641). Why had such glowing optimism characterized our outlook on education? This is difficult to say, but the Hechingers (1975:411) offer one possible answer:

> No rational assessment of American education is possible without an understanding of the close link between the nation's mood and the schools. The optimism of the frontier . . . the dream of an open society, the conviction that there are pragmatic solutions for all problems, the trust in efficiency and productivity . . . all of these often conflicting currents of thought have shaped American schools. They did so not because educators recommended it but because society willed it.

Unfortunately, the national mood has turned largely into one of malaise, and glowing testimonials to the American schools are no longer heard.

In fact, the state of American education has reached such a low level of esteem that even writers who profess to be optimists are issuing such dire warnings as the following:

> American schools are in trouble. In fact, the problems of schooling are of such crippling proportions that many schools may not survive. It is possible that our entire public education system is nearing collapse. We will continue to have schools, no doubt, but the basis of their support and their relationships to families, communities and states could be quite different from what we have known (Goodlad, 1984:1).

SCHOOLS IN DECLINE

There is a growing literature on the decline of American schools. Anxiety over the condition of our elementary and secondary schools is a relatively recent development spurred on, no doubt, by the growing literature on how American schools have been declining. Several reports upset the once-prevailing atmosphere of calm and optimism. Of course, shocks had occurred previously, particularly after the 1957 launch of the first Soviet satellite, *Sputnik,* which made people question America's alleged superiority in mathematics and science. But the public mood toward education soon relapsed into acceptance and complacency. Now, however, the decline of American education is more obvious and widespread.

Misbehavior and Fear

One of the major worries in the educational world in recent years is the apparent rise in student misbehavior. It is the schools' major problem in the opinion of students, teachers, and parents at every level: elementary, junior high, and senior high schools (Goodlad, 1984). One woman who taught school, left for eleven years, and then returned to the classroom found that although the amount of misbehavior was virtually the same as before, almost everyone tolerated and even encouraged it, and that misbehaving students defied their teachers and refused to be punished or corrected. The blame is placed on the teacher for being unfair (Niensted, 1979). Teachers object to these behaviors not only because they violate rules, but because they are means that students use to register their dislike of the school or teacher, distracting the teacher and other students from the process of learning. School observers generally agree that most elementary- and secondary-school teachers spend little time on teaching; discipline and other chores consume as much as three-fourths of their class time.

The school-related misbehaviors most studied in recent years are violence, vandalism, and various kinds of theft. It is widely believed that violence against teachers and other pupils has increased in recent years.

> During the last decade, violence, terrorism, and vandalism by students in our schools—and a few lawless outsiders—have more than tripled. More than 70,000 teachers are physically assaulted every year in the classroom and hallways of our schools. . . . Thousands of students arrive at school every morning to find older bullies intimidating, attacking, and robbing them of whatever they may have in their possession. As to school vandalism: a report of the National Education Association verifies that the destruction of school buildings and property has grown to an annual figure that would supply schoolbooks for the entire nation (Armstrong, 1978:40).

The National Institute of Education, which prepared a long report to Congress called *Violent Schools—Safe Schools* (1978), found that one out of every eight teachers hesitates to confront misbehaving students for fear of retaliation. Students too admit fear; about 600,000 report that they live in fear most of the time that they spend in school. More than one in five students confesses that he or she is afraid to use school restrooms because of the possibility of being robbed or attacked.

Transience

The problem of transience has never received much attention; truancy and dropouts, for instance, have attracted much more publicity. But transience also has important consequences. Maeroff presents a scenario for transience in the inner city and its relation to school:

> Life on the edge of poverty is life without stability. If there is not enough money to pay the rent, it may be easier to move. If the landlord refuses to make needed repairs or will not supply sufficient heat, it may be easier to move. If drug addicts take over part of a building and threaten the tenants, it may be easier to move. The effect on educational continuity can be disastrous. Some schools find their rolls turning over more than 100 percent a year (1982:72).

Research by Abramson (1974) indicates that this level of transience affects school performance. He looked at ten schools in New York City; fifth-graders classified as transient (that is, they transferred into their present school at some time after third grade) had reading scores that were a full year behind those of students who had remained at the same school during that period.

Scholarship

While violence and vandalism may be rising, academic performance is sliding downhill. Signs of decline are many: perhaps the best known is the Scholastic Aptitude Test (SAT). This exam is taken annually by college-bound high-

TABLE 4–1
Average Number of Months Gained or Lost in Achievement Test Scores by Students in Elementary Schools from 1964 to 1973*

Grade	Reading	Math Computation
8	−8	−18
7	−5	−14
6	−7	−12
5	−4	−9
4	−5	−4
3	−4	−2
2	+1	+4
1	+3	not available

*One school year equals ten months.
Source: Copperman, 1980:43.

school seniors and is scrutinized carefully by college admissions officers. The possible scores range from a low of 200 to a high of 800. Scores on the SAT reached a peak in 1963 when high-school seniors nationwide averaged 478 on the verbal SAT and 502 on the mathematical SAT. Then a long decline began; the SAT scores of college-bound high-schoolers hit bottom in 1980. From 1963 to 1980 the average verbal SAT score fell 54 points—from 478 to 424—and the average mathematical SAT score plummeted 36 points—from 502 to 466. Scores remained unchanged in 1981, and in 1982 the change in scores was minimal. During 1983, however, the average mathematical SAT score jumped 3 points—from 468 in 1982 to 471 in 1983—and the average verbal SAT score also increased—from 425 in 1982 to 426 in 1983. Although the increase in the mathematical score is the largest ever reported, SAT scores still do not approach what they were in 1960. It is, however, a hopeful sign that the decline in scores appears to have stopped; but whether the improved scores are the beginning of an upward slope is as yet unknown.

Not all grade levels, however, exhibit this downward spiral. At the very earliest levels—preschool and first and second grades—tests show that there has been a *gain* in proficiency since the early 1960s. *Sesame Street,* which is watched by over half of 3- to 5-year-olds, has boosted skills, as has the increased number of children who attend kindergarten. But students in the later years of elementary school and in all years of high school show a decline when compared to students of the 1960s. Table 4–1 shows the faltering achievement scores between 1964 and 1973, based on a Harcourt-Brace study.

Once these students reach college, deficiencies remain. Tests in New Jersey, for instance, showed that 39 percent of entering college freshman

> could not fully understand written prose and that 41 percent were unable to construct grammatical sentences. Each year, 40 to 60 percent of the entering

> students at the University of California are required to enroll in what used to be called "remedial" English (Jones, 1980:132).

Even more astounding is the fact that at a San Francisco junior college, more than 50 percent of incoming students read at a fifth-grade level or lower (Copperman, 1980)!

The failure of students to achieve in high school has been obscured by *grade inflation*: the number of A's and B's given to high schoolers has risen by about 25 percent over the last fifteen years, while actual learning has declined. This discrepancy has produced disturbing results. For instance, the valedictorian at Western High School in Washington, D.C., was denied admission to George Washington University. Despite top grades in high school, this student scored only 320 and 280 respectively on the SAT verbal and math tests. George Washington's dean of admissions commented, "My feeling is that a kid like this has been conned" (Jones, 1980:154). Many students never realize how low their achievement level is because they are surrounded by students equally below the norm (Maeroff, 1982).

Still, the public spends $87 billion a year on elementary and secondary schools. When students receive A's and B's, their parents and the general public assume that this investment will pay off. To find out later that many students have learned almost nothing can be shocking. In fact, some angry parents have filed suits against the schools. These malpractice suits have not succeeded, but some surely had merit.

> In June of 1972, a young white male who calls himself Peter Doe graduated from a public high school in San Francisco. His school records show that he has an average IQ, and that during his twelve years of public schooling he achieved average grades . . . and was promoted every year. His parents testify that they frequently complained to school officials that he did not seem to have adequate reading skills. They were repeatedly assured that he was reading at the average level and had no special or unusual problems.
>
> The first job Peter obtained after graduation was selling shoes. He lasted less than a week in this job because his reading skills were so poor that he could not do the minimal amount of paper work the job required. His reading skills were subsequently tested, and it was discovered that he was reading at a fifth-grade level (Copperman, 1980:17).

Many such students become functionally illiterate adults. A University of Texas study found that about one-fifth of American adults fit this label: they cannot calculate change, read a want ad, or address an envelope. Among high-school graduates, the figure is 13 percent and may be climbing, because 18- and 19-year-olds are more likely to be illiterate than people aged 30–39, even though 30–39-year-olds are less likely to be high-school graduates.

Although some students are learning little and mastering nothing, nearly all get promoted to the next grade each year. This practice, called *social promotion*, saves students embarrassment and allows them to stay with their age-mates but renders promotion meaningless. This was not always the practice. In the 1930s, one-third of students were held back a year during the first six years in school. Now not even one-tenth receive this treatment.

Students who get better grades than the social-promotion cases are helped along by an easier curriculum. Publishers have revised textbooks downward, using more pictures, larger margins, and lower levels of reading difficulty. High-school texts in general are now pitched at the level once thought appropriate for eighth-graders (Foote, 1980). Homework assignments have been cut in half, according to a New York panel studying changes that took place between 1968 and 1977.

Courses also have changed in recent years. Fewer English, history, math, and science courses are taught. Foreign-language instruction has dropped precipitously, partly because many colleges eliminated their language requirements. The fact that verbal SAT scores have fallen farther than math scores reflects the declining number of English and foreign-language courses. The traditional three R's (reading, writing, and arithmetic) have been replaced in part by a host of electives: driver's education, communication skills, film appreciation, and so on. Goodlad (1984) reports that in senior high schools, the most numerous course offerings are vocational.

Teacher Inadequacies

When discussing the inadequacies of students and curricula, commentators often refer to teacher inadequacies as well. And although most elementary- and secondary-school teachers are probably capable, qualified, and competent, some are not. There are estimates indicating that 20 percent of teachers have not mastered the skills they are supposed to be teaching: reading, mathematics, and writing. People who apply for teaching positions may be required to take minimum competency tests. In Pinellas County, Florida, in the St. Petersburg–Clearwater area, applicants need to be able to read at an advanced tenth-grade level and to solve math problems pitched at the eighth-grade level. In 1979, one-third of the prospective teachers who took the exams for the first time failed.

These dismaying figures suggest that schools of education use very low standards when deciding whom to award degrees to, and very low standards in their curricula as well. Furthermore, the students they attract are a decidedly unimpressive lot. Research by Timothy Weaver confirms

> a longstanding charge that one of the easiest U.S. college majors is education. Weaver found the high-school seniors who planned to major in education well below the average for all college-bound seniors—34 points below average in verbal scores in the 1976 Scholastic Aptitude Test, 43 points below average in math. Teaching majors score lower in English than majors in almost every other field (Foote, 1980:58).

Several reasons have been offered for this situation: the pay scales for teachers remain very low and women, who traditionally made up the bulk of teachers, have opportunities nowadays to get into more exciting or prestigious fields.

Urban Schools

Some schools have more serious failings than others. Academically, small communities seem to fare better than large cities. In New York State, the Department of Education maintains a standard reference point for reading and math. In 1978–1979, 58 percent of the sixth-graders in New York City equaled or exceeded this point on reading. In other large cities in the state, 64 percent passed. The figure was 77 percent in smaller cities, 82 percent in rural regions, and 84 percent in villages and suburbs.

One of the changes urban schools are undergoing is "white flight"; that is, white families are increasingly moving out of inner-city areas. Some of these white students are now attending public schools in the suburbs and rural areas where their families have moved. Others are going to private schools, which now account for 11 percent of the total elementary- and secondary-school enrollment. Urban public schools have been left to the poor and minorities, making America's school system very socially stratified. Generally speaking, about 60 percent of public-school students in major cities are black, Hispanic, or members of other minorities. Some cities allow their students to fall farther behind the national average the farther along in school they go. Newark, the largest city in New Jersey, is one of the more sobering examples. In 1978, the proportion of students who read at or above the national average for their grade should have been about 50 percent. Instead, the percentages were 42 among second-graders, 24 for third-graders, 18 for fourth-graders, and 13 for fifth-graders (Maeroff, 1982).

Recently, public opinion has taken these developments into account and become less supportive of education. Arguments over busing, school prayer, sex education, and the teaching of evolution have given citizens an excuse to vote against tax bills for schools that do not comply with their personal beliefs. The fact that most of the voters are white and fairly conservative does not make them very sympathetic toward today's schools—particularly if their children are already out of school. Having to rely on elections makes schools vulnerable. Maeroff (1982:195) asks:

> In what other area of public expenditure is the citizenry permitted the luxury of an election? Tax revenues are spent on welfare, public safety, health and hospitals, higher education, and defense without the public right of disapproval. The public schools just happen to have the misfortune of having their funding subject to election. . . . Imagine what would happen if they could vote on welfare payments.

Our discussion thus reveals that American schools face many problems. Now we will examine theories of how school delinquency and disruption (and delinquency in general) arise. Although three of the following four explanations are offered by social scientists, we begin with one that is not.

SCHOOLS AND DELINQUENCY: FOUR THEORIES

Loss of Teacher Authority

Copperman (1980), who is a specialist in reading development, presents a complex argument that links a series of school problems together. We will simplify it here and focus on those features that are most relevant to school delinquency. Figure 4–1 represents his overall argument fairly well. The teacher's authority occupies a central position in this theory and affects students' academic performance and school-related delinquency. Teacher authority depends on the authority wielded by the principal and the amount of support provided by parents. The extent to which the school uses "open classrooms" may also affect teacher authority.

Copperman believes that schools cannot provide much learning if the principal is weak. Only principals who exercise authority by concentrating on curriculum and teaching can bring about an environment conducive to learning. They must fire or force out inept teachers, train those who have potential, and support those who are already performing ably. Most principals, however, spend their time on other activities, which Copperman believes are less important.

Parents' support for school policies and practices used to be taken for granted, but modern-day parents are more likely to rally to their children's side.

> They are not reinforcing the teacher by making sure their children do their schoolwork every day. They are not nearly as concerned about their children cutting classes or using drugs. Some parents actively subvert the teacher's authority by denigrating the school or the teacher to their children. . . (Copperman, 1980:160–161).

When parents do not support teachers, their children's respect for teachers declines.

Open classrooms also have a bearing on teacher authority. A. S. Neill, who ran a private school in Britain called Summerhill, wielded great influence in the open education movement; later, the movement was carried on by Americans such as Charles Silberman, Jonathan Kozol, and John Holt. Their philosophy has replaced traditional teaching methods in many American school systems. Organizationally, open classrooms involve the following innovations:

> . . . children are permitted to study the things that interest them, virtually whenever they want to do so; a wide variety of learning activities are to be made

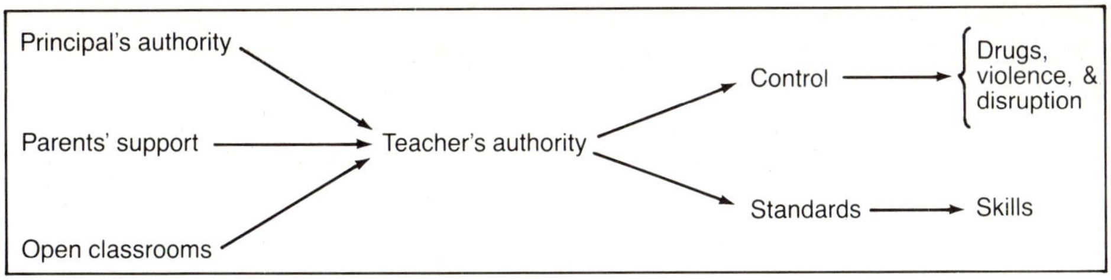

FIGURE 4–1
School Problems and Delinquency

> available to students within the classroom; during their learning activities children may move freely around the classroom, interacting with other students as they desire; the teacher is to behave in a democratic, nonmanipulative, warm, and respectful way toward his students, providing them with pleasant and enjoyable educational experiences (Copperman, 1980:66).

In high schools, the open education movement has spawned flexible scheduling, more electives, and lighter courseloads. At one time, students had a core curriculum to follow, and few electives were available. Students were assigned a predetermined set of courses, and these filled the student's entire day. Teachers imposed moderately stiff reading and writing requirements, tests, and homework. Students either did well on these tasks or faced the prospect of a low grade at the end of the term.

Copperman claims that modern students can choose not only electives but also teachers in the classes that are required. Teachers are thus put on the defensive: they must get a reasonably large number of students to take and like their courses, so their instruction must be entertaining and their assignments few and easy. This situation generates a popularity contest among teachers in which one of the ways to win is to inflate grades. And if one teacher inflates them, others are almost forced to follow. As a result, standards for students are relaxed. With life so easy, students are likely to become lazy and unmotivated. If they do not study, they do not worry, because they will receive good grades anyway. As teacher expectations decrease, students work less, learn less, and their skills erode, as the SAT and other tests show.

The loss of teacher authority also means that teachers no longer exert the inhibiting effect on student behavior in school that they once did. Students fear and respect teachers less. Flexible scheduling gives students more periods when they have no classes to attend. Teachers who see students in the hallways thus cannot be sure whether they are legitimately unscheduled or are just goofing off. Teachers generally give such students the benefit of the doubt, and students take advantage of this confusion to cut more classes.

This lack of control makes it easier for students to get away with behavior such as drug use, violence, and vandalism. If there is a great deal of free time and teachers are reluctant to intervene, deviant and disruptive behaviors are likely to increase. And they will continue if school officials refuse to suspend or expel the offending students, according to Copperman.

Regimentation and Revenge

Diametrically opposed to Copperman's view is the one proposed by David Greenberg (1978). Greenberg believes that no single theory explains the diverse kinds of delinquency, so he offers two: one for ordinary theft and the other for violence and vandalism. We will discuss only the second one, which is the one that relates to schooling. Greenberg begins by noting that as children grow older, especially as they enter their teens, they are given increasing freedom and independnce in the family and other settings. At school, however, the same rules apply year after year: "rules concerning such matters as smoking, hair styles, manner of dress, going to the bathroom, and attendance" (Greenberg, 1978:200). These rules bother students, who have come to expect authorities to begin treating them as adults.

Students who do well at school, are popular with their peers, and participate in extracurricular activities probably find school rules merely a minor annoyance. But those students who fare poorly academically, are not popular, and participate little, may find that school does not have much joy to offer and regard its rules as oppressive and intolerable. Such students find school frustrating, develop hostility toward it, and often drift into trouble.

In the 1900–1940 era, lower-class youths tended to drop out of school early and in large numbers, but more recently (1940–1985) many of them are remaining in school, in part because job prospects for young people with no diploma are bleak. If these students stay in school and do poorly, they typically do not get much respect, but they do get evaluated, ranked, and graded. Sometimes, teachers single them out for special abuse such as being called lazy or stupid in front of the entire class.

Faced with strict rules and degrading experiences in class, some students try to save face and regain their self-esteem by lashing out at the cause of their embarrassment: by attacking teachers or by vandalizing the school. Or they may try to reestablish their status in other ways.

> Common psychological responses to the irritation of the school's denial of autonomy range from affective disengagement to the school ("tuning out" the teacher) to smoldering resentment, and at the behavioral level, from truancy to self-assertion through the flouting of rules. Such activities as getting drunk, using drugs, joy-riding, truanting, and adopting eccentric styles of dress . . . can be seen as forms of . . ."conflictual validation of the self." By helping students establish independence from authority . . . these activities contribute to self-regard (Greenberg, 1978:201).

Greenberg thus believes that school rules breed frustration among students whose grades and popularity are low. This frustration may then bring about

ISRAEL

We often think of the United States as standing alone among nations, as the only one facing the problem of conflicting races or ethnic groups. Therefore, we are always quite surprised to find these conflicts breaking out elsewhere. Israel is an example of conflict stemming from immigration from different parts of the world and being most observable in the schools.

Since the establishment of the State of Israel in May 1947, the population has been more than trebled by an influx of immigrants from numerous and widely differing countries. There are now appoximately three and a half million inhabitants in Israel, among them 12 percent non-Jews, mostly Moslem Arabs. The major effort within the Jewish population has been concerned with the absorption of large masses of people which has been taking place for the last 30 years. Under prevailing circumstances this has entailed a heavy drain on economic as well as socio-cultural development, which increased difficulties in the process of integration. Suffice it to mention that this process occurred within a small territory and within a brief period of time. Invariably, immigration to Israel has meant for many, and particularly those who have come from Asia, North Africa, and countries of the Near and Middle East, a transplantation into competitive society, which is urbanized and industrialized on the pattern of countries in the western hemisphere. This sudden change has tended to disrupt the ordinary way of life of individuals, of families, and of whole groups. They have been thrown out of their normal rhythm and have encountered difficulties in reorienting themselves to the rhythm of the new environment.

We witness a clash of culture with all its inherent consequences. This process is especially felt among the various oriental communities as compared to their counterpart, namely those who have immigrated from European countries. . . .

[T]hree factors contribute to juvenile delinquency in Israel. These are the break-up of the family unit, the clash of cultures in a melting-pot setting, and the rapid development of a technological society. Each of these factors alone is of sufficient magnitude to create situations which can lead to delinquent behavior. Many individuals, however, must deal with all three simultaneously. . . .

Large numbers of children and young people in Israel often find themselves facing a sequence of frustrating situations. For instance, many children who belong to oriental Jewish communities find it difficult to keep pace with the ordinary school curriculum, although they are not mentally retarded. Many eventually drift away from school without finishing the prescribed grades in elementary school. They early become aware, albeit not intellectually, that their failure to finish school hampers their integration into Israeli society and contributes to their ultimate failure. Many of them hold a grudge against the school which, as they see it, prevented them from gaining the social status of their peers.

Source: David Reifen, "Israel," pp. 58, 80. Reprinted by permission of New York University Press from *Justice and Troubled Children Around the World,* volume I, edited by V. Lorne Stewart.

delinquency to shore up the students' battered self-esteem—the most likely delinquency being school vandalism and assaults on teachers.

Tracking

A small group of scholars has singled out tracking as an important cause of delinquency. Tracking refers to the grouping of students into college-preparatory and other categories variously called general, vocational, business, agricultural, or remedial. Students in the college-preparatory track traditionally take a foreign language, algebra or some other advanced math course, and a science course during their freshman year in high school. Other students take courses in other tracks. Thus, segregation and differentiation begin very early in students' high school careers.

The people who decide on which track a student should be placed include guidance counselors and teachers. According to several studies, these officials do not rely on students' academic ability alone when making this decision. Cicourel and Kitsuse (1963; 1968) found two types of error to be common: (1) low-ability students assigned to the college-bound program and (2) high-ability students placed in one of the noncollege tracks.

Type 1 students may have parents who push them into the college-bound track, or they may be informally sponsored by teachers or guidance counselors who believe them to be "serious, personable, well-rounded students with leadership potential" (Cicourel and Kitsuse, 1963:138). Type 2 students tend to be lower-class or members of a minority group (Schafer and Olexa, 1971). Kelly (1977) tried to find out how such errors might arise. He asked teachers to select those junior-high-school students who ought to be placed in a remedial reading program. He found that the teachers' selections were often questionable; many of the students chosen for the program had reading-test scores that were too high to warrant placement in it. After looking at many factors that could have influenced the teachers' decisions, Kelly concluded that the most influential one was whether the student had ever been in a remedial program. Thus, students who had become competent readers were stereotyped as incompetent by their teachers because they had once been placed in a remedial reading program and never recovered from the damaging effects of this label.

These labels are important because they may turn out to be irreversible: once assigned to a particular track, the student has little chance of ever being reassigned. Going from a noncollege to a college-preparatory track, for instance, is difficult because schools establish prerequisites: thus freshman algebra must be taken before one can take sophomore plane geometry; taking basic math in the freshman year, school officials argue, would not adequately prepare a person to jump into geometry as a sophomore. Schafer et al. (1972) found that only 7 percent of students switch from a college-preparatory track to a noncollege track or vice versa.

TABLE 4–2
Delinquency by Sex, Class, and Track Positions (Yule's Q)

Self-reported Act	Sex	Class	Track
Expelled from school	−.60	−.10	−.66
Placed on school probation	−.07	+.07	−.52
Skipped school	−.24	−.24	−.45
Stole book from library	−.21	+.08	−.39
Involved in gang fighting	−.57	+.08	−.61
Smoked cigarettes	+.06	−.02	−.57
Smoked marijuana	−.09	+.22	−.39
Shoplifted	−.14	+.07	−.46
Drank alcohol	−.14	+.13	−.45

Source: Kelly, 1975:268

Furthermore, the track that students occupy makes an important difference in their subsequent careers. It influences the people they associate with in and out of school, their grades, their participation in extracurricular activities, their self-esteem, their attitude toward school, their chances of failing, their attendance, their troublemaking while in school, and their involvement in juvenile delinquency elsewhere.

Schafer et al. (1972) found that a student's track has more effect on grade-point average than do variables such as social class, IQ, or previous grade-point average. This relationship may stem partly from grading floors in college-preparatory tracks (where almost no student gets a grade below B) and grade ceilings in other tracks (where almost no student gets a grade above B). And according to Schafer et al., noncollege-bound students get worse grades the longer they stay in school, while the grades of college-bound students consistently improve from their freshman to senior years. (It is possible that after Schafer et al. finished their work, grades of noncollege-bound students also improved, due to grade inflation.)

More important, though, is the link between track position and delinquency, an issue examined most thoroughly by Kelly (1975). In a self-report study of seniors from predominantly rural areas of western New York State, he compared track position, sex, and social class to see which factor predicted deliquency best. Kelly looked at three kinds of delinquency measures: ordinary offenses (gang fighting and shoplifting), school-related offenses, and status offenses. His findings appear in Table 4–2. Surprisingly, delinquency is more closely associated with track position than with sex, and social class and delinquency are related only quite weakly. Track position was most strongly linked to gang fighting, smoking, and school expulsion—one of each of the three types of offense. Thus, it appears as though school stratification may have some undesirable side effects for those students who fall into the noncollege tracks.

IQ and Delinquency

The relationship between IQ and delinquency has had a colorful research history. In the late nineteenth and early twentieth centuries, criminologists who had been trained in medicine or psychology made some inflated and, in some cases, inflammatory claims. Basically, they argued that people of low intelligence are (1) easily led into lawbreaking by the wiles of cleverer people, and (2) unable to realize that committing offenses in a certain way often leads to getting caught and perhaps punished. Some of this early research was remarkably shoddy; typically, only the IQ of offenders was measured, while researchers merely guessed at the IQs of the rest of the population. This guessing led to hugely overestimating the nonoffenders' IQs. Furthermore, these early IQ tests were not very valid or reliable in themselves, regardless of the question of sampling.

Later in the twentieth century, many scholars delivered severe blows to this simplistic argument. They felt that sociological factors were more important causes of crime and delinquency than biological and psychological factors could ever be (Vold, 1979). Therefore, they tried to dispel the remaining traces of biological or psychological thinking in criminology, including the idea that low IQs led people into delinquency. As evidence, Sutherland (1931) and other sociologists could cite the large-scale study of army draftees in World War I.

> The issue was conclusively settled insofar as adult crime was concerned by a precise scientific study made by Carl Murchison just after World War I. Murchison was Chief Psychological Examiner at Camp Sherman, Ohio, and therefore had access to the tests given to all draftees during World War I. He tested the prisoners at Ohio Penitentiary, at the invitation of the warden, and later was able to secure tests from men in nine or ten other prisons. He compared the scores of the prisoners with those of the soldiers, taking into account race, native or foreign birth, and region. The results unequivocally proved that prisoners and soldiers . . . had essentially the same range of mental test scores, that the great majority of both classes fell into the average range . . . (Cavan and Ferdinand, 1975:179).

Sutherland's critique seemed to put a damper on further theoretical consideration of IQ and delinquency until recently. Now researchers are consistently finding that there *is* a relationship between IQ and delinquency. Unlike the early research, today's studies reveal fairly modest differences—about eight points higher for nondelinquents. Evidence for such a relationship is extensively documented (for example, Caplan, 1965; Woodward, 1955; Merrill, 1947), but theories of delinquency ignore these findings, and just *how* IQ affects delinquency remains a mystery. One possibility, of course, is that IQ actually has no effect at all. People who favor this argument typically suggest that both IQ and delinquency are instead caused by some third variable, such as social class (Chambliss and Ryther, 1975). This hypothesis is commonly held, but it has little research support. Various studies show that within the same social class, students with lower IQs have higher rates of delinquency (for example, Moffitt et al., 1981; Wolfgang et al., 1972).

Another common argument is that lower IQs do not lead to higher rates of delinquency per se but merely to higher rates of getting caught; low- and high-IQ youths are equally delinquent, but low-IQ youths are not bright enough to avoid the police (Haskell and Yablonsky, 1978). This explanation also sounds plausible. If it is correct, then IQ and delinquency will be correlated when official data are examined but uncorrelated when self-report data are used. In fact, the evidence shows that IQ and delinquency are correlated just as strongly when self-report data are used (Weis, 1973; West, 1973; Hirschi, 1969), indicating that getting caught or not has nothing to do with the IQ/delinquency relationship.

Hirschi (1969) takes the position that IQ does indeed have an effect upon delinquency, but not a direct one; instead it is transmitted through school-experience variables. According to his view, IQ performance is a measure of how well a person does on paper-and-pencil tasks. For the most part, these tests measure verbal skills. The original purpose of IQ tests was to predict how well a person would do in school and, though they are certainly not perfect, they do have a reasonably good prediction record: students who perform well on IQ tests tend to get good grades.

School performance (grades) also has effects, particularly on how much the student will like school. Students who get good grades tend to find school more enjoyable than those whose grades are poor. Once students like school, they tend to be more accepting of its rules and regulations and its authority to impose them. Finally, students who can tolerate the school's authority are not as likely to break the rules. Acceptance of school authority makes such youngsters unlikely to become delinquent. Looking at the issue from the opposite side, we can say that low IQ leads to lower grades in school, lower grades lead to disliking school, disliking school leads to rejecting its authority to impose rules, and this rejection of authority leads some students into delinquency. This, then, is Hirschi's elaborate explanation of how IQ and delinquency are linked.

RESEARCH

Copperman's theory focuses on teachers' loss of authority. He believes that if they had more authority and could exercise more discipline, academic performance would improve and delinquent behaviors would decline. No social researchers have set out explicitly to test this theory, but some have compiled data that allow us to test it. Perhaps most relevant is the work by Coleman et al. (1982). They conducted a nationwide survey of nearly 60,000 students from more than 1,000 high schools. A large part of their work is devoted to comparing public and private (most of them Catholic) school students.

Coleman et al. point out that students' scholastic achievement is considerably higher in the private schools. They argue that there are two basic reasons for this difference.

> First, given the same type of student . . . private schools create higher rates of engagement in academic activities. School attendance is better, students do more homework, and students generally take more rigorous subjects (for instance, more advanced mathematics). The indication is that more extensive academic demands are made in the private schools, leading to more advanced courses and thus to greater achievement. This is a somewhat obvious conclusion, and the statistical evidence supports it. Second, student behavior in a school has strong and consistent effects on student achievement. . . . [The] greatest differences in achievement between private and public schools are accounted for by school-level behavior variables (that is, the incidence of fights, students threatening teachers, and so forth) (Coleman et al., 1982:178).

Thus, private schools have fewer behavior problems. Indeed, "the *average* public high school is outside the whole range of Catholic schools in the direction of more behavior problems" (Coleman et al., 1982:111). The researchers believe that the fewer behavior problems in private schools are in turn attributable to the disciplinary climate. Three-fourths of Catholic-school students say discipline in their school is strict and effective; only 40 percent of public-school students say the same about their schools. Because of the higher standards of discipline in the private schools, behavior problems such as absenteeism, cutting classes, threats to teachers, and fights among students are fewer (1982).

Although Coleman et al. control for various background factors, it still could be argued that Catholic-school students are less delinquent than public schoolers before they ever reach high school, and the difference in delinquency rates is due to selection, not socialization in school. Therefore it is important to look at some research that does not depend on comparisons between Catholic and public schools. The 1978 study of public education, *Violent Schools—Safe Schools,* is one such piece of research. It looked at the relationship among violence and several school characteristics and found that schools where personnel made the greatest effort to govern students and enforce rules consistently experienced the least violence. This proved true of junior high schools, senior high schools, rural, suburban, and urban schools. Surprisingly, this relationship was even stronger than the relationship between school violence and violence in the surrounding neighborhood. This evidence is certainly compatible with Copperman's theory.

In contrast to Copperman, David Greenberg argues that school is a frustrating and annoying experience for many students; the insensitivity and authoritarianism of teachers push some students into rebellion, violence, and school vandalism. There is some support for this approach; frustration caused by schools does appear to account for some delinquent behavior. We know this because of studies showing that delinquency *declines* after age 17 (when adolescents complete their schooling), on weekends and during the summer months (when school is out), and after youths drop out of school (Elliott, 1966; Elliott and Voss, 1974).

But questions have been raised about Greenberg's claim that school rules or regimentation cause student violence and vandalism. Perhaps the strongest doubts have been voiced by Toby (1980). Relying on the *Violent Schools* report, he argues that school violence is usually a product of too little discipline, not too much. Greenberg says student violence appears when student rights are ignored, but Toby says teacher attentiveness or responsiveness to student rights and desires is irrelevant.

> Rural schools are the least responsive and the safest; some of them paddle students and conduct strip-searches for drugs. *What makes violence likely is weak control.* Big-city junior high schools have high rates of assaults and robbery because they contain a handful of violent students whom they cannot control and cannot extrude, and because they have not devised credible rewards and punishments for the larger group of potentially violent youngsters who are susceptible to deterrence (1980:38).

The results thus indicate that part of Greenberg's theory may be valid, but part is somewhat questionable.

The same conclusion applies to tracking theory. We have already presented some data from Kelly's study of rural schools in western New York State (1975). He later carried out similar research at a school in a more urbanized setting in the eastern part of the state (1976). There, the results did not support his theory so consistently. Tracking correlated highly with some delinquency items (being put on probation by the school and being expelled from school) but not with others (cutting classes and misbehaving in school). Thus tracking may have more effect on school punishment than on delinquency per se.

Other researchers also have looked at tracking, though not always in connection with delinquency. First, they have found that tracking is not especially discriminatory. That is, if students with equal academic ability are compared, it appears that the track they enter is not significantly affected by their social-class background (Rehberg and Rosenthal, 1978; Heyns, 1974; Jencks, 1972). Secondly, students do not always know what track they are in. Both students and staff are often unsure what the tracks are (Polk, 1983). People in the noncollege track are most likely to misperceive their track and think they are in the college-preparatory track. Far from feeling stigmatized and frustrated, these students are unrealistically optimistic (Rosenbaum, 1980). Thirdly, the college track is becoming less popular; most students opt for the general track, and many of them will still be able to enter college (Boyer, 1983). And vocational classes are preferred to academic subjects (Goodlad, 1984). All of these findings contradict tracking theory, which claims that tracking is discriminatory and students in the noncollege track know it and feel humiliated and stigmatized.

Recently, Wiatrowski et al. (1982) looked at a national sample of 500 white males in high school and followed them for several years. They found that there was essentially *no* relationship between a student's track and (1) delinquency among tenth-graders, (2) delinquency among seniors, (3) amount of delinquency one year after high school, or (4) seriousness of delinquency one year after high school. All the correlations are under .10 and thus quite weak.

In a review of Wiatrowski's study, Kenneth Polk (1983) agrees that it shows tracking to be less important than tracking theory claims, but he also mentions that other school factors are important in producing delinquency; he looked at the relation between high-school grades and adult criminality. The four groups he compared were (1) youths with high grade-point averages (GPAs) and a record of delinquency, (2) youths with high GPAs and no delinquency, (3) youths with low GPAs and a delinquency record, and (4) youths with low GPAs and no delinquency record. When Polk (1978) looked at the adult lives of these people, he found that those who had been delinquent as youths were more likely to be criminals as adults, of course. But grades also made a difference in adult life. Those who had a low GPA but no record of delinquency were almost as likely to become adult criminals (40 percent) as were people with a delinquency record as youths and a high GPA (50 percent). These data suggest that high-school grades have long-term effects.

Polk's data are quite compatible with Hirschi's view of IQ and delinquency. Hirschi argues that IQ has an effect on grades; grades affect one's attachment to school; attachment to school affects one's tolerance of school authority; tolerance of authority then affects one's involvement in delinquency. Hirschi's argument hinges first on whether there is a relationship between IQ and delinquency. Wolfgang et al. (1972) provide some relevant data in Table 4–3. These data show that Philadelphia boys with no police contacts had a higher IQ than one-time offenders, and chronic offenders had the lowest IQ of all. Even after controlling for the variables of race and social class, the relationship between IQ and delinquency still held. Researchers also have found that grades are strongly related to IQ, and grades are a better predictor of future delinquency than IQ is (Rhodes and Reiss, 1969). Third, grades are strongly related to how much a student likes school (Johnson, 1979; Frease, 1973). Fourth, students who like school are less prone to engage in delinquency (Wiatrowski et al., 1981; Rankin, 1980). Each of these provides evidence supporting Hirschi's model.

TABLE 4–3
IQ and Achievement for One-Time and Chronic Offenders by Race and Socioeconomic Status (SES)

	LOWER SES		HIGHER SES	
	Whites	Nonwhites	Whites	Nonwhites
I.Q.:				
One-time offenders	103.7	95.5	109.0	99.2
Chronic offenders	93.1	87.4	98.0	90.9
Percent retarded:				
One-time offenders	4.0	11.2	1.8	7.9
Chronic offenders	14.6	30.4	5.8	17.9
Percent below average achievement:				
One-time offenders	39.8	68.1	21.7	66.7
Chronic offenders	73.7	86.0	44.9	78.3

Source: Wolfgang et al., 1972:93.

SUMMARY

There is a growing literature on the decline of America's elementary and secondary schools. Anxiety over schools is relatively recent, coming after a long period during which education was thought to be one of America's strengths. A major worry in the educational sphere nowadays is the apparent rise in student misbehavior—particularly violence and vandalism. Transience is another problem of some importance, though it is not well publicized.

Scholarship problems include declining scores on achievement tests such as the SAT, grade inflation, functional illiteracy, social promotion, simplified texts, and lower enrollments in key areas such as English, math, science, and history. Related to these problems are signs that there are quite a few teachers whose qualifications are questionable. And most of the problems mentioned above are more pronounced in urban schools.

The link between schools and delinquency has been approached from different directions. Copperman focuses on loss of teacher authority. This, he says, is caused by weak principals, unsupportive parents, and open classrooms and generally leads to less control in the classroom and lower academic standards. Lack of control in turn makes it easier for students to get away with behaviors such as drug use, violence, and vandalism. If there is a great deal of free time, students do nothing, and teachers fail to intervene, deviant and disruptive behaviors are likely to increase. Research by Coleman et al. and by Toby backs up some of these claims in a general fashion, but much more precise testing is needed.

Greenberg claims that the schools' rules and regimentation, teacher insensitivity, and authoritarianism in effect force students into deviance. These factors make students angry and frustrated, so they lash out by attacking the source of their anger: the teachers and the schools. The evidence for all this is mixed: school does seem to promote some frustration and delinquency, but violence and vandalism are not most common in the most regimented schools.

Tracking theory argues that students placed in noncollege tracks are stigmatized by such placement, and they react in many negative ways—including delinquency. There is some evidence that delinquency may be related to tracking (Kelly's study in western New York State), but other evidence (Wiatrowski et al.) suggests it is not. Other researchers find that there is little or no stigma attached to being in the noncollege track today.

Hirschi offers a theory of delinquency that involves low IQ. Low IQ leads to poor school performance (low grades), which leads to lower tolerance of school authority, which in turn provokes more delinquent and disruptive behavior. There is evidence to support each link in this chain of argument. Thus, Hirschi's theory looks promising so far. But much remains to be learned about the complex way in which school experiences bear on delinquency. Right now, we are only beginning to understand the picture.

DISCUSSION QUESTIONS

1. Why is discipline such a concern among teachers in elementary and secondary schools?
2. What evidence indicates a general decline in academic performance since the early 1960s?
3. How do such practices as grade inflation and social promotion mask learning deficiencies and inadequacies?
4. What have been some of the consequences of decreased teacher authority and control in the schools?
5. Why does Greenberg argue that school regimentation leads to student violence?
6. How may tracking in school be linked to delinquent behavior?
7. How may IQ indirectly affect delinquency through school experiences?
8. How are the findings of the Coleman et al. study and *Violent Schools—Safe Schools* consistent with Copperman's view of the relationship between teacher authority and delinquency?
9. What evidence reveals that school experiences can be frustrating and give rise to delinquent activities?
10. How may one account for the relationship between school experiences and adult criminal behavior reported by Polk?

TO BECOME SOMEBODY

In large cities, ordinary high schools lose up to 50 percent of their students as dropouts. Occasionally, there is an innovative alternative school with a committed teacher who tries to resuscitate their lives. The following excerpt shows how hard this can be to accomplish.

As if these personal difficulties were not enough to weigh me down, the program was falling apart. To begin with, the class was a catastrophe. I had foolishly allowed I.S. 44 to foist on me a large number of students who had no interest in attending any program. They agreed to my contract only because our class seemed like the least unpleasant alternative available. Many of the youngsters were already immersed in a criminal lifestyle of incredible complexity. Three of them, each not yet fifteen and standing barely five feet tall, had been arrested more than thirty times. Some of our students openly bragged of muggings and robberies in which they had participated and the various weapons to which they had access.

Most schools present themselves primarily as institutions designed to transfer to their students a certain body of skills and information. We have always treated The DOME Project as a vehicle for a much more comprehensive kind of personal and social development. We try to help our youngsters become happy, healthy adults with positive social values and the opportunity to lead productive lives. We want them to have the same kinds of options most parents wish for their children. How they exercise those options is ultimately their choice, but at least we try to convince them there are real choices to be made and real reasons to choose one kind of life over another.

We work hard to reinforce family ties, not replace or diminish them. By including parents and siblings in activities and decision making, we create a kind of extended family that gives each youngster a sense of belonging to a powerful and protective clan. Youth gangs often perform a similar function in neighborhoods where there is no other effective intermediary between the struggling nuclear family and society at large.

Most adolescents think they know what they want, and they are often able to resist or subvert whatever plans others may make for them. We offer youngsters school and work incentives, powerful role models, and a protective and nourishing environment. We create an extended family and positive peer associations in an attempt to alter or limit certain kinds of behavior. In the end, however, our success or failure will be determined by the extent to which the youngsters choose to participate.

The students we ended up with in 1974–75, with the lone exception of Ramon, showed little inclination to take advantage of what we had to offer. I am not certain why. Part of the answer may lie in the concept of balance. The forces of chaos in that class may simply have outweighed all the forces of order we could generate. A few especially hardened youngsters mixed in with a group open to change can function in a program such as ours. That year, as it turned out, we had too many youngsters who already believed the die had been cast for them. They had all been held back in junior high school the maximum number of times allowable and knew they would be kicked upstairs to high school at year's end no matter how much or how little progress they made. Most of them had acquired a sense of importance and identity through their criminal activities. They were not about to trade in this hard-won status for a pat on the head and a little praise from us.

Partly because many of my students were on probation from family court, I could get them to attend class regularly, but the quality of daily life in the classroom was unbearable. A more experienced staff would have had a tough time with this lot, but Bobby, Chris, and I were simply overwhelmed, and we paid a heavy price. By the time Bobby left to return to college in January, I was at the end of my rope. I needed help desperately, and the person I turned to was Ted.

Ted had left the day-care center a few months earlier and had not yet taken another job. While he wouldn't commit himself to anything more than helping me through the school year, just his presence and maturity took much of the pressure off me. Ted knew I was having a hard time, but I think he was genuinely shocked when he first witnessed the attitudes and behavior of some of my students at first hand.

> TED: I couldn't believe what I found in the class. The first thing those kids would do every morning was hunker down and hash over all the horror stories of what had happened the night before. They told the most incredibly gory tales of violence and brutality, of knifings and stompings and bloodshed. Their total fascination—just the looks on their faces—was awful. The tension in the room was unbelievable. There was a constant sense that from nowhere, for no particular reason, an explosion would occur.

Ted insists he took the job at The DOME because it was the best offer he had at the time, but I know better. He agreed to do it, against all his instincts for self-preservation, because I was in trouble.

The bright spot for me in each day was when our West Side High students came down for their special class. The course I designed for them was unreasonably ambitious, considering their very modest reading skills, but knowing the generally unpalatable remedial assignments they got in school I wanted to expose them to challenging and exciting works. First we read short stories by O. Henry, passages from Genesis, and poems by Robert Frost, Langston Hughes, and e. e. cummings. Then I decided to introduce my students to *Oedipus the King*.

Reading Sophocles with Lee, Michael, Isaac, Ernesto, Julio and a few others was a fascinating experience. It took us nearly two hours to read the first twenty-five lines. The vocabulary, the syntax, the setting were all so strange and to them [sic]. None of them had any idea where Greece was nor had any of them ever attended a live theater performance.

The following day we reread the same lines in just ten minutes and went on to complete two more pages before stopping. My students could now identify Thebes and Zeus and knew the meanings of *suppliant* and *oracle*, and they didn't complain quite so vehemently when I stopped to explain some details I felt were important.

By the third day, everyone had become deeply involved in the plot, especially Ernesto, who was ready to come to blows with anyone who challenged his right to read the part of Oedipus. They called Creon "Crayon" and Tiresias "Tire-ass," but they read the play with an intensity I suspect the ancient Greeks would have appreciated, shouting out their discoveries like children in a puppet theater warning the woodsman to beware of the wolf lurking behind the tree. I'm not sure how much they learned about classical Greek drama, but I never saw a group of students enjoy a play more thoroughly. We finished the whole play and then went back and reread it to get a feel for how it would sound without all the interruptions. I doubt whether any of those youngsters ever went on to read a second Greek tragedy, but I could derive some satisfaction from knowing they at least had learned the classical, literary derivation of the term *motherfucker*.

As much as I enjoyed working with my former students, their presence in the program contributed greatly to our problems. We had made them feel The DOME Project was an extension of their home and family, and then we had brought in a new group of students. The veterans reacted with the same petulant jealousy parents are warned to expect from their children when they bring a new baby home from the hospital. At first they tried to take out their anger on the new students, picking fights with them on the slightest pretext. When we put a stop to that, they gradually turned their resentment against the staff.

They knew they were behaving badly, and often felt guilty, but their feelings were hurt and they couldn't stand it. They started coming to The DOME high, partly to soften their feelings of guilt and anger and partly to embolden themselves for whatever confrontation might arise. They also got high to torment me, knowing how deeply I felt drug abuse was a sign of disrespect for our program and for themselves. I would send them home whenever I saw they were high, but some were better at concealing the condition than others. It became a kind of extremely unpleasant game they would play with me to see whether I could tell who had been smoking reefer and who had not.

I had been training these youngsters to become leaders in our program. They had helped define the range and character of activities we provided. Now they were undermining not only my authority but the major premises of cooperation and shared objectives upon which we had built the program. We had gone so far as to establish a leadership council empowered to make some important decisions but the council was unable to provide any constructive leadership in this instance because the council members were among the worst offenders.

Tension mounted day by day. Ted warned me we were heading for some kind of explosion. I agreed but couldn't figure out what to do to head it off. I kept trying to talk to the youngsters who were obviously unhappy, but nothing I said seemed to help.

One day I caught Lee smoking a joint in the stairwell of the church. Lee had almost killed someone with an axe at the dome site, and we had kept him in the program. He had walked out of high school, and we had taken him into our class. We had gotten him into West Side High, found him jobs, and befriended him in many ways. Despite these efforts, or perhaps because of them, Lee was one of those most disoriented by the arrival of the younger students.

I asked Lee to leave the building, but he just stood there as if he hadn't even heard me. I asked him again, more forcefully this time. Instead of leaving he walked into the classroom and sat down. Had I been a little less tired and in a better frame of mind, I probably would have given him a few minutes to find some way to leave gracefully. I was too upset, however, to respond rationally. I bolted after him, raised my voice, and ordered him to leave immediately. I could see the anger welling up in him, but my own fury was equally great.

Our confrontation had become the center of attention. The other youngsters were drawn to us like sharks toward the smell of blood. Lee was strong, strong enough so that I didn't look forward to grappling with him, but I was determined to move him out. As I started toward him, I didn't notice Lee taking a razor-sharp box cutter from his pocket. As I got close enough to put my hand on him, Lee stood up and suddenly lunged toward me. I grabbed him and pinned his arms, but he was still able to draw the blade across my back. Fortunately I was wearing a thick sweater. The point left only a long, ugly scratch from one shoulder blade to the small of my back. After I finally got Lee out to the street and on his way home, though, I realized I was trembling and horribly afraid.

The incident disturbed me deeply. I knew that Lee genuinely cared for me, but he had put himself, with my assistance, in a situation in which only the slightest alteration in circumstances might have resulted in his killing me. Something was dreadfully wrong with the direction the program was taking. If I didn't do something about it, the participants in the next incident might not escape so lightly.

Meanwhile, our younger students were watching carefully everything that was happening. Unlike the older program participants, they had no long-standing relationships to bind them to the staff. We had no way of predicting what they might do in any given situation. Some of them had begun to show some interest in improving their reading and writing skills or in getting into a high school in which they might have a chance to succeed, but we had done very little to change their fascination for and involvement in antisocial behavior.

TED: There was an atmosphere of violence that followed some of those kids wherever they went. It culminated in their thinking they could attack people without having to face any serious consequences. We had no stomach for hitting kids, yet some of them felt you weren't serious unless you were willing to back up your demands physically. In what way does belting a kid teach him anything you can use to rebuild a viable relationship? It may possibly have some deterrent effect on others, but you want a kid who did something wrong to learn his lesson, not be the lesson.

Nevertheless I realized by the end of the year that some of the most disturbed kids in the class, youngsters who probably didn't belong there in the first place, loved some of the people in the program. The relationships they established with us may have been the only decent ones they ever had in their lives.

Like Ted, I worried about these youngsters and how to reach them, and I particularly worried about Lee. I knew I couldn't allow him back in the program without communicating to everyone else my tolerance of his behavior. Yet I had never banished anyone before. Wasn't I, as Ted suggested, making him the lesson instead of teaching it to him? I knew throwing him out of the program was equivalent to pushing him out on the street. How would he survive?

> LEE: I always thought I must be here for a purpose, but I couldn't find out why. I used to ask myself, *Why was I born?* Things like that.
>
> I used to walk through the streets and wonder why I didn't have nobody walkin' with me, nobody to talk to. Other people always seemed to have family with them, but my family always seemed to be comin' down on me. I guess I felt more alone than most other kids.
>
> When I be doin' somethin' bad, I wouldn't be thinkin' about what could happen later. I'd just be thinkin' where to run.
>
> Afterwards, though, I'd feel bad inside, like I shouldn't have did that. I'd think, *Those people be out hustlin' at they jobs, and I'm over here takin' the money they work for.* I'd be thinking, *What's gonna happen to me if I keep doing stuff like this?*

In that pathetic voice I hear echoes of Michael describing conditions in the Vernon Hotel, Ernesto longing for some encouragement from his father, and Ramon hoping that some day he would have some skill or knowledge with which to make a useful place for himself in the world. None of these youngsters wanted charity or sympathy. They wanted a chance to be productive. They wanted to know what other people knew, do what other people did, and enjoy the kinds of relationships other people seemed to enjoy. To the extent their circumstances permitted, they were willing to work for those opportunities.

Our society, however, seems to begrudge these young people the room and time they need to grow. Many do not get the love and recognition essential to the development of a healthy personality. They grow up fearing they will never be valued, a worry they share with all adolescents to a certain extent, but the circumstances of their lives reinforce the sense that they have nothing to gain and, therefore, nothing to lose.

We all want recognition. If we can't attain it through talent or hard work, we may seek other routes. In an interview in *The New Yorker*, a New York City police officer who was laid off because of budget cuts was asked how he would support his family once his unemployment benefits ran out. He responded that he fully expected to get his job back, but if he didn't, he added, "At least I know how to use a gun." I have heard similar sentiments, time and again, from young people who see their hopes and dreams of making it in legitimate ways destroyed by a society that doesn't value their potential contribution.

Every youngster wants to grow up to be a star, but the mass of nonwhite urban adolescents are like extras milling around a set the producers have abandoned. They have no script, no role, and the filming has been moved to a different location. There can be little argument about the cost to everyone, from mugger to victim, from taxpayer to welfare recipient, of a socioeconomic system that allows so substantial a portion of its populace, and particularly its youth, to become extraneous.

Youngsters often turn to delinquent behavior for the simple but frightening reason that they don't see any alternative for themselves. They fail at school, although our schools must surely share some of the blame. They cannot find work, for there is no work for them to do. They are irresponsible but at least in part because they lack a role to play in our society that might carry with it some responsibility and teach them something about being response-able [sic].

It is hard for anyone, let alone confused adolescents, to maintain a fine sense of moral balance when they believe neither they nor their actions matter to anyone. These youngsters develop instead an opportunistic set of values that reflects both the moral fluidity of society and their lack of a stable position in it. I don't mean to suggest these youngsters have no principles to which they adhere, for that is not the case. Their standards for ethical judgment, however, are so different from those I derived from my middle-class upbringing that I often have to remind myself not to assume I know what these youngsters are thinking or what basis they may use for making decisions.

At the end of the 1974–75 school year I gave a little essay assignment to my class. The surprising response I got may help illustrate my point. I asked my junior high school students to comment on one of the aphorisms my father used to trot out whenever I began to feel sorry for myself: "I cried because I had no shoes until I met a man who had no feet." I assigned this topic to ten students in a setting where they could not consult with each other. I wanted to see how well each one could deal with the simple sentiment transmitted by the single sentence. The results really shocked me. Two or three students wrote about feeling sorry for themselves until they saw someone worse off, but the rest of the papers all conveyed a different message: "This means I cried because I had no shoes and my feet was cold and sore. Then I met a man who had no feet. I thought, *He don't need his shoes*, so I took them. After that my feet felt better."

Many of the youngsters with whom I work are so wrapped up in their own needs that they cannot see or relate to the needs of others. They steal, as Lee had done, simply because they don't have something they want and see someone else who has it. To them, their needs supersede the needs of everyone else. The same is, in one way or another, true of us all, but most of us respond to other constraints upon our behavior. Lee told me he felt bad about robbing a working man because he knew he was stealing not just a wallet but days or weeks of the man's labor, yet he did it just the same.

I stayed in touch with Lee after I forced him to leave The DOME. He carried crumpled in his wallet the letter I wrote him a few days after he tried to stab me. I tried to encourage him to stay in school, and I helped find him jobs when he dropped out. I also got him lawyers and appeared with him in court. None of it really helped, at least not to the point where it might have enabled him to hold himself together. Lee had no anchor. Rejection by his father and hatred of his stepfather had left him lonely and bitter. Alcohol and drugs had robbed him of his equilibrium. He became a person who felt he had nothing to live for.

Lee was not the only youngster we lost. During the years I have worked at The DOME Project, we have lost students to drugs, jail, and the cemetery. I have seen youngsters run away and waste away. We did what we could, but often we were powerless to help. There is only so much a small program can do to counteract pressures exerted by the rest of society.

Some failures are harder to endure than others, but the failure to help a child who is calling out to you is the hardest of all. I harden my heart. I say I did everything I could. I remind myself of all those still looking to our program for guidance and support. But sometimes I cannot screen out the pain. Then I think of Lee and remember the tone of panic in his voice as he ran away from his mother and me the last time we were in court together, and I hope he has found someone who can help him more than I did.

Source: John B. Simon, *To Become Somebody*. Boston: Houghton Mifflin, 1982, pp. 116–125.

REFERENCES

ABRAMSON, JACOB

1974 The effect of continuity of school environment on reading achievement of fifth-grade pupils. Paper presented at the Northeastern Educational Research Association meetings.

ARMSTRONG, O. K.

1978 The scandal in our public schools. *Saturday Evening Post* 750 (May/June):40–42, 112–113.

BOYER, ERNEST L.

1983 *High School*. New York: Harper & Row.

CAPLAN, NATHAN S.

1965 Intellectual functioning. Pp. 100–138 in Herbert C. Quay (ed.), *Juvenile Delinquency*. Princeton, N.J.: Van Nostrand.

CAVAN, RUTH SHONLE, AND THEODORE N. FERDINAND

1975 *Juvenile Delinquency*. Philadelphia: Lippincott.

CHAMBLISS, WILLIAM J., AND THOMAS E. RYTHER

1975 *Sociology*. New York: McGraw-Hill.

CICOUREL, AARON V., AND JOHN I. KITSUSE

1968 The social organization of the high school and deviant adolescent careers. Pp. 124–135 in Earl Rubington and Martin S. Weinberg (eds.), *Deviance: The Interactionist Perspective*. New York: Macmillan.

1963 *The Educational Decision-Makers*. Indianapolis: Bobbs-Merrill.

COLEMAN, JAMES S., ET AL.

1982 *High School Achievement*. New York: Basic.

COPPERMAN, PAUL
1980 *The Literacy Hoax.* New York: Morrow.

ELLIOTT, DELBERT S.
1966 Delinquency, school attendance, and dropout. *Social Problems* 13 (Winter):307–314.

ELLIOTT, DELBERT S., AND HARWIN L. VOSS
1974 *Delinquency and Dropout.* Lexington, Mass.: Lexington.

FOOTE, TIMOTHY
1980 Help! Teacher can't teach. *Time* 115 (June 16):54–63.

FREASE, DEAN E.
1973 Schools and delinquency. *Pacific Sociological Review* 16 (October):426–449.

GOODLAD, JOHN I.
1984 *A Place Called School.* New York: McGraw-Hill.

GREENBERG, DAVID F.
1978 Delinquency and the age structure of society. *Contemporary Crises* 1 (Summer):189–224.

HASKELL, MARTIN R., AND LEWIS YABLONSKY
1978 *Crime and Delinquency.* Chicago: Rand McNally.

HECHINGER, FRED M., AND GRACE HECHINGER
1975 *Growing Up in America.* New York: McGraw-Hill.

HEYNS, BARBARA
1974 Social selection and stratification within schools. *American Journal of Sociology* 79 (May):1434–1451.

HIRSCHI, TRAVIS
1969 *Causes of Delinquency.* Berkeley: University of California Press.

JENCKS, CHRISTOPHER
1972 *Inequality.* New York: Basic.

JOHNSON, PAUL
1983 *Modern Times.* New York: Harper & Row.

JOHNSON, RICHARD E.
1979 *Juvenile Delinquency and Its Origins.* New York: Cambridge University Press.

JONES, LANDON Y.
1980 *Great Expectations.* New York: Ballantine.

KELLY, DELOS
1980 The educational experience and evolving delinquent careers. Pp. 99–114 in David Shichor and Delos H. Kelly (eds.), *Critical Issues in Juvenile Delinquency.* Lexington, Mass.: Lexington.
1977 How the school and teachers create deviance. *Contemporary Education* 48 (Summer):202–205.
1976 Comparing college-bound and non-college-bound students in terms of deviant behavior. *College Student Journal* 10:20–27.
1975 Status origins, track position, and delinquent involvement. *Sociological Quarterly* 16 (Spring):264–271.

MAEROFF, GENE I.
1982 *Don't Blame the Kids.* New York: McGraw-Hill.

MERRILL, MAUD A.
1947 *Problems of Child Development.* Boston: Houghton Mifflin.

MOFFITT, TERRIE E., ET AL.
1981 Socioeconomic status, IQ, and delinquency. *Journal of Abnormal Psychology* 90 (April):152–156.

NIENSTED, SERENA

1979 Discipline for today's different children. *Phi Delta Kappan* 60 (April):502–503.

POLK, KENNETH

1983 Curriculum tracking and delinquency. *American Sociological Review* 48 (April):282–284.

1978 Schools and the delinquency experience. Pp. 180–195 in Delos H. Kelly (ed.), *Delinquent Behavior.* Belmont, Calif.: Dickinson.

RANKIN, JOSEPH

1980 School factors and delinquency. *Sociology and Social Research* 64 (April):420–434.

REHBERG, R. A., AND E. R. ROSENTHAL

1978 *Class and Merit in the American High School.* New York: Longman.

RHODES, LEWIS, AND ALBERT J. REISS

1969 Apathy, truancy, and delinquency as adaptations to school failure. *Social Forces* 48 (September):12–22.

ROBERTSON, JAMES OLIVER

1980 *American Myth, American Reality.* New York: Hill & Wang.

ROSENBAUM, JAMES E.

1980 *Making Inequality.* New York: Wiley.

SCHAFER, WALTER, AND CAROL OLEXA

1971 *Tracking and Opportunity.* San Francisco: Chandler.

SCHAFER, WALTER, ET AL.

1972 Programmed for social class. Pp. 33–54 in Kenneth Polk and Walter Schafer (eds.), *Schools and Delinquency.* Englewood Cliffs, N.J.: Prentice-Hall.

SUTHERLAND, EDWIN H.

1931 Mental deficiency and crime. Pp. 357–375 in Kimball Young (ed.), *Social Attitudes.* New York: Henry Holt.

TOBY, JACKSON

1980 Crime in American schools. *The Public Interest* 58 (Winter):18–43.

VIOLENT SCHOOLS—SAFE SCHOOLS

1978 National Institute of Education. Washington: U.S. Government Printing Office.

VOLD, GEORGE

1979 *Theoretical Criminology.* New York: Oxford University Press.

WEIS, JOSEPH

1973 Delinquency among the well-to-do. Doctoral dissertation, University of California, Berkeley.

WEST, D. J.

1973 *Who Becomes Delinquent?* London: Heinemann.

WIATROWSKI, MICHAEL D., ET AL.

1982 Curriculum tracking and delinquency. *American Sociological Review* 47 (February):151–160.

1981 Social control theory and delinquency. *American Sociological Review* 46 (October):525–541.

WOLFGANG, MARVIN, ET AL.

1972 *Delinquency in a Birth Cohort.* Chicago: University of Chicago Press.

WOODWARD, MARY

1955 The role of low intelligence in delinquency. *British Journal of Delinquency* 5 (April):281–303.

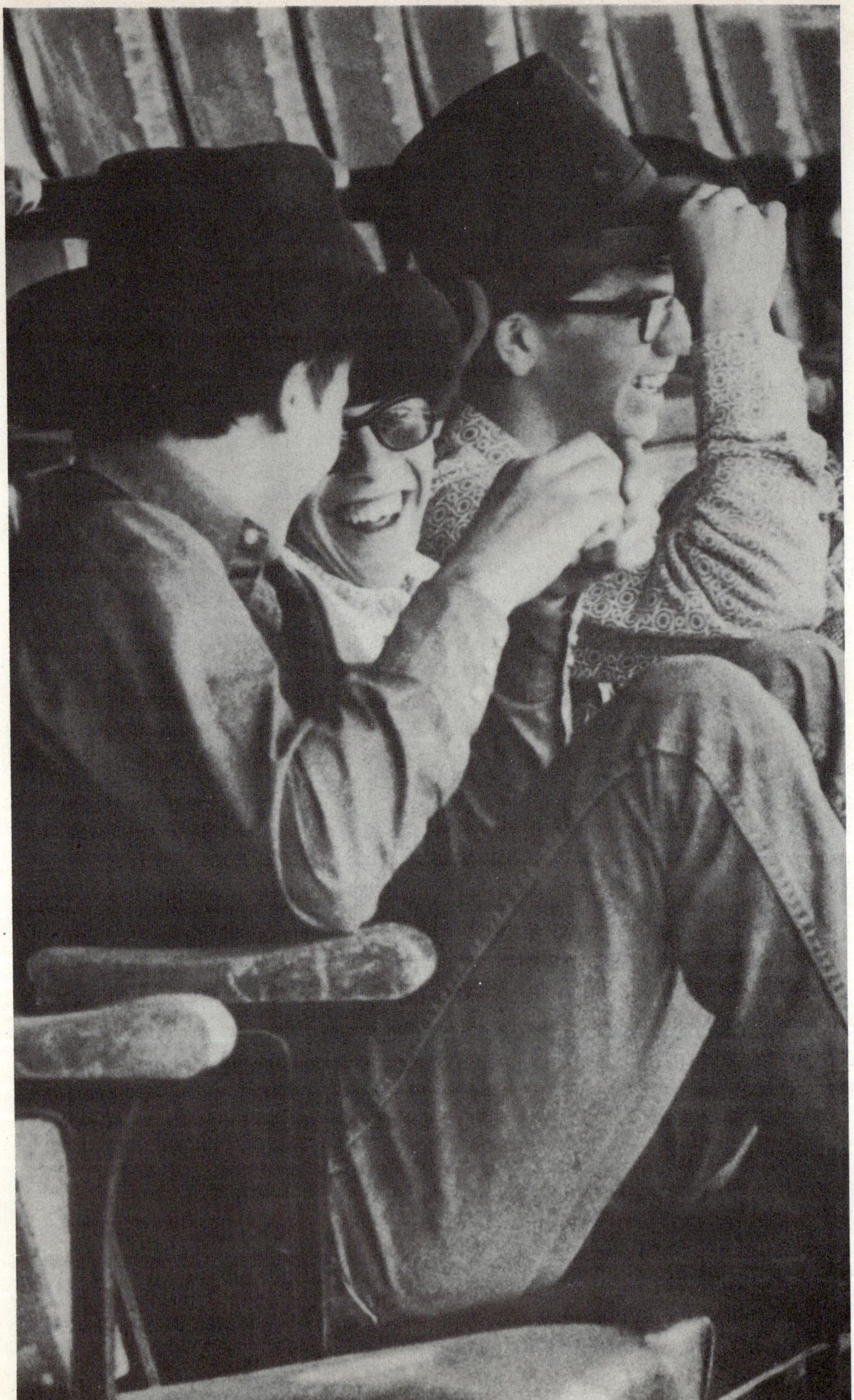

Adolescence, Peers, and Delinquency

5

ADOLESCENCE

Adolescence has different meanings and definitions, depending on whether it is approached from a biological, psychological, sociocultural, or historical viewpoint. Many aspects of adolescent life have been traced to biological changes; indeed, adolescence seems to be one stage in the life cycle particularly likely to be explained in biological terms. This is because puberty introduces some dramatic and obvious changes: genital and shoulder development in boys, menstruation and breast and hip development in girls, pubic-hair development in boys and girls, plus changes in voice pitch and sweat glands, the likelihood of acne, and major increases in weight and height. These changes take about four or five years, and not all of them begin at the same time in a particular youth. Nor do all youths experience puberty at the same age: there is considerable scholarly interest in the effects of early versus late development. Furthermore, girls begin puberty about two years before boys do. There have been some changes over the years (notably that puberty arrives much earlier in a girl's life now than it did a century ago), but, generally speaking, youths now go through the same biological changes that youths have always gone through. Hence, biological adolescence is a rather consistent and unchanging set of occurrences.

People knew about these phenomena years ago, of course, but they did not group them all together and give them a special name until 1904, when psychologist G. Stanley Hall coined the term "adolescence." Thus, the concept of adolescence is relatively new, and, because of Hall, the term has carried mostly psychological overtones. Even today, psychologists dominate the field of adolescence. First Hall and later Anna Freud developed the psychoanalytic perspective on adolescence. They characterized this period of life as a turbulent, emotional one, filled with storm and stress, brought on by the various biological changes in puberty. Such storm and stress were viewed as inevitable by the psychoanalysts and thought to be universal—not just limited to a particular social class, culture, or historical era. As psychoanalysts, however, Hall and Freud tended to see mostly disturbed youngsters who were in therapy; most youngsters did not receive such therapy or intensive diagnosis, so psychoanalytic samples were usually skewed toward the troubled and atypical youngsters. Thus it was concluded that adolescents in general suffer from rather serious problems: "emotional volatility, need for immediate gratification, impaired reality testing, failure of self-criticism, and indifference to the world at large" (Adelson and Doehrman, 1980:113). The recommended way to deal with such problem behavior was to provide a benign environment and wait for the adolescent to get the turmoil out of his or her system. This kind of thinking continues even today, as the following remarks indicate:

> Many teenagers have an inner radar that detects what irritates their parents. If we value neatness, our teenager will be sloppy, his room messy, his clothes repulsive, and his hair unkempt and long. If we insist on good manners, he will interrupt conversations, use profanity, and belch in company. If we enjoy language that has grace and nuance, he will speak slang. If we treasure peace, he will quarrel with our neighbors . . . and bully their children. . . . Rebellion against authority and against convention is to be expected and tolerated for the sake of learning and growth. . . . Adolescence is a period of curative madness in which every teenager has to remake his personality. He has to free himself from childhood ties with parents, establish new identifications with peers, and find his own identity (Ginott, 1969:23–25).

The psychoanalytic view of adolescence has long been the dominant, orthodox position. But it has been challenged by others, including what might be called the sociocultural view. The sociocultural theorists doubt that any universally true statements can be made about adolescents. These writers emphasize how different cultures deal with the adolescent period in different ways. The most famous work along these lines is Margaret Mead's early book on adolescents in Samoa (1928). She found that far from generating storm and stress, puberty in Samoa tends to arrive without much fanfare and to proceed quite smoothly. Mead attributes this in part to the Samoans' rather open, permissive attitude toward sexuality in general. (Biologically, of course, adolescence involves the development of primary and secondary sexual characteristics, so it is not surprising that attitudes toward sexuality and attitudes toward adolescence often overlap.)

A third approach to adolescence is more historical. The main idea behind this view is that adolescence varies from one period to another, depending on the circumstances people experience at the time. Before 1900, few youths attended high school, and not very many lived in large cities. Therefore, most adolescents spent much of their time with their parents and other adults, and school was a place of unequal opportunity, largely inaccessible to the lower class. Under such circumstances, adolescent life was very different from what it is now, when schools segregate youths from adults and are much more accessible to the lower class. Similarly, adolescence during the Depression of the 1930s or during World War II can be expected to have been very different from adolescence in earlier or later periods. Thus, the historical approach looks for the important and unique features of adolescence in each era and de-emphasizes its common or universal features, if indeed any exist.

PEER GROUPS

Adolescent peer groups have been a topic of considerable interest and concern in the second half of the twentieth century. We will look at some expressions of this concern, but first we need to look at why these peer groups should have begun to attract attention and take on special importance in the 1950s. Why was there no great outpouring of articles and books earlier on adolescent peer groups, say, in the 1930s or 1940s? What events or circumstances made the 1950s so distinctive in America?

One important difference was demographic. America experienced a baby boom that began in 1946 and continued until 1964. Rising birth rates occurred elsewhere in the world, too, but they generally lasted only a very few years. Continuing baby booms were experienced only in a few countries: the United States, Canada, Australia, and New Zealand. Each of these four countries was spacious, underpopulated, and had been spared the traumas of bombing and invasion during World War II.

In America there was a full decade and a half during the Depression and World War II (1929–1945) when many people simply did not feel that the time was right to bring children into the world. The end of World War II generally brought an end to this prolonged period and signaled the beginning of a new age of optimism and prosperity. This optimism encouraged people to marry; so did the booming economy.

> Encouraged by a thriving economy, and backed up by GI Bill veterans' benefits, more Americans married younger and faster than any other people in history. Everyone who could marry, it seemed, did. The change was startlingly rapid. As

> recently as 1940, as many as 15 percent of all women who reached their early thirties had never been married. But by 1960, only 7 percent were unmarried. All totaled, some 95 percent of all Americans of marriageable age were getting married—5 percent more than their parents, 7 percent more than the British, and 25 percent more than the Irish (Jones, 1980:23).

The high rate of marriage was an important factor in the high birth rates, but there were other factors too. For example, somewhat older people who thought the timing for childbearing was wrong during the Depression and war years now decided it was right. Many women over 35 thus contributed to the baby boom.

The size of the baby-boom generation can be estimated from the 1980 census. Persons aged 15–34 numbered just under 80 million. By contrast, the group aged 35–54 (which would be only slightly smaller if birth rates had been stable) numbered only 48 million. Thus, in the 1950s, the number of teenagers began to reach new heights and create new problems. They were a huge bulge in the population, one that the rest of the country was not very well prepared to cope with.

> The result of this [baby boom] has been provocatively stated by Professor Norman B. Ryder, the Princeton University demographer: "There is a perennial invasion of barbarians who must somehow be civilized and turned into contributors to the fulfillment of the various functions requisite to societal survival." That "invasion" is the coming of age of a new generation of young people. Every society copes with this enormous socialization process more or less successfully, but occasionally that process is almost literally swamped by a quantitative discontinuity in the numbers of persons involved: "The increase in the magnitude of the socialization tasks in the United States during the past decade was completely outside the bounds of previous experience" (Wilson, 1975:13–14).

Rising numbers were not the only factor involved in the rise of peer groups. Segregation, not racial or ethnic but segregation by age, also played a role. This was produced by sending more youngsters off to school. School may seem to be a normal, natural experience that all youngsters in America undergo, but this is a fairly recent development. All states do have laws requiring that children attend school until a certain age, usually 16. But in earlier years, not all youths went. Only one-third of persons aged 14–17 were attending high school in 1920 (Elder, 1980). This proportion climbed rapidly over the next twenty years, but even in the 1940s, Hollingshead found that lower-class youngsters were dropping out quite early. After dividing high-school-age youths into five social classes or strata, Hollingshead found that among 14-year-olds, one-third of those in the two lowest strata had quit school. He added, "*Before* the sixteenth birthday is reached, 64 percent of the class IV's and 75 percent of the class V's have left school" (1949:331), despite the fact that state law required them to remain in school until age 16. This all changed in the 1950s, when the proportion of youths attending school climbed into the 80-percent range (Elder, 1980). Thus, there were many more youngsters in America in the 1950s, and a much higher percentage of them were attending school. This meant new schools had to be built and new teachers had to be hired; it also meant that youths the same age were gathered together in record numbers—and were accompanied by very few adults. Empey calls schools of today "youth ghettos" (1982:43), and he finds age segregation pervasive.

> . . . kindergarten children are kept apart from first graders, first graders apart from second graders, and so on—not only in school but elsewhere. We are terribly conscious of the ages of childhood. . . (1982:47).

A third factor in the apparent rise of peer groups is the special treatment and consideration devoted to the baby-boom generation. Let us briefly mention three areas.

1. *Literature.* Dr. Benjamin Spock's book on baby and child care was first issued in 1946 (the year the baby boom began) and sold over a million copies for eighteen years in a row.
2. *Living space.* There was a very substantial migration to the suburbs.

   > In the twenty years from 1950 to 1970, the population of the suburbs doubled from 36 million to 72 million. No less than 83 percent of the total population growth in the United States during the 1950s was in the suburbs, which were growing fifteen times faster than any other segment of the country (Jones, 1980:38–39).

3. *Entertainment.* Though less than 1 percent of homes had television in 1946, 86 percent had a set by 1960. Hoola hoops and Barbie dolls also capitalized on the market created by the baby-boom generation. More significantly, though, this generation acquired its own music, rock and roll.

   > The music consolidated their group identity, bridging the emotions they all felt with peers who felt the same way. Rock was a language that taught the baby boom about themselves (Jones, 1980:62).

In the 1950s, there was a growing belief that young people as a whole were turning away from their parents and seeking closer ties with their peers or age-mates. (*Peers* are persons who are the same age but are not relatives.) One of the more important advocates of this argument is David Riesman (1950). According to him, the American family is not as closely knit as it once was; now it is only one part of the child's overall environment. Typical American children have higher status and more power than in previous decades, he wrote in 1950, and they face few if any economic hardships or deprivations. At the same time, parents have less power, less self-assurance and confidence, more doubts about how to raise children, and more doubts that they are superior to their children. These doubts encourage them to seek advice—perhaps from professionals such as psychologists, perhaps from the mass media, perhaps from their own children. Children learn norms of behavior from the media and put pressure on their parents to adhere to them: for example, parents should be permissive and use a minimum amount of discipline, and children should above all be well adjusted and popular within their peer group. Riesman's argument is that peers are becoming more important influences on a child than parents. Such children develop an insatiable need for approval, and peer-group approval is contingent on "going along." Therefore the child becomes an unthinking conformist, a pushover for the latest fad, and learns to "surrender any claim to independence of judgment and taste" (Riesman, 1950:73).

Bronfenbrenner (1970) also endorses this approach. He says that American children used to be well acquainted with many adults from different settings and walks of life. But nowadays, children spend most of their time at school or going to and from school. When they get home, their parents are often out, and the children do not know the other people in the neighborhood—an anonymity produced by urbanization. Society also has become age-segregated, as noted previously: parents and other adults want it this way, because they tell youngsters not to bother them, to spend time with the peer group instead. A substantial number of children follow this advice, but not always with positive results. According to Bronfenbrenner, peer-oriented youths have negative views of themselves, their peer group, and their future prospects; they also are more delinquent. In short, parents withdraw, leaving a social vacuum that children fill by turning to the peer group, which is composed of youngsters whose influence is largely negative. Bronfenbrenner (1970:121) writes:

> . . . if the current trend persists, if the institutions of our society continue to remove parents, other adults, and older youth from active participation in the lives of children, and if the resulting vacuum is filled by the age-segregated peer group, we can anticipate increased alienation, indifference, antagonism, and violence on the part of the younger generation in all segments of our society. . . .

A related argument is that teenagers have created their own subculture, a view developed most thoroughly by James Coleman in *The Adolescent Society* (1961). High schools play a key role in his theory. He maintains that occupational specialization and a need for higher levels of training (to become managers, engineers, and so on) keep larger numbers of people in school for many years. At school they are lumped together with people precisely their age and cut off from adults; there, they also manufacture their own culture—language, symbols, and values distinctly unlike those of adults.

A YOUTHQUAKE IN RUSSIA

James Coleman highlights the liberated, hedonistic, and superficial youth culture in America without hinting that it might arise elsewhere. But a few signs of it do occur in other countries—even in the Soviet Union, despite government fears that Western decadence will spoil Russian youths.

The Komsomol, or Young Communist League, used to sponsor sedate clubs where privileged youngsters could compare ideological notes and sing the songs of revolution. But instead of boning up on Lenin these evenings, young Russians are getting down with Donna Summer and turning the party into a party. "There weren't enough places to meet girls," explains Viktor Bashanov, 26, who helped start a Komsomol disco in Moscow, just a block from KGB headquarters. His hangout flashes with all the symptoms of "Saturday Night Fever," including strobe lights, beer and a baseball-capped deejay. Laughs Aleksandr Lazarev, shaking his booty in corduroy jeans and a black bodyshirt: "My mother worries that if I keep up this disco life, I'll never get married."

Restlessness: Swinging bachelorhood is far from the worst worry of Soviet mothers—or of the Communist Party. But the disco explosion is symptomatic of the increasing restlessness and Western-influenced values of the under-30 generation. Born to an affluence their parents never knew, many Russian youths are bent on conspicuous consumption, bored by political ideology and impatient with their system's shortcomings.

That may apply to youth the world over, but in the highly structured Soviet society, even a whiff of disaffection can cause alarm. Increasingly, official publications now inveigh against the "Philistinism" of youth. In the monthly Soviet journal Zvezda, for example, poet-songwriter Lev Kuklin reported he was shocked by technical students who asked him how much he "raked in" from his music and whether he owned a car, a dacha and a color TV. "Our children mirror our way of life," he wrote. "These young people's attitudes reflect a failure of our upbringing."

Disturbed by the rising level of youthful discontent, the Soviet Government is trying to defuse it by encouraging kids to dance, dance, dance. New discos proliferate faster than bouquets at Lenin's tomb; at last count, the Komsomol was operating 260 dance clubs in Moscow alone, more than double the number two years ago. The youth league, which is supposed to spread cultural "enlightenment," now interprets that duty very freely. At one recent evening in the House of Teachers Cultural Center, the "educational" content offered was a disco fashion show; while slides of John Travolta flickered across the screen, Komsomol members modeled such decadent designs as green satin jumpsuits for men and revealing sequined sunsuits for women.

The scene is even less square in the city's disco cafes, which are open to all. At the "Little Snowstorm," the throngs besiege the bouncer-doorman with a frenzy that would do justice to New York's Studio 54. Inside, they pogo to punk rock and sip champagne concoctions (at $4.50 a drink); outside they brawl on the sidewalk.

Protests: Beyond street-fighting, the Soviet Government sees numerous signs of dissolution among the young. The newspaper Sovetskaya Rossiya attributes the soaring divorce rate (nearly half of all marriages) largely to the "moral and civil immaturity of young people." Drug abuse is low by Western standards, but teen-age drinking is a deep concern; one survey indicated that 12 per cent of 14-year-old youths drink regularly. "Drinking problems are occurring in younger and younger age groups," lamented a recent issue of one Soviet magazine. Drinking often inspires juvenile delinquency—"hooliganism," in Soviet parlance—and, by some Western estimates, 59 per cent of all burglaries, 49 per cent of rapes and 12 per cent of murders are committed by criminals under 20.

Source: Lynn Langway and William E. Schmidt, "A Youthquake in Russia." *Newsweek* 96 (July 7, 1980):46.

At all the schools Coleman studied, students valued superficial and external things, such as physical attractiveness, cars, and clothes, and slighted academic achievement. For boys, the key to acceptance into the school's elite was membership in the football team. For girls, school activities performed a similar function. The school's elite is a model for other students to emulate, and Coleman found members of the elite were particularly sensitive to group pressures. In trying to account for the change in high-school students over the years, Coleman suggests that affluence has fostered independence from parents and that the mass media have made children more sophisticated, so they are less passive and obedient at home and at school. Thus, teenagers turn to peers for guidance, they scoff at academic competition, and they pursue popularity through dating, parties, and sports.

Quite simply, Coleman argues that teenagers are influenced more by peers than by parents, that their values are largely hedonistic and superficial, and that all adolescents belong to this society because they have been herded together in high schools. The schools are radically segregated institutions, cut off from the world of adults. Forced to stay there, teenagers cope by asserting their independence and having fun.

Jeanette Covington (1982) takes this argument one step further—into deviance and delinquency. She begins by noting that adolescence is a transitional stage between childhood and adulthood, and it must have its own set of norms, values, and expectations, just as childhood and adulthood have. But in periods of rapid social change or upheaval, there is likely to be *anomie*, a condition in which people cannot agree on what the norms and values (for adolescence, for instance) should be. Parents typically want to retain the same norms they have been used to while the youth was a child. They are resistant to the new role and they want to slow down the change as much as possible, but in so doing they create conflict with their adolescent. The adolescent finds that the norms and values parents want to maintain do not give him or her a sense of worth or accomplishment. Thus, the adolescent begins to question parental norms and values. At the same time, the adolescent's peers are undergoing the same experiences, and they begin to assume a crucial role in socializing him or her. They have the power to make the adolescent feel worthwhile and important. They also have some suggestions about how the adolescent can adapt to the normlessness of adolescence, how the adolescent can feel more grown-up and worthwhile. They point out that certain behaviors are symbolic of adulthood and are clear signs that the person is no longer a child: these behaviors have to do with drugs, sexuality, and autonomy. Wanting to be accepted and feel worthwhile and more grown-up, many youngsters turn to these deviant and delinquent activities recommended by the adolescent subculture.

Finally, some commentators claim that many youngsters belong not just to a large adolescent subculture or society but to delinquent gangs, whose primary goal is to commit offenses against persons and property. Adolescents who are delinquent are said to accept the delinquent role because they learned it early on, while associating with somewhat older delinquents. Soon they look upon delinquency as a way of life and finally a career. Committed to delinquency as a way of life, they feel compelled to commit more and more offenses.

Research

Much has been said about youths moving out of their parents' orbit, not being influenced by parents any longer, even being in open conflict with parents. In trying to determine the extent of the "generation gap," or the existence of one, we may begin by asking if youths and parents argue very much. There is not a greal deal of research on teenager-parent arguments, but John C. Coleman (1977; 1980) has looked into the issue. Adolescents and parents rated themselves and each other on a variety of traits and agreed that parents were more hardworking, quiet, and tidy, while the youths were more lazy, noisy, and untidy. On other traits, parents saw little or no difference between themselves and their children, but *the teenagers saw parents more positively*—that is, more patient, honest, reliable, unselfish, and grateful—*than themselves.* Coleman suggests that when conflict occurs within a family, it typically stems from everyday matters, not debates over morality or ideology. "Family squabbles are most likely to involve matters such as homework, money, and hair styles rather than basic values" (Hill, 1980:41). Offer (1969) agrees, saying that when youths rebel, they do so over little things, not world-shaking issues; these findings have been duplicated by Rutter et al. (1976) and Fogelman (1976).

In general, research points out that adolescents and parents tend to get along reasonably well, perhaps better in the teen years than in the preteens. Offer's (1969) study of typical adolescent boys found that a great majority of them (1) said that their parents approved of their future plans, (2) felt close to one of their parents, (3) said that they were disciplined by parents both fairly and reasonably, and (4) indicated that the worst feature of their home life was nothing more than sharing a room with a sibling or having only one car in the family. Hill sums matters up:

> The psychoanalytic position that rebelliousness is normal during adolescence enjoys considerable support from those who work with troubled and troublesome young people. Studies of more representative samples of the population, however, do not support this position. Adolescence is not, in general, a period of overt rebelliousness and familial conflict in industrial societies [according to] representative samples of parents and their adolescent offspring (1980:38).

Thus there is little evidence of adolescent revolt except for some domestic bickering over dress, sleeping hours, household chores, and the like.

The second question concerns whether parents or peers influence an adolescent more. Bowerman and Kinch (1959) conducted a study to see what changes take place as children pass from fourth through tenth grades. They looked at similarity (whose ideas the child's resembled more) and identification (who understood them more and whom would they rather be like when they grow up). As they proceeded from fourth to tenth grade, children tended to move closer to their peers on both similarity and identification. But even in the tenth grade, only about one-fourth identified with peers. Of course, this research is quite old, so the results might be different if the study were conducted today.

A more recent study of high schoolers (Cohen, 1980) found that youths do grow away from their parents and spend less time at home as they get older. But in moving from the freshman to the senior years, high schoolers do not reduce the importance they attach to pleasing their parents; nor do they lapse into a slavish conformity to the peer group during this period. In fact, Cohen found that popularity and peer acceptance become *less* important as one passes through high school. Conformity with peers peaks in about ninth grade (Berndt, 1979).

In looking at the question of parental influence versus peer influence, Brittain (1963) noted that parents have more influence when the issues involve future plans (education or occupation), while peers have more influence on issues such as what is attractive in the way of dress and grooming and what customs are appropriate for adolescents. Kandel (1980) also states that the influence of parents and peers varies, depending on the issue. On most issues, however, Kandel and Lesser (1972) found the adolescent's mother to be very influential. These same two researchers also found that American teenagers, in contrast to Danish teens, turn to peers for hedonistic activities rather than for advice.

One such activity is drug use. A great many studies show that people who use drugs tend to have friends who use them too (for a list of these studies, see Kandel, 1980). But this statement requires two qualifications. First, some people who use drugs tend to believe, often mistakenly, that their peers also use drugs (Kandel, 1980; Brown, 1982). Second, if two peers both use drugs, it is not always true that one of them has pressured the other into becoming a user; perhaps both were users first and only became friends later. Kandel (1978; 1980) has looked into this question carefully and discovered that influence (becoming like another person occurs after meeting) and selection (individuals associate because they are like each other) of peers are equally important factors in the similarity of peers' behavior. This is true not only for drug use, but for delinquency, political orientation, and educational plans. Thus, traditional models of influence, by failing to take selection into account, overestimate the amount of peer influence by 100 percent.

The major emphasis in theories of adolescent subcultures (Coleman's, for example) is on boys. But researchers have indicated that girls may in fact be more susceptible to peer pressure. Why should this be true? Blyth et al. (1982) offer one reason: girls consider more people to be significant in their life. The researchers traced this difference to the tendency of females to be more verbal and more oriented to people, while boys have traditionally been more interested in objects and tasks. Brown (1982) also found females to be more subject to peer pressure—particularly pressure to be socially active, to dress attractively, and to maintain a relationship with a boyfriend. Boys are under more pressure (from other boys) to engage in sexual intercourse than girls are, but this kind of pressure affects girls' behavior more than boys'.

One of the more common ways to test the relative influence of parents and peers is to present adolescents with a hypothetical situation in which they have a choice of two actions, one that their parents favor and one their friends endorse. Larson (1972) used this technique for a variety of situations, such as joining a club, going to a party, or pursuing a noncollege-bound track at school. He did *not* find that adolescents usually ignore their parents and follow their peers' wishes. He did find that adolescents' choices depended on the situation: most youths chose to enter or not to enter a given situation regardless of how parents or peers felt about it. These "situation compliant" individuals made up three-fourths of all the respondents. Most of the other one-fourth complied with parents more than peers by a ratio of three to one. Summing up, we can say that peer groups do not often dominate individual adolescents, and parents still have an impact on many of the decisions their children make.

The third question that has been raised is whether there is an adolescent subculture—a set of beliefs, values, and standards to which a great majority of adolescents adhere in opposition to adult standards. James Coleman (1961) popularized this idea. But it has not been substantiated by careful studies. For example, Jennings and Niemi (1975) looked at high-school seniors and their parents in 1968 and again seven years later. Not particularly far apart in political beliefs in 1968, they moved even closer together by 1975. And an especially sophisticated study of this issue by Bengston (1975) uncovered comparable results. He asked people from three generations of the same families to rank various values in order of importance to their lives: humanism (for example, devotion to bettering mankind), materialism (enough financial comfort to do what one enjoys), collectivism (religious participation, loyalty to family and loved ones), and individualism (an exciting life, excelling at something one enjoys). Bengston found that all three generations are about the same on the humanism/materialism dimension. On the collectivism/individualism dimension, however, the youngest generation was most individualistic. There were large differences within each age group, however, and the most interesting finding is that parents' values are closer to children's values than to grandparents' values. The bigger generation gap is thus between the two older generations!

The last question concerns delinquent gangs and groups. To begin with, do delinquents usually act alone or with others? If delinquency is principally the work of isolated individuals, then perhaps it ought to be the province of psychologists. If, on the other hand, most delinquent activities are carried out by groups, then sociology might have more appropriate explanations to offer. The answer to this question also has obvious implications for the kind of treatment that would be most appropriate for juvenile offenders—group therapy or individual therapy.

In 1967, Lerman published a study of boys aged 10–19 living in New York City slums. He determined that most of the boys who engaged in delinquency did not belong to a named group or gang. Less than 10 percent did; and for younger boys, those aged 10–13, the figure was especially low. Most of the boys involved in delinquency said that they usually spent their time alone or with just one or two others. Lerman (1967a) thus sees delinquency as an activity done in pairs or trios—not gangs.

James F. Short, Jr. (1967) has challenged Lerman's argument by noting that many gang members may pair off and commit offenses with each other but still remain part of the larger gang. And when the gang travels outside its territory or when it faces a hostile confrontation with some other gang, many members band together rather than splintering off into separate pairs or trios. Lerman's response is that (1) if gang members come together so rarely in one large group, then it is highly debatable that they are truly members of the gang and (2) no matter how loosely one defines membership, most slum-area delinquents are not part of a gang (Lerman, 1967b).

Other researchers have looked into the group nature of delinquency. Studies earlier in the century (for example, Shaw and McKay, 1931; Healy and Bronner, 1936) overestimated the amount of delinquency that could be attributed to groups. These studies relied on official data, and officials were more likely to arrest and refer youths to court if they congregated in packs. To counter this bias, Hindelang (1976) turned to self-report data to estimate group-delinquency rates. He found that some offenses were more likely than others to be committed when with associates; using marijuana and getting drunk, for instance, are primarily social activities. But a few are more often done alone (such as carrying a weapon). Research by Erickson and Jensen (1977) has produced similar findings: delinquency is usually group behavior. But these studies do not define "group" or say how many youths are typically involved in these collective activities. If Lerman is right, the typical situation involves a boy with only one or two companions; thus we would agree with Korn and McCorkle (1959) when they declare that most delinquency is companionate behavior—not group behavior.

PEERS AND MALE DELINQUENCY

Concern about peers and male delinquency has historically centered around gangs. The term "gang" has had several meanings over the years. At one time, it referred to a group of adult desperadoes bent on robbery and capable of cruelty and violence (Miller, 1981). The James gang, which wrecked and robbed trains in the late nineteenth-century West, contributed to early perceptions of what gangs were. In the early part of the twentieth century, however, sentimental songs softened and romanticized the term (Miller, 1981); one popular lyric lamented that "those wedding bells are breaking up that old gang of mine." "Gang" thus came to mean a group of close associates, with no deviant or criminal connotations. (The term continues to be used this way sometimes.) Then, in the 1950s, the definition changed again, referring this time to large groups of urban boys who fought each other in violent battles or "rumbles" like the Sharks and the Jets in the famous musical and movie *West Side Story*.

The study of delinquent gangs is still hampered by definitional problems. When Walter Miller asked police juvenile officers, social workers, and other presumed experts to define gangs, they agreed on the following traits: organization, leadership, turf, cohesiveness, and purpose. But do gangs really exhibit these characteristics?

1. *Organization:* Occasionally, a gang is organized. Perhaps the best example is the Vice Lords, a Chicago gang that took on the features of an organization because of jealousy over the publicity being accorded a rival gang, the Blackstone Rangers.

> The most important element in the new organizational scheme . . . was the creation of an administrative body called the "board" to deal with matters affecting the entire Vice Lord Nation. Further, regular weekly meetings were instituted with representatives from all the subgroups present. Finally, membership cards were printed with the Vice Lords' insignia—a top hat, cane, and white gloves. Every Lord in the Nation was required to pay an initial membership fee of 1 dollar, have his nickname written on the club's rolls, and carry his card with him at all times (Keiser, 1969:8).

The Vice Lords, however, appear to be very atypical! Short (1974) suggests that most gangs fall somewhere in the middle between crowds and mobs on the one hand and ordinary organizations on the other. Yablonsky (1959) goes much farther and says the gang is not even a group; it is a "near-group." It fits the needs of its members whose social abilities are so rudimentary that they cannot meet the minimal demands of a more organized or stable group.

2. *Leadership:* Nearly all commentators claim that gangs have clearly established leaders. In the militaristic or Mafia-style model, the top authority position

> is analogous to that of the highest ranking officer in a military unit; below him are lieutenants, sublieutenants, and so on. Decisions originating in higher echelons are transmitted through the ranks by chain-of-command system (Miller, 1981:297).

A second type of ideal leader is charismatic—that is, ruling by force of his unique personality. This leader is usually older, stronger, and revered by the gang's members. Miller says commentators believe that these ideal types are common, but in his experience, gang leaders are much more flexible and democratic. Krisberg says the only distinctive feature of gang leaders is their superior verbal ability. In the black gangs he studied, this verbal facility, or "gift of gab," enabled leaders to capture the attention of other members (1975:74). But older, more influential gang members said the leaders actually did not do anything.

3. *Turf:* Turf gangs identify with a particular territory or neighborhood.

> Classic youth gangs in traditional slum areas of older cities such as New York, Chicago, Philadelphia, and San Antonio identified with a particular block, neighborhood, district, or barrio. Boundaries were well defined and widely recognized (Miller, 1981:298).

Crossing turf boundaries and entering another gang's territory were dangerous risks at one time. But times have changed. Automobiles have increased the mobility of teenagers, and slum districts have been sliced up by highways and urban renewal, blurring the old dividing lines. And Simon et al. (1976) say that changes in politics and communications at the national and global levels have made the old communities fragile and ephemeral. Some well-defined turfs remain, of course, as in the barrios of East Los Angeles (Moore, 1978). And some gang members never leave their part of the city (Krisberg, 1975).

In some cases, *turf* refers less to territorial rights than to a particular line of business that one gang exploits and tells other gangs to leave alone. Among youth gangs, the most

> dramatic current manifestation of this practice is found in the activities of Chinese extortion gangs operating in San Francisco, Los Angeles, Chicago, New York, and other cities. These gangs have extorted hundreds of thousands of dollars from Chinese restaurant owners and other businessmen (Miller, 1981:299).

4. *Cohesiveness:* Are gangs very close, tight-knit organizations with loyal members bound to one another by mutual friendship and common interests? Early writers thought so. Thrasher (1927), for instance, depicted gangs filled with happy-go-lucky youngsters that performed positive functions, such as providing status for members. Modern writers are sometimes equally romantic. Brown (1978), for instance, claims that gangs provide very close relationships with people who will help in time of crisis. He quotes a gang member to support his argument:

> "Me and my homies are tight, we're blood. I know I can count on them, and they know they can count on me. If I need some clothes one of my homies will help me get them. After all, if I'm looking cheap it makes them look bad . . . and if it comes to a fight, I know my homies will be there. They stone bad and they don't let nobody get over on any of us" (Brown, 1978:41).

But most careful researchers disagree. Klein (1971) says that the gang members he observed were "dissatisfied, deprived, and making the best of an essentially unhappy situation" (1971:91). Short and Strodtbeck (1965) say that gang members tend to fail at school, on the job, and elsewhere; these failures, along with other social disabilities, make gang members anxious and insecure about their status, and such insecurities are heightened by constant challenges and insults by other gang members. Klein adds that there are good reasons why gangs are not cohesive: (1) the gang has few if any group goals; (2) the membership is constantly in a state of flux, turning over rapidly; and (3) group norms are practically nonexistent.

5. *Purpose:* Delinquent gangs are typically thought to exist for the purpose of committing offenses. Purpose is a state of mind difficult for gang researchers to measure; it is easier to study behavior—the extent to which gangs engage in offenses. Researchers have found that gang members spend most of their time on other pursuits—notably, just whiling away their time:

> Offhand, I can think of few categories of people who are less exciting to observe than gang members simply because, by and large, they just stand around and do nothing! Certainly, their involvement in delinquent episodes is so infrequent

> that one must wait many months before sufficient offenses have taken place to provide grist for the statistician's mill (Klein, 1971:123).

> Furthermore, gang delinquency constitutes only a small slice of the total delinquency pie. Gang members accounted for only about 6 percent of juvenile arrests in Philadelphia in 1968 (Pennsylvania Crime Commission, 1969). Miller (1975) notes that juvenile gang members made up 10 percent of arrests of juveniles in New York, Chicago, and Los Angeles in 1973. If this figure is approximately correct, it is particularly significant because Miller claims that the great majority of gang members reside in these three cities.

If the five characteristics listed above have been convincingly shown to be inaccurate or atypical of gangs and their members, then what traits *are* generally characteristic of them? Several have been suggested. First, many gangs are urban, lower-class, male groupings, with quite a few of them consisting of minorities, such as blacks, Hispanics, and Asians. Among the newest gangs are the Vietnamese. *Newsweek* reported that robbery, bombing, extortion and murder are part of an "upsurge in gang violence within the close-knit Vietnamese communities of central and southern California" (Morganthau et al., 1982:22). Second, gang members tend to have the normal adolescent problems, but in more severe form. The gang member "tends to be a *caricature* of the adolescent—more shy, more dependent on his peers, more ambivalent about appropriate role behaviors" (Klein, 1971:83). Not having very high IQs or very good social skills, gang members must learn to cope in other ways. Their third characteristic, therefore, is coping through aggression. There is "an underlying tone of aggression which characterizes so much of the interaction within the gang. . . . The gang boy is likely to come to the gang suspicious of the motives and the dependability of human relationships generally" (Short and Strodtbeck, 1965:233).

Finally, we should consider the question of what conditions give rise to gangs. The literature has long emphasized inner cities as the environment where gangs flourish, but Johnstone found gangs in several suburbs of Chicago. He studied those areas with the most gang activity and compared them to communities with less activity; he found gangs particularly prevalent in areas characterized by poverty, crowding (one or more persons per room), low occupational prestige, and high proportions of blacks (Johnstone, 1981). Johnstone speculates that poverty may not be the crucial variable—at least, not by itself. He argues that poverty may give rise to overcrowding in the home, which in turn makes the youngsters want to get out of the house. When large numbers of them congregate, the possibility that a delinquent gang will form increases. Why should areas with more blacks have more gangs? One possibility is that blacks have higher birth rates and shorter life expectancies. This means that blacks are on the average a bit younger than whites and thus more likely to be of the gang-member age.

PEERS AND FEMALE DELINQUENCY

When Thrasher (1927) conducted his study of more than 1,000 gangs, he claimed that only six were female. But female gangs have become much more common in recent decades, as Klein points out:

> While it is still true that female gangs as independent, self-originating, and self-perpetuating units are highly unusual, female "auxiliaries" to boys' groups seem quite common in all major cities. . . . Evidence from an independent study of ours in Los Angeles suggested that these girls' groups usually consist at first of the sisters and girl friends of male gang members, but that they soon take on a more diverse membership as the girls recruit new members among their own friends. The female gang is smaller (from 5 to 25 members), less seriously delinquent, and less stable than its male counterpart. It forms in response to the male structure and dissolves as the boys' group loses cohesion (Klein, 1971:77).

Murphy's (1978) study of a female gang in East Los Angeles found that most members were school dropouts who were affiliated with a male gang and who usually played the traditional roles of girlfriends or weapons carriers. Sometimes, however, they were swaggering and aggressive, as the following comment by a female gang member shows:

> "For me the great days were in junior high school, when I was fourteen or fifteen. I used to sniff paint, take downers, and I was always ditching school. I was a fighter, running the streets, looking for trouble. A group of us would walk down the sidewalk and we wouldn't move for anybody. We were too bad, we were from Primera Flats. The girls hung around in fours and fives for protection. You learn young that you don't be on the streets by yourself, you just don't" (Murphy, 1978:56–58).

Konopka's Theory

Most theories of female delinquency are not very gang-conscious. In fact, they usually ignore gangs and treat female delinquency as a more individual or personal problem. According to Konopka (1966), girls' delinquency is fundamentally different from boys', both in its nature and its causes.

> Almost invariably [the girl delinquent's] problems are deeply personalized. Whatever her offenses—whether shoplifting, truancy, or running away from home—it is usually accompanied by some disturbance or unfavorable behavior in the sexual area . . . (1966:4).

Konopka says girls desperately need friendship with other adolescents, especially boys. But some girls fail to achieve these friendships and suffer feelings of loneliness. Their self-esteem crumbles, so they try to lose themselves in a crowd or search frantically for romantic involvement, leading them to have sexual relations. According to Konopka, girls' delinquency is rarer than boys' and much more specialized: girls concentrate on sex offenses. The FBI's Uniform Crime Reports are in agreement on both of these claims: girls are more often arrested than boys for two offenses, prostitution and running away (and Cohen [1955] sees running away as a police euphemism for sex delinquency). But these findings may simply reflect the fact that parents, school officials, and other adults are more intolerant of sexual activity by female adolescents than by male adolescents. "Overt sexual activity in a girl has been considered deviant, whereas in a boy it has often been considered an expression of his masculinity" (Berlage, 1979:36).

Several self-report studies allow us to judge how distinctive girls' delinquency is. Hindelang (1971) found boys were more likely to engage in delinquency than girls were, and this was true of every offense studied. But the pattern was similar: what boys committed most, girls also committed most, and what boys were unlikely to do, girls rarely did. Girls did not dominate in sexual offenses; on the contrary, this was the offense where boys exceeded the girls by the largest margin. Sorensen (1973), whose work we discussed in Chapter 3, produced similar findings. He found that among Adventurers (nonvirgins who have no interest in a continuing relationship and who seek many different sexual partners), males outnumber females by about four to one.

Other studies agree that boys and girls follow the same pattern of offenses but girls commit fewer of each offense. Gold (1970:118), for instance, says: says:

> A more accurate picture of girls' delinquency showed it to be quite similar to boys', only smaller. The girls were less delinquent than the boys, trailing them significantly on every offense except the fairly infrequent ones of running away from home and hitting their parents. Except for those two offenses, however, the mixture of girls' offenses was not very different from that of boys.

Studies by Jensen and Eve (1976), Datesman and Scarpitti (1980), Weis (1976), Canter (1982), McDonough et al. (1981), Simons et al. (1980) all come up with the same results: females are less delinquent but commit much the same kinds of offenses as males do. They do not specialize in sexual or some other type of offenses. There is one exception to this similarity, however, which involves serious, aggressive, or violent offenses, as Table 5–1 indicates. Boys are much more likely to engage in such offenses as murder, robbery, and burglary than girls are; but on minor matters, boys and girls are fairly close (liquor laws, larceny-theft, running away). Similar kinds of results emerge

TABLE 5–1
Ratio of Males to Females Arrested for Selected Offenses in 1982 (persons under 18)

Offense	Ratio
Burglary	13.6:1
Robbery	13.6:1
Vandalism	10.9:1
Murder	10.7:1
Motor-vehicle theft	7.8:1
Arson	7.5:1
Aggravated assault	5.2:1
Drug-abuse violations	5.0:1
Disorderly conduct	4.4:1
Other assaults	3.6:1
Curfew and loitering	3.5:1
Liquor laws	3.2:1
Larceny-theft	2.8:1
Runaway	.7:1

Source: Webster, 1983.

from self-report research (Smith and Visher, 1980; McDonough et al., 1981; Weis, 1976; Canter, 1982).

Adler's Theory

We have established that there is more male delinquency than female delinquency. But are girls catching up to boys, and if so, is the women's movement responsible? Freda Adler (1975) is the most outspoken advocate of the liberation-causes-crime hypothesis. She says that women are becoming more active in serious, aggressive crimes and that because of the spread of liberated attitudes, women are becoming more masculine in general. She finds "a certain level of imitative male machismo competitiveness developing among criminal adolescent girls" (1975:98). And she claims that females are engaging in more armed robberies, muggings, murders, and other aggressive and violent crimes.

Giordano and Cernkovich (1979) set out to test Adler's theory; they compared incarcerated girls with high-school girls to see if offenders were more liberated in their attitudes. The authors looked at several dimensions of liberation:

1. Employment (desirability of women working; equal pay for equal work).
2. Family (the importance of getting married and having children).

3. Interpersonal relationships with males.
4. Etiquette (for example, should a boy help a girl put on her coat?).
5. Personality traits (do males and females have different characteristics?).
6. Appropriate behavior (what girls ought to be allowed to do).

Only on the sixth item were liberated attitudes and delinquency found to correlate. On the other five items, the more liberated girls were equally or less delinquent than more traditional girls. Also, Miller's (1973) study of female gang members notes that these girls are totally oblivious to the feminist movement. Finally, Berlage (1979:322) comments:

> No support was found for Adler's assumption that there has been a "masculinization" of female criminal behavior. The data support Weis' view that the "new female criminal" (a more versatile and serious offender who is equally adept at committing property crimes and acts of violence) is an invention.

Simon's Theory

But Adler is not the only criminologist to propose that liberation can induce females to commit crimes. Rita Simon (1975) also adopts this view, but she believes that liberation and moving outside the home and into the world are conducive to women committing property crimes rather than violent ones. She sees violence as a result of frustration, which spending all day at home increases. As women move out into the work world, however, they will engage in more property crimes, because they will have more opportunities to commit theft and fraud. Women will also commit more crimes because of liberated attitudes or "expanded consciousness" (Simon, 1975:2). Of course, we have already seen from the Giordano and Cernkovich (1979) study that this thesis lacks empirical support. James and Thornton, however, did discover a relationship between feminist attitudes and delinquency. Unfortunately for Adler and Simon, the correlation they report is neither strong nor in the predicted direction.

> We do not . . . report that girls who are approving of feminism in terms of fighting for equal rights and advocating change in traditional gender roles are more likely to engage in delinquency than are girls who support more traditional positions. The opposite appears true: favorable attitudes toward feminism inhibit involvement in property and aggressive crimes (1980:242).

Are Girls Catching Up?

On the question of whether girls' delinquency has been catching up to boys' in the past few years, researchers who have scrutinized the issue seem to say no (Steffensmeier and Steffensmeier, 1980; Canter, 1982). There are several ways to calculate "catching up." We can use the absolute number of offenses by which boys outnumber girls on arrests and see if the gap gets smaller as the years go by. Or we can take the percentage (relative number) of offenses boys account for and subtract from it the percentage of offenses girls account for and see if the difference gets smaller. If we do this for each type of offense in the Uniform Crime Reports for the years 1973 to 1982, we find that the only offense for which both the absolute gap and the relative gap decrease is motor-vehicle theft. And the reason for this decrease is that, for reasons unknown to us, boys' arrests declined considerably for this crime during the ten-year period; girls' arrests did not skyrocket. For the more serious offenses, neither the absolute gap nor the relative gap gets much smaller. There is no clear sign that female adolescents have been catching up to their male counterparts in delinquency in recent years.

SUMMARY

G. Stanley Hall coined the term "adolescence" in 1904, and psychologists have dominated the field since then, branding adolescence as turbulent, emotional, and filled with storm and stress. In the second half of the twentieth century, the emphasis has shifted away from adolescence per se and toward the peer group. Riesman argued that peer groups have become more influential than parents and that the child has become an unthinking conformist, surrendering his or her independent judgment. Bronfenbrenner said parents have withdrawn, leaving a social vacuum that children have filled by turning to the peer group, whose influence is mostly negative.

Coleman said that affluence has fostered independence from parents and the mass media have made children more sophisticated, so they are less passive and obedient at home and in school. They turn to peers, from whom they learn hedonistic and superficial values. Some commentators claim that this adolescent subculture may give rise to delinquent gangs, whose sole purpose is to engage in deviant behavior.

Researchers, however, have found that the gap between parents and teenagers is not so large as these theorists claim. Offer, for instance, found that most boys felt close to their parents, thought parental discipline was fair and reasonable, and agreed with parents on future educational plans. On the question of whether parents or peers are more influential, researchers found peers more influential on matters such as drugs, drinking, and dress, while parents have more impact on future plans. Even where drugs and drinking are concerned, though, the similarity between an adolescent and his or her peers is due as much to selection of friends as to influence of friends.

Research on the relationship between peers and male delinquency centers around gangs. There is a mythology about gangs that depicts them as organized, cohesive, and with strong leadership and an orientation to protecting their turf. Researchers have found that, by and large, these characteristics do not accurately describe what most gangs are or do. Some researchers have found that gangs do tend to appeal to minorities and lower-class youths in large cities, that gang members tend to have important problems as adolescents, and that they learn to cope by being aggressive, even against other members in the gang.

Female delinquent gangs are not as numerous as male gangs, but they are nevertheless numerous. They tend to have a rather small number of members per gang and to be affiliated with a boys' gang. They may play traditional female roles, helping the boys, or they may be more independent. Little research exists on them, however.

More interest has been devoted to female delinquency in general. Konopka argued that girls' delinquency is both rare and specialized in sexual offenses. Her theory agrees with the Uniform Crime Reports, but not with self-report research; which finds that girls are not specialists in sex offenses. Indeed, like boys, they do not appear to specialize in anything.

Adler advances the thesis that women are being masculinized and that liberation causes women to engage in more crime, especially aggressive and violent crime. But there seems to be little evidence to support either this theory or Simon's belief that expanded employment opportunities for women will cause them to commit more property crimes. Finally, there are several ways to measure whether girls are catching up to boys in the area of delinquency, and not all of them yield precisely the same conclusions. But, in general, analyses of official data in recent years suggest that girls are not catching up.

DISCUSSION QUESTIONS

1. What issues do youth define as most important to them? How do these differ from the concerns that adults view as major youth problems?
2. What explanations have been advanced to account for adolescent rebellion?
3. To what extent is adolescent behavior influenced by parental wishes and peer preferences? Use studies mentioned in the chapter to support your answer.
4. What does Bengston's study of generational differences in values tell us about the "generation gap"?
5. What is the link between friends' delinquency and one's own delinquency?

6. What are the five gang traits identified by Miller?
7. To what extent does gang membership affect participation in delinquent activities?
8. What factors have given rise to peer groups? Discuss your answer.
9. How and to what extent does female delinquency differ from male delinquency?
10. Why have some researchers suggested that the "liberation" of women has led to an increase in female involvement in crime and delinquency? Are these claims supported by most studies? Why or why not?

REFERENCES

ADELSON, JOSEPH, AND MARGERY J. DOEHRMAN
1980 The psychodynamic approach to adolescence. Pp. 99–116 in Joseph Adelson (ed.), *Handbook of Adolescent Psychology.* New York: Wiley.

ADLER, FREDA
1975 *Sisters in Crime.* New York: McGraw-Hill.

BENGSTON, VERN L.
1975 Generation and family effects in value socialization. *American Sociological Review* 40 (June):358–371.

BERLAGE, GAI INGHAM
1979 The study of the relationship between girls' social class, values, self-reported and official delinquency in one urban community. Doctoral dissertation, New York University.

BERNDT, THOMAS J.
1979 Developmental changes in conformity to peers and parents. *Developmental Psychology* 15 (November):608–616.

BLYTH, DALE A., ET AL.
1982 Early adolescents' significant others. *Journal of Youth and Adolescence* 11 (December):425–450.

BOWERMAN, CHARLES E., AND JOHN W. KINCH
1959 Changes in family and peer orientation of children between fourth and tenth grades. *Social Forces* 37 (February):206–211.

BRITTAIN, CLAY V.
1963 Adolescent choices and parent-peer cross-pressures. *American Sociological Review* 28 (June):385–391.

BRONFENBRENNER, URIE
1970 *Two Worlds of Childhood: U.S. and U.S.S.R.* New York: Basic.

BROWN, B. BRADFORD
1982 The extent and effects of peer pressure among high school students. *Journal of Youth and Adolescence* 11 (April):121–133.

BROWN, WALN K.
1978 Black gangs as family extensions. *International Journal of Offender Therapy and Comparative Criminology* 22 (April):39–45.

CANTER, RACHELLE J.
1982 Sex differences in self-reported delinquency. *Criminology* 20 (November):373–393.

COHEN, ALBERT K.
1955 *Delinquent Boys.* New York: Free Press.

COHEN, JERE
1980 Adolescent independence and adolescent change. *Youth and Society* 12 (September):107–124.

COLEMAN, JAMES S.
1961 *The Adolescent Society.* New York: Free Press.

COLEMAN, JOHN C.
1980 Friendship and the peer group in adolescence. Pp. 408–431 in Joseph Adelson (ed.), *Handbook of Adolescent Psychology.* New York: Wiley.

COLEMAN, JOHN C., ET AL.
1977 Adolescents and their parents: A study of attitudes. *Journal of Genetic Psychology* 130 (June):239–245.

COVINGTON, JEANETTE
1982 Adolescent deviation and age. *Journal of Youth and Adolescence* 11 (August):329–344.

DATESMAN, SUSAN K., AND FRANK R. SCARPITTI
1980 *Women, Crime, and Justice.* New York: Oxford University Press.

ELDER, GLEN H., JR.
1980 Adolescence in historical perspective. Pp. 3–46 in Joseph Adelson (ed.), *Handbook of Adolescent Psychology.* New York: Wiley.

EMPEY, LAMAR T.
1982 *American Delinquency.* Homewood, Ill.: Dorsey.

ERICKSON, MAYNARD L., AND GARY F. JENSEN
1977 Delinquency is still group behavior! *Journal of Criminal Law and Criminology* 68 (June):262–273.

FOGELMAN, K. R.
1976 *Britain's Sixteen-Year-Olds.* London: National Children's Bureau.

GINOTT, HAIM G.
1969 *Between Parent and Teenager.* New York: Avon.

GIORDANO, PEGGY C., AND STEPHEN A. CERNKOVICH
1979 On complicating the relationship between liberation and delinquency. *Social Problems* 26 (April):467–481.

GOLD, MARTIN
1970 *Delinquent Behavior in an American City.* Belmont, Calif.: Brooks/Cole.

HEALY, WILLIAM, AND AUGUSTA J. BRONNER
1936 *New Light on Delinquency and Its Treatment.* New Haven, Conn.: Yale University Press.

HILL, JOHN P.
1980 The family. Pp. 32–55 in Mauritz Johnson (ed.), *Toward Adolescence.* Chicago: University of Chicago Press.

HINDELANG, MICHAEL J.
1976 With a little help from their friends: Group participation in reported delinquent behavior. *British Journal of Criminology* 16 (April):109–125.
1971 Age, sex, and the versatility of delinquent involvement. *Social Problems* 18 (Spring):527–535.

HOLLINGSHEAD, AUGUST B.
1949 *Elmtown's Youth.* New York: Wiley.

JAMES, JENNIFER, AND WILLIAM THORNTON
1980 Women's liberation and the female delinquent. *Journal of Research in Crime and Delinquency* 17 (July):230–244.

JENNINGS, M. KENT, AND RICHARD G. NIEMI
1975 Continuity and change in political orientations. *American Political Science Review* 69 (December):1316–1335.
JENSEN, GARY F., AND RAYMOND EVE
1976 Sex differences in delinquency. *Criminology* 12 (February):427–448.
JOHNSTONE, JOHN W. C.
1981 Youth gangs and black suburbs. *Pacific Sociological Review* 24 (July):355–375.
JONES, LANDON Y.
1980 *Great Expectations.* New York: Coward, McCann & Geoghegan.
KANDEL, DENISE B.
1980 Drug and drinking behavior among youth. Pp. 235–285 in Alex Inkeles et al. (eds.), *Annual Review of Sociology.* Palo Alto, Calif.: Annual Reviews, Inc.
1978 Homophily, selection, and socialization in adolescent friendships. *American Journal of Sociology* 84 (September):427–436.
KANDEL, DENISE B., AND GERALD R. LESSER
1972 *Youth in Two Worlds.* San Francisco: Jossey-Bass.
KEISER, R. LINCOLN
1969 *The Vice Lords.* New York: Holt, Rinehart & Winston.
KLEIN, MALCOLM W.
1971 *Street Gangs and Street Workers.* Englewood Cliffs, N.J.: Prentice-Hall.
KONOPKA, GISELA
1966 *The Adolescent Girl in Conflict.* Englewood Cliffs, N.J.: Prentice-Hall.
KORN, RICHARD R., AND LLOYD W. McCORKLE
1959 *Criminology and Penology.* New York: Henry Holt.
KRISBERG, BARRY
1975 *The Gang and the Community.* San Francisco: R & E Research Associates.
LARSON, LYLE E.
1972 The influence of parents and peers during adolescence. *Journal of Marriage and Family* 34 (February):67–74.
LERMAN, PAUL
1967a Gangs, networks, and subcultural delinquency. *American Journal of Sociology* 73 (July):63–71.
1967b Reply. *American Journal of Sociology* 73 (November):515–517.
McDONOUGH, JOSEFINA FIGUEIRA, ET AL.
1981 Normal deviance: Gender similarities in adolescent subcultures. Pp. 17–45 in Margueritte Q. Warren (ed.), *Comparing Female and Male Offenders.* Beverly Hills, Calif.: Sage.
MEAD, MARGARET
1928 *Coming of Age in Samoa.* Ann Arbor, Mich.: Morrow.
MILLER, WALTER B.
1981 American youth gangs. Pp. 291–320 in Abraham S. Blumberg (ed.), *Current Perspectives on Criminal Behavior.* New York: Knopf.
1975 *Violence by Youth Gangs and Youth Groups.* Washington: U.S. Government Printing Office.
1973 The Molls. *Society* 11 (November/December):32–35.
MOORE, JOAN W.
1978 *Homeboys.* Philadelphia: Temple University Press.
MORGANTHAU, TOM, ET AL.
1982 Vietnamese gangs in California. *Newsweek* 100 (August 2):22.

MURPHY, SUZANNE
1978 A year with the gangs of East Los Angeles. *Ms.* 7 (July):56–64.
OFFER, DANIEL
1969 *The Psychological World of the Teenager.* New York: Basic.
PENNSYLVANIA CRIME COMMISSION
1969 *Gang Violence in Philadelphia.* Harrisburg: Pennsylvania Department of Justice.
RIESMAN, DAVID
1950 *The Lonely Crowd.* New Haven, Conn.: Yale University Press.
RUTTER, MICHAEL, ET AL.
1976 Adolescent turmoil. *Journal of Child Psychology and Psychiatry* 17 (January):35–36.
SHAW, CLIFFORD R., AND HENRY D. McKAY
1931 *Social Factors in Juvenile Delinquency.* Washington: U.S. Government Printing Office.
SHORT, JAMES F., JR.
1974 Collective behavior, crime, and delinquency. Pp. 403–449 in Daniel Glaser (ed.), *Handbook of Criminology.* Chicago: Rand McNally.
1967 Comment on Lerman's "Gangs, networks, and subcultural delinquency." *American Journal of Sociology* 73 (November):513–515.
SHORT, JAMES F., JR., AND FRED L. STRODTBECK
1965 *Group Process and Gang Delinquency.* Chicago: University of Chicago Press.
SIMON, RITA JAMES
1975 *Women and Crime.* Lexington, Mass.: Lexington.
SIMON, WILLIAM, ET AL.
1976 Continuities in delinquency research. Pp. 50–63 in James F. Short, Jr. (ed.), *Delinquency, Crime, and Society.* Chicago: University of Chicago Press.
SIMONS, RONALD L., ET AL.
1980 Contemporary theories of deviance and female delinquency. *Journal of Research in Crime and Delinquency* 17 (January):42–53.
SMITH, DOUGLAS A., AND CHRISTY A. VISHER
1980 Sex and involvement in deviance/crime. *American Sociological Review* 45 (August):691–701.
SORENSEN, ROBERT C.
1973 *Adolescent Sexuality in Contemporary America.* New York: World.
STEFFENSMEIER, DARRELL, AND RENEE HOFFMAN STEFFENSMEIER
1980 Trends in female delinquency. *Criminology* 18 (May):62–85.
THRASHER, FREDERIC M.
1927 *The Gang.* Chicago: University of Chicago Press.
WEBSTER, WILLIAM H.
1983 *Crime in the United States.* Washington: U.S. Government Printing Office.
WEIS, JOSEPH
1976 Liberation and crime. *Crime and Social Justice* 6 (Fall/Winter):17–27.
WILSON, JAMES Q.
1975 *Thinking about Crime.* New York: Basic.
YABLONSKY, LEWIS
1959 The delinquent gang as a near-group. *Social Problems* 7 (Fall):108–117.

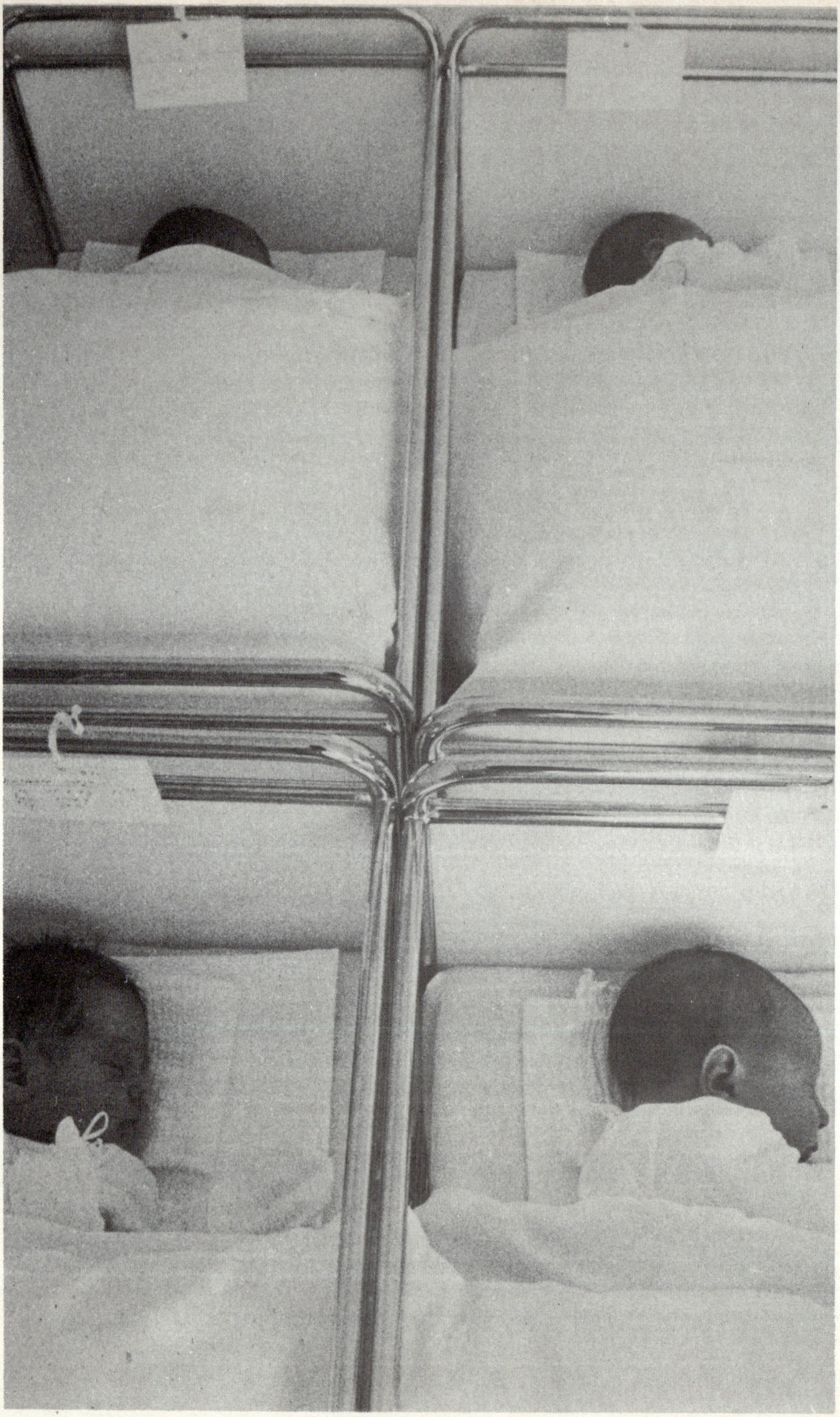

6 Biological and Psychological Theories

Why some youths misbehave while others do not is an issue that has been addressed by biological, psychological, and sociological theories. At the simplest level, biological theories seek the causes of delinquency in inherited traits; psychological theories assess personality structures; and sociological theories examine individuals only as part of larger social groups, categories, and social forces. We will devote this chapter to the biological and psychological perspectives and the next two chapters to sociological theories. Before examining these theories in detail, however, we will first look at the nature of theories in general.

WHAT THEORIES ARE

Theories are explanations. In their most rudimentary forms, theories are answers to the question, "Why?" As such, they may be very sophisticated and complex, or they may be quite simple. In general, simplicity is a virtue in a theory, because one of the main purposes of a theory is to take a huge mass of information (that we call "reality") and reduce it to a few simple laws, as Newton and Einstein did in physics.

Another desirable feature of a theory is that it be testable—that is, subject to testing that can either verify or refute it. Some theories are not testable, because their main concepts are either unclear or unmeasurable. For example, we will encounter concepts such as "reaction formation" and "differential association" that cannot realistically be detected, measured, or counted since we cannot constantly monitor the people being studied for several years. Other concepts are problematic because they have no clear, agreed-upon meaning; psychiatric diagnoses (for example, "schizophrenic" or "pathological") are particularly subject to this flaw.

If the theory is simple and testable, then we look for a third desirable feature: is the theory valid empirically? That is, do the research findings support the theory and its predictions? Of course, some theories give rise to many predictions, and the research tests could be carried out in many different settings and with many different samples and research procedures or methods. Which setting, sample, and method are chosen may depend on whether the researcher likes or dislikes the theory being tested. And people who test their own theories are notoriously prone to publishing only the most favorable results. Occasionally, researchers even cheat.

Finally, after determining the theory's validity, we may ask if the theory is logically coherent and consistent. What good would a theory be if it did not make sense and "hang together" as a set of ideas? Consider Peter Blau's theory about exchange and power (1964):

When A supplies B with particularly valued services, A can insist that B comply with A's demands. But A cannot demand so much if

1. B can supply other resources in return,
2. B can get the services from other sources,
3. B can use physical force or coercion, or
4. B can do without the services.

Whatever its other merits or flaws, this theory is consistent and unified. The various elements fit together and do not contradict one another.

We have listed what scholars like and dislike about theories. Now we should mention how ordinary citizens feel about them. First, one often gets the impression that the general public seems to think that theories are useless, impractical, speculative creations based upon nothing more substantial than guesswork. This kind of thinking reflects the American penchant for solving problems, "fixing what needs to be fixed," and not wasting time thinking about the causes. James Q. Wilson thus is quintessentially American when he argues that causal theories are meaningless when it comes to setting policies. He believes policies should be based on the intuitive feelings of the public:

> It is the duty of the statesman to try to take the confident instincts and immediate knowledge of the public and convert them . . . into reasonable policy proposals (Wilson, 1975:xvii).

The trouble with "immediate knowledge" is that it tends to reflect either stereotypes or long-discredited theories.

The second criticism leveled at theories by the public (especially students) is that there are so many theories; after reading them all, one ends up more confused than ever. It is indeed true that there are many explanations of delinquency. And it is certainly easy to become confused about which theorist made what claims. Furthermore, it is probably not desirable to have such a large number of theories competing for academic acceptance and respectability. Frankly, some of these theories should not be accepted or respected, because they contain serious deficiencies. We plan to spend this chapter and the next two detailing what the theories say, but we also will be noting what some of their basic inadequacies are. We would welcome a war of attrition among these theories!

SOME EARLY EXPLANATIONS

Why do some youths commit many delinquent acts and other youths none? Delinquency theories have wrestled with this question for many years. Some early explanations emphasized demonological causes—that is, they argued that supernatural spirits prompted various kinds of behavior. Spirits could do whatever they wanted, so anything that happened could be blamed on them. Moreover, spirits could inhabit anything—rocks, trees, even human beings. People who were thought to be possessed by spirits were called witches or warlocks and were subject to persecution. The demonological view declined after the Middle Ages, but it never died completely, resurfacing in full force in Salem, Massachusetts, in 1692:

> . . . the "witchcraft delusion" truly possessed the village of Salem. Every tavern, every household, every barn stable was swept up by the hysterical events. No woman dared talk freely with her husband or her neighbor or even her children for fear some inconsequential aside would be recalled in court testimony and used as evidence against her (Browning and Gerassi, 1980:38).

The Enlightenment of the seventeenth and eighteenth centuries gave rise to a new view of crime called the classical school. This view saw people as rational, intelligent individuals who are fully capable of making their own decisions and directing their daily lives in a perfectly sane and sensible way. If people engaged in delinquent or criminal behaviors, classical criminologists argued, they did so of their own free will. And their choosing to do so was rational—that is, they felt that the benefits produced by committing an illegal act would outweigh the penalties that might follow. The only way to reduce such activity was to make sure that society caught and punished offenders, thus instilling fear and discouraging them and others from offending in the future. Beccaria (1767), an early classical criminologist, simply took for granted that people were motivated by the desire to maximize pleasure and avoid pain. His concern was with bringing rationality into the justice system by making trials speedy, making punishment more certain and less arbitrary, extending the use of imprisonment, and eliminating capital punishment and other needlessly severe kinds of punishment that were then common. In short, the classical school (which is the basis of much modern law) had little to say about the causes of crime but much to say about criminal procedure.

BIOLOGICAL THEORIES

Lombroso and Positivism

The classical school held sway for more than a century before it was challenged by the positivist school of criminology. This approach was less philosophical and more scientific; that is, it relied on empirical methods to learn about the world (observation, experimentation, and so on). The first prominent positivist was an Italian physician, Cesare Lombroso (1836–1909).

American textbooks on crime and delinquency usually highlight a few of Lombroso's more incredible ideas, present these as his most important contributions, and then show how foolish they are. Among his harshest critics are Sutherland and Cressey, who claim that he delayed criminological thinking for fifty years "and in addition made no lasting contribution" of his own (1955:55).

Not all criminologists agree with this position. Wolfgang (1961), for instance, notes that Lombroso's influence has been both positive and long-lasting. American criminology owes an intellectual debt to him for each of the following:

1. The scientific study of the criminal or delinquent person. Earlier approaches, such as classical criminology, were more legalistic and philosophical, concerned with crime only in the abstract.
2. The comparisons of delinquents and nondelinquents to find differences between these two groups that might explain the variation in their delinquency.
3. The reliance on determinism rather than free will to explain delinquent activity. This line of thinking implies that forces act on people to lead them into deviance.
4. Emphasis on understanding the individual offender and on adapting treatment to the individual, not to the crime.

5. Sparking controversy and intellectual curiosity. By challenging criminological thinkers of his day, Lombroso forced them to confront his ideas, test them, and propose others.

As the prison doctor in Turin, Italy, Lombroso examined hundreds of prisoners each year. These examinations convinced him that criminals have many stigmata—distinctive features such as asymmetrical faces, enormous jaws, large or protruding ears, and receding chins. Influenced by Darwin's *Descent of Man* (1871), Lombroso (1876) proposed that these traits were *atavistic*—that is, they represented a reversion to a more primitive level of human development. These atavistic beings not only looked different but thought differently, having the mentality of primitive people. As throwbacks to an earlier stage of evolution, they were incapable of fitting into modern society or following its complex rules and expectations (Wolfgang, 1961). Their stage of development equipped them to live only in a much more primitive environment.

Lombroso mentioned three criminal types: the epileptic, the insane, and the born criminal. It is the last that has received most attention. Besides their physical quirks, born criminals were said to be insensitive to pain and to be characterized by

> a lack of moral sense, including an absence of repentance and remorse . . . and other manifestations, such as a special criminal argot, or slang, the tendency to express ideas pictorially, and the extensive use of tattooing (Wolfgang, 1961:251).

Lombroso's theory and research were both flawed. His samples of offenders included only prisoners; he did not compare random samples of nonoffenders with the offender groups. He defined criminals subjectively—as "the kind of men who . . . we believe to be criminal at heart" (Goring, 1913:21). In a replication of Lombroso's research, Goring concluded:

> We have extensively compared, with regard to many physical characteristics, different kinds of criminals with each other, and criminals as a class with law-abiding citizens. Our results nowhere confirm the evidence of physical-type criminals. In fact, both with regard to measurements and the presence of physical anomalies in criminals, our statistics present startling conformity with similar statistics of the law-abiding class. Our inevitable conclusion must be there is no such thing as a physical criminal type (1913:173).

Lombroso's theory of atavism turned out to be an unjustified leap of the imagination. Even those criminologists who initially embraced Lombroso's work later abandoned this part of his explanation of crime and delinquency (for example, Hooton, 1939; Sheldon, 1949). Lombroso is almost thoroughly rejected by criminology today, but some members of the public at large still believe that there are physical differences that set criminals apart from the rest of the population. Of course, there also are people who think there is some validity in the demonological view (hence the popularity of *The Exorcist*, *The Omen*, and similar films).

Physique, Temperament, and Behavior

William Sheldon (1949) carried on Lombroso's tradition by claiming that delinquency is related to body type. Indeed, he assumed that body type affects a person's entire personality or temperament. He classified people by how closely they approximated one of three ideal or extreme types: the *endomorphs,* who tend to put on fat, to be round and soft, and to have short arms and legs; *mesomorphs,* who have athletic and muscular physiques; and *ectomorphs,* who are basically skinny, with lean and fragile bodies. Sheldon hypothesized that each body build would exhibit a specific corresponding temperament. Endomorphs would be relaxed, comfortable, extroverted "softies." Mesomorphs would be more active, assertive, and aggressive. And ectomorphs would be introverted, overly sensitive, and chronically complaining about their health.

Sheldon claimed that mesomorphs have characteristics that make them the most suitable of the three types for delinquency. His research methods were questionable, but his work found support. More satisfactory research by Sheldon and Eleanor Glueck (1956) also found mesomorphs to be more prone than other types to engage in delinquency. But the Gluecks noted that mesomorphs also tend to feel inadequate, "not taken care of," and emotionally unstable (Shoemaker, 1984), which is quite different from the "macho" image of mesomorphs Sheldon proposed. The meaning of the mesomorphy/delinquency relationship remains unclear. Possibly, being muscular enables some youngsters to be admitted to gangs that engage in delinquent acts. Or perhaps muscularity allows an individual to dominate others through violence and threats. Or muscularity may be a sign of masculinity and physical toughness, so boys who develop muscles feel they should play the role of "tough guy." Finally, juvenile justice officials may regard mesomorphy in youths as a danger sign and treat them more severely.

Genetics and Crime

Genes do not determine behavior; how people behave is not something that is inherited. But genetic structure can influence hormones and enzymes, which in turn can combine with certain environmental factors to lead to aggressive or disruptive behavior. In attempts to assess the relative importance of heredity and environment, researchers sometimes look to two types of studies: the study of twins and the study of adoptees. We will look at twins studies first. There are two types of twins, *monozygotic* (identical) ones, who come from the same egg, and *dizygotic* (fraternal) ones, who come from separate eggs and are no more alike genetically than any nontwin siblings are. If there is a genetic factor in delinquency, then monozygotic twins should be more alike than dizygotics. Researchers call this *concordance*: both twins are delinquent, or both are nondelinquent. When one twin is delinquent and the other is not, this is known as *discordance.*

Over the years, quite a few twins studies have been conducted, and they usually have found more concordance among monozygotic pairs than among dizygotics. Thus researchers have generally concluded that these findings show the importance of heredity. Their work assumes that monozygotic twins are treated no differently than dizygotics. But this assumption is questionable:

> MZ twins tend to establish more similar environments for each other than DZ's do; they spend more time together, choose more often the same friends, are more closely attached to and dependent on each other, choose more similar occupations, and are typically cooperative, while DZ twins are typically competitive (Stott, 1982:193).

Furthermore, since monozygotic twins look alike, they tend to be treated alike; sometimes their parents dress them alike. Most people have great difficulty telling them apart. Thus, they come to think of themselves as alike. All of these factors show the influence of environment on making them behave more alike. Dalgard and Kringlen (1978) point out another factor: the reason why some twins (especially monozygotics) may both engage in delinquency is that they do so *together*; thus their delinquency can be traced to the simplest and most ordinary of social circumstances—they associate with each other a great deal.

Adoption studies also try to separate the influences of heredity from those of the environment. Adopted children tend to have no contact with their biological fathers; if they resemble their biological fathers in behavior, this presumably reflects the powerful impact that heredity has on behavior.

> The most comprehensive and best-designed study of adoptees for the investigation of a genetic factor in criminality has been that of Hutchings and Mednick (1977). From a file of all children placed for adoption in the city of Copenhagen, they took the 971 males born between 1927 and 1941 whose biological fathers could be traced. Their critical finding was that 48.8 percent of the criminal adoptees but only 31.1 percent of the noncriminal adoptees had a biological father who was in the criminal register (Stott, 1982:194).

At the present time, adoption research stands as an interesting line of inquiry, but it is too new and too little explored to be evaluated conclusively.

Chromosomal Abnormalities

Chromosomes are tiny structures found in all cell nuclei. They contain DNA and transmit the basic genetic material, genes (Shah and Roth, 1974). Most people have forty-six chromosomes, two of which determine the person's sex; males typically have an XY complement, while females have an XX. Sometimes, however, abnormalities occur, and the result may be either an XXX (a "superfemale," who is usually mentally deficient), an XO (a condition known as Turner's syndrome, in which females have no ovaries to produce female sex hormones), XXY (referred to as Klinefelter's syndrome, in which males usually have small genitals and are sterile), or an XYY. Criminological interest centers on the XYY males. Newspapers fanned the flames on this issue in the late 1960s, when they first reported that Richard Speck, convicted murderer of eight nurses in the Chicago area, had the extra Y chromosome. (It was later learned that he did not.) Some people argue that the extra Y chromosome causes aggressiveness and thus criminal activity. The ordinary male has one Y chromosome and the female none. In their research on different cultures, Maccoby and Jacklin (1974) reported that the one universal difference between the sexes is that males are more aggressive. If one Y chromosome produces such a difference, imagine what two Y's could do!

Witkin (1978) set out to determine whether XYY men do indeed have a higher crime rate than average men, then to determine why such a relationship exists (if it does). He studied tall men (the XYY complement is more common among males who are tall) in Copenhagen, Denmark, and was able to complete sex-chromosome tests on about 4,000 men; of these, only twelve possessed the extra Y chromosome. But five of the twelve had been convicted of one offense or more. This high rate (42 percent) contrasts sharply with the rate for other men (9 percent). This seems impressive until we learn that the XYY men did not commit very serious or aggressive crimes. The author concluded that XYY men are not especially prone to committing crime; they are just easily caught for the minor offenses they do commit. Witkin speculated that they get caught because of their low intelligence, a common trait among XYYs.

Blood Chemistry and Deviance

The final biological theory we will consider is that aggression may be related to blood chemistry. This seems to be true for males and females, humans and nonhumans:

> It has been known for centuries . . . that one can take a raging bull and convert it into a gentle steer by the operation of castration, which reduces the level of testosterone in the blood stream (Moyer, 1979:28).

More recently, studies of women and the premenstrual syndrome have been conducted. It has long been known that some women display a relationship between their mood and their stage in the menstrual cycle. Perhaps as many as 25 percent of women suffer from moderate to severe stress, which is known as premenstrual tension (Shah and Roth, 1974). Symptoms include abdominal pain, fatigue, irritability, headaches, depression, tension, and nervousness.

We do not know for sure what the behavioral consequences of this condition are, but a few studies have prompted interest. Dalton's (1964) is the the most controversial. She found that during menstrual and premenstrual days, an abnormally high percentage of women call in sick or undergo acute psychiatric admissions, surgical and medical admissions, and emergency accident admissions. Dalton also found a "highly significant" correlation between the menstrual cycle and deviance by girls and women. At least two interpretations are possible. Hormonal changes could cause more crimes during this stage or perhaps

> women are more likely to be detected in their criminal acts during this time. The adverse effect of menstruation was greatest among sufferers of premenstrual tension, with its concomitant symptoms of lethargy, slower reaction time, and mental dullness; and these factors would lead to easier detection during certain days of the menstrual cycle. . . . Premenstrual tension is also accompanied by irritability, lethargy, depression, and water retention, and these symptoms alone may be responsible for certain crimes—for example . . . violence and assault . . . (Dalton, 1961:1753).

In 1982, the premenstrual syndrome attracted a flurry of attention when a woman in Brooklyn, New York, was accused of beating her little child and said the case should be dismissed because premenstrual tension caused her to act irrationally. (She later abandoned this defense and pleaded guilty to a lesser charge.)

Biological criminology has come a long way since Lombroso's era. Research techniques have become more sophisticated, keeping pace with biology. But the advocates of this branch of criminology tend to lean toward less ambitious claims than their early predecessors did. Present investigators such as Shah and Roth (1974) suggest more modestly that *some* biological factors may have *some* effect under *certain* conditions. But what these effects are and how they are triggered remain unclear. In short, this field poses more questions than answers. Any promise of solving all crime and delinquency by isolating a biological cause has eroded due to consistent failures to locate such a factor. Nowadays, biological theories are increasingly complex and apply only to tiny segments of the population.

PSYCHOLOGICAL THEORIES

Biological theories were popular in the nineteenth century, when criminological theory was written mostly by physicians. But psychological theories began to be advanced early in the twentieth century. What distinguishes psychological theories of crime and delinquency from biological and sociological theories? Shoemaker (1984) suggests that there are several distinctive elements: (1) delinquency is regarded as a result of internal, underlying disturbances, (2) these disturbances develop in early childhood and tend to become permanent features of the individual's character, and (3) since the individual has the problem, he or she must be focused on if the problem is ever going to be solved.

Intelligence

One early view that attracted considerable backing in America claimed that many delinquents were feebleminded. Goddard (1912) fostered this notion in his biography of the Kallikaks.

> This family had two lines of progeny, one emanating from a "feebleminded" barmaid and the other from a "respectable girl of good family." The former line "produced" an assorted array of illegitimate children, prostitutes, alcoholics, and other deviants. The latter lineage consisted of a variety of governors, senators, doctors, and "good" people (Shoemaker, 1984:44).

Many psychologists administered IQ tests to prison and jail inmates early in this century. Their findings were included in Goddard's book *Feeblemindedness: Its Causes and Consequences* (1914). Estimates of the percentage of delinquents who were feebleminded varied from study to study, but the median percentage was 70. This extremely high figure, coupled with the assumption that very few members of the general population were feebleminded (less than 1 percent, Goddard speculated) seemed to indicate clearly that low intelligence fostered delinquency to a great degree. Goddard also offered several reasons why the feebleminded would be more likely than other people to get involved in delinquency. First, he said, the feebleminded often do not understand the difference between right and wrong. Second, those few who do know the difference still break laws because they lack self-control. Other writers offered a third reason: the feebleminded engage in delinquency because they fail to foresee the consequences of their acts, such as getting caught and punished.

The feeblemindedness argument was avidly accepted as an explanation of crime and delinquency for several years. But during World War I the U.S. Army began administering IQ tests to draftees, and the average scores they produced were not very high. Indeed, they were on the verge of "moronity" (one of Goddard's terms), with a mental age of 13, scoring about the same as samples of adult prisoners had in that era (Murchison, 1926). This research, along with a critical review of crime-and-IQ studies by Sutherland (1931), seemed to put the notion that low intelligence breeds delinquency to rest. Actually, all of the work on IQ at that time is suspect. Many people taking the tests did not have enough time to complete them, and many others were not given proper instructions. Furthermore, the tests contained some items that tested knowledge of specific areas, not general intelligence. And finally, the scoring was not done properly; thus, a great majority of normal people were scored as morons. Only in recent decades have IQ tests become more reliable and valid. (For a more recent discussion of developments in the area of delinquency and IQ, see Chapter 4.)

Psychopathy

There have been many definitions of psychopathy. To make matters simple, we might refer to *The Mask of Sanity*, by Cleckley, which lists the following symptoms of psychopathy (1955:13–14):

1. Superficial charm and "good" intelligence.
2. Absence of delusions and other signs of irrational behavior.
3. Absence of nervousness.
4. Unreliability.
5. Untruthfulness and insincerity.
6. Lack of remorse and shame.
7. Inadequately motivated antisocial behavior.
8. Poor judgment and failure to learn by experience.
9. Pathological egocentricity and incapacity for love.
10. Lack of feeling for other people.

Psychopaths are usually very capable of appearing to be warm, friendly, and likable. One such individual was Ferdinand Waldo Demara. He never graduated from high school, but as "the great imposter" (Crichton, 1959), he successfully passed himself off as a variety of persons. In the navy, he was on the verge of being found out for having forged papers, so he faked his own death by dropping his clothes at the end of a pier and leaving a suicide note. Then he used stolen credentials to pose as a psychologist with a Harvard Ph.D. and then dean of philosophy at a college in Canada, where he taught psychology courses and handled adminstrative chores very competently.

In the Korean War, Demara "earned" his commission in the Royal Canadian Navy, this time posing as a medical doctor. While aboard a destroyer, he was faced with a great crisis: three men were critically injured and required immediate surgery to live. Demara, who had read up on medicine, did some intensive reviewing, then operated throughout the night. He saved the three men and by dawn also had successfully treated sixteen others (Bartol, 1980). Eventually, Demara ceased this kind of activity, and a book and movie were made of his life.

Psychopaths are unpredictable and unreliable, but only some of the time. Their crimes stem from a cyclical impulsiveness. They generally commit offenses where the risks are high and the gains are small or even nonexistent. Some psychologists think that a key element of the psychopathic personality is a need for greater stimulation, thrills, and excitement (Quay, 1965). Some of these points seem to be applicable to Ted Bundy, a young man who received considerable notoriety on the West Coast a few years ago. In 1978, the FBI called Bundy perhaps the most prolific mass murderer in American history. He killed young women and teenage girls in a series of attacks from Washington state to Florida. These murders followed a pattern of impulsiveness: he would be inactive for a while, then there would be a period of furious activity, then another lull. One investigator referred to the offender as having "an alarm clock of madness in his head, ticking, ready to go off at certain intervals" (Larsen, 1980:24). Bundy was very capable of manipulating, charming, and exploiting people—even the governor of Washington state wrote a letter of recommendation for him. People who knew him described him as sympathetic, understanding, very tender; one person commented that "you can't help but have a great deal of affection for him" (Larsen, 1980:7). He also had a high IQ, had served as assistant director of the Seattle Crime Commission, and had entered law school. Later, after committing the crimes, he dropped hints to his captors: "The evidence is there. Keep diggin'. You'll find it" (Larsen, 1980:297). And he committed his final murders in Florida, deliberately crossing the entire country to get there after he had learned that Florida was the state where capital punishment is most popular. The Bundy profile thus resembles Cleckley's picture of the psychopath in many ways. But Bundy is also very atypical; very few criminals and delinquents can appear so friendly and sympathetic. Thus, we cannot expect to trace many offenses to psychopathy.

Fearlessness

Previously, in the section on biological theories, we mentioned that temperament has been linked to delinquency through body type. Usually, however, it is the psychological theories that discuss the importance of temperament or personality. Here we are going to look at the personality trait of fearlessness and its possible relationship to delinquency. Lykken (1982) contrasts the fearful with the fearless; the former avoid risk and stress by seeking out relatively sheltered environments. The latter, though, appear to have conquered fear; they welcome risk. Each society needs to have some people who are fearless, people who go on to become explorers, astronauts, or national leaders.

Not all fearless people pursue this path, however, as Lykken notes. He divides the fearless into two types, the hero and the disordered person. We are not sure what causes fearlessness, but it seems to occur early in life. Lykken suggests that whether the fearless person becomes a hero or a disordered person depends on how he or she is raised. Fearless children are difficult to rear. They are not afraid of antagonizing their parents, and parents may react by giving them less warmth and affection. The child thus becomes less interested in other people's feelings and less likely to adopt their beliefs, values, and sentiments. Such children may learn to use their daring and aggressiveness to win approval on the streets. Take the case of Al Capone, who at age 10 challenged a Marine Corps guard to fight:

> "Hey, you long-legged number three there! Get in step! You're holding 'em up. . . . " Crimson with shame and anger, the recruit ran up to the gate, making as if to spit at the boy through the bars. Al flew into a rage and, though the recruit was twice as big, challenged him to a fight. The corporal intervened, ordering the recruit back to the guardhouse. . . . [Al] swaggered up and down before his awed companions (Kobler, 1971:24–25).

Research shows that such offenders do not get sweaty palms in shock experiments because they take disaster lightly. The question, however, is how many offenders are like this. Lykken's research does not tell us; fearlessness could be a very rare trait.

Hyperactivity

Hyperactivity has been linked with juvenile delinquency (Berman and Siegal, 1976). Hyperkinesis (the medical term for hyperactivity) is thought to occur in 2–12 percent of grade schoolers, with a higher incidence among boys than girls. Signs of this disorder include excessive movement, short attention span, mood swings, fidgeting, and impulsiveness (Conrad and Schneider, 1980). Teachers recognize it when they say, "That boy just can't sit still for a moment." Hyperactivity is a new problem, or at least a new name for an old one. Gross and Wilson (1974) say that it is also now the most common psychiatric problem. Scores of clinics are dedicated to treating it, and they are backed up by sizable federal expenditures. Some commentators say that drug companies have largely created the problem, so they can supply the treatment and reap the profits.

> The pharmaceutical companies spent a great deal of time and money promoting stimulant medications for this new disorder. After the middle 1960s it was nearly impossible to read a medical journal . . . without seeing some elaborate advertising for either Ritalin or Dexedrine. . . . These same pharmaceutical firms also supply sophisticated packets of "diagnostic and treatment" information on hyperkinesis to physicians, pay for professional conferences on the subject, and

support research in the identification and treatment of the disorder (Conrad and Schneider, 1980:159).

Runaway Delinquents

Richard Jenkins (1969) has developed a typology of delinquency: the hyperactive child, the seclusive child, the overanxious child, the runaway child, the unsocialized aggressive, and the socialized delinquent. Here we will mention the runaway delinquent. Such children run away from home and stay away overnight; they do this often. They also tend to engage in stealing, particularly at home, after which they run away. Such children tend to be unhappy, discouraged, and seclusive. They may, however, associate with companions that adults generally consider to be undesirable; they may even become part of a juvenile gang, though usually only as hangers-on because they cannot gain acceptance as core members. They are too lacking in self-confidence to be accepted by the regular members. Jenkins traces their problems to their home life:

> The home background of the chronic runaway child is typically one of parental rejection from birth, and one of parental severity and inconsistency (Jenkins, 1969:1035).

In commenting on this type of juvenile, Wattenberg notes that such youths seem to greatly resemble the vagrants who populate "skid row" areas and wander aimlessly in large cities.

> These are the pathetic losers. In their pitiable search for a home of some sort, they can and do adjust somewhat passively to any institutional setting (Wattenberg, 1979:295–296).

Theories of Aggression

In 1939, five Yale psychologists proposed the now-famous frustration/aggression theory. According to Dollard et al., people who are frustrated will act aggressively, and people who engage in aggression were frustrated first. But this theory is problematic because neither frustration nor aggression was clearly defined; and no matter how they were defined, the two did not in fact always accompany one another. The theory has since been modified by another psychologist, Leonard Berkowitz, who defines aggression as:

> behavior whose goal is to inflict damage or injury on some object or person. The behavior may be overt (physical or verbal) or implicit (for example, wishing someone dead). Berkowitz says frustration results when behavior directed at anticipated goals or expectations is thwarted in some way. In a sense, any nonfulfillment of expectations may result in frustration. Thus, to be frustrated a

> person must have been expecting or anticipating the attainment of a goal or achievement. *Deprivation* of goals, achievement, or goods by itself does not necessarily qualify as a frustrating agent. People who are living under deprived conditions are not necessarily frustrated unless they actually *expect* something better (Bartol, 1980:187).

There are several elements of Berkowitz's version of frustration/aggression theory. First, frustration develops when a person experiences the blocking of some goal. Frustration involves dashed hopes and unfulfilled expectations. It is thus not a feeling or an emotion but an objective condition.

Second, frustration leads to anger. This, of course, is an emotion, and it can be aroused by causes other than frustration. Third, anger makes aggression more likely. If the anger is very strong, aggression is almost certain to follow. Anger increases a person's energy level and lowers one's inhibitions. Fourth, whether the person will resort to aggression depends on the presence of certain cues or stimuli and the person's learning history. This last hypothesis is Berkowitz's main contribution: there are certain cues in the environment that induce aggression if the person is already provoked.

These environmental stimuli assume various forms; Berkowitz has studied two types, words and weapons. In the weapons experiment, the subjects who were angered and who were in a room where a weapon happened to be present delivered more electrical shocks (that is, were more aggressive) to a fellow student than did other angered subjects in a room where there were no weapons (Berkowitz and LePage, 1967). Interestingly, the subjects voiced no suspicions about the weapons; indeed, they denied later that the weapons had any impact at all on their behavior in the experiment. It appears that some cues may increase the chances of aggression although the aggressor has no idea of this effect.

Redl and Wineman, in their book *Children Who Hate* (1951), take a psychoanalytic approach to aggression. They say that hyperaggressive children are impossible to live with and considered untreatable by child guidance workers. At the same time, these children are grossly and continuously traumatized. They are shunted from one foster home to another, warehoused in institutions, or subjected to homes where brutality, cruelty, and neglect are common practices, as the following example indicates:

> Between the ages of two to five he was shuttled about from foster home to foster home. Occasionally he lived with his mother in the home of maternal grandparents. When Larry was six, his mother moved to Detroit and married a man much older than she. Shortly thereafter Larry came to live with them. He was six and one-half at this time. The mother was weak, passive, detached. Her tie to Larry appeared to be on a very tenuous level. The stepfather was a short, squat, powerfully built man. He was severely alcoholic, profane, brutal. From the very beginning of Larry's entrance into the home, he became the butt for the stepfather's primitive bullying. The degree of sadism that the stepfather expressed

> toward Larry is almost unbelievable. He was beaten severely, threatened with a shotgun, booted, thrown into a drainage ditch in front of their home, and locked in a woodshed for long hours without food (Redl and Wineman, 1951:55–56).

Such children end up with psychological problems. On the one hand, their egos are weak. There are many signs of such weakness among the hyperaggressives, including the following eight:

1. They cannot tolerate even the slightest frustrations (such as having to wait a few seconds for a traffic light to change).
2. In coping with insecurity, anxiety, and fear, they react with total flight or with a ferocious attack.
3. They cannot resist even the slightest temptation to act unruly or delinquent.
4. When exposed to any kind of excitement, they cannot keep from joining in.
5. Faced with objects that have ordinary uses (such as clay for molding or chairs for sitting), they often see them as a way of satisfying primitive urges and impulses (such as throwing them).
6. They have no sense of how to care for or protect their property.
7. They feel panic whenever they are exposed to new situations.
8. They cannot control themselves when memories of past traumas are brought to mind. Again, Larry provides a good example:

   > [Being taken out of the group therapy room] was too much for Larry. Although usually docile and clinging to the adult and well aware that he is loved and well-treated, this spectacle of the head counselor actually removing him bodily played back into memories of brutality-loaded moments with his murderous stepfather. As if by a pre-arranged signal the moment the head counselor began to move him, he unleashed a torrent of counter aggression, and hooked his legs in a steely scissor grip on a nearby table. . . . "You want to twist my arm off, you want to kill me, you want to hurt my muscles, you want to choke me" all of which things, as we know from his case history, his stepfather actually did threaten to do (Redl and Wineman, 1951:104).

On the other hand, the authors also say that in some ways these children have very strong egos. They devise excellent defenses against guilt feelings: "he did it first"; "we were all in on it"; "he had it coming to him"; "I had to do it or I would have lost face"; and so on. Thus the efficient delinquent ego invents alibi tricks to appease its conscience (superego, in Freudian terminology) (1951:156). With so many problems to deal with, therapists treating these hyperaggressive children have a very difficult task. Redl and Wineman believe that only psychoanalytic insights make success possible.

SUMMARY

Theories are answers to the question "Why?" We evaluate them by how well they meet certain requirements. First, they need to be expressed simply; simpler theories make phenomena easier to understand. Second, they need to be testable, so that research studies can be conducted to either support or refute them. Third, the theory ought to be compatible with research findings. And finally, good theories are unified, consistent, and logically coherent, not full of contradictions.

In the Middle Ages, many people relied on demonological explanations, attributing crime and other ills to supernatural spirits. The Enlightenment gave rise to the classical school of criminology. According to this philosophical approach, crime is a product of free will (like all other behavior) and occurs when the benefits outweigh the costs. The classical school therefore proposed that punishment be made more certain, swifter, and less arbitrary.

Biological positivists challenged the classical school. Lombroso and other biological positivists adopted a scientific rather than a philosophical approach. They were interested in the causes of crime, not the criminal law or criminal justice system. Lombroso emphasized determinism rather than free will. He also compared criminals and noncriminals to see what made them different. His physical examination of prisoners in Italy led him to believe that criminals have many stigmata and that these represent a reversion to an earlier stage of evolution, making these criminals incapable of fitting into modern society. Much later, Sheldon also emphasized physical characteristics. He believed the mesomorphic body type is conducive to delinquency because people with a muscular build automatically have aggressive, assertive temperaments.

The Scandinavian countries have contributed significantly to our understanding of biological criminology, particularly in the area of genetics. Twins studies are common there, usually resulting in the finding that monozygotic twins have higher concordance on delinquency than dizygotic twins. But critics point out that this concordance could well be due to the fact that monozygotics tend to spend more time together. Adoption studies also try to separate heredity from environment, and, at first glance, they seem to show that heredity does influence the child's involvement in delinquency. But these data are still new, and much more critical analysis remains to be done. Chromosomal abnormalities have been addressed in the XYY controversy. The extra Y chromosome was thought to be a cause of violent crime, but subsequent research has shown that it is exceedingly rare and not related to violence anyway.

Among psychological theories, an early view that attracted attention claimed that delinquency was caused by feeblemindedness. Goddard said the feebleminded become delinquent either because they do not know right from wrong or because they have no control over their behavior. But Goddard's measurements of IQ, along with the army IQ tests used to refute his theory, were poorly designed, unfairly administered, and incorrectly interpreted.

Psychopathy has been pointed to as another psychological cause of crime and delinquency. As defined by Cleckley, psychopathy refers to a series of traits, including charm, intelligence, calmness, and insincerity. Ted Bundy, a mass murderer of women in the 1970s, fits the profile of a psychopath quite well, but the great bulk of offenders do not seem to be psychopathic at all, so as an explanation of widespread crime and delinquency, psychopathy is very questionable.

Fearlessness may be a factor in delinquency, as Lykken suggests, but the research on this topic is only in its very early stages. Hyperactivity has been linked to delinquency in young children, but it reaches its peak very early in life, so it may not have a long-range impact. Jenkins mentions runaway children in his delinquent typology. He argues that they become runaways and perhaps join delinquent gangs because they are completely rejected by their parents.

Finally, psychologists have looked at aggression. Berkowitz, an experimental psychologist, tried to improve upon frustration/aggression theory by defining frustration and aggression more carefully and by taking into account the influence of cues such as hostile words and weapons. Redl and Wineman focused more specifically on delinquent children. They argued that there are thousands of hyperaggressive preadolescents in each large city. These children are usually impossible for families to control and are considered untreatable by most child-guidance workers. The problems of such children are traceable to a consistently and grossly traumatizing home life. These children develop egos that are both too weak and too strong. They cannot control their impulses and urges, which result in a great deal of aggression. But their egos are very efficient (strong) when it comes to creating alibis to evade guilt feelings.

DISCUSSION QUESTIONS

1. What are theories?
2. What is the relationship between theories and scientific research?
3. What were the principal concerns of classical criminologists?
4. What plausible explanations may account for the relationship between body type and delinquency?
5. What are the major flaws in theories linking delinquency with genetic makeup, chromosomal abnormalities, and blood chemistry?

6. What types of personality traits have been identified as differentiating delinquents and nondelinquents?
7. Under what conditions is frustration expected to produce aggression?
8. What role does social learning play in explanations of aggressive behavior?
9. Which of the biological or psychological theories of delinquency appear to hold the most promise for future research efforts? Explain your answer.

REFERENCES

BARTOL, CURT R.
1980 *Criminal Behavior.* Englewood Cliffs, N.J.: Prentice-Hall.
BECCARIA, CESARE
1767 *Essays on Crime and Punishment* (1963). Indianapolis: Bobbs-Merrill.
BERKOWITZ, LEONARD, AND ANTHONY LePAGE
1967 Weapons as aggression-eliciting stimuli. *Journal of Personality and Social Psychology* 7 (October):202–207.
BERMAN, ALLAN, AND A. W. SIEGAL
1976 Adaptive and learning skills in juvenile delinquents. *Journal of Learning Disabilities* 9 (November):583–590.
BLAU, PETER M.
1964 *Exchange and Power in Social Life.* New York: Wiley.
BROWNING, FRANK AND JOHN GERASSI
1980 *The American Way of Crime.* New York: Putnam.
CLECKLEY, HARVEY
1955 *The Mask of Sanity.* St. Louis: Mosby.
CONRAD, PETER, AND JOSEPH SCHNEIDER
1980 *Deviance and Medicalization.* St. Louis: Mosby.
CRICHTON, ROBERT
1959 *The Great Imposter.* New York: Random House.
DALGARD, ODD STEFFEN, AND EINAR KRINGLEN
1978 Criminal behavior in twins. Pp. 292–307 in Leonard D. Savitz and Norman Johnston (eds.), *Crime in Society.* New York: Wiley.
DALTON, KATHARINA
1964 *The Premenstrual Syndrome.* Springfield, Ill.: Charles C Thomas.
1961 Menstruation and crime. *British Medical Journal* 2:1752–1753.
DARWIN, CHARLES
1871 *Descent of Man.* London: John Murray.
DOLLARD, JOHN, ET AL.
1939 *Frustration and Aggression.* New Haven, Conn.: Yale Univesity Press.
GLUECK, SHELDON, AND ELEANOR GLUECK
1956 *Physique and Delinquency.* New York: Harper.
GODDARD, HENRY
1914 *Feeblemindedness: Its Causes and Consequences.* New York: Macmillan.
1912 *The Kallikak Family.* New York: Macmillan.
GORING, CHARLES
1913 *The English Convict* (1972). Montclair, N.J.: Patterson Smith.

GROSS, M. B., AND W. E. WILSON
1974 *Minimal Brain Dysfunction.* New York: Brunner/Mazel.

HOOTON, ERNEST
1939 *The American Criminal.* Cambridge, Mass.: Harvard University Press.

HUTCHINGS, BARRY, AND SARNOFF A. MEDNICK
1977 Criminality in adoptees and their adoptive and biological parents. Pp. 127–141 in Sarnoff A. Mednick and Karl O. Christiansen (eds.), *Biosocial Bases of Criminal Behavior.* New York: Gardner.

JENKINS, RICHARD L.
1969 Classification of behavior problems of children. *American Journal of Psychiatry* 125 (February):1032–1039.

KOBLER, JOHN
1971 *Capone.* New York: Collier.

LARSEN, RICHARD
1980 *Bundy.* Englewood Cliffs, N.J.: Prentice-Hall.

LOMBROSO, CESARE
1876 *L'Uomo Delinquente.* Milan, Italy: Hoepli.

LYKKEN, DAVID T.
1982 Fearlessness. *Psychology Today* 16 (September):20–25.

MACCOBY, ELEANOR, AND CAROL JACKLIN
1974 *The Psychology of Sex Differences.* Palo Alto, Calif.: Stanford University Press.

MOYER, KENNETH R.
1979 What is the potential for biological violence control? Pp. 19–46 in C. Ray Jeffery (ed.), *Biology and Crime.* Beverly Hills, Calif.: Sage.

MURCHISON, CARL
1926 *Criminal Intelligence.* Worcester, Mass.: Clark University Press.

QUAY, HERBERT C.
1965 Psychopathic personality as pathological stimulation seeking. *American Journal of Psychiatry* 122 (August):180–183.

REDL, FRITZ, AND DAVID WINEMAN
1951 *Children Who Hate.* Glencoe, Ill.: Free Press.

SHAH, SALEEM A., AND LOREN H. ROTH
1974 Biological and psychophysiological factors in criminality. Pp. 101–174 in Daniel Glaser (ed.), *Handbook of Criminology.* Chicago: Rand McNally.

SHELDON, WILLIAM
1949 *Varieties of Delinquent Youth.* New York: Harper.

SHOEMAKER, DONALD J.
1984 *Theories of Delinquency.* New York: Oxford University Press.

STOTT, DENNIS
1982 *Delinquency.* New York: SP Medical & Scientific Books.

SUTHERLAND, EDWIN
1931 Mental deficiency and crime. Pp. 357–375 in Kimball Young (ed.), *Social Attitudes.* New York: Holt, Rinehart & Winston.

SUTHERLAND, EDWIN, AND DONALD CRESSEY
1955 *Principles of Criminology.* Philadelphia: Lippincott.

WATTENBERG, WILLIAM W.
1979 The juvenile delinquent. Pp. 287–298 in Hans Toch (ed.), *Psychology of Crime and Criminal Justice.* New York: Holt, Rinehart & Winston.

WILSON, JAMES Q.
1975 *Thinking About Crime.* New York: Basic.

WITKIN, HERMAN A.
1978 XYY and criminality. Pp. 275–291 in Leonard D. Savitz and Norman Johnston (eds.), *Crime in Society.* New York: Wiley.
WOLFGANG, MARVIN
1961 Pioneers in criminology: Cesare Lombroso. *Journal of Criminal Law, Criminology, and Police Science* 52 (November):361–369.

Sociological Theories: The Chicago School and Anomie

7

Biological theories of crime and delinquency were superseded by psychological theories. Then, in the 1930s, several prominent sociological explanations were proposed. There are several features that distinguish these early sociological theories from previous theories we have discussed. First of all, they assume that crime and delinquency occur because of social and environmental circumstances. Second, society's institutions are assumed to be plagued by disintegration and disorganization. Third, this leads individuals to be more likely to engage in delinquency. Fourth, the lower class is assumed to be responsible for the bulk of offenses (Shoemaker, 1984).

THE CHICAGO SCHOOL

During the 1920s and 1930s, American sociology in general and juvenile delinquency studies in particular were a tale of one city—Chicago. The University of Chicago sprang almost full-grown thanks to the Standard Oil money of John D. Rockefeller and the drive of the university's first president, William Rainey Harper. Rockefeller favored a small college devoted to moral and theological training, but Harper pushed for—and got—a large university with a distinguished and innovative faculty. One of Harper's many contributions was to create the first department of sociology in America. Columbia and other schools soon followed, but for many years none could match Chicago's program, faculty, or influence on sociology (Faris, 1967).

Several factors helped Chicago's sociology department to thrive. First, it was housed in a new university, where all academic departments started out on a relatively equal footing; sociology thus did not have to occupy the bottom spot usually assigned to the newest discipline. It competed for the top students with the other departments and often won. Second, Chicago was a dynamic city. From a mere fort in the swamps, it had grown to be the second largest city in the United States, specializing in meat packing (Carl Sandburg called it "hog butcher for the world"), steel, and railroads. The population increased from a few hundred to more than a million in only sixty years because people streamed in from the East Coast and, especially, from Europe. Population growth caused new and serious problems. By 1920, Chicago was famous not only for hog butchers but for criminals as well. "Al Capone, the czar of the underworld, became a celebrity sought out by visitors who desired to take in all the important local sights" (Faris, 1967:21).

Perhaps the key figure in the University of Chicago's sociology department from 1914 to 1933 was Robert Park. He had been a teacher, a newspaper reporter, and a secretary to Booker T. Washington before coming to the university. A wide traveler, he had developed a unique understanding of cities. He wrote:

> I expect that I have actually covered more ground, tramping about in cities, than any other living man. Out of all this, I gained, among other things, a conception of the city, the community, and the region not as a geographical phenomenon merely but as a kind of social organism (quoted in Faris, 1967:29).

Park insisted that graduate students use the city as their "laboratory" to explore the burgeoning metropolis and to develop an understanding of its people and the social changes Chicago was undergoing. Certain groups were focused on, such as hobos, the mentally ill, suicides, and juvenile delinquents. Many of the students' dissertations were *ecological*: they mapped out the rates of a specific behavior (such as suicide) in the various parts of the city. Others, under the influence of George Herbert Mead, were more *social-psychological* in nature, sometimes emphasizing deviants' own views of their situation.

Clifford Shaw and Henry McKay

Clifford Shaw and Henry McKay were the most prominent students of juvenile delinquency to come out of the University of Chicago, and they used both ecological and social-psychological approaches. The social-psychological works included life histories that Shaw helped offenders write while he worked as a probation officer for the juvenile court. These books—*The Jack-Roller* (1930), *The Natural History of a Delinquent Career* (1931), and *Brothers in Crime* (1938)—were read very widely, made Shaw famous, and undermined some of the older biological views of crime and delinquency.

> To a generation of readers who had been deeply influenced by genetic theories of criminality he brought the actual voice of the offender presenting his own version of his origins, his growth, and his orientation to the world. A more forceful mode of presenting the force of circumstances in the molding of human lives would have been difficult to devise. The result was a highly compelling insider's view of criminality, made available to a public of readers and students normally far removed from the situations that produce confirmed criminal offenders (Finestone, 1976:94).

Shaw and his associates depicted delinquency as a series of stages. The first of these was the gang or play group, which could be found in any neighborhood. In these peer groups, youngsters acquired the local values and attitudes. In certain areas, these values were criminal ones.

In the next stage, the boys first got involved in delinquent activity. Generally, these initial forays into lawbreaking were quite minor, involving acts no more serious than truancy, vandalism, or petty theft. Boys often won the approval of their peers for these adventures, particularly if they were not caught. In the third stage, delinquency became less playful and more systematic; youths began to think of themselves as deviants. In the fourth, they progressed to professional crime, adhering to the criminal code.

Although Shaw's life histories of offenders were read widely in America, they did not have a pronounced impact upon delinquency theory. Even Shaw and McKay paid far more attention to their ecological research findings when they developed their own theory. They found that delinquency conformed to the zonal hypothesis by Ernest Burgess (Park's colleague and Shaw's mentor): rates of deviance declined the farther away one got from the city center. Burgess divided Chicago into a series of concentric circles. At the center was the Loop, the downtown business district, where property values are the highest. Beyond the Loop, there was a "zone in transition," containing an inner ring of factories and an outer ring of

> first-settlement immigrant colonies, of rooming-house districts, of homeless-men areas, of resorts of gambling, bootlegging, sexual vice, and of breeding places of crime. In this area of physical deterioration and social disorganization our studies show the greatest concentration of causes of poverty, bad housing, juvenile delinquency, family disintegration, physical and mental disease. As families and individuals prosper, they escape from this area into Zone III, leaving behind . . . the defeated, leaderless, and helpless (Burgess, 1929:62).

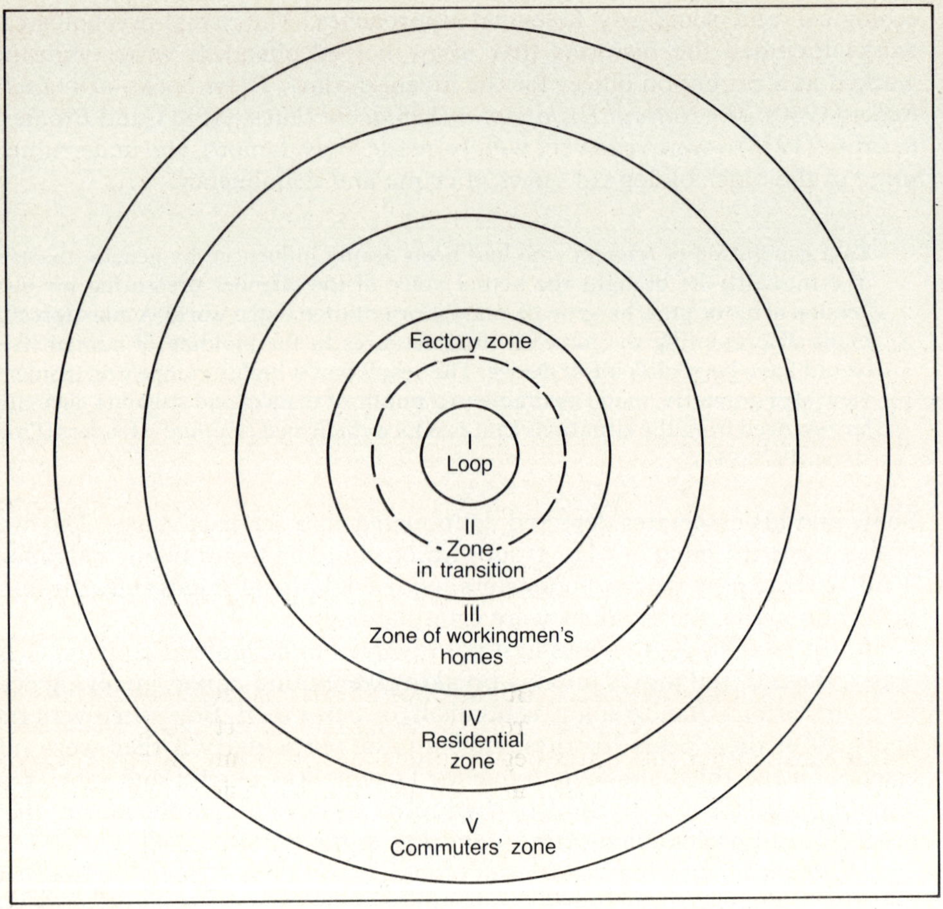

FIGURE 7–1
Concentric Zones
Source: Parks et al., 1928:51.

Zones III and IV were urban residential areas, and Zone V included the suburbs (see Figure 7–1).

Shaw and McKay found that all of the official measures of delinquency in Chicago and other cities followed this same pattern: reaching a peak in the first two zones and declining steadily as one moved farther away from the city center. And they discovered that areas high in delinquency also were characterized by high rates of families on relief, low rents, excessive infant mortality, many immigrants, and many adult criminals.

The Chicago sociologists had a ready explanation for these findings. Railroads, stockyards, and industry nearby made Zone II the least desirable area in the city but also the cheapest. Therefore, people naturally gravitated there if they were very poor, as many recent immigrants to America were. In the late nineteenth century, these areas were filled with German, Irish, and English immigrants; Scandinavians, Poles, Italians, and Jews arrived later. Then blacks came up from the South in hopes of landing jobs in Chicago's heavy industries. Each new incoming group was segregated in the slums of Zone II. They climbed out of them slowly.

What did these findings reveal about delinquency? The racial, ethnic, and economic segregation, the deteriorating buildings, and the high rates of delinquency and illness—all characteristic of Zone II—were interpreted in cultural and ecological terms by Shaw and McKay. Delinquency was not to be blamed on the biological or psychological inadequacies of the people who lived in Zone II. After all, they had not been very delinquent or criminal in the countries or regions where they lived previously. Many were rural European peasants who had never broken the law. Only after moving to the center of American cities did they or their children get involved in crime and delinquency.

Furthermore, the high rates of crime and delinquency did not appear to follow these people as they moved into zones farther from the central city. For instance, the Irish once comprised a large proportion of the official delinquents in American cities. But as they slowly achieved wealth and respectability, they moved away from the slums and poverty pockets and their crime and delinquency rates began to decline. The same pattern occurred with the Germans, Jews, Poles, and so on. (For a discussion of modern white ethnics in America, see Greeley, 1974.)

Shaw and McKay found that the rates of delinquency in given areas remain stable regardless of the race or ethnicity of the people who live in them. Areas high in delinquency at the turn of the century were still high thirty years later, even though none of the original residents were still living there. Communities themselves thus generated the amount of delinquency they would experience. The following outline summarizes this process.

1. Dilapidated areas create social disorganization. Cities such as Chicago were expanding industrially, their populations were exploding, and segregation was forcing the new immigrants into the slums. These immigrants did not know the city's geography or culture; they arrived with different languages and work experiences; and they immediately faced new and overwhelming problems of poverty, disease, and confusion.
2. Social disorganization allows cultural conflicts to arise. In the low-delinquency areas of the city, parents generally concurred on what values and attitudes were the "right" ones. They agreed on the importance of education, constructive leisure, and other child-rearing issues. These conventional goals and values were reinforced by local institutions such as

SOCIAL CONTROL AND DEVIANCE IN CUBA

Delinquency prevention has taken various forms and guises in the United States, from police patrols to Boy Scout troops. But it is clear that we have barely scratched the surface; a myriad of possibilities remains to be tried. Cuba has tried one of the most innovative ideas yet—it sends its youth out on military interventions to inspire patriotism, conformity, and revolutionary fervor.

Even though there has been an overwhelming amount of research and scholarly interest in the problem of juvenile delinquency, there has been a notable lack of discussion about these problems in Marxist societies. This deficiency is especially evident in the case of socialist countries other than the Soviet Union. . . . One point that should be mentioned is the feeling among many scholars that there could not possibly be a considerable amount of delinquency in a society under such tight control. [A closer look, however, shows that delinquency control is] not this simple. . . .

Cuban leaders, during the early stages of revolutionary rule, believed that they could make radical changes in the nation's culture and that social values could be transformed in much the same way as institutions were. They have learned, however, that institutional changes cannot be made so fast when they do not reflect the values held by the majority of the people. Likewise, radical changes in the fabric of society cannot be made without generating social disharmony, as evidenced by rising rates of divorce and delinquency. . . .

Cuban delinquency develops in many of the same forms and patterns found in other socialist and capitalist societies. It seems to be concentrated among lower-class urban, male youths, from broken or maladjusted homes, with low educational achievement. Property offenses form the largest category of juvenile crime, with consumer goods such as clothes, radios, and tape recorders being the articles most sought after by offenders. . . .Interesting features are the existence of gangs very similar in character to those found in capitalist societies and the influence of adults working in concert with juveniles. There do not seem to be any political motivations in Cuban delinquency except insofar as the government may label any antisocial act as being politically motivated.

Cuba is now in the midst of . . . increasing problems of urbanization. Overcrowding and shortages of consumer items are still felt among the urban population. . . . As Cuba develops its economy, new problems emerge. Shortages in available space in Cuban institutions of higher education will make entry progressively harder. Likewise, the need for skilled technicians and a bureaucratic cadre foretells the danger of creating new elite classes.

As armed threats from abroad and conflict have given way to stability and pragmatism, one of Cuba's main concerns seems to be the maintenance of revolutionary commitment among the youth who have not had to undergo the sacrifices of their elders. Recent Cuban foreign interventions have satisfied these concerns. [Another fear] is the possibility of generation gaps emerging, characterized by feelings of superiority among many of Cuba's youth.

Source: From *Social Control and Deviance in Cuba* by Luis Salas, pp. 14, 33–34. Copyright © 1979 Praeger Publishers. Reprinted by permission of Praeger Publishers.

the PTA, women's clubs, churches, and neighborhood centers. But no such consistency prevailed in high-delinquency areas. Although some people did promote the conventional value system, with the support of the churches and most families, these areas also contained people who held a criminal value system; they defined theft as an acceptable path to wealth. This value system could count on the support of criminal gangs, rackets, and semilegitimate businesses.

3. Cultural conflict allows crime and delinquency to flourish. Boys raised in low-socioeconomic, high-delinquency areas are exposed to both conventional and criminal value systems. They do not merely read or hear about criminal activities and organizations; they see them in operation on a daily basis. And successful criminals pass on their know-how to younger residents, who in turn teach those who are younger still. So delinquency becomes a tradition in certain areas. The term for this process is *cultural transmission.*
4. Allowed to flourish, delinquency becomes a full-time job or career. Boys dabble in delinquency very early in life, perhaps by age 5 or 6. Their initial offenses are trivial, but as the years go by, their acts become increasingly serious, and their delinquencies are almost always group efforts. Shaw claimed never to have met a delinquent whose first offense was committed alone. Eventually each youth learns to become a specialist and an expert in one particular kind of offense.

Shaw's and McKay's research findings were a vital contribution to understanding delinquency. Their theory was a great advance, too, but it is open to criticism. For example, the term "social disorganization" has often been pounced on by critics, who claim that areas where crime and delinquency flourish are not really disorganized at all; rather, they are organized to pursue criminal purposes. In fact, Shaw and McKay were well aware of this; some high-crime areas are indeed organized in this sense.

Shaw and McKay could more deservedly be criticized for seeing criminal careers, specialization, and expertise as inevitable. We will consider the career issue later; for now, we will discuss specialization. Delinquency is not an activity of large companies or government bureaucracies; it is not organized so that each worker is assigned a specific role to be performed for decades. Even organized crime allows its personnel to dabble in a variety of trades. Vincent Teresa (1973), for instance, revealed in his autobiography that as a member of the Patriarca "family" in New England, he engaged in murder, burglary, illegal gambling, black marketeering, con artistry, fencing, grand larceny, bank robbery, and counterfeiting. Bruce Jackson's book about the lives of criminals points in the same direction. He first planned to write chapters on drugs, robbery, punks, hustling, and so on. "But it all melds together; they're not separate in the life and there seemed no way . . . to separate them here" (1972:7). Adult criminals thus tend to be dilettantes, generalists; if they are, then delinquents are almost certain to be. And they are, as many researchers have pointed out. For example, a researcher studying delinquency in Flint, Michigan, wrote:

> Flint youngsters simply do not specialize. Among the 100 most delinquent of them, the fewest different varieties of offenses committed by anyone was four, and there were only 5 youngsters of the 100 who committed as few as four kinds (Gold, 1970:33).

The evidence on expertise also raises some doubts about the Shaw-McKay theory. Some of this evidence, ironically, comes from Shaw's most famous work, *The Jack Roller* (1930) (a "jack roller" is a person who commits strong-arm robbery against drunks and bums). This is a book about Stanley, a boy taught delinquent techniques by William, his half-brother, and Tony, the local gang leader. Stanley acquired a great deal of experience while young; he was arrested twenty-three times before he was 10. But despite all of his experience and first-hand instruction, Stanley never became an expert, never became a professional criminal, never joined a criminal organization. He did not progress beyond jack-rolling, at which he remained amateurish at best. After doing it for ten years, Stanley was foolish enough to rob a sleeping drunk and get arrested the next day in the same neighborhood while wearing the drunk's stolen trousers. Stanley is not unusual. According to Jackson, "With rare exceptions, people do not go to jail because they are guilty of something; they go to jail because they are too dumb or broke or clumsy or unlucky to stay out" (1972:3). Finally, there is the experience of two bank robbers cited in the memoirs of a con artist.

> The Marucca brothers were bank robbers. One time they decided to blow open a safe. . . . They used so much dynamite there was nothing left when they finished but a hole in the ground. They blew up the whole building.
>
> The best story I heard about Steven Marucca was when him and his brother went down through the roof of the First State Bank. . . . They see they're going to have to work all weekend . . . there's a lot to steal. Steve decides he'd better call his wife, Marie, and tell her he won't be home for a while. There's a phone

> that goes direct to the police station. If Joe don't stop him, he'd've picked up the phone in the vault and tried to call his wife (Lepara and Goodman, 1974:178–179).

Such evidence makes one skeptical about claims that offenders invariably become specialists and experts.

Nevertheless, Shaw and McKay's thesis has strongly influenced contemporary sociological thinking about juvenile delinquency. And while their works do have shortcomings, they broadened the focus of explanation beyond biological and psychological factors to include sociological and cultural ones. And their contributions are so extensive that each of the main sociological theories of today owes some ideas and inspiration to Shaw and McKay.

Edwin Sutherland

Another member of the Chicago school is Edwin Sutherland, whose most famous contribution to the study of juvenile dilenquency is his theory of *differential association,* first presented in 1939. Sutherland seems to have been strongly influenced by his talks with a professional thief, whom he refers to by the alias "Chic Conwell."

> I had worked for several years with a professional thief and had been greatly impressed by his statement that a person cannot become a professional thief merely by wanting to be one; he must be trained in personal association with those who are already professional thieves. There I seemed to see in magnified form the process that occurs in all crime (Sutherland, 1973:17).

Differential association theory is thus a process theory; it details the experiences a person must go through in order to become a delinquent. To arrive at his theory, Sutherland generalized from the professional thief's experiences to those of *all* offenders (including delinquents).

The theory was first presented in 1939, revised in 1947, and zealously defended thereafter by Donald Cressey, Sutherland's student, coauthor, and successor. The first principle of the theory is that delinquent behavior is *learned.* Sutherland thus rejected biological and hereditary factors as possible causes. He claimed that only a sociological explanation could account for a person's involvement in delinquency. The first point also dismisses the idea that an individual might think of committing an offense without being taught.

The second principle of Sutherland's theory states that delinquent behavior is learned while *communicating with others in intimate groups.* Over the years, movies, newspapers, television, and comic books have all been blamed for provoking delinquency, but Sutherland and Cressey (1978) believe that only small, face-to-face gatherings really have an influence; they would thus focus on family or peer groups as the most likely sources of initiation into delinquent values and activities. The third principle claims that the learning process includes two different elements: *techniques* (how to commit offenses) *and attitudes or rationalizations* (how to justify the offenses to oneself and others).

Sutherland's fourth principle states that rationalizations and attitudes toward the law are *learned from people whom we associate with and who hold attitudes that favor either obeying the laws or violating them.* Examples of attitudes favoring law violation are common, especially with respect to smoking marijuana, which is illegal. People opposed to the laws assert that such restrictions are senseless and discriminate against the younger generation, that marijuana does no more harm than alcohol, and that lawmakers are uninformed or "killjoys." Sutherland's fifth principle is the heart of differential association theory; it states that *people who are exposed more to verbal signs and suggestions favoring law violation than to ones favoring obedience will break the law.* Thus, parents who even hint that it is acceptable to fight, to treat women as potential conquests, to cheat on income tax returns, or to lie may foster delinquent children unless these comments are outnumbered by statements that favor obeying laws.

Finally, Sutherland mentions the factors of duration, priority, intensity, and frequency. The longer and earlier youths are exposed to a set of attitudes about delinquency (pro or anti), the more influenced they will be. Sutherland used the term "intensity" to refer to the degree of respect a person gives to some role model or associate. Thus, Sutherland argued, prison guards are not likely to become socialized into crime, despite all the positive things inmates have to say about a life of crime, because the guards do not respect or admire the inmates and therefore do not adopt their beliefs, values, and attitudes (Sutherland, 1973).

Sutherland's differential association theory has had a profound effect on crime and delinquency theory, although he developed it more than forty years ago. Perhaps the clearest sign of its acceptance is the variety of attempts to test or critique it (for example, Glueck, 1956; Short, 1957; Korn and McCorkle, 1959; Clinard, 1959). According to Gibbons (1979:56), "Sutherland's formulation has been the most popular [causal] perspective in American criminology." It pleased sociologists because it was explicitly sociological, general, and unified.

But popularity also brought criticisms, some serious and some rather frivolous (Cressey, 1969). Some researchers, for instance, complain that the key element of the theory (differential association) is untestable. To measure this, researchers would have to be constantly on the spot to count how many prodelinquency expressions and how many antidelinquency ones the individual hears over a period of months or years. This would be impossible.

A second criticism focuses on the time sequence: which comes first, differential association or delinquency? Some criminologists believe that delinquency occurs first; only later do delinquent youths select other delinquents as associates. Sutherland, though, insists that associates are chosen first, and then they socialize (or influence) each other into becoming delinquents. Research by Kandel (1978), mentioned in Chapter 5 with respect to peer influence, suggests two points: (1) friends' behavior is not an especially powerful predictor of an individual's delinquency and (2) influence (differential association) contributes no more to the relationship than does selection (picking associates who are delinquent *after* becoming delinquent oneself).

Perhaps the third most important charge leveled against differential association theory is that it implies that much more delinquency will occur than actually does.

> If delinquents were in fact radically differentiated from the rest of conventional youth in that their unseemly behavior was constrained through compulsion or commitment [to delinquent values], then involvement in delinquency would be more permanent and less transient, more pervasive and less intermittent than is apparently the case. . . . This accounting for too much delinquency may be taken as an observable consequence of the distorted picture of the delinquent that has developed . . . (Matza, 1964:21–22).

Differential association thus is faulted because it is completely unable to account for the facts that even the most delinquent youngsters are usually nondelinquent and that most youngsters eventually grow out of delinquency as they get older. Finally, one may question the truth of Sutherland's claim that delinquency requires a long period of instruction. How much training is needed to engage in fist fights, to commit acts of vandalism, or to steal hubcaps? Perhaps one of the most attractive elements about being a delinquent is how *little* learning it takes. As the research cited earlier suggests, low IQs are not a hindrance to committing offenses.

Walter Miller

Walter Miller is not a product of the University of Chicago, but his ideas are somewhat similar to the Chicagoans'. Much of his contribution focuses on delinquent gangs (see Chapter 5). Some of his research methods were interesting; for instance, he sometimes relied on unobtrusive observation (the subjects did not know he was collecting data about them). He would go to a pizza parlor, buy some food, sit down in a booth, and pretend to be completely absorbed in his meal and his newspaper. But in fact he was listening carefully to what the youths there were talking about. He took extensive notes that he later mined for theoretical nuggets. He came up with the following:

1. The lower class has a distinctive family structure. Most social scientists agree that social class has three elements: the occupational prestige of the father or both parents, the family income, and the parents' level of

education. Walter Miller, however, has substituted his own quite idiosyncratic view, in which social class is determined by family arrangement. Specifically, he says lower-class families are characterized by female-based households and serial monogamy. Women run the household, and they go through a series of husbands or lovers. Because there are inevitably periods when no man is in their lives, they have to fend for themselves and their children.

2. This family structure alienates boys, leading them to join all-male peer groups. Miller believes that boys grow up with the traditional belief that a boy ought not to be told what to do by his mother, aunt, or older sister. With no father or husband present, however, the boy is indeed subject to the control and authority of women. Resenting this, he seeks the company of other males who congregate on the corner or in other gathering places. In Miller's era, one of the favorite such places among lower-class boys was the pool hall.
3. In these all-male peer groups, the lower-class culture is created and transmitted. Boys form values and standards which mirror those of lower-class culture in general. While most social scientists see cultural items (material and nonmaterial) as traveling downward from the middle to the lower class, Miller says they travel upward. He says that 15 percent of the American population is "hard-core" lower class but that a total of 50 percent of the population is influenced by lower-class culture.
4. The lower-class culture, which is centuries old, revolves around six focal concerns: trouble, toughness, smartness, excitement, fate, and autonomy. These issues monopolize lower-class consciousness. Miller notes that middle-class people tend to judge each other in terms of achievement and its symbols. But there is little of this in the lower class, so people there tend to judge people by how much trouble they get into. Some members of the lower class claim that they want to avoid trouble with the law, but Miller says they covertly seek it. Members of criminal and delinquent gangs seek trouble overtly.

   Toughness, the second lower-class concern, includes physical strength, "macho" masculinity (scorn for the arts and sentimentality, plus treating women as objects), and bravery. The intense emphasis on toughness seems to be an overreaction to the absence of an adult male in the family. Smartness refers to the ability to outfox people on the street corner, to learn and take advantage of the weaknesses of one's opponents. Excitement, the fourth focal concern, involves a search for thrills, danger, or risk, prompted in part by the long periods of boredom and routine that lower-class people experience. Excitement often includes the use of alcohol and other drugs, trying to pick up women, and fights over women or gambling.

   Fate is another concern of lower-class people. Believing that they cannot control their future by setting and achieving goals, they turn to gambling, where they hope to hit the jackpot and avoid the drudgery of a conventional work life. Finally, there is autonomy. On the overt level, these people express resentment about external controls. Common expressions are "No one's gonna push *me* around" and "I'm gonna tell him he can take the job and shove it . . ." (Miller, 1958:12). But, on the covert level, they actually seek out restrictive settings where they are told what to do, because they identify these strong controls with being cared for.

5. Identifying with the focal concerns of lower-class culture leads to violations of the law. Lower-class adolescent boys in gangs get into trouble simply because they live up to the standards presented to them in lower-class culture.

Miller's theory is interesting and fairly original. There are a few questions, however, that can be raised about it. First of all, Miller implies that the United States has a large permanent underclass. This is questionable. Research for the years 1962 and 1973 has shown that when sons are compared with fathers, 40 percent of the sons were upwardly mobile (and only about 18 percent were downwardly mobile); furthermore, opportunities increased more for blacks than for whites (Featherman, 1979). Second, Miller implies that middle-class values have no impact at all on lower-class people. This is difficult to believe, given the large number of lower-class children exposed to middle-class images in school and on television. Third, Miller implies that lower-class gang members are thoroughly indoctrinated into lower-class culture and immune to middle-class values. Short and Strodtbeck (1965), however, found that lower-class gang members evaluate significant features of middle-class life just as highly as other boys do, including boys who are middle-class nondelinquents. And lower-class gang members do not evaluate elements of delinquent subcultures very positively. Finally, we presented data in Chapter 3 that showed that broken homes or female-based households are not very important factors in delinquency, particularly among boys and nonwhites.

ANOMIE THEORIES

Anomie theories are not based upon extensive field research. Rather, they were conceived by intellectual theorists (Merton, Cohen, Cloward and Ohlin) who were all products of or professors at Harvard or Columbia University. Neither school required its scholars to immerse themselves in the everyday lives of the common person. The city was not their laboratory; field research was not their specialty. Thus, anomie theory is different in many respects from the theories we associate with the Chicago school tradition.

Robert K. Merton

Robert K. Merton may never have met a delinquent. Indeed, he has shown remarkably little interest in crime and delinquency aside from one classic article, "Social structure and anomie" (1938), which he later expanded into a chapter in his book *Social Theory and Social Structure* (1957). Merton began this work with an enlightening discussion of the Robber Barons, a group of men—including John D. Rockefeller, Andrew Carnegie, John Pierpont Morgan, and Cornelius Vanderbilt—who built vast corporate empires and amassed huge fortunes in the late nineteenth century, sometimes by illegal means. The Robber Barons are as essential to understanding Merton's theory as "Chic Conwell," the professional thief, was to understanding Sutherland's.

According to Merton, American society has (1) cultural goals that are generally regarded as worth striving for and (2) institutionalized means or approved ways of reaching these goals. Merton argues that the main goal among Americans is wealth or financial success and that the socially approved means of achieving it include training, education, and a steady job. But the emphasis in America has been stronger on the goals than on the approved means. This imbalance between goals and means creates *anomie*—a breakdown of societal rules.

When anomie sets in, *innovators* have a chance to act. These are people who strive for the goals but do not value the rules or the approved means because society as a whole is not very rule-conscious. "The ends justify the means" becomes the ruling principle. The Robber Barons were among the most successful of the innovators; they used practically any means to gain wealth, including counterfeiting, embezzling, stock manipulation, hiring gangs to beat up opponents, building up monopolies, gouging customers, and corrupting government at all levels.

After introducing this line of argument, Merton turns away from the Robber Barons. He notes that official statistics show that most crime and delinquency is committed by people in the lower class. He thus argues (1) that people in the lower class want wealth and financial success as much as members of other classes do, (2) that people in the lower class are not allowed to use the legitimate or institutionalized means, and thus (3) some of them turn to illegitimate means, such as instrumental theft (theft to acquire something quite valuable or to make a large amount of profit), especially since (4) American society does not really emphasize the importance of obeying social rules.

Merton went on to point out that when society is in a state of anomie, several reactions, or "modes of adaptation," are possible besides innovation. These are conformity, ritualism, retreatism, and rebellion. Conformists accept the cultural goals and the institutionalized means. This is the most common response, even in anomic societies. Ritualism involves accepting the institutionalized means but rejecting the cultural goals. These people are not usually considered deviant. They scale down their aspirations and abide

TABLE 7–1
Frequency of Self-Reported Delinquency

Rank	Activity	Frequency
1.	Drinking	45,615
2.	Marijuana	36,872
3.	Smoking	33,802
4.	Drunkenness	28,159
5.	Truancy	13,858
6.	Defying parents	8,774
7.	Drugs	6,113
8.	Shoplifting	2,869
9.	Vandalism	1,532
10.	Petty theft	1,231
11.	Burglary	1,094
12.	Assault	632
13.	Running away	433
14.	Fights	413
15.	Auto theft	304
16.	Grand theft	246
17.	Robbery	232
18.	Armed robbery	137

Source: Erickson and Jensen, 1982:269.

almost compulsively by institutional norms (Merton, 1957). Retreatism involves rejecting both the cultural goal of getting ahead and the approved means. "In this category fall some of the adaptive activities of psychotics, autists, pariahs, outcasts, vagrants, vagabonds, tramps, chronic drunkards, and drug addicts" (Merton, 1957:153). Rebellion involves rejecting the goals and means and substituting completely new ones for them. But the most important mode of adaptation is innovation.

Does Merton have a valid case when he generalizes from the Robber Barons to juvenile delinquents? Some research casts doubt on this theory. For instance, many offenses committed by juveniles net them very little or no money, as Table 7–1 indicates. Of the eighteen delinquent acts in this self-report study, the only promising money producers seem to be burglary, grand theft, robbery, and armed robbery. These are among the less common delinquent acts; they rank eleventh, sixteenth, seventeenth, and eighteenth, respectively. Delinquency does not seem to be the lucrative career Merton claimed.

Albert Cohen

Albert Cohen, who both criticized and built upon Merton's work, is a crucial figure in modern juvenile delinquency theory. In the 1940s and 1950s, delinquency theory was not a stimulating area of study. No one was offering important ideas to advance beyond the earlier works of Shaw and McKay, Sutherland, and Merton. Then, in 1955, Cohen offered an interesting explanation of why boys turn to delinquent behavior. The response to his book *Delinquent Boys* was overwhelmingly favorable; and those few critics who disagreed with it felt compelled to construct rival theories of their own (for example, Walter Miller). Thus, one of Cohen's greatest contributions to delinquency theory was that he almost singlehandedly revived it.

Cohen's theory has been called a parable (Simon et al., 1976)—a simple, glib story with an obvious moral. There is much to be said, however, for theories that are so clearly and concisely written: theories are supposed to simplify reality. Cohen begins his story by describing what he believes to be the main characteristics of delinquents: that they are malicious, negativistic, and nonutilitarian. Their activities show that they have other traits as well, which Cohen terms versatility, short-run hedonism, and group autonomy.

Malicious behaviors are committed out of spite. Delinquent boys, according to Cohen, get their kicks from tormenting nondelinquent children, driving them out of playgrounds and gyms or chasing them home after school every day. They show the same kind of spite or malice toward their schools and teachers. Delinquents also are *negativistic*; that is, they think that their behavior is right precisely because it is wrong according to the norms or rules of the larger culture. The term *nonutilitarian* describes activities that do not produce a direct economic benefit. Cohen says delinquents steal things that they do not plan to eat, wear, or use. They simply steal for "the hell of it." Cohen's position—that delinquents are out for kicks—directly contradicts Merton's view that they are involved in instrumental theft.

Versatility refers to the wide variety of delinquent activities in which these boys dabble: stealing, vandalism, trespassing, truancy, and so on. They do not specialize in one activity. (On this point, Cohen disagrees with Shaw and McKay.) *Short-run hedonism* means that these boys are impatient, impetuous, and out for fun. They don't take kindly to rules, schedules, or organization, nor do they plan ahead, study, or practice. Future gains and goals are of no significance to them; they live for the moment. Finally, *group autonomy* refers to Cohen's belief that delinquents are close to the other members of the gang but hostile to outsiders such as parents, teachers, and other authorities. Cohen adds that delinquency is a male, urban, lower-class phenomenon. Having thus outlined the characteristics of delinquents, Cohen next explains how these traits were acquired.

He notes that Americans have different ways of evaluating their children. People such as middle-class parents, teachers, and social workers apply a set of values or standards which Cohen calls the "middle-class measuring rod." All children, not just middle-class children, are expected to live up to these. To his credit, Cohen is very explicit about what these values are:

1. "Ambition is a virtue; its absence is a defect and a sign of maladjustment. . . . It means . . . an orientation to long-range goals and long-deferred rewards. It means an early determination to 'get ahead' " (1955:88).
2. "The middle-class ethic is one of individual responsibility. It applauds resourcefulness and self-reliance, a reluctance to turn to others for help" (1955:89).
3. "Middle-class norms place a high evaluation on . . . skills and on . . . tangible achievements . . ." (1955:89).
4. "Industry and thrift . . . are admirable . . ." (1955:90).
5. "Rationality is highly valued, in the sense of the exercise of forethought, conscious planning, the budgeting of time . . ." (1955:90).
6. "The middle-class value system rewards and encourages the rational cultivation of manners, courtesy, and personability" (1955:90).
7. "The middle-class ethic emphasizes the control of physical aggression and violence, which are subversive of good personal relations . . ." (1955:91).
8. "One should not 'waste' time but spend his leisure time 'constructively' " (1955:91).
9. "Lastly, middle-class values emphasize 'respect for property.' . . . Things are to be husbanded, treated carefully, not wantonly wasted, carelessly abused, or destroyed" (1955:91–92).

Not all children find it easy to conform to these standards. Middle-class children, who (according to Cohen) learn these values at home, may live up to them effortlessly. But lower-class children often are not taught these standards (or not taught them as well) and may have greater difficulty adopting them.

At school, all children, regardless of their social class, are judged by their ability to follow these middle-class rules. Children who cannot do so tend to lose status or prestige. Teachers look down on them, as do many of their fellow students. So what do these lower-class youngsters do? First, several boys frustrated by their low status may get together and discuss what they can do about it. Cohen suggests that one solution they will consider is a delinquent subculture, a set of values and standards that completely reverses the middle-class norms. By making a complete change—from accepting middle-class norms to totally rejecting them (a process Cohen calls "reaction formation")—the youths would actually gain status in the eyes of lower-class peers. But they lose any respect they had in the wider society, and, once delinquent, they cannot turn back. In a nutshell, then, Cohen sees delinquency as a male, lower-class, subcultural phenomenon produced by status frustration and inability to live up to middle-class standards. It gets expressed as hostility toward middle-class norms and institutions: malice, negativism, and so on.

Critics have taken Cohen to task on several grounds. Perhaps the greatest weakness in his theory is his idea of "reaction formation." Frankly, there is little or no evidence that boys in the delinquent subculture completely and suddenly reject middle-class norms at some point to form their own diametrically opposite rules. Conversions like these are exceedingly rare. Much more reasonable suggestions are offered by Rodman (1963) and Rainwater (1970). Rodman says that people in the lower class share the middle-class values but "stretch" them to adjust to their impoverished and deprived situation. Rainwater adds, along the same lines, that people in the lower class "will live up to the norms if they possibly can" (1970:142).

Richard Cloward and Lloyd Ohlin

Cloward and Ohlin, like Cohen, view delinquency as a lower-class urban phenomenon. And like Merton, they say that delinquency occurs because of the great disparity between what such youths are taught to want and what is actually available to them. Youths who join a delinquent subculture want to achieve success, but since their legitimate path is blocked, they turn to illegitimate means—delinquency and eventually crime.

Cloward and Ohlin say that lower-class youngsters who want to make a lot of money but remain with their lower-class friends are the ones most likely to join the delinquent subculture. They want, in the terminology of the 1940s and 1950s, "big cars, flashy clothes, and swell dames" (Cloward and Ohlin, 1960:96). They do not have a compelling urge to acquire a middle-class status or way of life.

When a lower-class male adolescent senses that he is not headed toward financial success in later life, he may blame his failure on society or on himself. If he blames society, he will probably become alienated from it and consider its rules illegitimate, especially if he thinks he is capable and deserving of success; he will believe his failure is due primarily to the fact that the social system is closed, unfair, and discriminatory. If he feels this way, he may join a delinquent subculture where the rules are regarded by members as the only legitimate rules. Boys who discuss their alienation will soon come to realize how isolated they are from the rest of society, a realization that prompts them to become closer, more cohesive, more dependent on each other.

One of Cloward and Ohlin's two major contributions is their claim that there are three different kinds of delinquent subcultures. The other is their idea that just as there are differences in the availability of legitimate opportunities, there also are differences in the availability of illegitimate ones. Not everyone who wants to be a surgeon can become one, nor can everyone who wants to become a racketeer.

The kind of delinquent subculture that develops depends on the nature of the community and the opportunities it has to offer. One delinquent subculture is the *criminal* one. Here, there are illegitimate opportunities to become reasonably wealthy because the community has (1) adult role models

BROKEN EARTH

Cloward and Ohlin's theory can be applied widely, if it is altered slightly. Hostility and delinquency can erupt as a result of many different kinds of blocked opportunities. In the following excerpt about China, we read that youths are blocked from moving into a more promising environment—the city.

[One] factor holding down rural crime committed by youth is that even the most rambunctious youngsters suddenly find themselves saddled with grown-up responsibilities at the age of 16, when most begin work. After a punishing day of such activities as spreading buckets of mud weighing 50 pounds each over mulberry fields as fertilizer, few have the reservoirs of restless adolescent energy that lead to serious delinquency.

The one potentially violent crime that happened to me in China smacked more of youthful high jinks than deliberate violence. I was driving the road toward the famed resort city of Guilin. . . . Night had come quickly. About an hour outside of Guilin, a trailer parked on the right-hand side of the road came into the sweep of my headlights. In a moment we were up to it. I had caught a sense of vague, shadowy motion behind the trailer, so I gave it a wide berth, swinging far to the left. All at once, the night exploded. The road lit up momentarily as if a flare had been fired, and I heard a heavy whomp next to my ear. Etched on my retina was the image of a group of men, six in all, who had been standing in the lee of the trailer. I instinctively hit the brakes, but my driver yelled at me not to stop.

"What in the son of a turtle's egg was that?" I shouted, lapsing into the vernacular.

My driver, looking as grim as I was shaken, explained that groups of youth frequently lurk on the edges of roads at night and throw bottles, rocks and homemade cannon crackers at passing trucks. . . .

"If they just break your windshield or dent your fender, you can consider yourself fortunate. What we drivers really worry about is taking a shot in the head and having a possibly fatal crash. That's why most drivers keep their windows rolled up even on stuffy nights."

I quietly rolled my window up.

Trucks are inviting targets for casual vandalism, my driver went on to explain. There can be no reprisals from the driver, who, outnumbered five or ten to one, an only curse and continue on his way. . . . Truck drivers represent the freedom and opportunity that sedentary rural youth yearn for, the chance to go to the cities, to travel without restrictions, and the chance to work with machinery instead of their bare hands. This contrast fuels the resentment that occasionally ignites in rock-throwing incidents.

Source: Reprinted with permission of Free Press, a Division of Macmillan, Inc., from *Broken Earth* by Steven W. Mosher, pp. 152–153.

(successful adult criminals); (2) integration of age levels, so younger people learn how to commit offenses and how to handle themselves when they get caught; (3) cooperation between offenders and supposedly legitimate people in the community such as bail bondsmen, lawyers, and politicians; and (4) control of delinquents by adult criminals who make them cut down on unnecessary violence in favor of strictly money-making offenses.

A second kind of delinquent subculture is the *conflict* type. This type arises in disorganized slums, where many people move in and out, and where social and cultural rootlessness and conflict occur. Here, children are deprived of legitimate *and* illegitimate opportunities to achieve success. Adult criminals in the neighborhood are unsuccessful. There is no integration of different age levels, because older offenders have no impressive knowledge to pass along to younger ones. There is little cooperation between offenders and legitimate members of the community because local lawyers and politicians do not stand to gain by assisting adult criminals who are abject failures. Finally, adult criminals have neither the ability nor the inclination to make delinquents in the neighborhood reduce their violent activity. The lack of opportunities to succeed frustrates these boys. To vent their frustrations and to win a reputation for toughness, they turn to violence.

The third subculture is the *retreatist.* Some youngsters are eager to succeed in the criminal or conflict subculture, but they do not meet the standards. Nor do they live up to the requirements of the conventional culture. They find it impossible to make a name for themselves in any line of activity they attempt. They are "double failures." Eventually, they give up and turn to drugs—heroin in particular.

Thus, Cloward and Ohlin believe that delinquency stems from pressures to succeed and obstacles members of the lower class face in trying to succeed. Presumably, if there were equal opportunities for them to succeed via legitimate means, their delinquency rates would go down. This was the dominant ideology of the 1960s and the impetus for Mobilization for Youth, a program designed to provide jobs and organize lower-class communities.

Cloward and Ohlin's book *Delinquency and Opportunity* was well written and immensely popular during the 1960s and 1970s. And it has received some support from research in the field. Short et al. (1965) found that gang delinquents are more likely than other boys to think their opportunities are limited; they are more likely to agree to these statements: (1) "It's hard for a young man in our area to get a good paying honest job" and (2) "In this area it's hard to make much money without doing something illegal." On the other hand, all research casts doubt on the idea that delinquents are ambitious strivers. Invariably, these studies show that delinquent youths have lower-than-average levels of educational and occupational aspirations. All the theories in this chapter assume that delinquency is overwhelmingly a lower-class phenomenon, but as we have shown in the discussion on family and delinquency, the only type of delinquency in which the lower class is more active is predatory crimes against persons. Thus, all of the theories in this chapter are hampered and undermined by their reliance upon official data (which have shown class and delinquency to be related). Had the theorists known what we know now about class and delinquency, they would not have made the fundamental mistake of pinning their whole explanation on the assumption that delinquency is dominated by one class.

SUMMARY

The "scientific" study of delinquency in America began at the University of Chicago, a school founded by Rockefeller largesse and stimulated by a rapidly growing city. There, Shaw and McKay launched a series of studies that rejected earlier biological and psychological theories and that focused instead on the surrounding community. They depicted delinquency as a natural succession of stages boys pass through, particularly boys living in the zone in transition, where the newest immigrants settled. In this area of cultural diversity, poverty, and disorganization, criminal values and behavior were readily apparent to the local boys. And a life of crime and delinquency was an ever-present option, at least as lucrative and attractive as a conventional career.

Sutherland, also trained at Chicago, contributed the theory of differential association, a process theory that describes the way that delinquent behavior and values are learned. To Sutherland, the key to learning delinquency was the attitudes and values transmitted by the people one knows most intimately—the family and the closest members of the peer group. If these people express attitudes favoring delinquency more often than not, then the person will adopt those attitudes and act accordingly.

Miller claims that there is a distinctive lower-class culture that has existed for centuries. This culture is transmitted verbally by boys who hang out on street corners and who are alienated from their female-controlled families. This culture emphasizes the focal concerns of trouble, toughness, smartness, excitement, fate, and autonomy. Identifying with these focal concerns automatically leads to involvement in delinquent activities.

The anomie perspective as developed by Merton is unlike the Chicago school. Merton does not believe that there is a separate lower-class culture. Instead, he argues that there is only one culture in America and it stresses wealth or financial success for all. Not all are able to achieve it, however, since the legitimate means to success are often restricted to the middle and upper classes, thus forcing lower-class people to give up the chase or to go about it in illegal ways, primarily instrumental theft.

Albert Cohen has tried to combine the anomie and Chicago school theories in his book *Delinquent Boys.* He theorizes that lower-class youths, often poorly prepared at home, go to school and find themselves looked down upon by teachers and many fellow students for their inability to live up to the values contained in the "middle-class measuring rod." Hurt by this failure, they join together and create their own values. They form a subculture around these new values and violate the old ones. Their behavior becomes malicious, negativisitic, and nonutilitarian.

Finally, Cloward and Ohlin offer another mixed model. They follow the Merton tradition by saying that lower-class boys are searching for wealth and its trappings. They are barred from the conventional means, so they turn to delinquency. And if they live in a community where adult crime is rampant and flourishing, the boys may have an opportunity to achieve the wealth they seek in a criminal subculture. But if the community is disorganized and the adult criminals there are obvious failures, then the illegitimate opportunities of a criminal organization are lacking, and the boys may turn to a conflict subculture of violence to win a reputation and vent their anger. If they cannot succeed in either of these subcultures, they may resort to a third delinquent subculture, the retreatist, where the goal of wealth is totally abandoned and life centers around drug use.

DISCUSSION QUESTIONS

1. According to Shaw and McKay, how do communities generate delinquency?
2. What have been the major criticisms of Shaw and McKay's work?
3. What is the focus of Sutherland's theory of differential association?
4. What role do rationalizations play in learning delinquent behavior?
5. Why has differential association theory been criticized as being untestable?
6. What focal concerns did Miller use to describe lower-class culture?
7. According to Merton, what are the causes of delinquency?
8. According to Cohen, what are the main characteristics of delinquents?
9. What is the importance of the "middle-class measuring rod" in Cohen's theory of delinquency?
10. What are the distinguishing features of the types of delinquent subcultures described by Cloward and Ohlin?

CRIME AS WORK

There is a persistent tendency to portray delinquents as very committed to a delinquent career and as extremely proficient in carrying out their delinquent tasks. But a closer look shows that much of the activity is more crude than skillful and occurs in a context of fun and daring rather than painstaking commitment.

Experienced criminals relate their early delinquent behavior with a good deal of humor. Their recollections dwell on the aspect of adventure—the humor having to do with what now appears to them to have been a preponderance of daring over ability.

Their early technical skills are described as simple applications of everyday knowledge. A safecracker, now age fifty, recalls the first safe he opened:

> I had—like we hit a safe in the meantime, you know. When we were just kids; we got the safe open, it was a very cheap safe. We got it open and we had—we had a pretty fair bank roll for kids, you know. About two hundred dollars apiece when we split it up—about two hundred. Why that was just—that was—I just turned fifteen about a week before. We took it (the safe) in one of these stores—a small general store, and it was a cheap safe.
> HOW DID YOU MANAGE TO OPEN IT? Well, we used two or three screw drivers, that's how bad the safe was—we kept stepping over, you know, till we got it open. STEPPING OVER—WHAT'S THAT? Well, we started on the corner, you know. And then we drove another one in, you know, and kept stepping till we got it open. (no. 32)

The absence of technical sophistication is evident in the following example of teen-age house burglary:

> LET'S LOOK, IN FACT, AT HOW YOU'D GOTTEN AROUND. HOW DID YOU CHOOSE A HOUSE TO ENTER? Well, that's what I say—like for a time I'd walk around. Like let's say in the———district. They built that new district there. I'd walk around and I'd see a house with all the lights out. Well, I'd go up and knock at the door. If nobody answered, then I'd know right away. Then, if somebody did answer, well I'd just say, "Does so-and-so live here?" and most people would say, "Well, no, I don't know that person." The majority of times when I did knock I knew nobody was home anyway, because the lights were all out.
>
> SO WHAT DID YOU DO IF NO ONE WAS HOME? Well, I'd go in through the back door; just make a hole through the window and open the door. JUST BREAK THE WINDOW. Yeh, with a rock. DID YOU HAVE TO CARRY ANY TOOLS WITH YOU? No. WHAT TIME OF DAY WOULD YOU DO THIS KIND OF STUFF? Oh, usually in the winter between seven and nine. Six, seven, nine—around there.
>
> OKAY, LET'S SAY YOU'VE KNOCKED ON THE DOOR, NO ONE ANSWERS, YOU WALK IN AND IT'S DARK. DO YOU HAVE A LIGHT WITH YOU, OR HOW DO YOU OPERATE? Well,

> sometimes I used to carry a flashlight. Sometimes I used to turn the light on in the house. I'd go in the bedroom, turn the light on, walk around and turn it back off. You see, I wasn't there that long; I was just looking for the money, and if I didn't find it I'd leave. . . .
>
> NOW, DURING THIS TIME, WERE YOU ALSO HOLDING DOWN A JOB OF SOME SORT?
>
> Yeh. I was working at different jobs—for a month, maybe three months. Then I'd get fired or I'd quit. So then I'd be broke again and then I'd go back to stealing again, 'cause I couldn't get a job right away. (no. 21)

Early B & E's are referred to as "kick-ins"—applying physical force to doors and windows. Such technical "skills" were not learned in any formal sense, though they may have been prompted by social pressure:

> And these guys were kicking joints in and everything; like, from school, and we were getting razzed about being sissies, so we acted, or reacted, I guess, and we got to be pretty tough eggs ourselves during the next, well—in my case, the next forty years, or thirty-five.

Another example quoting my notes taken during an interview with [informant] no. 14:

> Number 14 went to a fair in Regina one summer and ran into one of the guys he had met at reform school. This friend had introduced him to another person—a former boxer. "They were quite the characters." The three of them spent the week in Regina, just talking and fooling around, and one of them came back to Moose Jaw with him. While having coffee in a cafe, his friend spotted a safe on the other side of the counter and said, "Did you ever open a safe?" Number 14 answered, "No." "Well, we can open this one." Apparently no. 14 had been somewhat reluctant, but that night they came back and "We hammered it open." They were caught at this and sentenced to the Prairie Penitentiary.

The neophyte's learning consists in part of an understanding of what one can reasonably expect police to do in specific situations. By providing opportunity for the observation of police behavior, the delinquent experience forms the basis for future reaction to the police:

> Anyway, I go up and they (the police) say, "Your partner's given us his version of your story, now tell us what you know." Well, I didn't go for this, because being brought up in the slums and that, I was suspicious of anything they said, without even knowing this tack that they used—this ploy that they use. I was just naturally, I wouldn't believe anything they said anyway. Because it was a conditioned thing in me from that environment. That they were bad and you didn't believe anything they said.

Delinquency is also associated with the reformatory experience, which seems to be a first formal step in the direction of the criminal career. Not only does it segregate the delinquent from his nondelinquent peers, but reformatory conversation, as my respondent's comments indicate, centers around crime, perhaps even more than in jails and penitentiaries. The following is quoted from my notes taken during an interview with [informant] no. 11:

> Number 11 goes into a long discussion on card tricks. He mentions that he worked in a factory for three years and did part-time stealing on the side. He started using drugs and was arrested for illegal possession of narcotics and sentenced to six months in a reformatory, and in there he felt his criminal education began: "And I went to a reformatory, and in there I would say my criminal education began, partially, that is."
>
> It is interesting that although no. 11 had been consistently engaged in delinquency and crime, and was recognized in the factory as one associated with the criminal element, he states that it was in the reformatory where he got "educated": "In the shop that I was working at, that is, in the reformatory, I got talking to one guy about laying notes. And he showed me a couple of ways of laying notes, and explained to me how lucrative it could be. And various other ways of B & E, heel man. . . ."

[Informant] no. 27 states that, in 1943, he spent six years in a penitentiary, and that before this term he committed a wide variety of offences. In referring to the penitentiary sentence, he says:

> Well, incidentally, that's where my education in determining my future—I think you'll agree that up till now I was rather aimless, which I was, you know. But actually, I had grown pretty bitter in there—I done a lot of time in the hole. I must have done thirteen months in a stretch in the damper. And got my ass paddled—when I came out, I was determined to get hold of a bank roll. My first experience was with the military. This time—by this time, I was relatively broke—I had maybe a hundred dollars—and I had *no contacts* because I had been away too long. And I had to go to work. But before I could get—got to work, I had to get clearance from the army. And I got my call-up notice, and was rejected for medical psychiatric reason. (LAUGHS AT THIS.)
>
> I got cleared with the army and—and I worked in the shipyards as a rigger until I could get back on my feet. Now here's where the narcotics begins.

The above quotation indicates that, despite having committed a wide variety of offences, no. 27 considered himself as "aimless." By this he seems to mean he had not yet established any skill identity. This corresponds well with our previous definition of the "bum." The six year penitentiary stretch resulted in what we might call "career crystallization." He was bitter and determined to be less aimless regarding crime. This determination was hampered by the fact that, having been in prison for so long, he had lost his previous contacts with other offenders. Both for reasons of finance and association, he worked legitimately until "I could get back on my feet." At that point, he had developed connections with a drug trafficker who wished to use no. 27's skills as a burglar. From here on, his criminal activities, as well as his associations, took on a routine pattern. He was known by twelve of the persons I interviewed, and was clearly considered a "rounder."

Source: From the book *Crime as Work* by Peter Letkeman © 1973 by Prentice-Hall, Inc. Published by Prentice-Hall, Inc., Englewood Cliffs, N.J. 07632.

REFERENCES

BURGESS, ERNEST W.

1929 Urban areas in Chicago. Pp. 114–117 in T. V. Smith and L. D. White (eds.), *Chicago: An Experiment in Social Science Research*. Chicago: University of Chicago Press.

CLINARD, MARSHALL B.

1959 Criminological research. Pp. 510–513 in Robert Merton et al. (eds.), *Sociology Today*. New York: Basic.

CLOWARD, RICHARD A., AND LLOYD E. OHLIN

1960 *Delinquency and Opportunity*. New York: Free Press.

COHEN, ALBERT K.

1955 *Delinquent Boys*. New York: Free Press.

CRESSEY, DONALD R.

1969 Epidemiology and individual conduct. Pp. 557–577 in Donald R. Cressey and David A. Ward (eds.), *Delinquency, Crime, and Social Process*. New York: Harper & Row.

ERICKSON, MAYNARD L., AND GARY F. JENSEN

1982 Delinquency is still group behavior! Pp. 265–277 in Rose Giallombardo (ed.), *Juvenile Delinquency*. New York: Wiley.

FARIS, ROBERT E. L.

1967 *Chicago Sociology, 1920–1932*. Chicago: University of Chicago Press.

FEATHERMAN, DAVID L.

1979 Opportunities are expanding. *Society* 16 (March/April):4, 6–11.

FINESTONE, HAROLD

1976 *Victims of Change: Juvenile Delinquents in American Society*. Westport, Conn.: Greenwood Press.

GIBBONS, DON C.

1979 *The Criminological Enterprise*. Englewood Cliffs, N.J.: Prentice-Hall.

GLUECK, SHELDON

1956 Theory and fact in criminology: A criticism of differential association. *British Journal of Delinquency* 7 (October):92–109.

GOLD, MARTIN

1970 *Delinquent Behavior in an American City*. Belmont, Calif.: Brooks/Cole.

GREELEY, ANDREW M.

1976 *Ethnicity in the United States*. New York: Wiley.

JACKSON, BRUCE

1972 *In the Life: Versions of the Criminal Experience*. New York: New American Library.

KANDEL, DENISE B.

1978 Homophily, selection, and socialization in adolescent friendships. *American Journal of Sociology* 84 (September):427–436.

KORN, RICHARD R., AND LLOYD W. McCORKLE

1959 *Criminology and Penology*. New York: Henry Holt.

LEPARA, PATSY, AND WALTER GOODMAN

1974 *Memoirs of a Scam Man*. New York: Farrar, Straus & Giroux.

MATZA, DAVID

1964 *Delinquency and Drift*. New York: Wiley.

MERTON, ROBERT K.

1957 *Social Theory and Social Structure*. New York: Free Press.

1938 Social structure and anomie. *American Sociological Review* 3 (October):672–682.

MILLER, WALTER B.
1958 Lower-class culture as a generating milieu of gang delinquency. *Journal of Social Issues* 14 (Summer):5–19.
PARK, ROBERT, ET AL.
1928 *The City*. Chicago: University of Chicago Press.
RAINWATER, LEE
1970 The problem of lower-class culture. *Journal of Social Issues* 26 (Winter):133–148.
RODMAN, HYMAN
1963 The lower-class value stretch. *Social Forces* 42 (December):205–215.
SHAW, CLIFFORD R.
1938 *Brothers in Crime*. Chicago: University of Chicago Press.
1931 *The Natural History of a Delinquent Career*. Chicago: University of Chicago Press.
1930 *The Jack Roller*. Chicago: University of Chicago Press.
SHOEMAKER, DONALD J.
1984 *Theories of Delinquency*. New York: Oxford University Press.
SHORT, JAMES F., JR.
1957 Differential association and delinquency. *Social Problems* 4 (January):233–239.
SHORT, JAMES F., JR., AND FRED L. STRODTBECK
1965 *Group Process and Gang Delinquency*. Chicago: University of Chicago Press.
SHORT, JAMES F., JR., ET AL.
1965 Perceived opportunities, gang membership, and delinquency. *American Sociological Review* 30 (February):56–67.
SIMON, WILLIAM, ET AL.
1976 Continuities in delinquency research. Pp. 50–63 in James F. Short, Jr. (ed.), *Delinquency, Crime, and Society*. Chicago: University of Chicago Press.
SUTHERLAND, EDWIN H.
1973 *On Analyzing Crime*. Chicago: University of Chicago Press.
SUTHERLAND, EDWIN H., AND DONALD R. CRESSEY
1978 *Criminology*. Philadelphia: Lippincott.
TERESA, VINCENT
1973 *My Life in the Mafia*. Garden City, N.Y.: Doubleday.

NO
TRESPASSING

Sociological Theories: Control and Labeling

8

INTRODUCTION

Anomie and Chicago-school theories share some important characteristics: both originated in the 1930s, relatively early in the history of American sociology; both are still quite popular and respected; and both focus on motivations. Since these two types of theories are about half a century old, we might expect that they have been replaced by more up-to-date thinking in the intervening years. But age seems not to have dimmed their luster, and evidence of their continued acceptance is widespread. All current delinquency textbooks and anthologies, for instance, honor them with numerous references and discussions, and contemporary theorists feel compelled to draw upon them and to treat them with deference when proposing new ideas.

When we call the anomie and Chicago-school theories motivational theories, we mean that both identify factors that *pull* or *push* youngsters toward delinquency. In the Chicagoans' cultural transmission theory, the key factor is other people who portray crime and delinquency as acceptable. In anomie theory, the factor is ambition or the desire to succeed (coupled with limited legitimate opportunities to do so).

In recent decades, two more bodies of sociological theory have emerged. These are control and labeling theories, whose *main* statements were offered after 1950. These theories partly reflect their favored methodologies. Control theory relies on self-report questionnaires. Labeling theory, on the other hand, relies on field research—observing deviant behavior in the deviants' "natural habitat."

Relying on these methodologies means that control and labeling theorists do not depend on official data. This, in turn, means that their theories do not have to begin with the assumption that deviance and delinquency are dominated by the lower class or explain what motivates people in the lower class to deviate. It is probably accurate to say that control and labeling are not really motivational theories at all.

Control and labeling theories also are more modest than anomie and Chicago-school theories. For instance, Sutherland (a Chicagoan) claimed that any theory is inadequate (and therefore must be revised) unless *every case* under study fits the theory perfectly. Control theory, on the other hand, acknowledges that it cannot predict perfectly who will be delinquent and who will not. It also admits to being unable to say what motivates people to become delinquent. Labeling theory not only admits it cannot predict delinquency perfectly; it does not want to try. Becker (1963), for instance, questions whether criminologists should have any interest in what causes people to break the law.

However, in spite of the similarities between control and labeling theories, they also are different in many ways. Labeling theory has very little interest in the causes of crime and delinquency. It is much more concerned about how officials in the criminal justice system react to offenses and offenders. Labeling theory also takes a definite political stance: it is on the side of the offender or the accused ("the underdog"). It is highly critical of the justice system. This political position was very popular among graduate students and young professors in the 1960s because it fit in with their overall political attitudes. Control theory, on the other hand, has long been concerned with the causation of crime and delinquency. Official reaction is something control theorists ignore almost completely. And there is no rooting for the underdog; control theorists have not been explicitly political or anti-Establishment.

CONTROL THEORY

Stake in Conformity

In 1957, Jackson Toby published an article called "Social disorganization and stake in conformity: complementary factors in the predatory behavior of hoodlums." This title may seem odd because the concept of social disorganization is connected with the Chicago school, while "stake in conformity" is linked with control theory, and if we compare purists from each theory (say, Sutherland versus Hirschi) the two approaches are contradictory. But Toby is not a purist, nor are Shaw and McKay, who also discussed social disorganization; there are elements of control theory and Chicago-school theory in each.

Toby examines theft in America, and the following summary of his ideas is one example of an early control theory:

1. Most thefts are committed by adolescent boys from poor neighborhoods. Both low age and low income are conducive to theft because they are typically associated with weak external controls. Adolescents, for instance, are in the process of breaking away from family ties and supervision but have not yet settled into steady employment or marriage; they are in a very emancipated period of the life cycle. Low-income slum neighborhoods also exert little external control over people because they are filled with families who must face many problems, including

   > chronic warfare in the household; death, desertion, or serious illness of the breadwinner; mental deficiency or disease; alcoholism; gambling; promiscuity; or too many children for an unkskilled father to support or a harried mother to supervise. . . . Preoccupied with their difficulties, they are simultaneously ineffective parents and apathetic citizens (Toby, 1958:542–543).

   Because families in this type of neighborhood are so beset with personal crises, Toby claims, the neighborhood lacks unity, fails to prohibit illicit businesses from starting up, permits children to do as they please much of the time, and shows little interest in building up the community.

2. Poverty, apathy, and social disorganization in a neighborhood are not the only causes of delinquency. Education also is important. Toby traces a person's social standing to his or her performance in school: people who end up on the bottom of the socioeconomic heap do so "largely because they did poorly at school" (1958:544). Parents are important because they strongly affect the child's attitude toward school.

   > Parents who see to it that their son keeps up with his work in primary school may make it possible for him to pursue a business or professional career later. Parents who permit their boys to flounder in the early grades unwittingly cut them off from the main path of social ascent (1958:544).

   Without parental encouragement, even capable youngsters will do poorly in school because they will lack incentive. Uninterested students tend to find school unpleasant, so they annoy teachers, play truant, and cause disciplinary problems. Many later quit school, get low-level jobs, find them boring, and quit.

3. Boys who are not committed to education or work loaf or hang out together. Like everyone else, they sometimes have an impulse to steal things; but unlike most other people, they often act on their impulses because they have little stake in conformity.

> For those with social honor, disgrace is a powerful sanction. For a boy disapproved of already, there is less incentive to resist the temptation to do what he wants when he wants to do it. Usually, the higher the socioeconomic status of the family, the more the youngster feels he has to lose by deviant behavior (1958:546).

And people with much to lose are not likely to risk losing it by getting caught in a delinquent act.

Internal, Direct, and Indirect Controls

While Toby emphasized education as a central element in social control, F. Ivan Nye focuses on the family. Indeed, Nye is best known today as a family sociologist. Nye notes that in their early years, children have no concept of right or wrong and therefore break rules quite often. Even after they have learned rules, they may continue to break them because delinquency is a quick and easy way to get what one wants. Generally speaking, Nye thus believes that delinquency is natural; conformity, on the other hand, is not at all natural; it must be explicitly taught and encouraged, usually by parents. What prevents delinquency and fosters conformity is social control. There are three types of social control: internal, direct, and indirect.

Internal control refers to the absorption and acceptance of norms and rules by the child as if they were his or her own; in short, the child develops a conscience. Every society relies upon this occurrence as the primary form of social control. It is an ideal form of control because it goes with the child everywhere and costs nothing. Were it completely successful, no other forms of control would be necessary. But it is not.

Direct control is what most people think of when they hear the word "control." It includes prevention, supervision, sanctions, and rewards by external agents—parents, teachers, police, and others. Some sanctions—such as punishment, disapproval, and ostracism—may be informal. Parents also can impose restrictions such as keeping children at home, setting up curfews, and forbidding children to play with certain individuals. Nye argues that parents exercise more direct control over girls than over boys, which largely explains girls' lesser involvement in delinquency. But direct control has some important limitations. First, it works only when adults are observing the youth's behavior. Second, parents' direct control may become excessive, causing children to become annoyed, angry, and resentful. As a result, indirect control is undermined.

Indirect control refers to a person's affection for parents and other conventional figures. Liking these people ought to make a youngster less prone to engage in delinquency; among other reasons, the child does not want to embarrass those he or she likes.

> College students frequently state that they do not want to embarrass their parents by "getting into trouble," and even more often they do not want parents to be

hurt and disappointed in their failure. The same probably holds true for some siblings, peers, and adult friends. This indirect control, however, can be exercised only when there is an affectional relationship to the conforming individual (Nye, 1958:6).

Nye believes that the family is the most important influence in a child's life. But delinquency depends primarily on family attitudes and feelings, not family structure. Parents who cannot get along with each other, who are moody, irritable, and frequently at odds, will tend to make life unpleasant for the children, who may respond by trying to escape to a more pleasant environment among outsiders. Similarly, parent-child conflict may eventually spur a child to engage in delinquency. Nye is quick to say, however, that the crucial factor is how the child feels about the parents, not vice versa. When children reject their parents, delinquency is fairly common.

Nye also cites religion as an institution that may act as a form of social control over youngsters. He assumes that people who attend church regularly are socialized more effectively into the prevailing norms of society. The idea that religion offers a blueprint for conformity did not originate with Nye, of course; it dates back at least to the nineteenth century when Karl Marx berated religion for being an "opiate of the masses."

Finally, Nye discusses factors that affect the amount of freedom from the family an adolescent has. These include role changes and spatial mobility. Nye argues that, in general, youths who have a great amount of freedom are more able to engage in delinquency. Those who have little freedom are so frustrated that they also may commit more delinquency. Less delinquency occurs when children are accorded a moderate amount of freedom. Role changes occur in the transition from childhood to adulthood, and American society has no very clear signposts for determining when a person has passed from one status to the other. Adolescents are often eager to assume some of the benefits attached to the adult role, and parents are sometimes just as eager to keep them in the child role. This conflict can weaken parental control.

Spatial mobility is probably a more important factor than is generally supposed. Control theory assumes that the farther away from the family and peers a youth is, the more likely he or she is to "live it up." In a society where moving from place to place is common and parents are often not in the vicinity, delinquency should be correspondingly high, simply because supervision is so low that even if one is caught, the fact may never get back to one's parents.

Drifting into Delinquency

The American judicial system uses a simple decision model: the defendant is either guilty or not guilty. This clear-cut distinction has seeped into customary usage, and people nowadays are called criminals or delinquents as if their offenses were the crucial element of their personality—their *master status.* According to David Matza, another control theorist, delinquency theorists make the same mistake: they exaggerate the differences between delinquents and nondelinquents and imply that they are fundamentally two different species.

Matza says subcultural theorists (Miller, Cohen, and Cloward and Ohlin) see delinquents as part of a subculture that is completely committed to misdeeds, engaging in delinquency because they believe in ideas that require such behavior. These youths are normal in all respects except that they belong to this subculture, which teaches them it is right to be delinquent. Matza finds this hypothesis hard to believe.

Matza criticizes subcultural theories for failing to account for *maturational reform,* which refers to the fact that many youths engage in delinquency but reduce or stop such activity as they become older. Subcultural theories persistently maintain that youths are committed to misdeeds, having sworn to go out and steal, vandalize, and assault. Why do many delinquents modify their behavior as they reach the age of 20 or 25? Subcultural theories are unable to supply an answer.

Furthermore, Matza notes, if delinquents were really as committed to misdeeds as subcultural theories claim, they would engage in delinquency nearly all of their waking hours. In fact, even the most delinquent youths spend most of their time in conventional, nondelinquent activities; they devote relatively little time to delinquency. Matza cites other considerations that undermine subcultural theories. First, a truly antagonistic subculture must have the support of adults; children cannot realistically create one alone. And Matza maintains that parents are almost uniformly in favor of their children growing up to be nondelinquent. Even parents who engage in crime want their children to enter more respectable lines of activity. Second, Matza notes that many delinquents who are caught know they have done something wrong and feel sorry about it. They do not fit "the gross stereotype of the delinquent as a hardened gangster in miniature" (Matza, 1964:41).

If, as Matza says, delinquents think delinquency is wrong, why do they engage in it? Matza suggests that youths pick up cues in conversations with other youths that imply that these other youths really think delinquency is acceptable. The individual comes to believe that he or she is the only one who does not want to be delinquent. Thinking this way, he or she is reluctant to take the humiliating role of the "chicken," the one who backs out of a delinquent escapade, as in the following example:

> A possible plan was discussed as to how we might steal the package. Tom could go to the office and gain admittance on the pretense of looking for an important letter. Then Art and I, masked and armed, would rush in, tie Tom and the clerk, and make off with the package. We had lost sight of the fact that the package contained money. We were simply discussing the possibility of playing an exciting prank with no thought of actually committing it. We had played many harmless

pranks and had discussed them in much the same way before; but the knowledge that there was danger in this prank made it a subject to linger over.

After about an hour and a half of talk, I started to take off my shoes. As I unlaced them, I thought of how it looked as if I were the one to kill our interesting project. I foolishly said something to the effect that if Tom was going downtown, I thought I would write a letter that was already overdue. Tom was anxiously awaiting a letter that should be in that night. He suggested that I go down also as it was a very decent night. I consented and Art decided to join us. I sat down and wrote the letter—meanwhile we continued our talk about the money package.

My letter finished, something seemed to change. We found further inaction impossible: we had either to rob the post office or go to bed. Tom brought out his two guns; I hunted up a couple of regular plain handkerchiefs, and Art added some rope to the assortment. At the time we were still individually and collectively playing a game with ourselves. Each of us expected one of the other two to give the thing the horse laugh and suggest going to bed and letting the letters wait till morning. But it seemed that we forgot everything—our position in school, our families and friends, the danger to us and to our folks. . . .

"Have you got enough guts to go through with this thing?" I asked, turning to Art, who was behind me.

"If you have," he answered.

Frankly, I felt that I had gone far enough, but for some unknown reason I did not throw out a remark that would have ended it all then and there. And Art didn't. He later said that he was just too scared to suggest anything . . . (Thrasher, 1936:300–303).

Youths also can be delinquent without being committed to delinquency if they believe the circumstances are exceptional. Normally, such youngsters may accept conventional rules and laws but occasionally their acceptance of the law if overridden by some other factor, such as an attack on or a provocation of the youth. When this happens, the youth drifts between commitment to lawfulness and to delinquency. When the youth drifts in this way, delinquency is possible but not inevitable. Whether delinquency will occur depends on factors such as the youth's mood.

Bond to Society

Travis Hirschi took over from Matza, his mentor, and fashioned the most widely read version of control theory. In *Causes of Delinquency* (1969), he combined the principles of control theory with a painstaking empirical test of control theory, anomie theory, and the Chicago-school theory. According to Hirschi, delinquency should not be seen as a surprising phenomenon. Rather, it is something all of us would engage in if obstacles were not thrown in our path by a disapproving civilization. These obstacles or controls are chiefly attitudes that are quite effectively implanted in most people but less effectively instilled in others. These others have a relatively weak bond to society; their minds are not set so firmly against delinquent activities.

Hirschi mentions four ties to society: attachment, commitment, involvement, and belief. *Attachment* is an emotional element; it refers to the extent that a person cares about other people. *Commitment* is a more rational quality, referring to the degree of one's investment in conventional activities. *Involvement* refers to the time spent in conventional activities; if these occupy a youngster's entire day, delinquent incidents cannot take place. *Belief* (in the moral validity of conventional norms) is almost self-explanatory: people who think it is wrong to violate a particular law will probably not violate it.

Not only do different ties to society exist, but there also are different parts of society to which a person may be tied. Although "control theories sometimes suggest that attachment to any object outside one's self, whether it be the home town, the starry heavens, or the family dog, promotes moral behavior" (Hirschi, 1969:30), Hirschi thinks that the attachments most significant for predicting delinquency are those to parents, schools, and peers—the primary agents of socialization. Children attached to parents are less likely to become delinquent, Hirschi says, because positive feelings toward parents promote acceptance of the parents' values and beliefs; children avoid delinquency and other behavior that would jeopardize that affection. Hirschi's argument also applies to peers—that is, the closer one's ties to one's peers, the less delinquent one will be (even if one's friends are sometimes involved in delinquency). This directly contradicts the apparently more reasonable Chicago-school notion that closeness to delinquents makes a person more likely to engage in delinquency.

Hirschi's views on attachment to school were covered in Chapter 4, but we will summarize them again. He argues that attitudes toward schooling and teachers are an important intervening variable in the relationship between IQ and delinquency. Youths with high IQs generally receive better grades than other students do. Getting better grades in turn makes school a more interesting and enjoyable experience, so youngsters with better grades like school more than their peers do. Liking school makes it easier for them to accept or at least endure school rules and authority, which makes them less likely to engage in delinquency.

Commitment, unlike attachment, involves success, achievement, and ambition rather than respect, admiration, or identification. Anomie theory argues that thwarted ambition generates unbearable frustration, which causes delinquent behavior—theft, in particular. Control theory suggests, on the contrary, that ambition or motivation to achieve keeps people on the straight and narrow path, because they know that getting into trouble will hurt their chances of success.

Involvement in conventional activities was viewed as a means of preventing delinquency as early as Biblical times, when sages counseled that "idle hands are the devil's workshop." In modern times, such thinking has prompted city planners to call for more and better playgrounds to keep children off the streets, based on the assumption that if such facilities are available, youngsters will spend their time in them and have little time for delinquent pursuits.

Finally, Hirschi looks at belief in the moral validity of conventional norms. Quite simply, he maintains that there is only one belief system in America, and it centers around conventional values; there are no subcultures that regard theft and assault as proper or permissible. But there is variation in the acceptance of these conventional values; some people accept them strongly and others more weakly or lukewarmly. Those whose acceptance is weak feel relatively free to violate the norms, at least on occasion.

RESEARCH ON CONTROL THEORY

How well does control theory measure up against the pertinent research data? Some data, noted in Chapters 3–5, are consistently supportive of control theory (such as Sorensen's data linking parental attachment and nondelinquency in the realm of sexual behavior). But additional studies are worth mentioning. First, we should note the relevance of parental supervision to delinquency. Hirschi regards supervision as a kind of attachment; Nye calls it direct control. But whatever its name, parental supervision is a central element in control theory. In their research on Seattle youths, Hindelang et al. (1981) used the following items as measures of supervision:

1. As far as my father is concerned, I'm pretty much free to come and go as I please.
2. When you're away from home, does your father know where you are and who you're with?
3. As far as my mother is concerned, I'm pretty much free to come and go as I please.
4. When you're away from home, does your mother know where you are and who you're with?
5. I could stay away from home overnight and no one would ask me where I'd been.

Among white males, about one-half of those with minimal supervision committed twenty-one or more of the delinquent acts under study. By contrast, among those boys receiving the most supervision, only 11 percent were so involved in delinquency (see Table 8–1). Very similar results held for black males. (There were no data on females.) In an earlier study by Hindelang (1973) and in Hirschi's own research (1969), attachment to parents was measured more directly (as affection rather than supervision), and it proved a good predictor in both investigations: boys who identified with and respected their parents were noticeably less delinquent. Canter (1982) found that the

TABLE 8–1
Parental Supervision and Self-Reported Delinquency

	White Males			
	Least Supervised	**Level 2**	**Level 3**	**Most Supervised**
Very Delinquent	48%	27%	14%	11%
Not As Delinquent	52	73	86	89
	100%	100%	100%	100%
	Black Males			
	Least Supervised	**Level 2**	**Level 3**	**Most Supervised**
Very Delinquent	46%	18%	11%	11%
Not As Delinquent	54	82	89	89
	100%	100%	100%	100%

Source: Hindelang et al., 1981:129–130.

more a youth feels part of the family, the less delinquent he or she is likely to be. Conger (1976), however, found that attachment to parents discourages delinquency only if the parents react positively, not punitively, when communicating with the child.

As for attachment to peers, Hirschi (1969) found that the closer a boy is to his peers, the less delinquent he is likely to be. Linden and Hackler (1973) discovered that boys with close ties to conventional peers are indeed rarely delinquent. Those with more distant ties to conventional peers are twice as likely to engage in delinquency. On the other hand, what about closeness to deviant or delinquent peers? This question is absolutely crucial to Sutherland's differential association theory, which insists that closeness to deviant peers makes delinquency inevitable. In control theory, though, this issue is a minor one, but control theory says that closeness, even to deviant peers, fosters nondelinquency. The data in Table 8–2 are rather remarkable because

TABLE 8–2
Self-Reported Delinquency and Attachment to Peers

	Strong or Moderate Attachment to Deviant Peers	**Weak or No Attachment to Deviant Peers**	**Strong or Moderate Attachment to Conventional Peers**	**Weak or No Attachment to Conventional Peers**
Delinquent	27%	24%	19%	38%
Nondelinquent	73	76	81	62
	100%	100%	100%	100%

Source: Linden and Hackler, 1973:38.

they show that Sutherland and common sense are wrong; close ties to deviants do *not* make a person more delinquent. On the other hand, they do not make a person less delinquent either, so the data do not actually support control theory.

Occasionally, one reads in delinquency textbooks that attachment to peers in general makes a person more delinquent. The studies usually cited as evidence for this, however, do not really measure attachment to peers but factors such as whether a person would continue to associate with a friend who got in trouble (Elliott and Voss, 1974) or whether a person would hide a friend who was in trouble (Empey and Lubeck, 1971). These studies measure tolerance of delinquency, perhaps, but not attachment to peers. Thus, they do not constitute evidence against control theory.

Commitment is the second element of the bond to society in control theory. Control theory argues that a youth will not become delinquent if he or she has an investment in some conventional line of activity and aims to achieve high position, prestige, or income. Anomie theory, however, disagrees. It proposes that ambition leads to *more* delinquency because youths will do anything they can to succeed, including becoming delinquent. Merton, for example, writes, "In this setting, a cardinal American virtue, 'ambition,' promotes a cardinal American vice, 'deviant behavior'" (1957:146). But most researchers conclude that anomie does not fit the available data well. Johnson's findings, for instance, show that anomie plays "literally no role whatsoever" in causing delinquency (1979:105). A large contingent of researchers (Elliott, 1961; Clark and Wenninger, 1962; Hirschi, 1969; Hindelang, 1973; Short, 1964; Gold, 1963; Spergel, 1961) has found the same thing: ambition makes people *less* delinquent, as control theory predicts.

Involvement is the third element of the bond to society proposed by Hirschi. But it turns out not to have an impact on delinquency. Even Hirschi's research shows this. Why don't television, newspapers, football, baseball, or hobbies use up a youth's entire time and therefore discourage delinquency? The main reason is probably the fact that delinquency is not a full-time role; it requires so little time that anyone, no matter how involved, can manage enough free moments to engage in it. Thus, using up a child's free time is a questionable strategy for preventing delinquency.

The last element of Hirschi's bond to society is belief in the moral validity of social norms. He argues that everybody adheres to the conventional belief system and that no one accepts a criminal value system, though some people believe less strongly than other people. Let us consider segments of this argument one by one. Striking evidence for the first hypothesis comes from Short and Strodtbeck (1965), who found that delinquent gang members in Chicago positively evaluate conventional activities and goals such as working for good grades at school, reading good books, and having a steady job. These same gang members evaluate criminal activities (such as knowing where to sell stolen goods) far less positively. Thus, they adhere to a conventional value system, as control theory argues. But they and other delinquents adhere to it noticeably less strongly than other people, as other research demonstrates (Hirschi, 1969; Hindelang, 1973, 1974; Hepburn, 1976; Silberman, 1976; Wiatrowski et al., 1981).

As for religion and delinquency, control theory suggests there ought to be a relationship. And Nye found that there is a link between church attendance and delinquency. But this was subsequently questioned in a well-known article by Hirschi and Stark (1969), called "Hellfire and delinquency." The authors concluded that delinquency was not related to either church attendance or belief in the supernatural world. This view remained dominant for several years, until Higgins and Albrecht (1977) found that church attendance was fairly strongly related to all seventeen of the indicators of delinquency they studied. They proposed that the delinquency/religiosity relationship may depend on regional differences. (The Hirschi and Stark study took place near San Francisco, while the Higgins and Albrecht study was conducted in Atlanta.) This line of reasoning was later confirmed by Stark et al. (1980:44):

> only in communities where the majority profess religious faith, and thus where religion is an integral part of everyday life, does individual religious commitment limit delinquency. In communities where religion does not receive overt, customary expression, variations in individual religiousness do not influence delinquency.

LABELING THEORY

Labeling or interactionist theory is not limited to crime and delinquency; instead, it is often applied to other forms of deviance such as mental disorders, alcoholism, drug abuse, and suicide. Furthermore, recent statements of labeling theory show little interest in the causes of crime and delinquency. Rather, they focus their attention on the ways officials respond to these behaviors.

The Dramatization of Evil

Labeling theory in large part developed in the 1960s, but a few writings appeared in earlier decades. One of its first expressions was Tannenbaum's *Crime and Community* (1938). Tannenbaum began by rejecting the "dualistic fallacy"—the assumption that delinquents and nondelinquents are two fundamentally different kinds of people. He argued that, over the years, criminologists have imputed undesirable qualities to delinquents and criminals (atavistic physical features, intellectual inferiority, and so on). Such accusations are untrue, Tannenbaum maintained; delinquents are instead quite well adjusted to their social groups.

Delinquent activity, he went on, begins as random play, or adventure; children certainly do not think of their play as delinquent behavior. But despite its innocent beginnings, a play group may later turn into a delinquent gang, typically because conflict breaks out between the group and the community. The adults in the community who are annoyed with the group (which perhaps is considered too noisy) try to subdue or crush it. This effort usually fails, however, and the children become more defiant. They refuse to be pushed around and turn to fellow gang members for support.

As a labeling theorist, Tannenbaum stressed the importance of meanings, definitions of the situation, and attitudes. When conflict between the gang and the community breaks out, both sides resort to name-calling. The adults call the youths' activity delinquent or evil. Their attitudes harden, and they insist the activity can no longer be tolerated.

> There is a gradual shift from the definition of the specific act as evil to a definition of the individual as evil, so that all his acts come to be looked upon with suspicion. In the process of identification, his companions, hangouts, play, speech, income, all his conduct, the personality itself, become subject to scrutiny and question. From the community's point of view, the individual who used to do bad and mischievous things has now become a bad and unredeemable human being. From the individual's point of view, there has taken place a similar change. He has gone slowly from a sense of grievance and injustice . . . to a recognition that the definition of him as a human being is different from that of other boys. . . . The young delinquent becomes bad because he is not believed if he is good. There is a persistent demand for consistency in character (Tannenbaum, 1938:17–18).

Thus, calling a child a delinquent makes it much more likely that he or she will accept the description and live up to it. According to Tannenbaum, name-calling and stereotyping lead a child to isolate himself or herself from the rest of the community and associate with other youths who have been tagged with the same label. These youths thus stick together and function as a group.

Finally, Tannenbaum falls back on the old adage that juvenile correctional institutions are "schools for crime": a youth goes to a reformatory and is thrown in with hundreds of others, all of whom have been delinquent on the outside, all of whom have tales to tell about their delinquent exploits. Never having been exposed to such bravado before, the youth is impressed, eager to soak up the fascinating details of these imaginative stories. After being released and sent home, the youth can dazzle the rest of the gang with the tales he or she heard in the institution. At the same time, the returned youth learns that he or she is now defined by the community as a delinquent. People in the community expect the youth to act in accordance with that label; they will not believe that the youth has turned over a new leaf. With community attitudes so resistant to change, the youth will probably pursue a criminal career. Tannenbaum offered a simple solution to this scenario: adults should do nothing to the children. Left to their own devices, youths would continue to engage in delinquency now and then but not graduate into crime and delinquency full-time.

Primary and Secondary Deviation

Edwin Lemert is most famous for developing the ideas of "primary deviation" and "secondary deviation." *Primary deviation* is deviance that people engage in occasionally in various situations; it is excused, "rationalized, or otherwise dealt with as [part of] a socially acceptable role. Under such circumstances, normal and [deviant] behaviors remain strange and somewhat tensional bedfellows in the same person" (Lemert, 1951:75). This situation may change, however, and the person may step into a deviant or delinquent role. This role and the definition of oneself as a delinquent are affected by several factors: how much delinquency the person engages in, how visible such acts are to the rest of the community, how serious the reactions of other people are, and how aware the delinquent is of their reaction. If the delinquent behavior is very visible and if the societal reaction to this behavior is very obvious and very negative, then the youth will see himself or herself very differently and will have difficulty holding onto his or her past self-image and roles. The youth will have to choose new roles, which may be more deviant or less deviant than the old ones. If they are more deviant, the youth has reached the stage Lemert calls *secondary deviation:*

> When a person begins to employ his deviant behavior or a role based upon it as a means of defense, attack, or adjustment to the overt and covert problems created by the consequent societal reaction to him, his deviation is secondary. Objective evidences of this change will be found in the symbolic appurtenances of the new role, in clothes, speech, posture, and mannerisms, which in some cases heighten social visibility, and which in some cases serve as symbolic cues to professionalization (Lemert, 1951:76).

Lemert sees secondary deviation as a possible outgrowth of a long process, a dynamic relationship between the person's deviation and the society's reaction to it. If the individual is eventually stigmatized, efforts to control him or her will shift from informal to formal, legal ones, and the individual will be redefined as delinquent.

> The sequence of interaction leading to secondary deviation is roughly as follows: (1) primary deviation; (2) social penalties; (3) further primary deviation; (4) stronger penalties and rejections; (5) further deviations, perhaps with hostilities and resentment beginning to focus upon those doing the penalizing; (6) crisis reached in the tolerance quotient, expressed in formal action by the community stigmatizing of the deviant; (7) strengthening of the deviant conduct as a reaction to the stigmatizing and penalties; (8) ultimate acceptance of deviant social status and . . . the associated role (Lemert, 1951:77).

Lemert claimed that not all persons labeled criminal or delinquent accept these roles. How receptive they are to such labels depends on their social class. If a youth comes from a family where the parents are powerless and poor, he or she is more likely to accept the assigned delinquent role, especially if either parent is, say, alcoholic. This occurs because the "close identification between parents and children in our culture means that the status and self-conceptions of family members are readily transferred to" the children (1951:318). Also, lower-class parents may be frustrated by their situation and disturbed by inner conflicts. They may be quick to label their children bad or worthless, overreacting to qualities in their children that remind them of traits they despise in themselves. This leads them to reject their children and, when trouble occurs, to turn them over to community agencies such as the juvenile court.

Once the child arrives in juvenile court, what happens? Lemert says that the court and related agencies give rise to new meanings of deviant behavior and new definitions of the individual's character:

> Court hearings, home investigations by social workers, clinical visits, segregation within the school system and other formal dispositions of deviants under the aegis of public welfare or public protection in many instances are cause for dramatic redefinitions of the self and role of deviants . . . (1951:70–71).

Lemert asserts that having a juvenile court record formally establishes the youth's status as a deviant and segregates him or her from the rest of the community. Jail experience and contacts advance this process, making the youth more certain than ever to think of himself or herself as truly delinquent. Lemert takes it for granted that institutions do not bring about rehabilitation. Instead he believes they do the opposite—that is, they promote recidivism.

Tannenbaum and Lemert provided the first writings on labeling theory, but they never presumed that an explanation of deviance ought to be limited to the labeling process. Nor did they presume that persons labeled criminal, delinquent, alcoholic, and so on were entirely innocent. Instead, Tannenbaum and Lemert added labeling principles to already existing explanations, most notably those of the Chicago school. Lemert in particular was aware of the complexity of the process of becoming delinquent. As an early labeling theorist, he was quite careful not to lapse into overstatement. And several decades later, his work is still highly respected.

Moral Entrepreneurs

In the 1960s, there was a new intellectual ferment. A charismatic young president entered the White House, a new focus on civil rights developed, to be followed by student protests a few years later. In sociology, labeling theory assumed new prominence and popularity; it was anti-Establishment, liberal, unconventional, and "hip." Its guru during the sixties was Howard Becker, who achieved fame with two books, *Outsiders* (1963) and *The Other Side* (1964).

Becker began by attacking other social scientists. He claimed that their research centers around the question the general public usually asks about deviants—namely, "Why do they do it?" Social scientists assume that such a question is answerable because rule breaking is inherently deviant and some characteristic of rule breakers makes them do it; in other words, it is assumed that they are a particular kind of person. Becker also argued that social scientists adopt the values of persons in control, those who make the decisions about who is deviant and should be institutionalized. Thus, social scientists are accused of playing a part in the oppression of deviants.

Becker said that deviants are not a homogeneous group. Some who are labeled deviant have actually not broken any rules, and others have broken rules but have never been caught or officially labeled. As a result, social scientists study people who have little in common. Therefore, Becker focused on how people acquire their labels. He argued that whether an activity is deviant or not depends *on how other people react to it*—not on the nature of the activity itself. In other words, behavior is neither moral nor immoral in and of itself. Rules are not always enforced regularly or consistently; some are even allowed to lapse completely. When rules are enforced irregularly, the groups who bear the brunt of enforcement are the poor and powerless:

> Boys from middle-class areas do not get as far in the legal process when they are apprehended as do boys from slum areas. The middle-class boy is less likely, when picked up by the police, to be taken to the station; less likely when taken to the station to be booked; and it is extremely unlikely that he will be convicted and sentenced (Becker, 1963:12–13).

Next, Becker considered the process of becoming deviant. The first step is to commit a deviant act (even if it is unintentional). The offender may have no idea that others see it as deviant. The next crucial step in the process is getting caught, which puts the person in a new light and gives him or her a new status or label as a "whore," a "lunatic," or a "juvenile delinquent." Once labeled, a person is presumed likely to engage in such behavior again and again. Police will round up suspects (including this person) if a similar act occurs in the city at some later time. People expect the criminal or delinquent to commit other offenses too. Thus the stigma (negative label) becomes generalized; a person who is accused of one kind of deviance is expected to lie, cheat, and steal as well.

Deviance, Becker asserted, is a *master status;* regardless of what other qualities a person has, being labeled delinquent, for instance, will carry the greatest weight in the minds of others who evaluate the person. This may lead to a self-fulfilling prophecy: the labeled person may not be heavily involved or interested in the deviant activity, but calling the person delinquent may force him or her to sever ties with conventional groups and jobs and turn to illegal activities to make a living. Thus, deviance becomes an outgrowth of other people's reactions, not a simple continuation of the original deviant act.

The final step in the process of pursuing a deviant career is to join an organized deviant group, where each member learns to rationalize deviant activities. Delinquents, for instance, learn to regard their victims as unworthy people; con artists think of their victims as "suckers" or people with larcency in their hearts. Members of deviant groups learn reasons for continuing to engage in deviant behavior, and tips are passed along on how to commit acts adroitly and avoid capture.

Becker devoted special attention to people he called *moral entrepreneurs*—crusaders who set their sights on an activity they regard as especially repugnant, then expose it to public attention. They tend to categorize behavior as good or bad; they think that whatever is bad should be stamped out by any available means. The wrath of moral entrepreneurs has been directed at alcohol drinking, prostitution, gambling, domestic violence, and various sexual activities. Historically, these moral crusades were led by upper-class entrepreneurs, who had enough influence to see their views enacted into law. Since reformers typically see their mission as a holy one, the movement may have ties to a particular religious group or organization.

When legislation is passed, moral crusaders recede into the background and law enforcers assume a central role. Unlike the moral entrepreneurs, the police or other enforcers know from experience that the "evil" will not be eradicated, so they eventually give up trying to enforce the new laws. Instead, they focus their attention on how deviants respond to them. The offender who displays a hostile attitude may be arrested, while more cooperative offenders are released without further penalty. Police enjoy great latitude and discretion in deciding whom to arrest—another example Becker used to show that deviance is not inherent in a given behavior but results from the application of negative sanctions.

Radical Nonintervention

Edwin Schur (1971; 1973) focused on three elements in the labeling process: stereotyping, retrospective interpretation, and negotiation. *Stereotyping* is a quick mental classification of individuals or groups, and exaggerates the differences among people. It also involves jumping to conclusions—that is, taking a single cue and making a sweeping judgment on it: X did this, so he or she must be *that kind of person.* Schur maintains that stereotyping is rampant in juvenile courts, which run background investigations on juveniles and their families. If a juvenile comes from a broken home, the court may jump to the conclusion that he or she is not being properly raised and therefore ought to be institutionalized.

Retrospective interpretation involves labeling an individual in a certain way and then viewing him or her in an entirely new light. This sometimes occurs in the mental-health field, where a person is admitted to an institution and cast in the role of a patient; all of his or her activities will then be taken as further evidence of mental imbalance. In Rosenhan's (1973) famous experiment, eight sane people pretended to have a mental illness and were placed in psychiatric wards. Then, they acted normally, showing no signs of mental disorder. But not one of them was ever discovered by the hospital staffs. Instead, staff members distorted their normal and mundane personal histories into terms reflecting schizophrenia! (Interestingly, though, other residents perceived that these people were not mentally disordered.)

Psychiatry is notorious for retrospective interpretation—"almost anyone's life course could yield up enough denigrating facts to provide grounds for the record's justification of commitment" (Goffman, 1961:159)—but the juvenile justice system also is subject to it. Schur suggests that this susceptibility may be due to "the extreme vagueness with which delinquency and alleged predispositions to delinquency are defined (Schur, 1973:123). When examined with a cynical eye, almost every child has something in his or her background that may suggest future trouble and delinquency.

Negotiation is the third key term Schur uses when discussing the labeling process. This occurs often in criminal courts, where defense and prosecution bargain with each other over the charge, plea, and sentence. The juvenile justice system has not been so amenable to such negotiation, however, because juveniles have traditionally had so little power or influence. The paternalistic philosophy of the juvenile court assumes that the judge and probation officer have the child's best interest in mind when making a decision. With so much discretionary power, however, court officials can be quite arbitrary, basing judgments on irrelevant and biased considerations.

Schur suggested that this process makes the youth likely to get caught up in a deviant or delinquent role that becomes a crucial part of his or her identity and increasingly difficult to disavow. Many people believe that "once a delinquent, always a delinquent," making delinquency a status the person cannot change. According to Schur, the label acquired from being sent to juvenile court stays with a person for many years thereafter.

Furthermore, the juvenile justice system has allowed a large amount of bias to seep into its decision making. Lower-class, male, and black youths are more likely to be officially labeled delinquent because they lack the resources to fight the juvenile justice system's machinery. Thus, Schur feels that they are singled out unfairly.

Schur took a tolerant view of delinquency, arguing that most of it is insignificant and benign—not violent, aggressive, or harmful to other people; punishment is unnecessary, as are most delinquency laws. He believed these laws are actually counterproductive, producing more delinquency than they deter. Schur said society should permit the widest possible diversity of behavior and not require individuals to adapt to society's standards. He supported what he called "radical nonintervention," meaning that children should be left alone whenever possible.

RESEARCH ON LABELING THEORY

Testing labeling theory is often difficult because different parts of it generate different predictions. The labeling theorists insist that deviants are no different from anyone else. But they also claim that labeling may turn a person into a full-fledged deviant—that is, someone who engages in deviant behavior frequently and regularly. At issue, however, is whether labeling affects the relationship between, say, an offender and the community. Two studies are worth noting.

Schwartz and Skolnick (1962) report results from a study of the indirect consequences of legal sanctions. They hypothesize that:

1. The imposition of a sanction actually may be an incentive to violate the law;
2. Deprivations or benefits may accrue to nonsanctioned persons simply because of their relationship to the defendant;
3. The social position of the defendant will either aggravate or alleviate the effects of a sanction.

Their findings are interesting because they show that legal accusations have a variety of consequences that are contingent upon "the nature of the accusation and the characteristics of the accused" (1962:142). In other words, just as labeling theory predicts, nonlegal factors (e.g., the accused's social class, amount of social support available) do have an effect on legal processes.

Landy and Aronson (1969) report the results of two separate experiments that reveal labeling effects. Subjects were read a description of a crime of negligent automobile homicide. In both experiments about one-half of the subjects were presented a description of an "unattractive *victim*" ("a notorious hoodlum and ex-convict who had been convicted of assault and extortion" [1969:145]), while the remaining subjects read about an "attractive victim" ("a senior partner in a successful stock brokerage firm and an active member of the community welfare board" [1969:145]). Then subjects were told to sentence the defendant in each case. As was predicted, persons who had killed attractive victims were sentenced to longer prison terms. Moreover, when Landy and Aronson manipulated the defendant's "attractiveness," "unattractive defendants" received the longest prison terms. Again, nonlegal factors affected decision making.

Just how powerful labeling effects are is not easy to determine. Poole and Regoli (1985) are currently involved in research that begins to assess this issue. They have asked three sorts of questions:

1. How do persons who think their deviant status is known only to themselves behave?
2. How do these persons' activities differ from those of persons whose deviant status is publicly recognized?
3. What is the effect of audience reactions on the activities of these two types of actors?

Labeling theory would predict that the activities of actors who believe their deviant status is known would differ from those who think their deviant status is known only to themselves. And to some extent Poole and Regoli find support for this position. But their most salient finding is simply that when audiences know about one's deviant status, the interactions between the audience and deviant are exacerbated *regardless* of whether the deviant is aware of his or her status or not. In other words, as long as an audience defines a condition as real, that condition will have real consequences.

SUMMARY

Control and labeling theories are relatively new theories that developed, for the most part, after 1950. Control theory relies on self-report questionnaires, while labeling theory favors field research. Use of these methodologies means that neither theory depends on official data; thus, neither assumes that deviance and delinquency are dominated by the lower class.

But differences between labeling and control theories are more pronounced than their similarities. Labeling theory has little interest in the causes of crime and delinquency. It is much more concerned with the way criminal justice officials react to youngsters. Labeling theory also takes the side of the deviant and therefore views the criminal and juvenile justice systems in a critical light. Control theory, on the other hand, is concerned with causation and does not favor either the delinquent or the justice system.

One of the early control theorists was Toby, whose work combined principles of Chicago-school theory with those of control theory. He argued that parents affect a boy's attitude toward school. Without parental encouragement, the boy will lack incentive and find school unpleasant, so he will annoy teachers, create disciplinary problems, drop out, and have an unstable work career. With no commitment to school or work, such a boy has nothing to lose by engaging in delinquency.

Nye switched the emphasis from the school to the family. He claimed that there are three kinds of control: internal, direct, and indirect. Internal control refers to acceptance of social norms by the child as if they were his or her own. Direct control includes prevention, supervision, and sanctions by parents, teachers, and police. Indirect control derives from the child's affection for his or her parents; the child hesitates to engage in delinquency for fear that such behavior will embarrass or disappoint them. Although the family is a crucial source of control, Nye claimed that religion also makes a difference; the church socializes people to be obedient.

Matza talked less about control theory than about the flaws of subcultural theory. He believed that subcultural theory errs when it claims that delinquents are committed to misdeeds. Matza contended that they are not really committed to either the conventional or the criminal belief system. Instead, they are drifting. They engage in delinquency, but they do so partly because they mistakenly believe that their companions are committed to delinquency. Their companions do in fact give cues that they are committed to it, so the youth thinks he or she is the only member of the group who is not. He or she must go along with the group's delinquent escapades or take the humiliating position of being the one who tries to back out.

Hirschi offered a more recent statement of control theory. He separated the bond to society into four components: attachment, commitment, involvement, and belief. He considered attachment to parents, peers, and school a barrier to delinquency because the youth does not want to lose their affection by getting into trouble. Commitment reflects how much a youngster believes he or she stands to lose by engaging in delinquency (reputation, future job prospects, and so on). Involvement implies that time used in conventional activities reduces the likelihood of delinquency. Belief in the moral validity of conventional norms reduces delinquency because people tend to behave in ways that do not violate their strong beliefs.

Labeling theory began with Tannenbaum, who stressed the dramatization of evil. He said delinquency begins as random play, which later turns into delinquent gang activity if adults in the community try to subdue the children's activities. This conflict gives rise to name-calling, which makes it more likely that the child will in fact live up to the label. Institutionalizing the child will also backfire, Tannenbaum argued, because the child will be expected to behave as a confirmed offender afterward; no one will believe that he or she has become a law-abiding person.

Lemert became famous for developing the terms *primary* and *secondary deviation*. Primary deviation is excused or considered part of a socially acceptable role. But this status may change, and the child may step into a delinquent role (secondary deviation), depending on the extent of the child's delinquency and how visible it is to the rest of the community. If it is very visible and the community reaction is very negative, the youth may come to see himself or herself as delinquent.

Becker emphasized the role of moral entrepreneurs, crusaders who single out a particular issue, call it reprehensible, and try to outlaw it. Such crusades are usually led by upper-class reformers who have political influence.

Schur focused on stereotyping, retrospective interpretation, and negotiation. Stereotyping emphasizes the differences among groups and the similarities of people in the same group. It is common in the juvenile court, where quick judgments are made on the basis of race, family status, sex, demeanor, or some other background characteristic of the juvenile. Retrospective interpretation involves labeling a person and then viewing him or her in an entirely new light. Thus putting a label on someone allows officials to reinterpret the person's past and say that there were early signs that the individual was bad or abnormal. Negotiation is most prominent in criminal courts where it is known as plea bargaining.

DISCUSSION QUESTIONS

1. According to Toby, how may school experiences help youths develop a "stake in conformity"?
2. What are the differences between direct and indirect controls?
3. How may delinquents "drift" into delinquency?
4. In Hirschi's version of control theory, in what four ways may individuals be "tied" to society? Explain each.
5. What does the research evidence indicate about the effect of ties to parents and peers on one's delinquency?
6. What is Lemert's conception of the sequence of interaction leading to secondary deviation?
7. According to labeling theory, how does the concept of "master status" help us to understand the development of deviant careers?
8. According to Becker, what role do "moral entrepreneurs" play in the creation of deviance?
9. What are the three elements in Schur's model of the labeling process?
10. How does labeling theory fare in light of empirical research findings? Explain your answer.

WHY FREDDY GOT HIS GUN

Control theory emphasizes a person's ties to conventional society. When these are weak or broken, there is little to prevent the person from turning to crime or delinquency. Sometimes, the person simply rejects school, work, marriage, and conventional peers. Sometimes, they reject him. In either case, the future is bleak, as the story of Fast Freddy indicates.

Spring 1979

Fast Freddy Thompson comes out of the Chinese takeout restaurant at Broadway and 48th Street, his left hand rubbing his eyes, his right hand carrying a plate of shrimp fried rice. It is just eleven o'clock, but Freddy is bone-tired, and if he didn't have some jive job interview with Burger King at noon, he would have stayed in bed all day. But his mother, Little Louise, a five-foot bundle of perpetual fury, had stood over him shouting curses from nine o'clock until he finally crawled from under the sheets just before ten.

Now, on the last Wednesday in April, he stands yawning in the sunlight and wishing that he hadn't gone last night to Mahogany, a cool discotheque on Fulton Street in Brooklyn. He wishes, too, that he had the money to go to California, but most of all he wishes he had a job.

"It's going to be the same old shit," he says. "They ain't going to have nothing." Then he sees T.L., a buddy from the old days on Hancock Street when they had a singing group and had glided through the ghetto garbage with the certain knowledge that they would never stumble, never fall. But T.L. has just spent his nineteenth birthday on Riker's Island, and now he has three front teeth missing and the posture of a graying man. They begin to slap five, to talk loudly, to strut, to preen, for they know that they must bring each other, swiftly, into a circle of affection, for only then can they pretend that the dreams of the Dukes of Hancock Street still live.

"You lookin' good, my man."

"Man, you the joint."

"You got a job, man. You got a slave?"

"No, man. Nothing. Just trying to survive. Hustling. Selling reefers. Whatever."

"I just been chilling out, man. Just watching the world. I hear they hiring at Burger King."

"Sheet. I ain't gonna bust my chops for no chump change."

"You got that right," says Fast Freddy. And soon there is nothing else to say.

"Got to book," says Thompson, turning on his red Adidas.

To the casual observer, Fast Freddy Thompson should have no trouble getting a job. He is a clean-cut nineteen-year-old. He stands six feet two inches, speaks reasonably well, and seems intelligent. For a time he thought he would become an athlete. He thought, at thirteen, that he would use his height and strength to get away from the Bed-Stuy blues. And so basketball became his passion, and basketball stars his heroes. He looked at all the games he could on the broken TV set his father had bought on credit from Macy's. And he spent the summers on the school yard's playing grounds, breaking only for Kool-Aid and sleep. He stayed coiled in himself, never speaking much, never sharing his dreams with anyone. For he was a believer then. He knew he could do it, for he was tall and strong and fast. He ran so well that he had gotten his nickname, "Fast," one summer night when, having stolen an orange from a fruit stand owned by a Jamaican, he out-ran the dog that the old man had sent after him. But his size, which he thought would bring his escape, brought him defeat instead. For he was too big for his age, and at fourteen, embarrassed by being at least six inches taller than everyone else in his eighth-grade class, he quit. His father, a giant who he said would have "whipped his ass back into school," had by then retreated into the ramblings of the mad. He spent his nights hitting his head against the living-room wall, with a grin on his face and a tic in his neck. One morning he left and didn't come back, and years later, Little Louise said that he had found his peace in Dalton, Georgia, and his name was never mentioned again.

Thompson worked at odd jobs in supermarkets and filling stations waiting for his mind to catch up with his body. But his mind atrophied while selling gas, and his body stopped growing. Moreover, he found out that without college there could be no life in basketball, and so he formed with two other dropouts the Dukes of Hancock Street, for although he had no voice, that was the only other dream he had, the only way he thought he could beat the hand that life had dealt him. And so, night after night, he tried to get his broken falsetto closer to that of Smokey Robinson, while Little Louise looked at him with complete disdain. She could no longer control him. He could lift her up with one hand, and so her voice became her weapon, and the bitterness of her curse wounded him deeply.

"Moms always saying, 'Make something of yourself, you no-good bum,' but she can't tell me how."

So he watched his mother grow into a virago, for she had lost one man to madness, and she was losing another, and she did not know what to do. She became tight. Controlled. Wary. Until some imagined slight, some thwarted expectation, caused her dam to burst and her fury to touch all around her. Except Big Louise, Freddy's younger sister. At six feet one inch and 200 pounds, she lived through her seventeen years with laughter, went to church, and studied hard. She was her mother's hope.

By the spring of 1979, when he moved to 122nd Street and Seventh Avenue—a fire had burned them out of Bed-Stuy—Fast Freddy was living in "a nowhere time." There were no more heroes in his life. Not even "Dr. J." "The dude is cool and all, but I can't relate to all that shit anymore." And music was now simply something he listened to when he wanted to get high or danced to when he wanted to get higher.

His meal of shrimp fried rice finished, Thompson heads east on 42nd Street for the Burger King on Third Avenue. His mood has grown sullen because he is convinced that today will be another exercise in rejection. Then he sees a bald, heavyset man coming toward him, and he stops in recognition and pride, for the man, Charles McGregor, sprang to ghetto fame when he played a junkie in *Superfly*, the first of the spate of seventies movies that tried to make heroes out of black criminals. McGregor's portrait of that despairing addict was etched out of his own experience, and because the man of the screen was his namesake, Fast Freddy Thompson became a McGregor fan. To reach his present position as actor, lecturer, and, above all, mentor to a host of black youngsters, McGregor had to spend 26 years in prison. He didn't waste all of them. He taught himself to read, and his life story, *Up From the Walking Dead*, was published by Doubleday.

"How you doin'," says Fast Freddy.

"Hanging in there. Working hard," says McGregor. "And you?"

"Tryin' to make it," says Fast Freddy. "Tryin'. It ain't easy."

"You can do it, brother," says McGregor, as Fast Freddy walks away.

On the lecture circuit, McGregor tells black students, "From ten to eighteen, study the three R's: reading, writing, and arithmetic. But at eighteen, when you become an adult, you must be prepared for three more R's: right, wrong, and responsibility." The message gets him some applause, but he worries about reaching the ones who should be listening. "Many kids in high school have already chosen their direction. We can help them along, but we have no strategies for the street kids, and they are multiplying every day." It is in this growing mass that Freddy finds himself, and he has begun to sense that the laws enacted over the past decade seem only to help the black trained, the black mobile, the black bright. The festering sore of envy has already begun to run as Freddy walks toward the subway after having been told that the Burger King job was taken.

Summer 1979

It is the last Wednesday in June, and Fast Freddy Thompson is as "clean" as he can be this morning. His dungarees are starched until the pleats stand out as sharply as weapons. He's changed his customary Adidas for a Florsheim brown, and he's wearing his only tie—a black one—bought two years ago to attend the funeral of B.J., a boyhood friend shot dead while robbing a bodega in the Bronx. Thompson is on his way to the Vocational Foundation on East 23rd Street. This private, nonprofit organization was established in 1937 to find jobs for young people who were in trouble with the law or were having difficulties in the marketplace. It has its work cut out, for in the third quarter of 1979, the unemployment rate for sixteen- to nineteen-year-olds in New York City was 34.1 percent. And many people thought that it was higher. Yet the foundation's executive director, George Carson, thinks he can make a difference in the lives of his charges. He has fought the youth-unemployment battle for a long time. He believes. He sees Fast Freddy and directs him to a member of his staff who questions him, tests him, and tells him to call back tomorrow.

Thompson goes home early. He resists the pressure from his buddies to "hang out" in the streets. He sleeps and calls the foundation at nine the next morning. They send him to a job on West 28th Street. The firm makes zippers. Thompson lasts one week."What went down?" I ask.

"They was hassling me, man. I couldn't take all that stuff." And the "stuff" was simply orders given in the gruff style that supervisors lay on the underlings. But to Thompson, the sound behind the words meant more than the words themselves. It told him that he was at the bottom, and maybe he would have to stay there. "I ain't licking anybody's ass no more."

The Wednesday that Thompson went to the Vocational Foundation was the day on which the United States Supreme Court ruled, in the Brian Weber case, that private employers could seek to eliminate "manifest racial imbalance" in traditionally white-only jobs by giving specific preference to black workers. I ask Thompson what he thinks about that decision. "I don't know nothing about that. All I know is that I want a job that will pay me and not abuse me." And what was he worth? "What is any man worth? I got to have something to live on. I got to give my Moms a little something. Give my lady a little something. I got to keep clean. Add all that up. That's what I'm worth. But it don't make no difference anyway, for if it's not for you, you don't get it. Like they say, if the dice don't roll, you don't reach your goal." And what about education and discipline, I ask. What about the belief that in this country your life can become better by steady, sure mobility? "That's all crap," says Thompson. "All I know, my man, is that it's all luck. It's all chance."

I meet Lucinda, Freddy's "gold charm." She is seventeen years old, out of school, and "tired." The baby fat has not quite disappeared, although the eyes are already shaded with cynicism. "I seen it all," she says proudly. "Just ask me. I'm a ghet-to girl." When she walks with Freddy she holds on to him as if she's afraid that he'll suddenly disappear.

"Damn," says Freddy, "why you always hold me so tight?"

"You niggers here today and gone tomorrow," says Lucinda. She chews gum all the time and pops it loudly in her left cheek. She loves cats and wants more than anything else to be a nurse. But she doubts that she will ever become one. "It's all the system. They tell you that you have to go to school for it, but school don't really teach you how to care for a person." And so she spends her days in wandering commutes between Crown Heights, where she lives, and Harlem, where her lover lives. But there is one side to her that cuts across the moon face, the seeming gentleness. Because she spends so much time on the subways, she thinks she has an a priori right to space. So she sprawls. And when reproved, she delights in frightening old women with the muted curses that she throws their way. So, almost unnoticed, she has begun her spiral of bitterness. She tells me that she can't stand the well-dressed blacks she sees on the streets. "Ain't I got rights too?" she says. "How come the same black people keeping it all for theyself? Just because I poor, don't mean I don't want nice things. Government won't give me no job. Nobody hiring." How does she see herself a year from now? "Doing the same thing I always do. I don't like New York noway. When you poor here, people look at you like you nothing. I stare them the hell back. They ain't no better than me." She says that her friends have a little game going in Crown Heights or wherever the pickings look good. They do it for divertissement, for fun, for daring, for those nice things they can't afford. They mug old black women. "I don't do it, though. I figure it could be my relative or something. But they the onliest ones around there with money, you know. Social Security. And they can't run."

Fall 1979

I don't hear from Thompson for weeks, and I think that he's dispirited about finding a job. When he finally calls, I find out that he's been on Riker's Island. For fighting in the streets. His mother refused to put up all the money for his bail, but his "gold charm" came through, and he was released.

"Where'd you get the money?" I ask Lucinda.

"Some of my godmothers gave it to me."

When I look at her, she smiles and says, "My girl friends taught me how. I had to hit just two of them to get the money." There is nothing further to say.

"If you gonna get it together," I tell Thompson, "you have to go back to school. You've got to get that piece of paper."

"Go back to school. Go back to school," he taunts. And suddenly his voice is whiplash: "Is that all you have to tell me, man? I want a job that I can make me some good money. Will school do that for me? When? I want something good, *now,* but I ain't ever gonna find it."

He may be right. William Raspberry, the columnist, says that many young black people have "already become a permanent jobless and useless underclass, immune from the fluctuations of the general economy." In January, President Carter announced a $2-billion plan to help the Fast Freddies of this country enter the world of work. But even if Congress gets around to doing something about this plan, will all that money, *alone,* work? Herbert Hill, a University of Wisconsin professor and labor analyst, thinks not. "The complex and accumulated problems of black ghetto youth cannot be solved by anti-bias measures or by an expanding economy." So what have we spawned? A new generation of black youth who never enter this country's labor force, who may want to work but have no skills, and who, by now, are so afraid to compete in an American world of effort and reward, of planning and achievement, that failure has become a cushion for their sundered egos. They think that it is ordained, in the rhythm of things, since they are black.

But when they see other blacks wearing the mantle of the successful, the confluence of excuses becomes a war stirring in their souls.

Fall breezes stir the brown, dead leaves through the Brooklyn streets as Fast Freddy and Lucinda meet me at Nostrand Avenue and Eastern Parkway.

"She's got news," he says.

"I'm two months," she says. It is a boast that is tinged with fear.

"What you going to do?" I ask.

"Do? Nothing, I guess. I'm so damn happy."

"Money? What about money?"

"Welfare, what else. Gonna have to go on down." And suddenly her laughter is high-pitched, poised on the edge of panic. "Ain't it funny," she says. "When I was young, I used to couldn't wait to get us off welfare. Me, Li'l Bro, and my mother. Looks like that ain't gonna happen now."

Two days later, I pass Thompson on his new beat in Bryant Park. He, too, is shouting "Loose joints," but his heart is not in it, and he smokes more than he sells. He has lost his summer charm, and he no longer wants to find a job: "That nine-to-five bullshit is not for me, man. I tried it, and it ain't for me." He has become ordinary now, a street person sinking slowly and moving farther away from the world of any work. "I got to get my hands on some real bank."

"How you going to do that?"

"I don't give a shit. Any which way. Don't make me no difference. Black, white, young, old. You got it, and I can get it. I'm gonna try to get it."

Winter 1980

I go on vacation, and so I do not see Fast Freddy for several weeks. One morning I run into him at the Nedick's in Pennsylvania Station. He's alive, brimming with enthusiasm, and happy to report how he is getting it all together and how the baby is making Lucinda more beautiful. He's a young man on the balls of his feet, checking everything out and knowing that he has many oats left to sow. I notice, though, that he is very high, and he tells me that he's on his way to meet Lucinda. I wonder at the change, and I think that maybe some new world is opening up.

Meanwhile, I see that for another young man it's the end of his time. Robert Bilodeau, a city cop, was shot hours before in a Harlem alley by a man carrying a handgun. As we pass the newsstands, I look at the headlines and ask Freddy what he thinks about the violence in the city.

"Yeah," he says. "It's something else out there, man. It's bad for everybody." We walk in silence for a while. And then he says, "But I don't see why they make so much fuss when a cop gets hit. He's doing his job, man. Just doing his job. Nobody forced him to take it. I can't get a job, and if I get killed, ain't nobody going say nothing, right? Well, I don't think a cop's life is worth more than mine."

We are meeting Lucinda at the Nedick's in the subway at Eighth Avenue, and as we walk up Eighth, a redheaded whore, still out with the morning light, stops to adjust the straps on her green high-heeled shoes. Thompson slows down. His high working. His youngman juices flowing.

"You looking good, mama," he says. "Real, real good." She ignores him. "You can make me forget heaven," he says.

"Ain't no freebies here," she says. "You got to pay to squeeze *this* Charmin."

It is all good-natured. Two denizens of the Empire City sharing an early-morning laugh. He gives her a joint. She blows smoke in his face.

"I'll check you out later," he says.

"Bring money, honey," she says.

We walk into Nedick's. Lucinda is already there in a gray cloth coat. She is beginning to look matronly. A bit unkempt. She is tinkering with something, and when I look closely, I see that it's a blank check belonging to one L. Weinstein, and that she is writing herself a check for $110. With some residual high-mindedness coursing through me, I say, "You'll get yourself in trouble."

"Sheet," she says.

"How're you going to cash it?"

"A check-cashing place in Harlem."

"Just so?"

"If they don't know you, they'll tell you to go and come back with a cop."

"So?"

"No problem," she says. Blithely. Undisturbed. "I know one or two cops who will go there with me if I give them half."

"Will you?"

"Why not? I'll still have more than I got."

I drink my 45-cent orange drink in silence. Lucinda and Freddy are talking in a corner. They are enjoying each other and obviously talking over something important. A young man, shabbily dressed, walks into the shop, his Sanyo cassette over his right shoulder, blasting the McFadden and Whitehead hit: "Ain't no stopping us now. We're on the move. . . . We've got the groove. . . ."

And he sings along, his head thrown backward, his upper torso moving with the drums, and as he sees two young white men coming toward him, he bellows his song of liberation, of defiance even, in their startled faces. They slow down, check him out quickly, their eyes darting over his clothes, his torn sneakers, and then smiles, ever so disdainful, begin to play at their lips, for they know that as high and as illiterate as the singer is, he can always be stopped.

Freddy calls me over, and we move slowly into a corner.

"I got something to show you," he says as he smiles and unzips his Hong Kong-made nylon bomber jacket. I see the handle of the Saturday-night special in his belt before I realize what it is.

"Got it cheap," he says.

"What you gonna do with it?"

He shrugs. His eyes seem bright, and I can sense the exhilaration racing through him.

"Whatever," he says. "It's real life out there, right?"

And suddenly I knew that I had no right to continue to interfere in his life. There was nothing I could do for him. He was young and black and poor. His city glittered, and he had to make his way in the world.

Source: Orde Coombs, "Why Freddy Got His Gun," *New York,* May 26, 1980. Reprinted by permission of the author.

REFERENCES

BECKER, HOWARD S.

1964 *The Other Side.* New York: Free Press.

1963 *Outsiders.* New York: Free Press.

CANTER, RACHELLE J.

1982 Family correlates of male and female delinquency. *Criminology* 20 (August):149–167.

CLARK, JOHN P., AND EUGENE P. WENNINGER

1962 Socio-economic class and area as correlates of illegal behavior among juveniles. *American Sociological Review* 27 (December):826–834.

ELLIOTT, DELBERT S.

1961 Delinquency, Opportunity and Patterns of Orientations. Unpublished doctoral dissertation. University of Washington, Seattle.

ELLIOTT, DELBERT S., AND HARWIN L. VOSS

1974 *Delinquency and Dropout.* Lexington, Mass.: Lexington.

EMPEY, LAMAR T., AND STEVEN G. LUBECK

1971 *Explaining Delinquency.* Lexington, Mass.: Lexington.

GOFFMAN, ERVING R.

1961 *Asylums.* New York: Doubleday.

GOLD, MARTIN

1963 *Status Forces in Delinquent Boys.* Ann Arbor, Mich.: Institute for Social Research.

HEPBURN, JOHN R.

1976 Testing alternative models of delinquency causation. *Journal of Criminal Law and Criminology* 67 (December):450–460.

HIGGINS, PAUL C., AND GARY L. ALBRECHT

1977 Hellfire and delinquency revisited. *Social Forces* 55 (June):952–958.

HINDELANG, MICHAEL J.

1974 Moral evaluations and illegal behavior. *Social Problems* 21 (February):370–385.

1973 Causes of delinquency: A partial replication and extension. *Social Problems* 20 (Spring):471–487.

HINDELANG, MICHAEL J., ET AL.

1981 *Measuring Delinquency.* Beverly Hills, Calif.: Sage.

HIRSCHI, TRAVIS

1969 *Causes of Delinquency.* Berkeley: University of California Press.

HIRSCHI, TRAVIS, AND RODNEY STARK

1969 Hellfire and delinquency. *Social Problems* 17 (Fall):202–213.

LANDY, DAVID, AND ELLIOT ARONSON

1969 The influence of the character of the criminal and his victim on the decisions of simulated jurors. *Journal of Experimental Social Psychology* 5 (2):141–152.

LEMERT, EDWIN M.

1951 *Social Pathology.* New York: McGraw-Hill.

LINDEN, ERIC, AND JAMES C. HACKLER

1973 Affective ties and delinquency. *Pacific Sociological Review* 16 (January):27–46.

MATZA, DAVID

1964 *Delinquency and Drift.* New York: Wiley.

MERTON, ROBERT K.

1957 *Social Theory and Social Structure.* New York: Free Press.

NYE, F. IVAN
1958 *Family Relationships and Delinquent Behavior.* New York: Wiley.
POOLE, ERIC D., AND ROBERT M. REGOLI
1985 A study of the effects of self-labeling and public labeling. Unpublished manuscript.
ROSENHAN, D. L.
1973 Being sane in insane places. *Science* 179 (January):250–258.
SCHUR, EDWIN M.
1973 *Radical Nonintervention: Rethinking the Delinquency Problem.* Englewood Cliffs, N. J.: Prentice-Hall.
1971 *Labeling Deviant Behavior.* New York: Harper & Row.
SCHWARTZ, RICHARD, AND JEROME H. SKOLNICK
1962 Two studies of legal stigma. *Social Problems* 10(2):133–142.
SHORT, JAMES F., JR.
1964 Gang delinquency and anomie. Pp. 98–127 in Marshall B. Clinard (ed.), *Anomie and Deviant Behavior.* New York: Free Press.
SHORT, JAMES F., JR., AND FRED L. STRODTBECK
1965 *Group Process and Gang Delinquency.* Chicago: University of Chicago Press.
SILBERMAN, MATTHEW
1976 Toward a theory of criminal behavior. *American Sociological Review* 41 (June):442–461.
SPERGEL, IRVING
1961 An exploratory research in delinquent subculture. *Social Service Review* 35 (March):33–47.
STARK, RODNEY, ET AL.
1980 Rediscovering moral communities. Pp. 43–52 in Travis Hirschi and Michael Gottfredson (eds.), *Understanding Crime.* Beverly Hills, Calif.: Sage.
TANNENBAUM, FRANK
1938 *Crime and the Community.* New York: Columbia University Press.
THRASHER, FREDERIC
1936 *The Gang.* Chicago: University of Chicago Press.
TOBY, JACKSON
1958 Hoodlum or businessman: An American dilemma. Pp. 542–550 in Marshall Sklare (ed.), *The Jews.* New York: Free Press.
1957 Social disorganization and stake in conformity: Complementary factors in the predatory behavior of hoodlums. *Journal of Criminal Law and Criminology* 48 (May-June):12–17.
WIATROWSKI, MICHAEL D., ET AL.
1981 Social control theory and delinquency. *American Sociological Review* 46 (October):525–541.

9 Origins of the Juvenile Court

Using the law to protect the welfare of children is a modern idea in America. Traditionally, the state and organized institutions played a relatively unimportant role in the lives of children; rarely, for instance, did government involve itself in family matters. Beginning in the nineteenth century, however, laws began to be used more and more ambitiously as an instrument of social policy (Haskins, 1968). In response to new perspectives on the place of children in society, there were increasing demands that the state should take responsibility for improving the lives of children. As the special needs of children came to be recognized, new regulations such as child-labor laws and compulsory school attendance were enacted. In addition, agencies and institutions whose stated goals were the protection and enhancement of children's lives were formed.

Although much of this early interest in children was motivated by humanitarian concern, the reforms it brought about also served to control the children of immigrants and the lower classes. Their swarming, ragged presence on city streets made these children highly visible to a worried public. For the first time, Americans were forced to confront large numbers of children who apparently had no home or lived an undisciplined existence. Thus, the new concern for children was paradoxically bound up with a fear that many of these children threatened the well-being of society. A typical example of such a fear was expressed by John L. Hart, principal of the New Jersey State Normal School:

> About one-half of our poor can neither read nor write, have never been in any school, and know little, positively nothing, of the doctrines of the Christian religion, of moral duties, or of any higher pleasures than beer-drinking and spirit-drinking, and the grossest sensual indulgence. . . . They have unclear, indefinable ideas of all around them; they eat, drink, breed, work, and die; and while they pass through their brute-like existence here, the rich and more intelligent classes are obliged to guard them with prisons, cages, and all kinds of receptacles for the perpetrators of crime (Hart, 1879:252–257).

American responses to poor people have long been ambivalent. On the one hand, protecting, nurturing, and providing for those who need help. On the other hand, difficult children were much feared, and it was thought that they must be prevented from prospering and assuming power (Diamond, 1966).

Nineteenth-century child-oriented legislation transformed many children into nonpersons. They were shunted into factories, almshouses, orphanages, and houses of refuge, where they were often treated inhumanely, and no attention was paid to their individual needs. All too often, the legal system hid these problems from public view, taking away the children's freedom, and occasionally their lives, in the process.

Thus, in the guise of better preparing children for life or of removing them from circumstances of poverty and crime, institutions were created that in fact often did these children more harm than good. And as legal means were used to broaden society's control over its children, the power of those who managed these institutions assumed the dimensions of parental control. In fact, this institutional control was frequently more awesome, more total, than parental authority—and less open to surveillance and judgment.

The prime concern of this chapter is to show how social and legal developments fostered the ideology that problem children are best controlled by the state. We will do this by examining the role of the law in the emergence of child-care institutions and by describing similarities in the child-labor legislation, case law dealing with corporal punishment in schools, and the judicial role in formulating institutional policies and practices. An important corollary task lies in relating these formal operations to life outside the law. Thus, we will also examine the connection between legal and administrative activities and the behavior of children both before and after their institutionalization. This will include looking at the issues involving indeterminate sentencing, status offense jurisdiction, judicial due process, and the detention of children in adult jails.

To accomplish these tasks, we must consider several questions. What were the origins of and justifications for the institutionalized control of children? Have these justifications changed? What latitude have institutional officials been allowed in their authority over children? What concerns have motivated reformers as they struggled with the problems of institutionalized children? What has happened to erode trust in institutional authority and in the laws regulating this authority? How has the legal response to institutional control reflected developments in society at large?

THE EARLY HISTORY OF INSTITUTIONAL CONTROL

Some of the earliest recorded attempts to deal with the phenomenon of delinquency in the United States in a public, institutional manner occurred in the early years of the nineteenth century. People at this time began to be aware of the child as a distinct cultural phenomenon and to regard childhood as a stage of growth in human development that deserved the care and attention its pliant nature demanded (Aries, 1962). Yet in the midst of developing cities such as New York, Philadelphia, and Boston, conflicting aspects of juvenile behavior gained public notice. There, the juvenile delinquent—the child rooted in evil and on the verge of a life in crime—stood in sharp contrast to the innocence of childhood. Reformers launched interventionist efforts to save the delinquent, to relieve the circumstances of his or her development, and to guide him or her firmly toward the path of righteousness. But this path proved to be often convoluted by the anxieties of the well-intentioned reformers. Juvenile delinquents were not simply innocent children gone wrong. They were to be restrained from activities that ran counter to social norms, and these restraints sometimes reached awesome dimensions.

Based on chancery jurisdictions (where the court rendered decisions on the basis of what was considered fair in a particular situation) exercised in England, the doctrine of *parens patriae* allowed the state, as benevolent parent, to assume responsibility for the care and development of its children. As a parent, the state enjoyed wide latitude in its efforts to redeem the delinquent child. One of the earliest judicial expressions of *parens patriae* was occasioned in 1838 by a distraught father whose child had fallen victim to the "benevolence" of the Philadelphia House of Refuge. Mary Ann Crouse had been committed to the House of Refuge by her mother, who alleged "that the said infant by reason of vicious conduct, has rendered her control beyond the power of said complainant, and made it manifestly requisite that from regard to the moral and future welfare of the said infant she should be placed under the guardianship of the managers of the House of Refuge" (4 Wharton 11). The child's father disagreed, arguing that the commitment procedures had been unfair. The child herself had been allowed neither defense nor trial. The mother charged her daughter with incorrigibility, still regarded as an offense by the juvenile court today; the child was accused of being uncontrollable and therefore was committed to the state for guidance. While the child today can take advantage of certain procedural safeguards, Mary Ann Crouse had none. *Parens patriae* reigned supreme in the court's decision:

> The object of the charity is reformation, by training its inmates to industry; by imbuing their minds with principles of morality and religion; by furnishing them with means to earn a living; and above all, by separating them from the corrupting influence of improper associates. To this end, may not the natural parents, when unequal to the task of education, or unworthy of it, be superseded by the *parens patriae*, or common guardian of the community? It is to be remembered that the public has a paramount interest in the virtue and knowledge of its members, and that, of strict right, the business of education belongs to it (4 Wharton 11).

The first House of Refuge in America, founded in 1825 in New York, stands as another example of the mixture of concerns underlying the concept of *parens patriae*. In 1824 it was estimated that there were more than 9,000 children under 14 years of age living in poverty in New York state. This fact led to concern for the welfare of these children but also to a fear "that this mass of pauperism will (quite soon) form a fruitful nursery of crime, unless prevented by the watchful superintendence of the legislature" (New York State Board of Charities, 1901:942). One of the main instruments of this "superintendence" was the New York House of Refuge. Designed to save children from a life of crime, the House soon revealed an orientation toward saving society from the children.

The reformers' attitude toward delinquency was rooted in an equation of poverty and crime. Poverty was linked with idleness, which was a reprehensible moral quality that produced all forms of vice—most notably crime. The managers of the House of Refuge translated this equation into a severely regimented existence for its inmates. At the House, even in the reformers' minds, hostility mixed with benevolence to provide a peculiar atmosphere for the children:

> These little vagrants, whose depradations provoke and call down upon them our indignation are yet but children who have gone astray for want of that very care and vigilance we exercise toward our own. They deserve our censure, and a regard for our property, and the good of society, requires that they should be stopped, reproved and punished (New York Society for the Reformation of Juvenile Delinquents, 1832:81).

Common to most Houses of Refuge or juvenile asylums was an emphasis on repentance and punishment. The children accused of crimes were not only to be persuaded of the error of their ways; they were also to suffer for them. Expiation in the form of punishment provided the most convenient method of conversion and, it seems, a suitable form of justification for the reformers.

In his analysis of the New York House of Refuge, Sanford Fox (1970) found a profound negative core of fear in the reformers' attitudes, particularly toward the poor, and most especially the immigrant poor. This fear was expressed as a strong hostility toward the delinquent. The Quaker devotion to education, an attitude shared by the Progressives in the early twentieth century, was applied to control rather than develop the delinquent child. As part of the severe regimen imposed by juvenile correctional institutions, education came to form a part of the ambivalent posture of the reformers toward the delinquent.

Fox's insight into the early nineteenth-century New York reformers applies equally well to the subsequent leaders in juvenile reform. Mary Carpenter, one of the foremost spokespersons for the concept of *parens patriae* and the founder of the Ragged Schools, gave voice to the societal fear of the threat posed by delinquency. In her book *Reformatory Schools for the Children of the Perishing and Dangerous Classes, and for Juvenile Offenders* (1851), she argued that reform schools were the most effective agencies for preventing juvenile crimes. In the face of opposition to her innovation, she appealed to an element inherent in both the popular culture and the reformers' beliefs—fear of the menace of the "dangerous classes." Charles Loring Brace borrowed the idea from Mary Carpenter that the "dangerous classes" posed one of the greatest threats to modern society. He argued so strongly for placing delinquent children in the rural West for reformation that the Western states rallied to protect themselves from the children to be imported (Hawes, 1971).

The concept of *parens patriae* stemmed largely from the nineteenthcentury fear of the delinquent child; yet to the public, *parens patriae* spoke only of benevolence and confident hope in the young, explaining that they, the ultimate hope for the future, deserved the best. The reformers thus viewed the increased control of the state over the lives of children as a positive expression of society's concern. The state's intensified regulation of the child's life took a variety of forms: compulsory school attendance, restrictions on child labor, and strict supervision of leisure activities, for example. Traditionally, childhood misbehavior had been viewed as a problem that called for punishment. Now, as Aries has noted, "It was recognized that the child was not ready for life, and that he had to be subjected to a special treatment, a sort of quarantine, before he was allowed to join the adults" (1962:412).

Progressive reformers thus sought new solutions to the growing problems of juvenile delinquency. The most significant was the creation of the juvenile court in Chicago in 1899, a culmination of the nineteenth-century campaign to separate youthful and adult offenders (Hurley, 1907). Like the earlier Houses of Refuge, the juvenile court was an attempt to supervise problem children closely; yet unlike those previous efforts, this new form of supervision was to occur within the child's own home and within the community—not, except in the most troublesome cases, in institutions.

One of the central concerns that motivated Illinois reformers was the problematic relationship of delinquent children to the industrial schools designed for their reformation. A child, once committed, was, in effect, under the guardianship of the industrial school until age of majority. Each county was required to pay a fixed monthly sum to support each child committed from that county. Therefore, many communities were reluctant to prosecute children except in cases of major offenses, and many unruly children continued to roam the streets until they were eventually committed for criminal acts.

Reformers also focused attention on those children confined in jails and forgotten in almshouses. The 1898 report of the Illinois state commissioners illustrates the breadth of this concern:

> There are at the present moment in the State of Illinois, especially in the city of Chicago, thousands of children in need of active intervention for their preservation from physical, mental and moral destruction. Such intervention is demanded, not only by sympathetic consideration of their well being, but also in the name of the Commonwealth, for the preservation of the State. If the child is the material out of which men and women are made, the neglected child is the material out of which paupers and criminals are made (Mennel, 1973:129).

Outraged by the plight—and by the potential threat—of so many needy children, philanthropic reformers joined hands with penologists and lawyers to create the new juvenile court. It began with an 1899 Illinois legislative act "to regulate the treatment and control of dependent, neglected, and delinquent children." According to this act, a delinquent child was an individual "under the age of 16 years who violates any law of this State or any City or Village ordinance." A dependent or neglected child was one

> who for any reason is destitute or homeless or abandoned; or dependent upon the public for support; or has not proper parental care or guardianship; or who habitually begs or receives alms; or who is found living in any house of ill fame or with any vicious or disreputable person; or whose home, by reason of neglect, cruelty, or depravity on the part of its parents, guardian or other person in whose care it may be, is an unfit place for such a child; or [one] under the age of 8 years who is found peddling or selling any article or singing or playing any musical instrument upon the street or giving any public entertainment (Abbott, 1938:392–401).

Perhaps because the juvenile court movement was primarily spearheaded by social workers, the court's procedures were to be civil rather than criminal. In theory, children were to be treated rather than punished, and the judge was to assume the role of a wise and kind parent. As the new court was envisioned, its most important provisions were the segregation of juvenile offenders from adult offenders at all procedural stages, the hiring of probation officers who would provide friendly supervision over the children in their care, and informal civil court proceedings (Hurley, 1907).

The juvenile court reaffirmed and extended the *parens patriae* doctrine. As Timothy Hurley, president of the Chicago Visitation and Aid Society, commented, "The fundamental idea of the Juvenile Court is . . . a return to paternalism. It is the acknowledgement by the State of its relationship as the parent to every child within its borders. Civilization for years lost sight of this relationship and as a consequence the utter demoralization of society was threatened" (Hurley, 1907:56).

This paternalistic philosophy meant that reformers gave more attention to the "needs" than to the rights of children. In their campaign to meet what they perceived to be the children's needs, concerned reformers enlarged the ideal of the state as parent to include the handling of children in the judicial system.

In the state's expanded role as parent, perhaps the most important component of the new court organization was its system of probation, "the keystone which supports the arch of juvenile law" (Hurley, 1907:225). Probation officers were to perform two crucial tasks: presentence investigation and postsentence supervision. Harvey H. Baker, the first judge of the Boston Juvenile Court, described these duties:

> The probation officer investigates the case and reports to the judge all available information about the family and other features of the environment of the boy, the boy's personal history at home, in school, at work, and on the street, and the circumstances attending the particular outbreak which got him into court. The boy himself is scrutinized for indications of feeble-mindedness or physical defects. . . . The judge and probation officer consider together, like a physician and his junior, whether the outbreak which resulted in the arrest of the child was largely accidental, or whether it is habitual or likely to be so; whether it is due chiefly to some inherent physical or moral defect of the child, or whether some feature of his environment is an important factor; and then they address themselves to the question of how permanently to prevent the recurrence (1910:332).

Despite the key role of the probation officer in the juvenile court, the Illinois laws of 1899 and 1901 expressly provided that these court officials could not be paid from any public money. During the first twelve months that the Illinois juvenile court was in operation, 1,095 children were put on probation with no funds to provide for their care. To plug the gap, settlement workers and private associations scrambled to raise funds and offer their services on a volunteer basis (Thurston, 1910).

In theory, the range of the probation officer's mission was enormous. As David Rothman has noted, "probation officers had the tasks, incredible as they were, of correcting the child's difficulties and at the same time correcting faults in the family and in the community" (1979:50). Progressive idealism magnified the probation officer's potential to bring about such change. Richard Tuthill, an early juvenile court judge in Chicago, claimed that "with the great right arm and force of the law, the probation officer can go into the home and demand to know the cause of the dependency or the delinquency of the child. . . . He becomes practically a member of the family and teaches them lessons of cleanliness and decency, of truth and integrity" (Rothman, 1979:51). Thus probation officers were bound to be nosy and officious.

The importance of the probation officer's role reflected the juvenile court's commitment to rehabilitate rather than incarcerate young offenders whenever possible. Although institutionalization was still an available recourse for the troublesome child, probation in the child's own home was more often the alternative chosen by court personnel. Like the expansion of the definition of delinquency to include noncriminal conduct such as guilt by association, incorrigibility, and idleness, the reliance on probation mirrored the reformer's interest in rehabilitating both the child and his or her home. As Ellen Ryerson has accurately commented, "While the reformers undoubtedly wished to avoid incarceration, they also wished to avoid the alternative of nonintervention" (1978:44–45).

Ideally, probation was to extend for an indeterminate length of time, since it was impossible to tell how long treatment would be needed. Frequent visits to the child's home, school, and neighborhood would enable the probation officer to spark the rehabilitation of the child and his or her family. The indeterminate probation period granted the state an active, extended role in molding children under its surveillance—a necessity if the children of the immigrant poor were ever to conform successfully to middle-class standards. The ambitions of juvenile court supporters focused on transforming the child's natural environment and his or her family. Reforming the child's habits and attitudes in an artificially controlled setting, the residential institution, had become a less desirable alternative.

Because of its innovative approach, the juvenile court movement spread quickly throughout the nation. Despite its speedy reception by both jurists and legislatures, "the legal sensibility of the country proved far more tractable than reality" (Ryerson, 1978:78); creating the juvenile court had proved to be much easier than making it work. The promise of the all-encompassing child-caring role envisaged by court personnel crumbled as municipal officials who rushed to establish their own juvenile courts quickly discovered that the new institution frequently failed to live up to its goal. In many cities, juvenile courts simply did not function in their prescribed tasks. In virtually all states, reformatories and penal institutions were still filled with hundreds of children; and in many jurisdictions where detention homes had not been provided for court use, children were still confined in jails, often with adult criminals, to await hearings (Hoffman, 1922). Responses to a 1918 Children's Bureau questionnaire that sought information on the workings of the new court system indicated that in most jurisdictions in the United States special provisions had not yet been made to handle children coming before the courts. The report of one court provided commentary on the blending of old ways and new: "65 were sent to jail; 40 were placed in a chain gang; 12 were sent to a reformatory and 1 to an orphanage; 156 were fined; 156 were placed on probation" (Belden, 1920:13). This report was not atypical; many judges still clung to their old attitudes and dealt out the old punishments. Moreover, this Children's Bureau study reported numerous other deficits in the court's operation: inadequate probation service, general unavailability of treatment facilities, inept record keeping and a failure to use the data that did exist, and unqualified judges who lacked either proper legal training or an understanding of children.

These problems were made more acute by staffing and financial deficits. While court officers were ideally to be trained, experienced, and sympathetic, in practice the courts neither attracted nor retained highly qualified individuals. Top-flight judges were decreasingly attracted to the juvenile court bench as time passed, and enthusiasm for the court waned (Polier, 1964). In many jurisdictions, particularly in large cities, a system of rotation was put into effect in which judges sat in a particular court no longer than three months at a time. Such a system hindered the judge's thorough grasp of individual cases and ensured that the fate of a child was often passed from one individual at the court to another—a situation that often paralleled the outside world where the child was shunted from an inadequate home to one foster home, then perhaps to another, and finally to an institution before the cycle began anew.

Personnel problems extended to the probation staff. The range of demands on these officials' time precluded a thorough knowledge of individual cases. As sociologist Thomas Eliot pointed out in his 1914 study of the juvenile court, "The probation officer was forced to become a jack-of-all-trades or first-aid man. He secured for the child shoes, job, club, book, medicine, as the case demanded, in addition to supplying the primary need of moral education. Usually he had no time or thought to go deeper than the immediate need" (1914:13). Although courts employed more full-time professional probation officers as time passed, their performance was still hindered by impossibly large caseloads that made complete investigation and treatment impossible. Indeed, when courts did increase their probation staffs, a simultancous and somctimcs disproportionately great increase in caseloads sometimes resulted (Haller, 1970). As a consequence of these large caseloads, juvenile offenders were often required to make brief appearances at their probation officer's station. This visit replaced the idealized home visit and was usually far too hurried and perfunctory to promote a meaningful relationship between the adult supervisor and the young offender. Ironically, these office visits, which were often conducted in groups to save time, brought troublesome children together and provided them with avenues for further delinquent escapades.

In addition to lapsing into impersonal relationships with probationers, probation officers—particularly those from the ranks of police forces—often at best did not comprehend the rehabilitative goals of the juvenile court and at worst did no more than shuffle papers and emphasize the punitive aspects of probation. Belden commented in her 1918 survey, "It is evident from the character of the replies of many of the police probation officers that they considered their duties in connection with children to be limited to conveying a child to an institution or jail, arresting or swearing out a petition against him, or presenting evidence in court. The constructive side of case work for children under their supervision did not appear in many of their reports" (1920:55).

Like the attitudes of judges, those of probation officers reflected the entrenchment of previous practices. Despite the aura of novelty, evidence quickly and persistently indicated that the juvenile court too often merely continued lackluster, heavy-handed legal responses to problems posed by dependency and delinquency. One national authority on juvenile delinquency asked rhetorically, "How many of these courts are anything other than criminal courts in which the ordinary punitive justice is, at the whim or the pleasure of the presiding judge, tempered with mercy? In how many of them is the presiding judge the wise and understanding father rather than the stern, if not vengeful, agent of outraged law?" (Murphy, 1929:81). From the juvenile court's inception, youths accused of major offenses were left in the adult criminal system. As Sanford Fox has noted, developments in the treatment of juvenile offenders, from the House of Refuge movement through the juvenile court's establishment to the current concern with removing status offenders from the court system, have continued to focus on "petty offenses and salvageable offenders" (1970:1191).

The issue of dealing with the child as a criminal and thus stigmatizing him or her for life was a crucial issue from the early days of the court. Concerned individuals objected that the new juvenile court system involved criminal proceedings and consequently required the protection of the constitutional rights of the accused. In a 1909 article, Julian Mack, a Chicago juvenile court judge, argued that incarceration was punishment for a crime and such punishment "could be inflicted only after criminal proceedings conducted with due regard to the constitutional rights of the defendant" (1909:114). Mack warned that the enthusiasm for the juvenile court movement obscured this important consideration. However, litigation challenging the constitutionality of the juvenile court, particularly the absence of procedural safeguards and the extension of the *parens patriae* doctrine, consistently failed in courts still employing the logic reminiscent of the 1838 *Crouse* decision. Because the legislation creating the new court had described the proceedings as civil rather than criminal, courts of review tended to affirm this view unquestioningly. The 1905 case *Commonwealth* v. *Fisher*, decided before the Pennsylvania Supreme Court, provided a model defense of the new proceedings:

> There is no probability, in the proper administration of the law, of the child's liberty being unduly invaded. Every statute which is designed to give protection, care, and training to children, as a needed substitute for parental authority, and performance of parental duty, is but a recognition of the duty of the state, as the legitimate guardian and protector of children where other guardianship fails. No constitutional right is violated (213 Pennsylvania State Reports 54).

In a 1908 decision, *Ex parte Sharpe,* the Idaho Supreme Court concurred in this estimate of the juvenile court's rehabilitative powers: "Its object is to confer a benefit both upon the child and the community in the way of surrounding the child with better and more elevating influences, and of educating and training him in the direction of good citizenship" (15 Idaho 127).

Others, however, did not so readily accept the extension of the state's authority at the expense of the individual and the family. A Pennsylvania judge, Edward Lindsey, wondered whether the constitutional safeguards of minors and the relationship of parent and child had "completely broken down." He emphasized that "in case of commitment to an institution, there is often a very real deprivation of liberty nor is that fact changed by refusing to call it punishment or because the good of the child is stated to be an object" (1914:145). Lindsey also noted that the parties involved in cases before the juvenile court were in most instances "unable through poverty or ignorance or both to make a contest." Lindsey's point, of course, was that this court was largely designed for the lower class and controlled by the upper classes. *Parens patriae* has rarely touched the powerful classes and, as Lindsey noted, if the concept were ever "so applied, it will undoubtedly be largely modified." But despite indications that the juvenile court was less than successful in meeting its goals, many reformers could not "let go of their favorite prescriptions" (Rothman, 1980:278); rather, they simply reiterated the ideal.

Although a handful of court personnel and concerned citizens began as early as the 1920s to question whether the juvenile court should be abolished, most individuals favored improving the existing institution. However, reform efforts languished while the nation was embroiled in the Depression and World War II. Then, as delinquency rates climbed again in the 1950s, disaffection with the juvenile court intensified (Lunden, 1964).

CONTEMPORARY HISTORY

As early as the 1930s, as disillusionment with the juvenile court began to solidify, concern over staggering arrest rates was accompanied by fears that those children who were brought before the court were significantly harmed by the stigmatization that resulted from judicial processing. The product of this process was explained by Lawrence G. Brown, a sociology professor: "Appearance in court places a stigma on the child and gives him a pernicious definition of himself" (1930:25). Accordingly, because of the court's potentially harmful influence, juvenile cases were more frequently handled out of court, generally by a probation officer or by referral to a social service agency. And the use of the term *juvenile delinquent* was avoided in many jurisdictions because it is a negative label. The New York Family Court Act of 1962, for example, applied the term only to those children between 7 and 16 who had committed an act that would be considered criminal if committed by an adult. For those children who were habitually truant, disobedient, or incorrigible, who were beyond parental control, the court utilized a new label, "Persons in Need of Supervision" (PINS). As Paul Lerman (1973) has noted, however, distinctions between "delinquents" and children "in need of supervision" have tended to be more symbolic than substantive. That children accorded both labels are often placed in the same reform schools and detention facilities is one piece of evidence that neither the public nor court and institutional officials have distinguished meaningfully between the terms.

Public concern with the rising rate of juvenile delinquency, perceptions of the damaging effects of labeling children as "delinquent" or "in need of supervision," and conservative critiques of rehabilitation have produced in the past two decades a sense of the "rupture between the theory and practice of juvenile court dispositions. While statutes, judges, and commentators still talk the language of compassion and treatment, it has become clear that in fact the same purposes that characterize the use of the criminal law for adult offenders—retribution, condemnation, deterrence, incapacitation—are involved in the disposition of juvenile offenders too" (President's Commission on Law Enforcement and Administration of Justice, 1967:80).

The Challenge of Crime in a Free Society, a 1967 report prepared by the President's Commission on Law Enforcement and Administration of Justice, concluded that the "great hopes originally held for the juvenile court have not been fulfilled. It has not succeeded significantly in rehabilitating delinquent youth, in reducing or even stemming the tide of delinquency, or in bringing justice and compassion to the child offender" (1967:80). In assessing the reasons for this failure, the commission laid much of the responsibility on the "community's continuing unwillingness to provide the resources—the people and facilities and concern—necessary to permit them to realize their potential and prevent them from acquiring some of the undesirable features typical of lower criminal courts in this country" (1967:80).

Often the only avenues open to court personnel have been to place juvenile offenders on probation with minimal supervision, to release them outright, or to confine them in warehouselike institutions. Staggering caseload volumes in most urban courts have resulted in brief interviews, assembly-line "treatment," and supervision in the form of phone calls and a few perfunctory visits. As Judge Justine Wise Polier of the New York Family Court has noted, "surveillance, not constructive and skilled supervision," has been the major activity of probation officers. Given the absence of training of court personnel, the lack of support services, and the overwhelming caseloads, Judge Polier has concluded, "The absence of treatment services throughout every area of court responsibility repeatedly reduces the social court to an institution that sanctions community neglect of the individual and so becomes the official executioner of his hopes and potential for change" (1964:42). In her 1964 review of the New York City juvenile court system, *A View from the Bench,* Judge Polier asserted:

> The value of diagnostic studies and recommendations is too often reduced to a paper recommendation. In shopping for placement, probation officers are forced to lower their sights from what they know a child needs to what they can secure. Their sense of professional responsibility is steadily eroded. The judge, in turn, becomes the ceremonial official who in many cases approves a disposition which he knows is only a dead end for the child. . . . The lack of appropriate services and facilities for delinquent children and to a much greater extent for neglected children has contributed more than any other single factor to negating the purpose of the court (1964:30, 42).

Despite the rhetoric of rehabilitating juvenile offenders, protection of the community has often been the paramount goal of judicial personnel charged with controlling threatening behavior. In *The Borderland of Criminal Justice,* Francis Allen has argued that it is "inaccurate and deceptive to describe the juvenile court's operation as rehabilitative or therapeutic; rather, the cases that come before it are being adjudicated primarily because the behavior in question threatens the security and well-being of the community" (1964:34–35). Indeed, the rehabilitative ideal has often led to increased severity of penal measures. For example, the indeterminate sentence, tied to individualized treatment, often leads to a lengthened period of imprisionment that becomes essentially incapacitative rather than therapeutic.

Somewhat paradoxically, the concern with protecting the community by punishing young offenders has gone hand in hand with a heightened attention to individual rights and a renewed skepticism regarding the benevolence of state intervention. In the following section, we will examine the series of Supreme Court cases that led to stronger safeguards of individual rights in juvenile court processing. It is important to note that these decisions were not grounded solely in legal considerations. Rather, the Supreme Court's rulings "drew substantially on an accumulated body of empirical knowledge about how the system of juvenile justice really worked" (Schur, 1973:4).

Kent v. *United States* (1966) was the first juvenile court case to reach the Supreme Court. The case involved a juvenile court judge's decision to waive jurisdiction and transfer the case from juvenile to adult court without a hearing. The situation allowed Justice Abe Fortas, chief spokesman on the bench for the juvenile courts, an opportunity to criticize the court procedure as it then operated. Indeed, it was Fortas's opinion that first stripped away much of the rhetoric of *parens patriae* to reveal the harsh reality of juvenile court procedure. Fortas well understood that the child—faced with the tremendous scope of discretion enjoyed by the juvenile court judge and awarded none of the criminal rights enjoyed by adults—found himself or herself in a particularly disadvantageous position. *Parens patriae* had allowed the juvenile court to escape the requirements of due process. The theory had given the court protection against challenge and, perhaps, against justice:

> There is evidence that there may be grounds for concern that the child receives the worst of both worlds: that he gets neither the protection accorded adults nor the solicitous care and regenerative care postulated for children (*Kent* v. *U.S.*, 383 U.S. 556).

In the *Kent* decision, Fortas felt that the reality was the loss of liberty that could befall a child in juvenile court. Whether transferred to another court, placed in a reformatory, or given a form of probation, the fundamental element at issue was the child's liberty. It was this criterion by which the application of due process to the juvenile court was to be gauged.

The *Kent* decision dealt with the issue of whether the juvenile court could (without a hearing) waive jurisdiction on a juvenile and send him on to the criminal court. The need for a hearing remains clouded even today. The decision definitely did hold that such a hearing was necessary in the District of Columbia. However, it is not at all clear whether the decision limited itself to the District by statutory interpretation or whether the Court was voicing a constitutional right that must be honored by all the states. As a result, several states have seen *Kent* as directive, while others have refused to apply the decision to their juvenile courts.

Fortas's opinion in *Kent* set the stage for *In re Gault* (1967). Through his analysis of the 1966 case, Fortas established a critical perspective on juvenile court law and procedure. Social agencies which carried the judicial powers of deprivation of liberty were now to be held to a strict accounting. The test was long overdue.

Even today, the elements of *Gault* can still shock. Taken into custody on suspicion of making a lewd phone call, Gerald Gault was never confronted by Mrs. Cook, the woman who made the complaint, was afforded no aid in his defense, was allowed no protection against self-incrimination, and was subjected to the shabbiest of judicial procedure. His mother learned of his arrest only through neighbors. Throughout the incident, both the police and the court acted with almost no regard for due process. Everything was justified under the doctrine of *parens patriae*: that this experience was for the child's own welfare.

Gerald Gault's "welfare" required that he be committed to the Arizona Industrial School for an indeterminate sentence. Under usual court procedure, this commitment would end at age 21, unless authorities of both court and institution should terminate this rehabilitation at an earlier age. Therefore, Gerald Gault, who was 15, could have been deprived of liberty for six years!

The Arizona Supreme Court upheld the procedures and decision of the juvenile court. For the members of the Arizona high court, the necessary flexibility of the juvenile system negated many of the elements urged under due process. Specific notice of the charge, therefore, could violate privacy and create a stigma. Better not to divulge the specific charge until the time of the hearing. The child did not require counsel since the probation officer (in this instance, the arresting officer) and the parents would protect the child's rights. His safety and well-being were the objects of the court's concern. In this spirit, the protection against self-incrimination was not necessary; and since the juvenile court enjoyed exclusive jurisdiction, neither appeal of the court decision nor transcript of the proceedings was needed. Finally, since the court did not see evidence that Gault denied the charges, the issue of confrontation of witnesses need not even be discussed. The juvenile court had acted properly and fulfilled the mandate of *parens patriae.*

As in the *Kent* case, Justice Fortas was unimpressed by any appeal to *parens patriae.* He repeated his statement in his previous decision that "the basic requirements of due process and fairness" must be satisfied in juvenile proceedings. After citing numerous cases relevant to the proceedings, Justice Fortas summed up his introduction with the statement that "neither the Fourteenth Amendment nor the Bill of Rights is for adults only" *(In re Gault,* 387 U.S. 3). From this premise he went on to dissolve the aura that surrounded the juvenile court and proceeded to challenge the very essence of its operation. The court's pleas that its activities worked for the good of the child were shown to be suspect. The court's procedure was shown, in fact, to violate fundamental rights. In Fortas's own words, "Under our Constitution, the condition of being a boy does not justify a kangaroo court" *(In re Gault,* 387 U.S. 28).

Fortas argued that the proper goal of the juvenile court—its desire to pay attention to the status of the child and to provide a therapeutic method of treatment—would not be impaired by constitutional requirements. In fact, he felt that the essentials of due process would express a fair and responsive attitude toward the juvenile—an attitude that the child could acknowledge and respect. Fortas then set out the essentials of due process as they apply to the adjudicatory hearing in a juvenile proceeding. The child, in the view of the Supreme Court, has a right to counsel, and to court-appointed counsel if necessary. With the aid of counsel, the child can present his or her defense and confront witnesses, who must present testimony under oath, through cross-examination. The child also has the right to confront his or her accuser and a right against self-incrimination. Since his or her freedom is at stake, this right has a special urgency. Finally, in order to make use of the available elements of defense, the child has a right to timely notice of the charges against him or her.

The spectrum of rights elaborated in the *Gault* decision is impressive and coincides with the more general investigation of the court system that the decision contains. However, Fortas's opinion has noticeable limitations that now underlie much of the investigation that goes on within the judicial system. The *Gault* decision has been limited to the adjudicatory hearing, where the guilt or innocence of the child is determined. It does not extend, for instance, to the intake hearing, where initial decisions to invoke juvenile court jurisdiction are made; nor does it affect the final stage of the process, the disposition hearing, where decisions concerning what is to be done with the child are made. *Gault*'s emphasis on due process and fundamental fairness, however, does have implications for these proceedings and is currently of great concern to the state and national juvenile court movements.

A subsequent case, *In re Winship* (1970), dealt with the single narrow question whether proof beyond a reasonable doubt is among the essentials of due process and fair treatment required when a juvenile is charged with an act that would be considered criminal if committed by an adult. Recalling *Gault*, Justice William Brennan delivered the opinion of the Court: in addition to affirming that "civil labels and good intentions" do not render due-process safeguards unnecessary, the Court rejected the argument that "the protection of proof beyond a reasonable doubt would risk destruction of beneficial aspects of the juvenile process" (*In re Winship*, 397 U.S. 365, 366).

The next juvenile court case to come before the Supreme Court involved the issue of jury trial for juveniles (*McKeiver* v. *Pennsylvania*, 1971). Proponents of this right for juveniles point out that children convicted by the juvenile court are subject to incarceration. While *Gault* never specifically converted the juvenile court to criminal status, it did rob this court of its "civil" label. Since a jury trial is a constitutional right afforded those accused in criminal proceedings in which their liberty is at issue, perhaps juveniles should have the same right; their liberty also is at stake.

In denying application of this criminal right to the juvenile court, Justice Harry Blackmun spoke for the majority when he expressed the fear that introduction of the juries would

> remake the juvenile proceedings into a fully adversary process and will put an effective end to what has been the idealistic prospect of an intimate, informal protective proceeding (*McKeiver* v. *Pennsylvania* 403 U.S. 543).

The majority was fully aware of the imperfections of the juvenile court system. The child, in the Court's opinion, deserved an "intimate, informal protective proceeding." But the proceeding should also ensure due process and fundamental fairness. *McKeiver* v. *Pennsylvania* basically asked where a juvenile proceeding in accord with due process ended and a criminal trial began. The Court felt that addition of more adult rights into the proceeding had to be undertaken with great caution.

As Justice Blackmun elaborated in his opinion, the majority did not view a jury trial as one of those adult rights that are fundamentally necessary to a juvenile proceeding. In fact, the majority played down the value of the jury in *any* trial, whether juvenile or criminal. In their view, the jury trial does not assure competence in the fact-finding function of the proceedings. In the context of the juvenile proceeding, the right to a jury trial could be a distinctly negative factor since it carries with it the traditional delay, formality, and clamor of the adversary system. The majority felt that states might allow jury trial in their own juvenile proceedings if they wished, but such a decision would be in no way based on constitutional mandate.

The dissenting justices attacked the very premise of the majority opinion; informality was no excuse for oppression, they said. While the dissenters appreciated the need for drawing the line between juvenile and criminal proceedings at some point, jury trial was not the proper issue for that purpose. The dissenters effectively pointed to a then-recent decision rendered by Judge De Ciantis in the Rhode Island case *In re McCloud* (1971):

> The child who feels he has been dealt with fairly and not merely expediently or as speedily as possible will be a better prospect for rehabilitation. Many of the children who come before the court come from broken homes, from the ghettos; they often suffer from low self-esteem; and their behavior is frequently a symptom of their own feelings of inadequacy. Traumatic experiences of denial of basic rights only accentuate the past deprivation and contribute to the problem. Thus, a general societal attitude of acceptance of the juvenile as a person entitled to the same protection as an adult may be the true beginning of the rehabilitative process (*McKeiver* v. *Pennsylvania,* 403 U.S. 562).

The dissenting members of the Court did not dispute the need for a juvenile court system. Rather, they demanded that the juvenile court squarely face the realities and implications of its procedures. Primary among those realities and implications is the loss of liberty that the child can suffer, and it is this issue that forms the most effective challenge to the court's existence. To paraphrase Justice William Douglas, if the juvenile court cannot justify its discretion to deprive children of their freedom without full adversary proceedings, then the fundamental issue of deprivation of liberty is sufficient to force the court into the status of a criminal court (*McKeiver* v. *Pennsylvania,* 403 U.S. 572).

Finally, in *Breed* v. *Jones* (1975), the Court unanimously ruled that the Fifth Amendment's prohibition against double jeopardy forbids criminal prosecution of a juvenile after he or she has been tried in juvenile court for the same act. In this case, the juvenile was made a ward of a California court based on factual findings that sustained a charge that the juvenile had committed an act that, if committed by an adult, would constitute the crime of robbery. The juvenile was ordered detained pending a dispositional hearing.

On the date scheduled for that hearing, the court announced that it intended to waive jurisdiction and transfer the case to the appropriate criminal court. Following a hearing at which the court determined the child did not warrant treatment as a juvenile, the case was transferred to criminal court where the juvenile was tried and convicted of robbery. On appeal, the Supreme Court overruled the lower court.

RECENT DEVELOPMENTS

Disillusionment with the juvenile justice system in recent years has been most evident in the radical changes proposed by a thirty-five member committee of judges, social scientists, educators, and social workers assembled under the auspices of the Institute of Judicial Administration and the American Bar Associations's Joint Commission on Juvenile Justice Standards. In 1971–1976, this commission prepared twenty-four volumes of material analyzing all facets of the juvenile justice system. Having found tremendous disparity among juvenile courts in the handling, sentencing, and treatment of juveniles, the commission recommended (Flicker, 1977):

1. Removal of the traditional rehabilitative model on which the concept of "treatment" services for juveniles has long rested.
2. Use of "determinate" rather than "indeterminate" sentencing.
3. Removal of status offenders (the phrase currently used to describe children "in need of supervision") from court jurisdiction.
4. Creating guidelines to regulate the disposition of cases.
5. Termination of the juvenile court jurisdiction over children who are neglected or abused by their parents.
6. Phasing out correctional institutions.

The commission disposed of the questions arising in *Kent* and *Gault* concerning the extent to which the state could adequately perform in its parental role, given the lack of personnel, facilities, and proven rehabilitative techniques, by suggesting that since court personnel are apparently unable to diagnose or predict behavior adequately, simply enlarging court staffs would be futile. And, the commission implied, communities that were unwilling to supply the necessary manpower and material resources for the juvenile court's proper function in the halcyon years of its infancy would not be inclined to do so now (Mayo and Isralowitz, 1980:134–135).

In suggesting that indeterminate sentences be replaced by determinate ones, the commission advocated a system of set penalties for specific offenses, with allowances for mitigating circumstances; the time limits would be established by legislation. Like many of the commission's other recommendations, this suggestion echoes the 1967 Presidential Commission's concern for the "potential arbitrariness and unfettered judicial discretion in dealing with human lives that informality establishes" (1967:85).

Although the 1971–1976 commission carefully considered the position that "institutionalization was inherently coercive and antithetical to legitimate treatment goals," it recognized that there are a "dangerous few" individuals who pose a serious threat to the community for whom institutionalization may be the only appropriate disposition. The commission emphasized, however, that such confinement not be grounded in rehabilitative principles: "Rather, incarceration must be based upon traditional criminal law factors, including the age of the offender, seriousness of the offense, prior record, and aggravating and mitigating circumstances of the crime" (Gilman, 1980:147).

SUMMARY

The creation of the first juvenile court in 1899 in Chicago was based on hopes of reducing the criminal responsibility of children and protecting them from the stigma attached to criminality. The distinctive features characterizing the development of the juvenile court can be attributed to the efforts of Progressive reformers, who focused interest on the young offender rather than on the offense. The early juvenile reform movement emphasized the court as a treatment center rather than as an instrument for social control, using the ancient English judicial doctrine of *parens patriae,* whereby the king—and now the state—has the power to act as a parent for the purpose of protecting the best interests of the child.

The establishment of a separate juvenile court is popularly viewed as a rejection of penal concepts and criminal proceedings for juveniles, for the juvenile court is formally considered as a civil court. Recent scholars have contended, however, that the progressive reformers were reacting less to our punitive heritage than to rapid urbanization, industrialism, and the influx of immigrant cultures that allegedly threatened rural and small-town values. Arguing that reform of children was more likely if they were removed from "immoral" parents and a "vicious" environment, these "child savers" erroneously and naively assumed a harmony of interests between juvenile offenders and agencies of social control. Their acceptance of middle-class values and paternalism remains a characteristic of current juvenile courts, which often perceive strivings for autonomy by minors as deviant behavior.

A series of cases decided since the 1960s by the United States Supreme Court has provided guidelines and legal constraints under which juvenile courts must operate. The first case in which the Court directly addressed procedures in juvenile courts was *Kent.* This case challenged the District of Columbia Juvenile Court Act, which allowed arbitrary waiver of juveniles to adult courts for criminal charges. The Supreme Court called for a hearing, assistance of counsel, and reasons for the waiver. In noting disapprovingly that juvenile courts, by operating as civil tribunals under the doctrine of *parens patriae,* denied to minors constitutional rights while severely curbing their liberties, the Court paved the way for the landmark decision delivered soon in *Gault.*

The *Gault* decision, applicable only to adjudicatory proceedings that could result in commitment to a state institution as a delinquent, held that due process requires the right to adequate and timely notice of charges, the right to counsel, the privilege against self-incrimination, and the right to confront and cross-examine sworn witnesses. Next, the case of *Winship* established that the more stringent standard of "proof beyond a reasonable doubt," rather than the "preponderance of the evidence," was an ingredient of due process during adjudication when a juvenile has been charged with an offense which would be a crime if committed by an adult. An apparent trend to extend to juvenile courts all criminal trial procedures was curtailed when the Court held, in *McKeiver* v. *Pennsylvania,* that the right to trial by jury was not constitutionally required in delinquency proceedings. But continuing the trend established by *Gault,* the Court later held, in *Breed* v. *Jones,* that a youth adjudicated delinquent in juvenile court cannot be prosecuted again as an adult without violating the constitutional ban on double jeopardy; waiver to adult court must be made prior to an adjudicatory hearing.

Most recently, the IJA-ABA Joint Commission on Juvenile Justice Standards issued recommendations reflecting the tension that exists in juvenile court proceedings: protective care and reformation of the child versus punishment by and the protection of society. These recommendations were consistent with the Supreme Court decision that formal legal requirements governing juvenile courts be aligned with those in adult criminal proceedings. The commission's recommendations take the view that youths who act like adults should be entitled to the same rights as adults in legal proceedings. In this way, both the youth and society are afforded protection.

DISCUSSION QUESTIONS

1. How have societal responses to control delinquent children reflected ambivalent attitudes toward them?
2. What were the origins and justifications for the institutional control of children?
3. What were the major assumptions and procedures employed in the Houses of Refuge to save children from crime?

4. What concerns motivated reformers who led the juvenile court movement?
5. How has the doctrine of *parens patriae* been used to justify intervention in the lives of children? Give examples.
6. What special role were probation officers supposed to play in the juvenile court system?
7. What problems emerged in the operation of the juvenile court that led to a general questioning of its continued existence?
8. What major rights were established for juveniles in the following United States Supreme Court cases: *Kent, Gault, Winship,* and *Breed* v. *Jones?*
9. What were the conflicting opinions presented in *McKeiver* v. *Pennsylvania* concerning the right to a jury trial in juvenile court proceedings?
10. How have legal responses to institutional control of children reflected the developments of society at large?

REFERENCES

ABBOTT, GRACE
1938 *The Child and the State,* volumes 1 and 2. Chicago: University of Chicago Press.

ALLEN, FRANCIS A.
1964 *The Borderland of Criminal Justice: Essays in Law and Criminology.* Chicago: University of Chicago Press.

ARIES, PHILIPPE
1962 *Centuries of Childhood: A Social History of Family Life* (translated by Robert Baldick). New York: Vintage Books.

BAKER, HARVEY H.
1910 Proceeding of the Boston juvenile court. Pp. 318–327 in Hastings Hart (ed.), *Preventive Treatment of Neglected Children.* New York: Charities Publication Committee.

BELDEN, EVELINA
1920 *Courts in the United States Hearing Children's Cases: Results of a Questionnaire Study Covering the Year 1918.* Washington, D.C.: U.S. Government Printing Office.

BROWN, LAWRENCE G.
1930 Social causes and cures for delinquency. *Yearbook of the National Probation Association: 1930.*

CARPENTER, MARY
1851 *Reformatory Schools for the Children of the Perishing and Dangerous Classes, and for Juvenile Offenders* (reprinted 1969). New York: A. M. Kelley.

DIAMOND, BERNARD L.
1966 The children of Leviathan: Psychoanalytic speculations concerning welfare law and punitive sanction. *California Law Review* 54:357–369.

ELIOT, THOMAS D.
1914 *The Juvenile Court and the Community.* New York: Macmillan.

FLICKER, BARBARA D.
1977 *Standards for Juvenile Justice: A Summary and Analysis.* Cambridge, Mass.: Ballinger.

FOX, SANFORD J.
1970 Juvenile justice reform: An historical perspective. *Stanford Law Review* 22:1187–1239.

GILMAN, DAVID
1980 Rethinking juvenile justice: The standards project. *Child Welfare* 59:145–151.

HALLER, MARK H.
1970 Urban crime and criminal justice: The Chicago case. *Journal of American History* 57:619–635.

HART, JOHN L.
1879 *In the School-Room (Philadelphia, 1879).* Cited in Herbert G. Gutman (ed.), *Work, Culture, and Society in Industrializing America: Essays in American Working-Class and Social History.* New York: Knopf, 1976.

HASKINS, GEORGE L.
1968 *Law and Authority in Early Massachusetts: A Study in Tradition and Design.* New York: Archon.

HAWES, JOSEPH M.
1971 *Children in an Urban Society: Juvenile Delinquency in Nineteenth-Century America.* New York: Oxford University Press.

HOFFMAN, CHARLES W.
1922 The fundamental principles of the juvenile court and its part in future community programs for child welfare. Pp. 13–23 in U.S. Children's Bureau, *Proceedings of the Conference on Juvenile Court Standards.* Washington, D.C.: U.S. Government Printing Office.

HURLEY, T. O.
1907 *Origin of the Illinois Juvenile Court Law: Juvenile Courts and What They Have Accomplished,* 3rd edition (reprinted 1977). New York: AMS Press.

INSTITUTE OF JUDICIAL ADMINISTRATION/THE AMERICAN BAR ASSOCIATION
1977 *Juvenile Justice Standards Project, Standards for Juvenile Justice: A Summary and Analysis.* Cambridge, Mass.: Ballinger.

LERMAN, PAUL
1973 Delinquent without crimes: The American approach to juvenile status offenses. Pp. 257–286 in Norman K. Denzin (ed.), *Children and Their Caretakers.* New Brunswick, N.J.: Transaction Books.

LINDSEY, EDWARD
1914 The juvenile court movement from a lawyer's standpoint. *Annals of the American Academy of Political and Social Science* 52:140–148.

LUNDEN, WALTER A.
1964 *Statistics on Delinquents and Delinquency.* Springfield, Ill.: Charles C Thomas.

MACK, JULIAN W.
1909 The juvenile court. *Harvard Law Review* 23:104–122.

MAYO, LEONARD W., AND RICHARD E. ISRALOWITZ
1980 The American juvenile justice system: An evaluation of standards. *Child Welfare* 59:131–144.

MENNEL, ROBERT M.
1973 *Thorns and Thistles: Juvenile Delinquents in the United States, 1825–1940.* Hanover, N.H.: University Press of New England.

MURPHY, J. PRENTICE
1929 The juvenile court at the bar. *Annals of the American Academy of Political and Social Science* 145:80–97.

NEW YORK SOCIETY FOR THE REFORMATION OF JUVENILE DELINQUENTS
1832 *Documents Relative to the House of Refuge,* Nathaniel Hart, ed. New York.

NEW YORK STATE BOARD OF CHARITIES
1901 Report of the secretary of state in 1824 on the relief and settlement of the poor, *Thirty-Fourth Annual Report, 1900* (Albany, New York). Cited in Robert H. Bremner, *Children and Youth in America: A Documentary History,* part I: *1600–1865.* Cambridge, Mass.: Harvard University Press.

POLIER, JUSTINE W.
1964 *A View from the Bench: The Juvenile Court.* New York: National Council on Crime and Delinquency.

PRESIDENT'S COMMISSION ON LAW ENFORCEMENT AND ADMINISTRATION OF JUSTICE
1967 *The Challenge of Crime in a Free Society.* Washington, D.C.: U.S. Government Printing Office.

ROTHMAN, DAVID S.
1980 *Conscience and Convenience: The Asylum and Its Alternative in Progressive America.* Boston: Little, Brown.
1979 The Progressive legacy: Development of American attitudes toward juvenile delinquency. Pp. 34–68 in LaMar T. Empey (ed.), *The Progressive Legacy and Current Reforms.* Charlottesville, Va.: University of Virginia Press.

RYERSON, ELLEN
1978 *The Best Laid Plans: America's Juvenile Court Experiment.* New York: Hill & Wang.

SCHUR, EDWIN M.
1973 *Radical Nonintervention: Rethinking the Delinquency Problem.* Englewood Cliffs, N.J.: Prentice-Hall.

THURSTON, HENRY W.
1910 The juvenile court as a probation institution. Pp. 333–347 in Hastings Hart (ed.), *Preventive Treatment of Neglected Children.* New York: Charities Publication Committee.

CASES

Breed v. *Jones,* 421 U.S. 519 (1975)
Commonwealth v. *Fisher,* 213 Penn. State Reports 54 (1905)
Ex parte Crouse, 4 Wharton 11 (1838) (Pennsylvania)
Ex parte Sharpe, 15 Idaho 127 (1908)
In re Gault, 387 U.S. 1 (1967)
In re McCloud, 109 Rhode Island Reports, appeal 1304 (1971)
In re Winship, 397 U.S. 358 (1970)
Kent v. *U.S.,* 383 U.S. 541 (1966)
McKeiver v. *Pennsylvania,* 403 U.S. 528 (1971)

The Contemporary Juvenile Court

10

JUVENILE JUSTICE PROCESSING: AN OVERVIEW

What happens to a juvenile who breaks the law or is in need of supervision, confinement, or treatment? The answer may depend upon where the juvenile lives, his or her age, family situation, and numerous other variables. Perhaps the only constant factor is that the juvenile is handled by the juvenile justice system. This system varies from state to state and community to community, depending largely on interpretations of the statutes that outline how juveniles will be processed when they become the responsibility of the authorities. A juvenile justice system consists of separate agencies—each run by different directives and administrative heads, each governed by different legislative mandates that are translated into policy guidelines and routinized procedures—which are primarily devoted to attaining their own objectives. An agency's objectives, though theoretically concerned with juvenile justice, are more practically oriented around services and procedures that only it can or should provide.

The juvenile justice system is patterned after the criminal justice system, and its design is constantly reviewed and redrafted by national, state, and local legislatures. It seems amazing that the system functions as well as it does, for the juvenile justice system "lacks one essential element for it to function as a system: a true manager" (Streib, 1978:21). Streib indicates that since no agency within a system has the power to control the activities of the other agencies in that system, the agencies may work at cross-purposes in any combined effort; certainly this charge is not entirely untrue. But to understand the combined efforts of the juvenile justice system, we must first recognize that the system is actually only a flow or process of one agency's contact with a given juvenile case that leads either to the termination (exit from the system) of the case or the transmission of the jurisdictional authority in the case to the next agency in the flow.

A case typically flows through the system by first being reported to law enforcement, then being processed by court intake, formally charged by the prosecutor, tried in a court hearing, and possibly assigned to some form of corrections activity. At any point in this flow, of course, a case may be diverted, dismissed, or terminated in some other way, returning the child to the outside world.

The Police

The police generally represent the outer layer of the juvenile justice system. For many juveniles, this is the only contact they will ever have with the system, while for many others it is only the first stage of processing. Somewhere between 2 and 3 million juveniles will have police contacts during a year; however, this is generally a redundant count since a given youngster may have multiple police contacts in a year. Most police-juvenile contacts are the result of citizen complaints; based on observations in three cities, for example, Black and Reiss (1970) found that of 273 police-juvenile encounters (excluding traffic violations), 78 percent were citizen-initiated and 22 percent were initiated by police on patrol. Similarly, Terry's (1967) examination of 9,023 juvenile offenses at the police level in one city revealed that only 16 percent were police initiated; fully 84 percent were the result of citizen complaints or calls.

Even though the police may not be the first persons to process a juvenile into the system, they represent the first public agency to be contacted. Even when insisting that a juvenile be processed, most citizens ask the police to initiate processing rather than go directly to the juvenile courts. The police then intervene and make the first formal determination of whether and how to process the juvenile.

During their initial contacts in the field, the police have a vast amount of discretion concerning whether to take a child into custody; in the majority of cases, they decide not to do so. However, an officer may also choose to take a case into court or police custody, to exercise an option that leads to termination, such as counsel and release, or to refer the case to a nonjuvenile justice agency.

If a child is taken into custody, statutes commonly address the question of what the police should do next. Some states require the arresting officer to notify a probation officer or other official designated by the juvenile court; however, most states simply require that the police promptly notify the arrested child's parents.

In some jurisdictions, a juvenile who is taken into police custody is taken to the police station for initial screening either by a regular police officer or a specially trained juvenile officer. The police may conduct a lengthy investigation and make a decision. This process could, like the field decision, lead to a termination of the case, enrollment in alternative programs, or a referral to court for formal intake.

Court Intake

One of the traditional features of the juvenile court system is the case-screening process known as intake. Intake screening procedures are generally designed to weed out cases that do not warrant a formal court hearing, such as:

1. Matters over which the court has no jurisdiction.
2. Cases where the evidence against the child is insufficient.
3. Cases not serious enough to require juvenile court adjudication.

But some intake operations actively seek to "adjust" particular cases that may best be handled informally outside the court system. The intake department may also order social-background investigations, medical or psychological diagnoses, or other studies that might be used to determine the suitability of juvenile court involvement. Even probation supervision is sometimes ordered on an informal level through intake. The intake department can therefore be regarded as an operation that performs on an unofficial level all of the functions of the court. Informal hearings, adjudications, and probation supervision are frequently administered at the intake level, without referral to a judge.

If the intake procedures result in a decision to submit the child to a formal court hearing, a *petition* is filed. This document sets forth, among other things, the specific charge that a delinquent act has been committed; that the child is dependent, neglected, or abused; or that the child is in need of supervision. It serves to notify the child of the claims made about his or her misconduct or status. The petition may be viewed as the counterpart of an indictment in criminal prosecutions and a complaint in civil litigation.

Most states impose limitations on who may sign the petition. For example, California authorizes only a probation officer to sign and file the petition, while Texas restricts the making of the petition to the prosecuting attorney alone. Furthermore, most states distinguish between who may sign a petition—generally anyone who has knowledge of the facts of the case and believes that they are true—and who has the formal authority to file it. (On the other hand, Illinois allows any adult to sign the petition against the child.) The latter power is generally vested in the prosecutor, who must countersign as well as file the petition.

The prosecutor's primary function is to evaluate the case in terms of legal sufficiency. In any case in which a minor is alleged to qualify for prosecution in the juvenile court, the prosecutor submits a petition to the court. If the prosecutor decides not to file the petition, his or her decision in the matter is regarded as final, and the case is dismissed. If the prosecutor does file the petition, it is usually followed by a report by the intake (probation) officer on the behavior patterns and social history of the minor cited in the petition.

Court Hearings

The proceedings in a juvenile court are civil in nature rather than criminal, and the general rules relating to civil proceedings apply to juvenile court for the most part. Juvenile court proceedings, however, are generally nonadversarial and thus there are some differences in procedures.

The Adjudication Hearing Adjudication determines whether the child has actually committed the offense of which he or she is accused. If delinquency is alleged, the required standard of evidence is *proof beyond reasonable doubt*—as is needed to sustain a criminal charge in an adult court. When the juvenile appears to be "in need of supervision," proof in most states is established by a preponderance of evidence. Hearsay is inadmissible at the adjudication hearing. (Inadequacy of evidence is a frequent basis for appeal.) The juvenile has the right to confront and cross-examine witnesses and is entitled to the due-process safeguards of adequate, timely, written notice of the allegations and sufficient time to formulate a response. The right to refuse to testify is also assured under the Fifth Amendment. The juvenile is entitled to counsel to protect his or her legal rights.

To be valid, confessions must be voluntary, corroborated by someone other than an accomplice, and preceded by the Miranda warning. The Miranda warning consists of the set of rights that a person has when accused or suspected of having committed a specific offense. He or she must be informed of the rights prior to interrogation, as stated by the U.S. Supreme Court in deciding *Miranda* v. *Arizona* (1966). These rights include: (1) the right to remain silent; (2) the right to have an attorney present during questioning; and (3) the right to have an attorney provided free of charge if the suspect cannot afford to hire one. If the suspect waives these rights, any statement he or she makes may be used in court against him or her. Generally, this warning is also given to the juvenile's parents so that they may assist in protecting their child's constitutional rights. A juvenile is not constitutionally entitled to the right of trial by jury, and only nine states accord a child this right under certain circumstances; fairness is the applicable due-process standard for juvenile proceedings. After hearing all of the evidence, the court may dismiss or continue the case (without judgment pending further investigation) or sustain the petition. If the petition is sustained, the court sets a date for the dispositional hearing, or the judge may ask for the social investigation report and make an immediate disposition of the case.

The Dispositional Hearing The dispositional hearing has retained many of the informal aspects that characterized the juvenile court system prior to the *Kent* and *Gault* decisions (see Chapter 9). The judge, the probation officer, the prosecutor, the defense attorney, and the child's parents typically discuss the available options, and hearsay evidence and opinion are thus admissible at this stage. Depending on community resources, the judge may have a considerable range of dispositional alternatives, ranging from dismissal to commitment to a state or local correctional facility. The judge may, in order to obtain further social studies or because of a change in the juvenile's status, elect to withhold disposition and continue the case. Or the court may release the child into the custody of his or her parents, or place him or her on probation. If probation is the disposition, then the juvenile may be referred to the probation department for formal or informal supervision. A child may also be removed from the custody of his or her parents and placed under the court's authority. The child may then be placed in a public or private facility or foster home. Whatever the disposition, however, it generally sets forth the facts on which the court has exercised jurisdiction and indicates the basis for the court's decree.

With this overview of case processing in the juvenile justice system in mind, we now turn to an examination of the scope of juvenile court jurisdiction, identifying those categories of youths who are subject to court intervention.

JUVENILE COURT JURISDICTION

As conceived and implemented by its supporters, the juvenile justice system was meant to prevent future criminal conduct by applying techniques and services designed to reform and rehabilitate the youthful offender. Broad statutory authority was deemed necessary in order to allow the court to intervene in a wide range of situations and to bring many juveniles under its jurisdiction, so that it might use the full range of its resources to decide who required treatment. The legal construct of "delinquency," therefore, was defined as a class of behaviors considered injurious to the community in general—such as property crimes and crimes against the person—and of

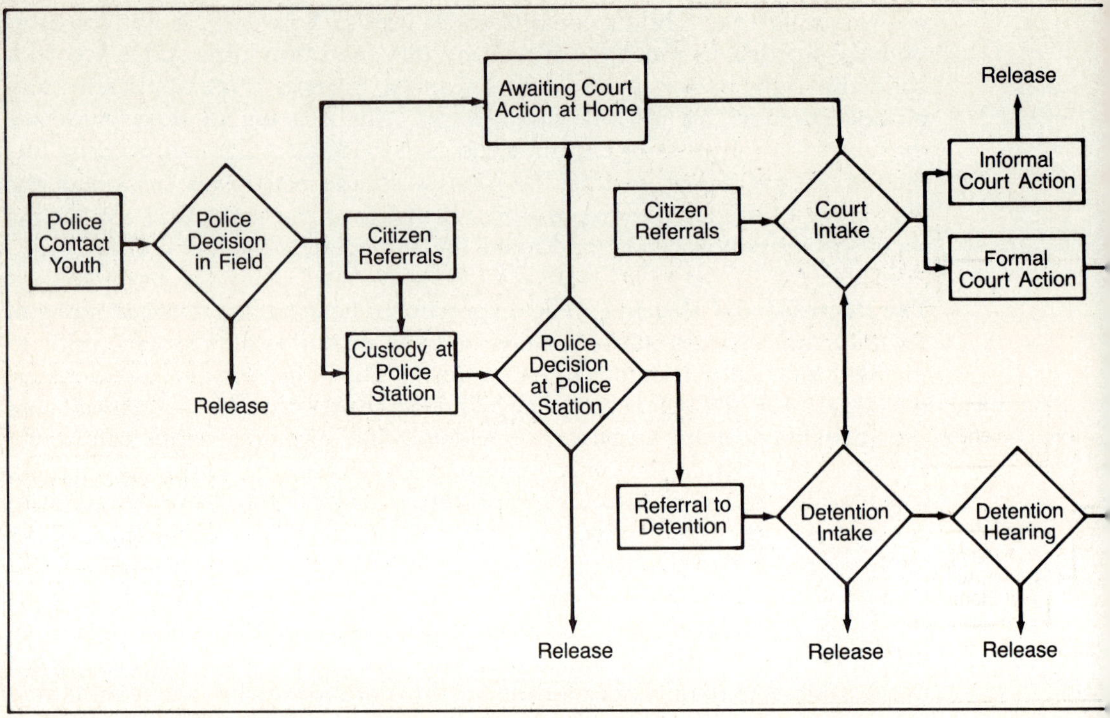

FIGURE 10–1
Structure and Process of the Juvenile Justice System

behaviors characterized as harmful to the juvenile's own welfare. Traditional statutes defining the limits of the juvenile court's delinquency jurisdiction used such terminology as "habitually so deports himself as to endanger the morals or health of himself or others"; "growing up in idleness or crime"; "associates with vagrant, vicious, or immoral persons"; "engages in indecent or immoral conduct"; "living in circumstances of manifest danger of falling into habits of vice or immorality"; "who, by reason of being habitually wayward or habitually disobedient, becomes an incorrigible or uncontrollable child." Therefore, the state, acting as *parens patriae* (see Chapter 9), could intervene in the juvenile's life virtually as it pleased. Such broad jurisdiction was fundamentally based on the assumption that "[n]atural parents would be expected to be concerned with the whole gamut of undesirable behavior—from criminal activity to smoking cigarettes . . . " (Miller et al., 1976:58).

The definitions of juvenile court jurisdiction can be confusing (see Figure 10–1). The term encompasses the notion of a valid exercise of power over a class of identified children. Today, the juvenile court's power is typically exercised over youths charged with conduct that would be criminal if com-

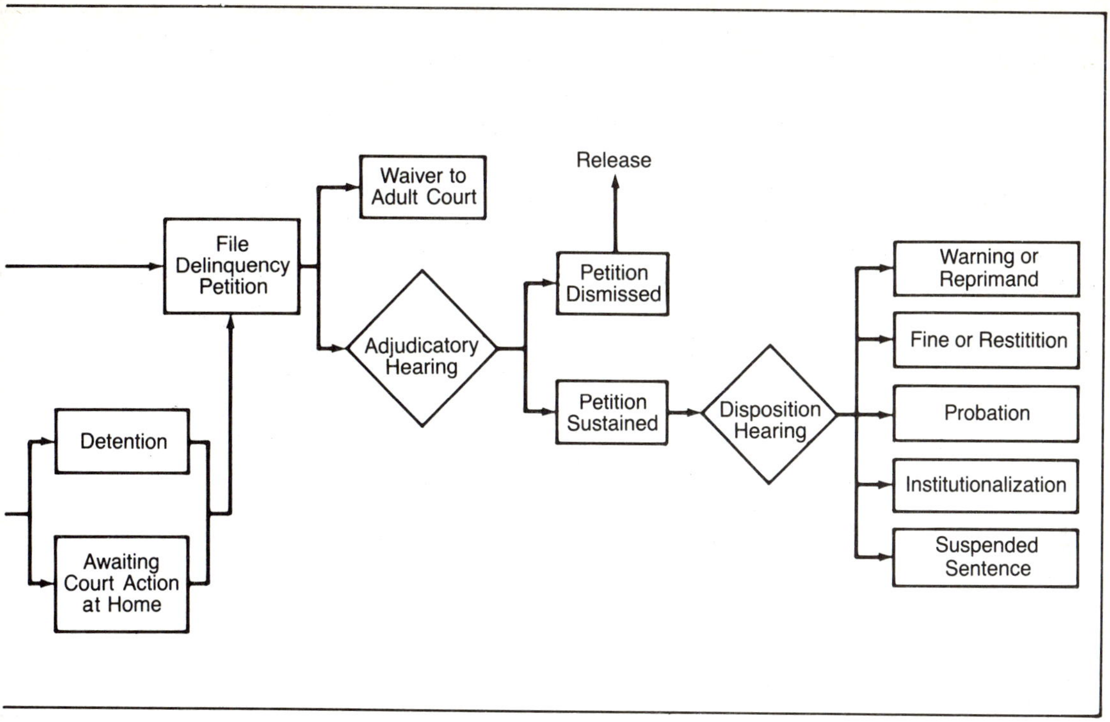

mitted by an adult (delinquency jurisdiction); youths charged with misbehavior or conduct that would not be criminal if performed by an adult (status offense jurisdiction); and youths who come to the court's attention because of parental deficiencies or misconduct (dependent, neglected, and abused children).

WAIVER OF JUVENILE COURT JURISDICTION

The juvenile court has evolved as a civil forum whose dispositions are ideally directed toward the treatment, rehabilitation, and the best interests of the child. At times, however, the jurisdiction of the juvenile court is not thought appropriate for certain young offenders. Thus, nearly every state provides for the prosecution of some juveniles as adults in criminal court. The procedure whereby a child winds up in criminal court is variously referred to as *transfer of jurisdiction, waiver of jurisdiction, certification as an adult,* or *determination of fitness.*

Whatever a given court terms this procedure, the decision to cause a child to be prosecuted as an adult is potentially its most extreme sanction. Although a young person may conceivably benefit from the procedural safeguards available only in the adult courts, the trade-off is considerable. A juvenile transferred to adult criminal court faces the exposure of a public trial and a public record that may bar him or her from military service or public or private employment. He or she is also subjected to the possibility of long-term incarceration, harsher conditions of confinement, the loss of civil rights, contact with adult felons, and the loss of whatever individualized rehabilitation and treatment programs are available through the juvenile court. In addition, young people who are confined in adult prisons will almost certainly be hardened by the experience. If they are not exploited due to their age and size, they will likely become more aggressive simply out of a need for self-protection or survival (Community Research Forum, 1980).

Largely because of these damaging consequences, some commentators have argued that juvenile courts should retain jurisdiction over *all* juveniles and that procedures permitting or mandating the transfer of young people to adult prosecution should be abolished. Other observers caution that the transfer process is a necessary vent for public frustration and anger at highly visible and violent juvenile crimes (Stamm, 1973). Abolishing the possibility of transfer in such circumstances could ultimately help to undo the juvenile court system altogether. When the means to extract retribution for violent crime are denied, political and community pressure to lower the maximum age of juvenile court jurisdiction or to otherwise exclude entire classes of juveniles from the jurisdiction of the juvenile court becomes almost irresistible. It has been proposed that the transfer mechanism is an essential safety valve "permitting the expiatory sacrifice of some youths to quiet political and community clamor and to preserve a more benign system for those who remain" (Feld, 1978:519).

We will not try here to resolve the question of whether transfer of jurisdiction has a legitimate place within the juvenile court framework. Instead, we will simply proceed on two basic premises. First, a mechanism for transfer is a political reality in most states; if there is to be any change in this mechanism, most states could be expected to move to facilitate transfer rather than to abolish it. Second, given a choice between the rehabilitative philosophy of the juvenile court and the sanctions of the adult penal system, the juvenile court is preferred for those who can benefit from it.

In considering the criteria used in transfer decisions, we will first review the Supreme Court decision in *Kent* v. *United States* (1966). We next examine various statutory schemes that bypass the *Kent* decision by directly or indirectly placing the option for adult prosecution in the hands of prosecutors, rather than of juvenile court judges. These procedures are then discussed in terms of their consistency with both the due-process requirements of *Kent* and the rehabilitative philosophy of the juvenile court.

The Impact of *Kent* v. *United States*

Kent v. *United States* (1966) was the first case arising from the juvenile justice system to reach the United States Supreme Court, and it was the point of departure for a procedural revolution in juvenile court decision making. The central figure in the case was Morris A. Kent, Jr., a 16-year-old who was charged with housebreaking, robbery, and rape while on probation under the jurisdiction of the District of Columbia Juvenile Court. Kent's attorney requested a transfer hearing and access to Kent's social service records, which the juvenile court held. Although the District of Columbia's transfer statute required a "full investigation" by the court, the judge failed to rule on the request for a hearing and, without notice, transferred Morris Kent to the criminal jurisdiction of the district court. At the trial, he was found guilty of housebreaking and robbery but innocent of rape by reason of insanity. He was ordered to serve his sentence as a psychiatric patient at St. Elizabeth's Hospital in the District of Columbia.

In reviewing Kent's appeal, the Supreme Court first recognized that there is no constitutional requirement for a separate juvenile court system. But when such a system is authorized by statute, the Court held, a juvenile may not be deprived of his or her constitutional benefits without ceremony. Specifically, the Court stated that there is no place in our legal system for reaching a verdict of such tremendous consequences without a hearing, without effective assistance of counsel, and without a statement of the reasons for the decision.

The unprecedented *Kent* decision initially evoked considerable discussion, with commentators and courts alike taking the position that the due-process safeguards it announced applied only in the District of Columbia because they derived solely from an interpretation of the District of Columbia code. For the most part, the controversy subsided when the Court decided *In re Gault* in 1967. The *Gault* opinion, which like *Kent* was authored by Justice Abe Fortas, held that although *Kent* relied upon the language of the District of Columbia code, the basic requirements of due process and fairness apply to all juvenile court transfer proceedings. A fair summary of the effect of these decisions is that a state is not required to create a juvenile court, but once it does so, the essentials of due process must be afforded those who fall within its jurisdiction.

A host of questions concening the transfer procedure, however, remain unanswered. Because the Court specifically declined to review the merits of the juvenile court's transfer decision in *Kent,* the case provides only limited guidance in establishing criteria for evaluating the appropriateness of transfer. The interpretation and application of transfer criteria have been elusive as well.

Like most state statutes, the District of Columbia Code made transfer dependent on suitability to treatment within the juvenile justice system.

Eight factors in the code were identified to guide District of Columbia Juvenile Court judges and to ensure some uniformity in their transfer decisions:

1. The seriousness of the alleged offense.
2. Whether the alleged offense was committed in an aggressive, violent, premeditated, or willful manner.
3. Whether the offense was against person or against property.
4. The merit of the complaint.
5. Where the codefendants are adults, the desirability of trying the entire action at one trial.
6. The sophistication and maturity of the juvenile.
7. Previous contacts with the juvenile court.
8. The likelihood of reasonable rehabilitation of the juvenile.

The inclusion of these standards in the appendix to the *Kent* opinion reflects the apparent approval by the Supreme Court of their use in determining the propriety of juvenile court jurisdiction (*Kent* v. *U.S.*, 383, U.S., 556–567). A number of states have incorporated these criteria in their juvenile codes almost verbatim.

In reality, though, the transfer criteria are highly subjective, and the decision to transfer often results from uneven judicial discretion. Various surveys have concluded that transfer may depend on such factors as the rebelliousness of the juvenile and the attitudes of the community toward the alleged offense (Stamm, 1973). The decision may also be influenced by the space available in the area's juvenile facilities, rather than by an objective determination of whether the young person cannot benefit from them.

As a practical matter, a juvenile is most likely to be transferred if he or she is nearing the maximum age of juvenile court jurisdiction, is accused of a relatively serious offense, and has a prior record of arrests. Such factors are certainly relevant to the juvenile court's disposition but may be overstressed when considering transfer to the adult court. Age, for example, does not necessarily require that the offender be transferred to adult court or released outright after his or her eighteenth birthday; juvenile court jurisdiction can, by statute, be extended beyond the eighteenth birthday in certain circumstances. If the youth still needs treatment when he or she exceeds the age of juvenile court jurisdiction, civil commitment may be appropriate; if he or she no longer needs treatment, there is no reason for continued confinement. The seriousness of the alleged offense is also a questionable criterion upon which to base transfer. There are indications that some serious offenders—particularly juveniles who have committed a homicide—may in fact be more receptive to the treatment concepts of the juvenile court than others who have committed lesser offenses (Vitiello, 1976). At the least, a single serious offense should not disqualify one from an attempt at rehabilitation. Perhaps juvenile court resources now being devoted to detention and supervision of status offenders could be better directed toward innovative treatment approaches for the serious offender within the juvenile court system.

Post-*Kent* Developments

In the more than fifteen years since *Kent* was decided, juvenile court transfer procedures in every state have been scrutinized for compliance with *Kent*'s due-process requirements. During this period, legislatures in some states have removed some or all transfer decisions from the juvenile court and instead placed them within the control of the prosecutor. One contributing factor in this development has been continuing public demand for retribution and protection in the wake of purported increases in juvenile crime. Another is the limitation of juvenile facilities in terms of physical capacity, personnel, and the availability of the specialized, individually oriented treatment programs that are supposedly the hallmark of the juvenile justice system. The fact that the recognition of procedural rights for juveniles has made the transfer process slower and more deliberate, and its outcome less certain, has also undoubtedly contributed. For some or all of these reasons, states have increasingly considered alternative, more streamlined methods to transfer juveniles.

An example is the District of Columbia Court Reform and Criminal Procedure Act of 1970 (D.C. Code §16–2307). This appears to have been enacted in direct response to *Kent* and has influenced reforms in a number of states. The act redefined the term *child* to exclude from the jurisdiction of the juvenile court persons who have reached the age of 16 and who are charged with murder, forcible rape, first-degree burglary, armed robbery, or assault with intent to commit any of these offenses. Although this procedure is sometimes referred to as the "legislative method" of transfer, this term is inexact because it is the prosecutor who decides whether to charge the young person with one of the "adult" offenses. At least one state has opted for a statute that permits the prosecutor even greater latitude. Nebraska allows the prosecutor to bring an action in either the adult court or the juvenile court in all felony cases, and in misdemeanor cases if the young person is 16 or over (Neb. Rev. Stat. §43–203 [3] [b], 43–202.01).

While these statutory provisions may indeed streamline the transfer process, they are also potentially arbitrary. A prosecutor is traditionally more responsive to political pressure than a judge is, and more likely to ignore the rehabilitative possibilities of the juvenile court. Furthermore, the prosecutor is an adversary who has been sworn to protect society's interests. It is unreasonable to expect him or her to weigh the interests of the child against those of the state objectively.

Until the Supreme Court decides that the *Kent* due-process protections apply to transfer proceedings regardless of who controls the decision, unreviewable discretion by prosecutors and its accompanying arbitrariness will likely continue. A number of common arguments support a judicial determination of transfer and oppose prosecutors' control over the decision either directly or indirectly through a "legislative method" of transfer. First, the decision to transfer is of critical importance to the juvenile, and due process and simple fairness demand that it be made only after a full hearing. Second, the automatic exclusion of some juveniles from juvenile court jurisdiction on the basis of the offense they are charged with is incompatible with the treatment premise of the juvenile court system. Third, a prosecutor is neither as objective nor as expert as a judge to act in the best interests of the child. Finally, transfer decisions by prosecutors have been held to be unreviewable, thereby inviting abuse.

The burden is on the juvenile court, the community, and the state legislatures to demand appropriate facilities to treat serious juvenile offenders. If such facilities are available, the pressure to move these young people into the adult prison system is considerably reduced. If we continue to incarcerate youths in adult facilities, we may not only have pushed them down a one-way path, we have done injury to the very fabric of our society.

Having established the scope of juvenile court jurisdiction, we will now examine the procedures and current issues surrounding three key decision points in the juvenile court process: (1) detention; (2) court intake; and (3) court dispositions.

DETENTION

The term *detention,* as used here and in juvenile court statutes, means the temporary care of children in physically restricting facilities pending adjudication, disposition, or implementation of disposition. Logically, one might expect that court intake (decisions establishing court jurisdiction) would precede the decision to place the youth in physical custody. However, juvenile courts generally are not organized to gather and assess relevant facts and to make official decisions regarding jurisdiction over cases immediately, and the detention decision is not postponed until this is done. Instead, a custody decision is usually made first.

A source of confusion about detention intake stems from the fact that the phrase is used to designate different kinds of decisions. Sometimes it refers to an initial decision to hold a youth (sometimes for a very brief period, sometimes for a more extended one) until a formal decision is made to proceed with legal action (court intake). At other times, the phrase is used to designate formal confirmation of an earlier holding decision. The critical factors affecting detention decisions are (1) the screening procedures, (2) the criteria for detention, and (3) the time limits on the length of detention.

Screening Procedures

The initial decision to take a child into custody is usually made by a police officer. If the police do not return a juvenile to his or her home, a second decision concerning detention is usually made by a probation, intake, or other court official designated to screen detention admissions. Some states, however, allow the police officer making the arrest to place the child in detention directly.

In many jurisdictions, an intake worker or other official decides that a particular case is to be dismissed, referred to court for adjudication, or processed informally (nonjudicially). If detention intake and court intake are combined, this worker also makes the decision, perhaps reviewed later, that a youth referred to court is to be placed in secure detention, returned home to await hearing—with or without conditions—or placed in some other setting. Some courts, even those with clear policies and procedures, do not have intake staff on duty during hours when they are needed. For example, a study of minors booked into San Francisco's Juvenile Hall reported that 73.9 percent of all admissions took place between 5:00 P.M. and 8:00 A.M., with 40.6 percent of them between 5:00 P.M. Fridays and 8:00 A.M. on Mondays (Bay Area Social Council, 1968). Children taken into custody during such hours often are detained until staff arrives to make court intake decisions.

Standards proposed by the IJA/ABA Joint Commission (1977b) require that intake officials take all necessary steps to process the juvenile's release from a secure facility or place the juvenile in a nonsecure setting. If a juvenile is detained, the intake official must document the reasons why a less restrictive alternative has not been selected.

Detention Criteria

Kent has made court personnel aware of the enormous discretion exercised by the courts at critical stages in juvenile proceedings. When proceedings may result in incarceration, such a stage has clearly been reached.

Typically, state codes use imprecise phrases to grant broad discretion to detain. Thirty-one states allow detention to ensure presence at a subsequent hearing, and only eight of these have any additional requirements—for example, that the child has been taken into custody for a serious offense or has a history of failure to appear. Twenty states allow a child to be placed in detention solely because there is no parent available to provide care and/or supervision. Mississippi adds the requirement that there be no reasonable alternative to custody, and Florida limits the place of detention to crisis homes only. Thirty-eight states provide that a child may be detained only if detention is necessary to protect the personal safety or property of others. Only eight of those states additionally require that the probability of the harm to others be serious, or the offense be of a serious nature. A mere three states call for a probable-cause determination to justify detention on this basis. Thirty-seven states also allow detention to protect the health and safety of the juvenile. Only Alabama requires that the threat of harm be substantial, while five states require that the threat to the child's welfare be immediate. While most state statutes contain at least broad guidelines concerning the decision to detain, some provisions altogether fail to guide the decision maker. For example, several states allow detention if release is "impracticable" or "inadvisable."

Given the broad jurisdiction of a juvenile court, ambiguous intake procedures and policies result in detaining large numbers of referrals needlessly. Moreover, these conditions produce marked variations in the use of detention in different jurisdictions. Saleebey (1975), for instance, gathered data on admissions to secure detention in thirty-three large U.S. cities in 1973. The detention rates per 100,000 youths aged 10–17 ranged from a low in Birmingham, Alabama, of 599 to a high in Memphis, Tennessee, of 8,299. Ferster et al. (1969) collected detention data for five of the largest cities in the United States and from four smaller communities. Of those taken into police custody, the percentage detained ranged from 11 percent to 33 percent. And of those juveniles subsequently referred to court, the percentage detained ranged from 20 percent to 74 percent. Finally, a survey of admissions to secure detention for nineteen counties in Michigan in 1972 calculated a detention rate based on the number of juvenile arrests in each county that year. Among the counties studied, the detention rate ranged from 8 percent to 52 percent (John Howard Association, 1974).

As the data indicate, many courts appear far more willing than others to accept youths referred by a police officer, other official, parent, or other citizen—at least for some period of time (Rubin, 1970). This is not unexpected; Levin and Sarri (1974) report that fifteen states have no statutory requirement that a court order be secured in order to place a child in detention. Thus, youths are detained for extended periods without any judicial opinion that they are within jurisdiction.

Fortunately, most states give detained juveniles the right to a detention hearing. A hearing is constitutionally required to justify continued detention. Pretrial detention without a hearing violates the fundamental fairness guaranteed by the due-process clause of the Fourteenth Amendment. Since the majority of states do not accord the juvenile the right to bail, a detention hearing is crucial to avoid arbitrary confinement. If there is neither a hearing nor an opportunity for release on bail, the detention of the juvenile is essentially punitive custody prior to any adjudication of guilt. Without a judicial determination of the need for detention, the juvenile is subjected to punitive confinement.

In recent years, both federal and state courts have held that as a matter of federal constitutional law, a juvenile may not be detained pending trial on charges of delinquency without a prompt determination of probable cause. However, in June 1984 the Supreme Court reversed these lower court rulings in *Schall* v. *Martin*. The justices upheld a New York statute authorizing the pretrial detention of an accused juvenile who, if released, may pose a "serious risk" by committing the equivalent of an adult crime. While the statute provides for a detention hearing, a formal finding that there is probable cause to believe that the youth committed the offense for which he or she was arrested is not required prior to the detention of the child.

Time Limitations

Delay in the processing, adjudication, and disposition of juvenile cases often compounds the disadvantages of detention.

> Detention is a waiting period. During the entire course of his confinement a child is troubled by his immediate placement and he wonders what's going to happen to him. The time lapse between admission, a quickly scheduled court hearing, and immediate disposition *we* may consider as short-term, but to a detained adolescent this period can seem an eternity. He has not volunteered to be in his circumstances and being in unnatural surroundings he can be expected to be on edge. Resistance must be anticipated and considered to be perfectly normal (Perkins, 1968:55–56).

Several states have recognized and addressed this problem. Twenty-eight states allow detention for a limited time unless a petition is filed. The limits range from 24 hours to 10 days, with most states imposing a 24–48-hour limitation. Almost all of the time limits exclude Saturdays, Sundays, and court holidays. Other states require a detention hearing within a certain time of the initial placement in detention, deemphasizing the role of the petition as a focal point. Thirty-one states specifically limit the duration of detention before a detention hearing. Nineteen of those states set the limit at 48 or 72 hours.

Fifteen states limit the time between initial detention and the adjudicatory hearing. This limit ranges from 5 to 30 days, with 30 days being most common. Most states allow some extension if a good cause is shown. Illinois limits the time between the detention hearing and the adjudicatory hearing to 10 judicial days for delinquents and status offenders and 30 days for nonoffenders. Eight states place some type of limit on the duration of post-adjudicatory/predispositional detention, with a minimum of 15 days to a maximum of 45 days.

The IJA/ABA Juvenile Justice Standards Project compiled time limits believed necessary to reduce the delay, yet still minimize the risks of inappropriate release (1977b:13). Each of the limits includes weekends and holidays:

1. Arrest—release within 2 hours, or transportation to a juvenile facility.
2. Intake—release or petition for detention to be filed within 24 hours.
3. Hearing—if custody continues, hearing to be held within 24 hours of filing of petition.
4. Review—detention decision to be reviewed by the court every 7 days.
5. Adjudication and disposition—cases dismissed if:

a. adjudication is not completed within 30 days of arrest if the juvenile is released, and within 15 days of arrest if the juvenile remains in detention for more than 24 hours following a court order of detention; or
b. final disposition is not determined and carried out within 30 days of adjudication if the juvenile is released, and within 15 days of adjudication if the juvenile remains in court ordered detention following adjudication. These latter time constraints may be extended or waived only in limited and specified circumstances.

6. Appeal—decision within 90 days when juvenile held in detention.

Secure Detention: Children in Jail

The National Center for Juvenile Justice (1977) estimated that in 1975, approximately 558,545 juveniles were detained in secure detention facilities in forty-two states for which information was available. Of these, 94,589 (16.9 percent) were held in adult jails. The study compared states according to the proportion of juveniles held in either jails or juvenile detention centers. Twelve states held more than half of their detained offenders in adult jails, and six of the twelve held more than three-quarters in jails. The average stay for juveniles detained in jails was 5 days; for those detained in juvenile detention centers, 10 days. It is important to note, however, that facilities holding persons less than 48 hours were not included in this survey. Thus, we do not know how many juveniles were detained for relatively short periods of time.

Statutory Approaches to the Use of Jail The states have adopted diverse statutory approaches to deal with the practice of jailing juveniles. Only Pennsylvania and Maryland prohibit the jailing of any child except juveniles certified to adult court. Only sixteen states and the District of Columbia prohibit jailing on the basis of a child's classification as a status offender or nonoffender (a dependent, neglected, or abused child). Other states impose various restrictions or conditions on jailing. Typical restrictions, employed alone or in combination, often permit jailing only if: no other detention facilities are available (seventeen states), adequate supervision of the juvenile is provided by the jail (nine states), there is a court order (eighteen states), the child would be a menace to other juveniles in detention (nine states and the District of Columbia) or to the community (eight states), or the particular facility has been approved for use by juveniles (eight states).

A few states make all children—be they delinquents, status offenders, or nonoffenders—subject to jailing on the basis of age: Colorado (over age 14), Illinois (over age 16), Michigan (over age 15), New York (over age 10), Oklahoma (over age 12), Oregon (over age 14), South Dakota (over age 15), and Utah (over age 16). Other states prohibit jailing of juveniles of specific ages if they fall into one or more specific categories. These states include Iowa (delinquents under age 14), Louisiana (delinquents under age 15), Minnesota (delinquents under age 14), Ohio (delinquents and status offenders under age 15), Virginia (delinquents under age 15), Washington (delinquents under age 16 and some runaways and status offenders), and West Virginia (delinquents under age 14). The District of Columbia permits the jailing of delinquents over 16 years old. States that permit the jailing of children on the basis of age may require that other conditions exist, such as: adequate supervision of the youth, by court order only, if no juvenile facility is available, if the adult facility is an approved facility, or approval of the state division for youth.

Finally, the vast majority of states require that jailed juveniles and adults be separated. The type and degree of separation vary considerably and are frequently ambiguous. Twenty-six states require "physical" separation. Three states require "sight and sound" separation. Montana requires that the juvenile be "physically and visually" separated from adults. West Virginia requires "sight" separation but not "sound" separation (presumably conversation is possible between adult and juvenile inmates although they cannot see each other). Arkansas prohibits the placement of juveniles in any facility where "regular contact" with adult criminal offenders (or suspects) is possible. Finally, Florida and Minnesota restrict the detention of juveniles to "separate cells." (In effect, those states requiring physical or sight-and-sound separation frequently place juveniles in a separate cell.)

The Nature of Jails and Their Effect on Youth

Few people would dispute that most jails are extremely old and generally deteriorated. The physical plant of the typical jail is inadequate to meet the needs of adult prisoners, if not unsafe for habitation. A former administrator in the U.S. Department of Justice during the early 1970s provided the following assessment:

> Jails are festering sores in the criminal justice system. There are no model jails anywhere; we know, we tried to find them. . . . Jails are, without question, brutal, filthy cesspools of crime—institutions which serve to brutalize and embitter men . . . (cited in Goldfarb, 1975:23).

The harmful effect of jailing has been the object of study by many different organizations. The most widely known harm is physical and sexual assault by adults in the same facility, including inmate trustees who may have access to juveniles in "separate" quarters in the jail. The cases of assault and rape of juveniles in jails are too many to be enumerated and too common to be denied. Even short-term, pretrial, or relocation detention in an adult jail exposes male and female juveniles to exploitation and victimization. In addition to physical and sexual abuse by adults, juveniles also suffer harm not directly related to contact with adults. The President's Commission on Law

Enforcement and Administration of Justice identified the following problems of jailing youths in adult facilities:

> Jail detention is characterized by enforced idleness, no supervision, and rejection. It is a demoralizing experience for a youngster at a time when his belief in himself is shattered or distorted. Repeated jailing of youth has no salutary effect on the more sophisticated youngster; on the contrary, it reinforces his delinquency status with his peers and his self-identification as a criminal. Enforced idleness in a jail gives the sophisticated juvenile ample time and reason for striking back at society (1967b:122).

There seems to be a clear recognition that contact with alleged or convicted offenders is only one narrow aspect of the harm that incarcerated children suffer. Much of the harm is psychological in nature and flows from the simple act of being placed in an adult penal facility. A study of juvenile-detention practices in Wisconsin sheds some light on the potential consequences of this situation (Wisconsin Health and Social Services Department, 1976). The Wisconsin researchers toured thirty jails and found that in twenty of them, specially designated cells or cell blocks were reserved for juveniles. Although this segregation was part of an effort to avoid the harmful effects that could result from interaction between juveniles and adults, the researchers pointed out that a significant side effect was that the juvenile sections were in worse condition than the adult cells. In two of the jails, when they were overcrowded with adults, juveniles were put into maximum security or holding cells to prevent contact with adults. The researchers concluded that this situation typifies how the juvenile may be subjected to harsher holding conditions than adults due to the overall physical design and original purpose of a jail. Simply, the jail environment is typically geared to dangerous or unruly offenders who must be restrained. In an adult jail or lock-up, architecture and building materials, staff orientation, and security hardware are developed with the most serious offenders in mind and are almost always inappropriate for the majority of adult inmates, let alone juveniles. Thus, not surprisingly, recent state experience in separating juveniles from adults in jails has often resulted in living conditions for juveniles equivalent to isolation in the most undesirable areas of the facility (isolation cell, drunk tank, and so on). Having been built for adults who have committed criminal acts, jails do not provide an environment suitable for the detention of juveniles; they are not designed to take into account the child's perception of time and space or his or her naïveté about the purpose and duration of this stay in a secure facility. The lack of sensory stimuli, the extended periods of absolute silence, the outbreaks of hostility, the foul odors and public commodes, and inactivity and empty time can be intolerable for a child (Children's Defense Fund, 1976).

While similar conclusions were reached by a National Assessment of

Juvenile Corrections study (Sarri, 1974), the major indictment was that jails generally lack basic necessities for physical and mental health. For example, a 1972 survey of the nation's jails (National Criminal Justice Information and Statistics Service, 1975) revealed that fewer than 5 percent of small jails (holding fewer than 21 inmates) and roughly 30 percent of medium-sized jails (housing 21–249 inmates) provided in-house medical services. Juveniles are usually detained in small or medium-sized jails. Moreover, an American Medical Association survey of medical facilities in 1,431 jails found that more than half provided only first aid (Community Research Forum, 1980). Such findings are important, since one source has indicated that of 31,323 youths remanded to detention facilities in New York City over a five-year period, approximately 50 percent required medical care (Children's Defense Fund, 1976). In adult jails and lock-ups, the physical and mental ailments of juveniles, including drug reactions and diabetes, often go unnoticed. The consequences of such neglect are shockingly cruel.

Alternatives to Secure Detention

In many parts of the country, secure detention continues to be used for reasons other than the protection of the community from youths who are viewed as likely to flee jurisdiction or commit dangerous offenses while awaiting court disposition. These reasons include punishment, the administrative convenience of the court, and lack of available social services for youths and their families—in our view, misuses of secure detention. In jurisdictions where such misuses occur, many youths placed in secure detention need not or should not be so held.

While major special-interest groups have called for the prohibition of detaining juveniles in jails and lock-ups, the issue has provoked only sporadic concern among the public at large and minimal action toward its resolution. Some observers argue that the low levels of public awareness and of official action result largely from the unavailability of data and the low visibility of juveniles in secure detention. These phenomena, in turn, are perpetuated by official rhetoric that cloaks the practice of jailing juveniles in a variety of time-worn, ill-conceived rationales—public safety, protection of juveniles from themselves or their environments, and lack of alternatives—that collapse under close scrutiny. For example, the threat-to-public-safety argument has been soundly refuted in two significant research efforts. In a study conducted by the Children's Defense Fund (1976), 449 jails in 9 states were surveyed. It was found that fewer than 12 percent of the children detained in jails were alleged to have committed a dangerous act. The great majority of the child detainees, 70 percent, were alleged to have committed minor offenses or property offenses, and 18 percent were not alleged to have committed any criminal offense. And a study of juvenile detention and alternatives in Scott County, Iowa, revealed that of 1,243 youths arrested in that county in 1977, only 36 juveniles were charged with offenses that would normally be considered serious crimes against persons; an additional 30 youths were arrested for carrying a concealed weapon (Schwartz, 1979). Only these 66 youths could be considered threats to the safety of the community. Yet some 436 juveniles—42 percent of those arrested in 1977—were detained in the Scott County jail; the study notes that only 5 percent of arrested juveniles normally need be detained if adequate services are available. Furthermore, in Scott County, 84.5 percent of all male juvenile detainees and 98 percent of female juvenile detainees were released within three days or less. Such a short term of detention leads one to question exactly what was gained by keeping these children in jail. Based on the above data, the study concludes that the vast majority of juvenile detainees did not need to be detained at all.

In recent years, several alternatives to secure detention have been tried. They range from simply increasing the proportion of youths released to their parents or guardians pending hearing to intensive prehearing supervision in the community, specialized foster homes, and group homes. Unfortunately, little research has been conducted on these various alternatives to determine the characteristics of juveniles served, program costs, and measures of effectiveness. A major exception is the national study conducted by Pappenfort and Young (1980). In 1976, they assessed fourteen programs used as alternatives to secure detention for youths awaiting court action in ten states and the District of Columbia. They found that youths in certain programs would simply have been sent home to await hearings if an alternative program had not been available. Juveniles in alternative programs tended to wait longer for adjudication than those in secure detention. A few programs were used as a form of informal probation to provide a testing period prior to adjudication (in one city a program was scornfully referred to as an "alternative to disposition"). But most of all, in addition to holding juveniles who might commit new offenses or run away, alternative programs were being used as a treatment resource for youths who were unlikely to do either. As a result, the symptoms of "overreach" may be appearing in certain jurisdictions through alternative programs. Just because new programs are available, juveniles who previously would not have been involved with the juvenile justice system now find themselves admitted to it.

This situation sometimes appears to be accompanied by transfer of one of the traditional uses of secure detention to the newer alternative programs. That is, secure detention has been used to control juveniles who need child-welfare services that have not been available in the community. As alternative programs become increasingly used by juvenile courts, there are real dangers that (1) the programs will be diverted from their main task of protecting communities and juveniles in the period prior to adjudication and (2) an increasing number of youths who need social services will be labeled alleged delinquents or status offenders in order to receive them.

COURT INTAKE

While most state statutes regarding intake are deliberately broad, some jurisdictions have formulated specific guidelines that intake officials should consider in deciding whether to file a petition or adjust a case informally. Those used by the Maryland Department of Juvenile Services are fairly typical (Maryland Courts and Judicial Proceedings Code Ann. 3–810 [1978]).

1. Seriousness of the offense.
   a. Intent.
   b. Severity of personal injury.
   c. Extent of property damage.
   d. Value of property taken, whether or not recovered.
   e. Whether the offense is isolated or not.
2. Impact of the offense on any individual or the community.
3. Previous number and nature of Department of Juvenile Services, police, and juvenile court contacts.
4. Age and maturity of child. (Was the violation committed because of an immature impulse or was it premeditated? What is the child's degree of awareness regarding the severity of the violation?)
5. Attitude of child. (Does the child admit his or her involvement in the violation?)
6. Attitude of parents toward child's responsibility regarding the offense and toward discipline of the child. (A possible lack of parental control or concern may be reflected by the time of day the offense occurred, for example.)
7. Degree of incorrigibility under parent's supervision. (Does the child normally obey reasonable guidelines set by parents?)
8. School attendance and behavior pattern.
9. Available social factors. (Is the child involved in gang activities? Does he or she have a bad reputation in the neighborhood?)
10. Resources and ability of family and community to provide appropriate care, treatment, and rehabilitation.

The seriousness of the offense is perhaps the most important element considered. A number of courts, as a matter of policy, may specify that certain offenses may not be adjusted or, more generally, that no felony offense may be adjusted. The range of available adjustments at the intake stage is limited only by the availability of resources in the community and the imagination of the intake staff. If a child has been referred to the court on a minor charge and the intake worker determines that court intervention is not necessary but that the child needs to be impressed with the seriousness of his or her actions, the worker may deliver a lecture to the child. To make the warning more impressive, the child may be taken before a judge for a stern reprimand.

A common practice is to delay the intake decision, with the understanding that no petition will be filed if the child makes restitution, apologizes to the complainant, completes a work detail at the police station, obtains employment, attends school regularly for a certain number of days, or takes some other action. If the child or his or her parents are viewed as needing professional assistance, they may be required to participate in a series of counseling sessions to avoid a court appearance.

Another standard practice in juvenile courts has been the use of informal probation in cases in which the child and family are willing to comply with requirments suggested by probation personnel in the absence of any formal court order. Problems with informal probation have arisen, since supervision of the child by probation personnel is conducted in much the same way as supervision of adjudicated children. Unfamiliar with juvenile court procedures, children and their parents sometimes agree to informal probation, not realizing that they have the right to a court hearing before the probation staff has authority over them.

A possible alternative to informal probation is a short-term intervention, particularly when the child is in conflict with his parents or school personnel. For example, an intake worker acts as mediator, listens to all sides in the dispute, helps to point out the problem areas, and recommends solutions that involve all parties to the conflict.

In some communities, youth-service bureaus and other diversion agencies provide another alternative to juvenile court. These programs offer counseling, drug treatment, job assistance, recreational programs, educational assistance, and other services. They were conceived, in part, to replace the screening and referral functions of juvenile court. In some communities, the police and schools make referrals directly to these agencies, bypassing juvenile court intake altogether.

JUVENILE COURT DISPOSITIONS

The juvenile court system emerged from a pervasive belief that the goal of rehabilitation could be best achieved if juveniles were treated with maximum flexibility, informality, and discretion, especially at the dispositional or sentencing stage. Under the concept of *parens patriae,* it is entirely up to the court to decide which disposition will best serve the interests and welfare of the child. Broad dispositional power is both justified and necessary in a system whose prime interest is the welfare of the minor. Time and again, the statement is made that the dispositional decision is likely to be the most important aspect of a juvenile court case.

The purpose clauses of most juvenile codes address the need to treat the individual brought before the court. The following clause, from the Standard Juvenile Court Act, is typical:

> Each child coming within the jurisdiction of the court shall receive, preferably in his own home, the care, guidance and control that will conduce to his welfare and the best interests of the state, and . . . when he is removed from control of his parents, the court shall secure for him care as nearly possible equivalent to that which they would have given him (National Council on Crime and Delinquency, 1959:329).

At the dispositional phase of the juvenile court proceeding, then, the juvenile court's philosophy of treatment and rehabilitation is put to the test. At this stage, the court is required to order a plan of treatment that meets the individual needs of the child.

Dispositional decisions are made about a relatively small number of juveniles, and those who are evaluated for various dispositional outcomes have already been "sifted" through several decision points. In 1977, for example, it was estimated that police made 2,452,318 juvenile arrests nationwide. Of these, 1,150,800 (46.9 percent) were referred to juvenile court. An additional 250,905 cases were referred to court by parents, citizens, community agencies, or other juvenile justice agencies (such as probation and corrections departments). Of the 1,401,705 cases referred to juvenile court intake, 646,885 (46.1 percent) were subsequently certified to juvenile court for an adjudicatory hearing. Of these, 490,085 (75.8 percent) cases had petitions sustained and were scheduled for dispositional hearings (Black and Smith, 1981). Still, these 490,085 cases represent only 18.1 percent of all juveniles initially arrested or referred to juvenile court by others.

Although the disposition is the heart of the juvenile process, it has received scant attention in Supreme Court decisions. The Supreme Court's decision in *In re Gault* (1967) (see Chapter 9) was limited to the adjudicatory stage of delinquency cases; and the Court has not extended the scope of that decision to apply to the dispositional process. However, this area of law is currently the subject of extensive litigation and legislative revision.

Presently, juvenile court statutes permit the court to make one of numerous dispositions ranging from counsel and release to commitment in an adult correctional facility. Typically, however, these statutes provide the court with little guidance as to which disposition will be appropriate for a particular youth. This absence of guidelines is a major concern today, when many states are still able to place runaways or truants in correctional institutions and jails, sanctions that are totally out of proportion to the acts committed. The Institute of Judicial Administration/American Bar Association Juvenile Justice Standards Project has recognized the importance of establishing guidelines and limiting judicial discretion at the dispositional stage. This project recommends that the court

> . . . employ the least restrictive category and duration of disposition that is appropriate to the seriousness of the offense, as modified by the degree of culpability indicated by the circumstances of the particular case, and by the age and prior record of the juvenile. The imposition of a particular disposition should be accompanied by a statement of the facts relied on in support of the disposition and the reasons for selecting the disposition and rejecting less restrictive alternatives (IJA/ABA, 1977a:6).

Institutionalization

The need for clearly defined dispositional criteria is best illustrated by an overview of current jailing and institutionalization practices. The President's Commission on Law Enforcement and Administration of Justice (1967a) succinctly described the plight of many juveniles institutionalized for the ostensible purpose of treatment under the state's *parens patriae* authority:

> Institutionalization too often means storage—isolation from the outside world—in an overcrowded, understaffed, high-security institution with little education, little vocational training, little counseling or job placement or other guidance upon release. Programs are subordinated to everyday control and maintenance (1967a:80).

Lack of dispositional guidelines is an especially serious problem in light of a growing body of literature that demonstrates that institutionalization *per se* is harmful. Research by the National Assessment of Juvenile Corrections (Sarri, 1974) and the Children's Defense Fund (1976) have indicated the following:

1. Large facilities require regimentation and routinization in order for staff to maintain control and restrict individual handling.
2. Smaller facilities allow staff to offer a more constructive and controlled environment.
3. Large facilities convey an atmosphere of anonymity to the individual resident and tend to engulf a child in feelings of powerlessness, meaninglessness, isolation, and self-estrangement.
4. Larger facilities reinforce the image of rejection of the individual by society, compounding the problems of reintegration into society.
5. Since institutions have a tendency to fill to capacity, larger facilities increase the risk of needlessly incarcerating more youths.

Of equally grave concern is the fact that institutionalization is not an effective means of rehabilitation. Generally, studies reveal that institutionalization is no more effective in reducing recidivism than alternatives that do not involve incarceration, and some studies indicate that institutionalization may actually increase recidivism (Vinter et al., 1975). Further, studies affirm that many incarcerated youths, particularly status offenders, do not require secure confinement. Not only is institutionalization harmful, it is also expensive:

> Analysis of the comparative costs of institutionalization versus nonincarcerative dispositions also provide cogent reasons for preferring the latter. . . . [A] comparison of institutional costs and the costs of nonincarcerative dispositions revealed that the overall daily cost for a juvenile in an institution is ten times more than the cost of juvenile probation or aftercare (National Council on Crime and Delinquency, 1967:73, 235).

These findings all lead to the conclusion that, at best, large institutions offer mere custodial care. Further, increased deviance is promoted by institutionalization. Troubled children, especially status offenders, deserve the individualized care and treatment that can only be provided at the local level in small, community settings.

Court Decisions/Litigation In recent years, courts and commentators have increasingly recognized that individuals involuntarily committed to institutions have the "right" to treatment (such as therapy and social services) and, conversely, that committed individuals who do not in fact receive treatment thereby suffer a violation of their rights. In 1966, the United States Court of Appeals for the District of Columbia Circuit became the first federal court to recognize the right to treatment as a basis for releasing involuntarily committed individuals (*Lake* v. *Cameron,* 1966; *Rouse* v. *Cameron,* 1966). While these cases involved persons involuntarily confined for mental illness, Kittrie (1969) has argued that the "right to treatment" concept applies with equal force to the confinement of children in jails. The juvenile justice system is based on the goal of rehabilitation, and the juvenile courts have always been considered similar to social welfare agencies, designed to provide treatment and assistance for children under the deliberately broad juvenile codes.

The United States Supreme Court has never definitively ruled on whether there is a constitutionally based right to treatment. But the Court has apparently based the right to treatment on the principle that restriction of fundamental liberties through involuntary confinement must follow the "least restrictive alternative" available. This principle was stated by the Supreme Court in *Shelton* v. *Tucker* (1960):

> In a series of decisions this Court has held that, even though the governmental purpose be legitimate and substantial, that purpose cannot be pursued by means that broadly stifle fundamental personal liberties when the end can be more

> narrowly achieved. The breadth of legislative abridgement must be viewed in the light of less drastic means for achieving the same basic purpose (364 U.S. 479, 488).

Under this rationale, the state violates the individual's constitutional rights if it fails to confine and provide treatment in the least restrictive setting possible.

Furthermore, juveniles who are victims of assaults by other inmates may sue for violation of their right to be reasonably protected from violence in the facility. Several courts have held that confinement that subjects the incarcerated to assaults and threats of violence constitutes cruel and unusual punishment. On the other hand, if juveniles are kept in isolation in order to protect them from assaults, they may nevertheless suffer such sensory deprivation and psychological damage as to violate their constitutional rights. Either way, then, the impact of incarcerating juveniles may directly conflict with the purpose of the juvenile justice system, which was expressly created to remove children from the punitive forces of the criminal justice system. To expose a girl or boy to coercive institutional conditions is to jeopardize his or her emotional and physical well-being. Reform of the various state laws that permit the jailing of juveniles to continue is absolutely necessary to protect the children of America.

Probation

Probation may be defined as the conditional freedom granted by a judicial officer to an alleged or adjudicated offender as long as the person meets certain conditions of behavior. Probation is usually an available disposition for every juvenile offender, regardless of the nature of the offense; all but four states (Nevada, Washington, West Virginia, and Wisconsin) provide for probation as a dispositional alternative in their respective juvenile codes. The theoretical rationale behind probation is the concept that deviant behavior may be better corrected by trying to rehabilitate the juvenile in the community than in an institution. The major goal of probation is rehabilitation and reintegration, and the principal figure in accomplishing these objectives is the juvenile court probation officer. A number of juvenile courts have no probation services at all; those that do, typically have such huge caseloads that counseling and supervision take the form of occasional phone calls and perfunctory visits, instead of the careful, individualized service that was intended. Furthermore, it has been well documented that juvenile probation workers frequently lack professional training. As a result, probation is often more a process of verifying behavior than of correcting it (President's Commission on Law Enforcement and Administration of Justice, 1967b:136–140).

Generally, there may be some restrictions imposed in any given juvenile court probation order—for example, obedience to all laws, regular attendance at school, periodic visits to the probation officer, remaining within the community, and being home at night by a set hour. The judge has the statutory authority, usually phrased in the broadest of terms, to shape these conditions. For example, the Alabama juvenile code states that if a child is found to be delinquent or in need of supervision, the court may "place the child on probation under such conditions and limitations as the court may prescribe" (Alabama Code S12–15–71 [c][2], 1979). Unfortunately, this leeway in decision making may result in the arbitrary and capricious imposition of conditions on juveniles (Best and Birzon, 1963).

Since probation has historically been viewed as a "favor" to a person convicted of a crime, conditions of probation were rarely subject to judicial review until fairly recently. Now, however, it is generally agreed that probationary conditions for both juveniles and adults are subject to certain limitations. For example, in juvenile court, a major goal of probation is to rehabilitate the child by treatment and guidance while the child remains an active and useful member of the community. If probation conditions do not promote this end, they should not be used or permitted.

Fines and Restitution

Thirty-two states authorize restitution and seventeen permit the use of fines as dispositional alternatives for juveniles. Restitution is a court requirement that an offender pay money or provide services to victims of the offense or to the community. A fine is a court requirement that the offender pay a specified sum of money to the court. Both are commonly imposed as conditions of probation, but there are some problems in the use of these measures.

Fines often bear little relationship to rehabilitation of the offender; they are clearly punitive in character. Thus, they are inconsistent with the goals of the juvenile justice system and undesirable as dispositions by the juvenile court (Piersma et al., 1975). And restitution has been used so often that the courts are apparently no longer concerned about whether or not it serves to reform or rehabilitate the offender (Schwarzenberger, 1971).

Occasionally, the juvenile court may attempt to impose responsibility for payment upon the child's parents. Not only is it questionable that a court that has adjudicated the child delinquent has jurisdiction to compel payment by the parent, but it is also doubtful that payment by the parent can have any rehabilitative effect on the child. The function of the juvenile court, in brief, must be to provide for care and guidance of the child, not to satisfy civil damage claims.

Duration of Dispositional Orders

Since youths adjudged delinquent are thought to be in need of treatment, many people think that a youth's best interest will be served if treatment continues until it achieves desired results. Seventeen states and the District of Columbia permit the juvenile or family court to exercise jurisdiction over a juvenile found delinquent until he or she reaches the age of 21, regardless of the offense. Some allow the same jurisdiction over status offenders and nonoffenders.

Other state statutes provide that the court may commit a juvenile for an indeterminate period up to a statutory maximum, which does not vary with the seriousness of the offense. Many of these provisions also provide for extensions of the dispositional period. Still other statutes provide that the court may commit a juvenile for a specified period of time, but these usually reserve the right to extend the duration of the order of commitment. A few states provide that a juvenile may be committed until the objectives of the dispositional decree have been met.

Statutes that limit the duration of disposition orders represent the best approach. Dispositional orders of indeterminate duration may cause the child to remain institutionalized or on probation for a time greatly disproportionate to the seriousness of his or her conduct, his or her need for treatment, or the maximum period of confinement statutorily authorized for an adult convicted of the same offense. Statutory limitations on the duration of dispositions can avoid this abuse.

Revocation of Probation and Changes in Dispositional Orders

The Supreme Court has held that a previously sentenced adult probationer is entitled to a hearing when his or her probation is revoked (*Morrissey* v. *Brewer,* 1972). An adult probationer, however, does not have an unconditional right to counsel at revocation proceedings (*Gagnon* v. *Scarpelli,* 1973). The right to counsel depends upon the particular circumstances of the case. The Court has noted that if the probationer asserts that he or she has not committed the violation or if he or she admits the violation but alleges mitigating circumstances that make revocation inappropriate, counsel should usually be appointed (*Gagnon* v. *Scarpelli,* 1973). The ultimate decision to appoint counsel should be based on a determination of whether or not the probationer appears capable of effectively representing himself or herself. Based on this test, juvenile probationers should almost always be entitled to the right to counsel, since they generally lack the maturity and expertise to present their arguments effectively without the assistance of counsel.

Most juvenile codes recognize the right to a hearing on the revocation of probation, and some even guarantee the right to counsel. Most of the statutes also require adequate notice of the hearing and notice of the factual basis for the alleged violation of probation; these latter provisions guarantee that juveniles will be informed of the charges against them in order to prepare a defense. Some statutes adopt clear and convincing evidence as the applicable standard of proof for revoking probation; others adopt the preponderance-of-evidence standard; and still others require proof beyond a reasonable doubt. Several codes adopt no specific standard of proof at all.

The fact that most states recognize the juvenile's right to a hearing before revocation of probation indicates a trend toward recognition of the right to counsel. Because the juvenile faces serious consequences in revocation proceedings, these rights deserve further recognition and protection. Even if a violation is admitted by the probationer, an attorney can more effectively present evidence of mitigating circumstances, should there be any. The nature of these circumstances may dissuade the judge from revoking probation on the theory that the juvenile is not a danger to society and can be better rehabilitated outside of an institution.

The system of revocation is easily and justly criticized, because its improvement would not be difficult. Every revocation proceeding should comply with constitutional due-process safeguards. Even if the juvenile admits the violations, the question of proper disposition requires a hearing. A violation of probation conditions does not, in itself, mean that the juvenile is a risk to society. The individual states ought to protect their probationers' rights in the revocation process by appointment of counsel and by stricter adherence to constitutional requirements.

Aftercare

Aftercare, or *parole,* refers to the release of an individual from an institution before the period of commitment is scheduled to end. Juvenile parole has its origins in the early House of Refuge practice of requiring child inmates to work for several years in private homes after their term of incarceration. It was the responsibility of the receiving family to feed and clothe the youngster and also to decide when he or she had earned complete freedom (Hussey, 1976). Today, the decision to parole and the determination of conditions of parole are generally made by the staff of the institution where the juvenile is confined. However, entrusting the important decision of whether to grant parole to the absolute discretion of institutional staff raises some serious concerns. When coupled with the traditional provision for indeterminate sentencing, such discretion allows institutional officials to exercise great power over a juvenile's life for a long period of time. While juvenile codes generally do not deal with aftercare, some statutes require judicial review of any modifications of disposition. These provisions seem better designed to protect juveniles' rights because the review affords juveniles the opportunity to be heard in matters of vital concern to them.

PUBLIC ACCESS TO JUVENILE COURT PROCEEDINGS AND RECORDS

Because of the rehabilitative goals of the juvenile court system, legislatures have traditionally enacted statutes that limit access to juvenile court proceedings and juvenile court and arrest records and that allow for the eventual expungement or destruction of those records. In recent years, a growing number of persons involved in the juvenile justice field have expressed support for public trials and, in many instances, public records. A public trial is likely to lead to greater public exposure of the names and addresses of children who are accused of juvenile delinquency. We briefly discuss the arguments for and against public trials and public records below.

The Right to Public Trial

More than 80 percent of the states currently limit access to a juvenile trial to persons with a specified interest in the proceeding—usually only members of the youth's family or other persons whose attendance the youth desires, as well as persons who may have a general or specific interest in juvenile justice. In the remaining handful of states, the general public is not excluded from the trial, except in those instances where the court finds that exclusion would be in the best interest of the child.

Supporters of public trials argue that the secrecy that surrounds juvenile court proceedings has failed to provide the protection for children it was intended to offer. Private trials, they contend, merely establish a secretive atmosphere where the judge rules supreme. Persons are excluded from hearings not out of concern for the youth, but out of a desire to protect the court from scrutiny that would bring its faults and weaknesses to the public's attention. In essence, advocates of public trials argue that existing provisions only perpetuate outdated procedures and commonplace deprivations of children's rights. Furthermore, a public trial would satisfy the community's curiosity with respect to the disposition of juvenile offenders.

Opponents of public trials do not argue with any but the last of these reasons. However, they favor an attempt to place other safeguards on the process—for example, (1) allowing a youth a public trial upon request; (2) establishing a citizens' monitoring committee that would routinely view court hearings; (3) rotating judges every year in order to avoid the abuse of power that commonly occurs when any one judge holds his or her position for a long period of time. They also suggest that public trials and the resulting publicity will interfere with the rehabilitation process (Howard, Grisso, and Neems, 1977). Furthermore, there is genuine concern that public trials will lead to dispositions based on public pressure rather than on the needs of the child. Although most supporters of public trials would not disagree with these positions, they would suggest that such safeguards would not help to solve the existing problems.

Confidentiality of Juvenile Court Records

As mentioned previously, almost 80 percent of all states have laws that provide for private trials of juveniles; and the vast majority of these states also insist that court and arrest records are to be maintained separate from those of adults and are not to be available to the general public. Advocates of such provisions generally base their arguments on the theory that the juvenile system is designed to rehabilitate youths and that rehabilitation is fostered by protecting children from the stigma that tends to adhere to a criminal prosecution; the best way to prevent this stigma from touching a juvenile is to assure that the information about his or her association with the juvenile court will remain confidential. On the other hand, those persons who believe that juvenile records should be made public base their arguments on: (1) the claim that provisions of confidentiality are typically used to thwart the rights of the child, rather than to promote them; (2) the public's need to know; and (3) the increase in serious youth crime.

In fact, though, these provisions have been singularly ineffective; members of the military, prospective employers, and representatives of educational institutions have generally had little difficulty in obtaining information about a youth's past record. Oddly, it appears that those who need access to juvenile court records the most frequently have the most trouble receiving it. Lawyers who defend children typically complain that provisions of confidentiality of juvenile court records are most often used to thwart defense efforts to prepare adequately for court hearings. Quite commonly, a child's lawyer must obtain a court order to view his or her client's records. Furthermore, when counsel is granted access to these files, he or she may not be allowed to photocopy them but may have to copy necessary information by hand.

Another matter of concern is the disclosure of social files. Unlike the court file, which may contain only the petition and other documents of the court process, the social file is likely to hold highly subjective personal observations and evaluations. The stigma arising from erroneous or hasty characterization in these files may be disastrous (Volenik, 1975). Thus, even if trials are public, many people believe that social files should always be kept in confidence.

Media Involvement

A serious issue that is intricately linked with those of public trials and public records is media involvement in the juvenile court proceeding. A number of states attempt to forbid publication by the mass media of the names of or other identifying information about juveniles accused of committing crimes. But such a provision does not typically prohibit the presence of the mass media at hearings. In fact, certain statutes allow the media to attend hearings and to publish information about them (though not information specifically identifying the juvenile). These kinds of provisions are particularly popular with individuals who contend that private trials make abuses of authority by the juvenile court judge more likely. These critics often suggest that allowing the media to monitor hearings would effectively restrain abuse of power.

While this position has obvious merit, it overlooks pertinent Supreme Court decisions that have largely eroded the state's power to limit publication of lawfully obtained information. In *Davis* v. *Alaska* (1974), the Supreme Court ruled that a trial court had erred in issuing a protective order that prohibited cross-examination of a juvenile, a key prosecution witness, concerning his prior juvenile court adjudication as a delinquent and his present probation status. The trial court's order was based on a state statute protecting the anonymity of juvenile offenders. The Supreme Court held that the defendant's Sixth Amendment right to confront witnesses must prevail over the state's interest in protecting juveniles from adverse publicity.

Two years later, in *Oklahoma Publishing Co.* v. *District Court* (1976), the Court struck down a state court injunction prohibiting the news media from publishing the name or photograph of an 11-year-old boy who was being tried before a juvenile court. Despite a state statute closing juvenile trials to the public, the judge had permitted reporters and other members of the public to attend an initial hearing. Afterward, the juvenile court attempted to block publication of information obtained at the hearing. The Supreme Court, however, held that once information was "publicly revealed" or "in the public domain," its publication or broadcast could not be restrained.

A more recent case decided by the Supreme Court, *Smith* v. *Daily Mail Publishing Co.* (1979), further eroded the principle that the media should refrain from disclosing the identity of a juvenile. In West Virginia, a statute prohibited newspapers from publishing, without a written court order, the name of any child in connection with a juvenile court proceeding. But three radio stations and two newspapers carried identifying information about a 14-year-old boy who shot and killed a classmate at school. West Virginia sought to justify its statute on the grounds that it would protect the anonymity of the juvenile offender and further the child's rehabilitation as a result. The Supreme Court here concluded that if information is lawfully obtained (as it was in the West Virginia case), the state may not prohibit its publication except when necessary to further an interest more substantial than the one advocated by the state.

Destruction of Records

Well over half the states currently have provisions that allow for sealing or destroying juvenile court records. Typically, they allow for the sealing or destruction of only social files or arrest records; the docket sheets and official court files will be maintained, although they may be sealed or placed in a totally restricted area.

Many persons argue for the complete destruction of all records, theorizing that unless the records are utterly destroyed, certain information will inevitably become available and harm the youth. Other persons, though, argue that total destruction of records may place a youth in a more vulnerable position than leaving them intact would. This argument is based on the theory that, in many instances, the conduct that brought a juvenile to the attention of the court may be far less serious than the label that is attached may imply. For example, a youth may be charged with and adjudicated for assault after what may have been no more than a schoolyard brawl. Without detailed records, such a youth may be unable to show that his or her offense was a minor one.

SUMMARY

In most cases, police officers, parents, social agencies, probation officers, school officials, and private citizens are legally empowered to refer minors directly to juvenile court. In practice, however, initiation of formal court proceedings is almost always the result of a decision by the police, and statutory provisions grant the police nearly complete discretion regarding the referral decision.

Most juvenile court legislation grants both police officers and social welfare agents the discretion either to release a youth, after apprehension for an alleged offense, to his or her parents or to transfer custody to a detention facility. Statutes seldom specify any criteria for detention, though most states place strict limits on the time a juvenile may be detained prior to a hearing by a judge or other appropriate official who must determine if there is probable cause to believe the minor is guilty of the charge(s) and if the minor warrants detention until the initial hearing of the facts. Most statutes prohibit minors from being detained in jails; in practice, however, it has been estimated that some 500,000 juveniles annually are processed through local jails meant for adults only.

Most states allow juvenile courts the discretion to waive any, or specifically designated, types of cases involving a juvenile's misconduct to adult criminal courts prior to adjudication. Waiver laws governing the transfer of youths to adult courts are the province of the state legislatures and vary among the fifty states. Each state has its own age offense limitations; in many states, the criteria are unusually broad—for example, the best interests of the child and/or the public. Social investigation reports, generally made by probation officers, are standard features of almost all juvenile courts; these reports contain detailed information about the juvenile's family environment and history, circumstances of the alleged offense, school records, and frequently prior or current psychological evaluations by social workers or psychiatrists.

Typically, states require two hearings for juvenile cases: an adjudicatory hearing in order to determine guilt or innocence regarding the charges; and a dispositional hearing to determine the appropriate disposition if the youth is adjudicated delinquent, abused, neglected, dependent, or a status offender. The usual dispositional options provided by state statutes after an adjudication has been made are probation and institutionalization in public or private facilities. Most juvenile courts also have options to supervise a youth informally without a judicial finding of guilt; this may be done by an intake official or by order of the court.

If probation is the disposition, the exact length of probation generally depends on the discretion of the probation officer according to an assessment of the youth's need and compliance with the conditions of probation. If institutionalization is the disposition, it is usually the facility that decides when a youth is ready to be released to the community, theoretically on the basis of his or her successful completion of a therapeutic or reformative program.

All juvenile hearings are typically held in private with the public barred, either by statute or judicial discretion, from observation of any proceedings. Some states do, however, allow reporters to attend juvenile hearings, although in practice these provisions are often superseded by judicial discretion. Most states have provided, either by statute or common consent, that the names of juveniles will not be revealed in the media. Finally, the majority of states have provisions that allow for sealing or destroying juvenile court records.

DISCUSSION QUESTIONS

1. What are the major decision points in juvenile justice processing?
2. What types of behavior are subject to juvenile court jurisdiction?
3. What criteria are used in decisions to waive juvenile court jurisdiction?
4. What factors contribute to the vast variation in detention rates in juvenile court jurisdictions?
5. What are the arguments against the detention of children in jails?
6. What are some potential alternatives to secure detention? What problems may be involved in expanding alternative programs?
7. What types of information are considered in court intake decisions to adjust or refer a case to court?
8. What are the major dispositional alternatives available to juvenile court judges?
9. How has the principle of "right to treatment" been applied to institutionalized juveniles?
10. What are the arguments for and against public access to juvenile court proceedings and records?

THE CHILD SAVERS

The early juvenile court envisioned a nonadversary process, in which all interested parties had the same goal in mind—what was best for the child. That system, however, has gradually given way to a system more like the trial of adult defendants, where there are two sides fighting it out: the defense and the prosecution. The following case in New York City is a good example of the modern practice.

The putative murderer, a fifteen-year-old boy named Angel Sanchez, is "known to the court." Translated from the jargon, this means that Angel, at the time he allegedly committed his murder, was on parole, awaiting trials for three other crimes of violence. Not a few in the court wonder why the little bastard has been let loose so many times to do his thing again, but their wonderment is strictly pro forma: this kind of nonsense happens all the time. . . .

At 10:15 this Thursday morning, Detective Richard J. Joyce of Manhattan Homicide Zone One is interviewed by Charles Emma, an attorney employed by the Corporation Counsel of the City of New York, in room 5B4 of the Family Court. The tone and substance of this interview might suggest to an ignorant observer that its purpose is to prepare an indictment that will lead to the arraignment, trial, conviction and sentencing of a teenage murderer. Not so. Were Angel Sanchez a year older—were he sixteen instead of fifteen—Detective Joyce's interview would be taking place a few hundred yards away in Manhattan's Criminal Court at 100 Centre Street, where adult offenders are indicted by assistant district attorneys. But because Angel is a juvenile, he is, according to the law, incapable of committing a crime. He will be charged instead, in the document that Charles Emma is drafting in pencil, with "an act which, if done by an adult, would constitute the crime of MURDER 2nd as defined by 125.25 of the Penal Law, a Designated Felony Act, pursuant to section 712 of the Family Court Act." Consequently, there will be for Angel no indictment, no arraignment, no trial, no verdict, and if, after all these events that do not happen, he is found to have killed a man, there will be no sentence and no prison. In their place, Angel faces a petition which will be supported by Corporation Counsel first at a brief intake hearing before a judge, and then at a longer fact-finding hearing before another judge in this civil court which is admonished to think first of the welfare of the child who stands before it. Should a finding be made against the respondent (never a defendant) at the conclusion of this hearing, there will eventually be a dispositional hearing before the same judge, at which time Angel may be locked away for years by a maneuver known as a placement with a training school. Some there are in Family Court who have no use at all for this pollution of the language of the law.

Emma's interview with Joyce is encouraging. There seems no doubt that the kid did it, and that the case can be proved in court. Joyce has with him the arrest report, prepared at 1:00 that morning in the 7th Precinct. In the large block reserved for "details," the booking supervisor, with a fine disregard of the euphemistic language of juvenile law, has typed: "Deft did stab one Jose Rodriguez thereby causing his death." In handwriting he has added: "Mother Juanita ntfd." Other information, entered in the appropriate blocks, reveals that the location of the "occurrence" was a park at Norfolk and Houston streets on Manhattan's Lower East Side, that the complainant's name is "People," that the arrested party was neither fingerprinted nor photographed—the law then forbade such records in the case of a juvenile—and that he had no funds in his possession. His race is "H" (though many Hispanics might object to being considered a race apart, the classification has less to do with genetic science than administrative ease), his weight is 105 pounds, and his height is 4 feet 9 inches.

"Angel," says Detective Joyce, "has a complex about his height." He also has scars on his face, the result of a fire.

Joyce gives to Emma a Police Department complaint report, filed by Police Officer George Allen of the 7th Precinct. According to this report, on June 29 Officer Allen "at approx. 2205 hours responded to a 10-85 at Bellevue Hospital where the undersigned was informed of a felonious assault. At 2315 hours complainant"—the complainant at this point was not "People" but José Rodriguez—"was pronounced DOA by Dr. Godfrey of Bellevue Hospital."

"Could it have been an accident?" Emma asks.

"The knife was thrust four inches into his heart," Joyce replies. The assumption is that no one can accidentally propel his heart four inches deep onto someone else's knife. Still, it seems that Rodriguez, twenty-four years old at the time of his demise, was a junkie.

"Was it self-defense?" Emma asks.

"I may have said to Angel that it looks like self-defense," Joyce says. This is, for Emma, a matter of concern. He hopes Tom Curtis will not hear of it. "Tom Curtis," Emma says, "is a damn good lawyer," and a damn good lawyer is likely to challenge the admissibility of the written confession that Joyce obtained from Angel at 2:00 A.M. that morning.

Eight days will pass before Curtis sees a copy of Angel's confession. After Joyce had read the boy the so-called Miranda warning of his rights, and another policeman had translated the warning into Spanish for his mother, Angel took two pieces of paper and wrote:

"This junkie was walking in the park at Norfolk St. between Houston and Stanton. She droped her purse and I pick did up. And the knife felt out. I pick up the knife and Jose who was staning next to me said don't steal from the lady. I said Jose I don't steal from nobody. I'am not like you stealing from all my friends. He said shut the fuck up. How are you talking like there. Jose went to hit me the pocketbook. I pick up the knife opened and I poinied it at him. He swung the pocket book again. Has he swung his body came right into the knife. I saw blood coming from his chess I was worried about him but people in the block will not let go. Somebody told my mother that I was in troublen. She came running and got me. I'am came back to the block. And my mother saw *Det.* Joyce and told me to give myself up. I told *Det.* Joyce what happened.

"I'am making this statement of my own free will. I was advised of my right and my mother was present."...

By 11:15 Emma has finished the draft of the petition. Bearing the docket number D-2414/77, which means that it purports to be the 2,414th delinquency petition to be filed in New York County Family Court so far this year, it charges that Angel "did with intent to cause the death of one JOSE RODRIGUEZ, did cause the death of such person by stabbing him with a knife, and such death was caused under circumstances evincing depraved indifference to human life, in that he recklessly engaged in conduct which created a grave risk of death to said person." Emma takes it to a typist, who will stamp on the finished document "Designated Felony Act Petition," which means that this is a particularly serious case and must be treated in a special manner conceived by the New York State legislature only last year in response to what the legislators take to be a cry from the voters that somebody must do something about all this juvenile crime. Emma thinks that with luck the petition will reach Intake A by the 1:00 lunch break.

In Intake A, on the fifth floor, Judge Philip W. Thurston presides. A seemingly amiable man in his sixties, he has a toothy grin which he flashes at the unfortunates assembled before him—whether in human commiseration or in reflex defense against the serial horrors that command his daily attention, no man can say. It is Thurston's job, this month, in this Part, to give brief audiences to all parties who have a claim on the court's time, excepting cases involving child abuse, which because of their special urgency are rushed to a Part reserved for them alone. Thurston has numerous options available to him for each case that is called before him, but his principal responsibilities are three: he must assign counsel to the participants in each case; with the help of his clerk, he must schedule these cases for hearings according to the time that is available on the calendars of each of the Parts in the court; and in matters involving children accused of offenses, he must determine, with the help of a Probation officer, whether they are to be paroled to their homes while awaiting a hearing, or remanded either to the Juvenile Center in the Bronx, a place of secure detention, or to one of the city's agencies or shelter care homes....

...the Sanchez case is called. Angel's mother enters, chewing her fingernails, followed by an interpreter and by Tom Curtis, who, like all Legal Aid lawyers, carries a sheaf of files and a fat yellow-covered book on family law. Angel is brought in from a detention room, in handcuffs; one of the court officers takes a position behind him. Angel is a dark-skinned, compactly built boy, but he *is* astonishingly short. Disconcerting as the scars on his face are, he has limpid brown eyes and an alert demeanor, and might be taken, by an unwary observer, for a cute little nine- or ten-year-old. When it becomes clear that the handcuffs are to stay on, Curtis objects—uselessly, because the Administrative Judge has ruled that violent children are to be so restrained.

Curtis informs the court that Angel's father is flying up from Puerto Rico tonight to hire a private lawyer, which means that the case must be adjourned until the next day. Privately, Curtis is somewhat miffed; although he doesn't really need a complicated murder trial added to his case load, he has had a lot of experience with Angel and understands the boy's problems. Besides, as everyone in Family Court knows, private lawyers do not fare well in this court. Most private lawyers strenuously resist appearing here, where they feel they are treated badly and due process seldom applies. It is true, they *are* treated badly, even rudely on occasion, by judges and court officers, but it is also true that most of them are unfamiliar with the peculiar vagaries of family law (hearsay testimony, for instance, is permitted in child abuse cases, much to the detriment of the parents whom the private lawyers defend), and many seem unfamiliar with a basic premise of trial practice, which is that the business of a defense lawyer is to defend his client vigorously, and not condescend to him or, having predetermined his guilt, conspire with judge and prosecutor to arrive at a semblance of equity. Curtis correctly assumes that by virtue of his experience with this kind of law and with this particular court, he can defend Angel more effectively than a private lawyer can, but he doesn't want to be put in a position where Angel's mother wants him and the father wants someone else. . . .

Curtis wonders whether Angel's seemingly uncontrollable violence results from a prescribed drug, methyltestosterone, he has been taking. Two years ago, Angel and some other kids attempted to light a fire for an indoor barbecue by throwing gasoline on the briquets; the gasoline fumes collected in the room and finally exploded, leaving Angel badly scarred. To enable his hair to grow, and to enable him to mature sexually—for Angel's principal problem is his stunted growth—he has been taking large doses of male hormones, which may have a side effect of making him violent. Curtis thinks, too, that brain damage may be a possibility: "So many of our clients were born to mothers who have no idea at all of prenatal care. The mothers are fourteen years old, have lived for years on a diet of Pepsi and Cheez Doodles, and as soon as possible they feed their infants Pepsi and Cheez Doodles, too—when they remember to feed them at all. Some of these mothers were junkies when they were pregnant. We get psychiatric reports on these kids, their average IQ is maybe 65 to 75, just barely the minimum to function, and the psychiatric reports say 'minimal brain damage.' It's the usual diagnosis, nobody knows what it means, maybe we're all 'minimally brain damaged' to some extent. The only doctor these kids have is the Emergency Room at Bellevue, when they get a leg cut off. Often the first doctor they see is the doctor at Juvenile Center, when they get arrested."

If any of these factors apply, Curtis thinks that Angel must be considered one of the victims of his acts, a boy who deserves treatment rather than punishment. If he can get the court to agree, then it is legally the court's responsibility to see that Angel is properly treated, but in this area, as in so many others, the court is inefficient and has few resources to draw upon, so if Angel is to get what he needs, it will be up to Curtis and the Legal Aid social workers to arrange it. This extralegal function, which occupies much of the Legal Aid attorneys' time, was anticipated by the framers of the Family Court Act, which defines the defenders of juveniles as "law guardians."

First, however, Curtis will have to persuade a judge that Angel is not in fact a hardened criminal. Considering Angel's present legal position, this will be difficult:

Angel faces trial on a charge of assault with a knife. Like many street kids, he carries an illegal weapon called a "double-oh-seven," a folding knife that opens with a flick of the wrist. Corporation Counsel has talked about "attempted murder," about Angel's cutting the throat of another boy, when, says Curtis, he only scratched the boy's shoulder in a fight over a girl. Such scrapes between acquaintances are so common in New York City that they rarely draw an arrest; Curtis thinks that if Angel had been an adult, there never would have been a case.

Angel is scheduled to stand trial for intimidation with a sawed-off rifle. He and a friend had been in a hardware store. The proprietor, says Curtis, "thought they were stealing stuff and beat the shit out of the other kid. Angel returned the next day with the rifle and threatened the man's life." In a pre-trial hearing, Curtis managed to suppress the rifle—meaning it could not later be used in evidence—because the police had not taken Angel to the station, as they are required to do, and had not read him his Miranda rights. "The police are anxious to suppress reality out there," Curtis says.

Angel is faced with another charge of attempted murder. A group of kids tried to kill another in the lobby of a movie theater. Seemingly the most serious of Angel's prior dilemmas, Curtis believes it the least worrisome. Angel is innocent of this one, he says: "We know who did it." After the assault, Angel calmly went back into the theater to see the rest of the movie—it was about the life of George Jackson—which, says Curtis, he would have been unlikely to do had he been guilty. . . .

Though Tom Curtis, that [next] morning, has reason to think he will not act as Angel's lawyer in the Rodriguez case, he has already been to the scene of the crime. "On the scene you can intuit a lot," he says, "and what you get by intuition is often more important than the hard evidence. . . ."

The park where José Rodriguez had been killed the night before is a small one at the corner of Houston and Norfolk streets. A chain fence surrounds it, but the gates are missing. There is an ugly brick gazebo in the middle, with reeking toilets on either side; in the shade and stench of urine that this structure offers, winos sleep on benches. Angel had mentioned some possible witnesses to the killing—two girls he doesn't know, who were sitting on a metal stump, and a man he does, who was shooting a basketball at a rim without a net—and Curtis hoped, since the other side will try to find these people, that he could prove the killing took place around a corner of the gazebo, out of their sight. But he found a red stain on the asphalt, which might be blood, and the stain is, unfortunately, in plain view of both the stump and the basketball rim. . . .

On the morning of July 1 . . . when Angel's case is recalled in Intake A, Curtis learns that the father, who lives with a woman in Brooklyn . . . has no money for a private lawyer. He learns, too, from Angel that when Detective Joyce asked if he wanted to make an oral confession, Angel refused; Joyce then said, "Well, why don't you write it, then?" Curtis tells Judge Thurston that he will ask for a probable cause hearing to suppress this confession and asks for a hearing to be held before some other judge than Joseph A. Doran, who now presides in

Part IV, the Designated Felony Part, and who will conduct the fact-finding hearing. Curtis knows Doran, a judge who normally sits in the Bronx, only by reputation—he is supposed to be bright, but also the most prosecution-minded of the judges—and dreads having to try Angel's case before him. He has another worry, as well:

Curtis: "I would object to it being put down for a probable cause in that Part of the court. I would point out to the Court that the standard of evidence that is set out by Section 739b of the Family Court Act and by reference by the Criminal Procedures Law are such that very often materials which would not be admitted in a full fact-finding or preliminary hearing are admitted at a probable cause hearing. I would therefore think that my client's rights would be prejudiced if the judge sitting in the Designated Felony Part, who in all likelihood will be the trial judge, were to hear the probable cause hearing also."

Thurston: "Motion is denied, counsel."

Inwardly, Curtis seethes. The judge hears all this inadmissible evidence. How is he to put it out of his mind during the trial? It's got to influence him. Aloud, he says: "Would the Court expound upon the reasons for denying my motion?"

Thurston: "As I understand the statute here, once the parties are here and everything is ready, the case then goes to the Designated Felony Part, period."

Curtis: "I think the aspects of the judge there—"

Thurston: "I think a lot of things should be changed, but I am not the legislature, counsel."

Curtis: "This is not the beginning of a trial. This is in fact a separate hearing. I would note my objection."

Thurston: "Certainly." He offers him a date in Part IV: July 7 or 8.

Curtis: "I would note that a delay of that nature is clearly outside of the three-day limit set by 739b of the Family Court Act."

Thurston: "I don't think that section or three days applies to homicide cases, counsel."

Curtis: "Your honor, I have my calendar in front of me. I have ten cases on the 8th, including a number of delinquencies with hearings in Part III. I would ask for the 5th or the 6th."

Thurston: "Counsel, it's either the 7th or the 8th."

Curtis: "Can the Court explain why I can't have the hearing within the three days required by the statute?"

Thurston: "I don't think it applies to homicides, in my estimation."

Curtis: "My client has been incarcerated now through the Court since yesterday."

Thurston: "Well, you know his history very well, counsel."

Having lost that one, Curtis tries another: "I understand that my client made a written statement to the Police Department."

Thurston: "This case is adjourned to July 7, 1977, Part IV, Designated Felony Part, for a probable cause hearing. Remand of respondent is continued."

Curtis: "I understand that my client has made a written statement which I gather is in the custody of the Police Department, your honor."

Thurston: "If so, you are entitled to it. Do you know anything about it?" Thurston is speaking now to Larry Schwartzstein, who is the head of Corporation

Counsel in the Manhattan court. Schwartzstein will prosecute this case. Most law guardians have little regard for him; they believe he is ambitious to be a judge, which is why he usurps the important cases—because if you want to be a judge, it looks good to have won important cases. Schwartzstein, however, is no fool, and brushes Curtis's ploy aside.

Schwartzstein: "I am in the process of investigating it. Between now and over the weekend I will attempt to obtain not only the statement but also some medical documents and turn them over to Mr. Curtis." It is a generous-sounding statement, but it means only that Curtis will have to sweat awhile before he sees the confession and the autopsy, without which he cannot prepare his defense.

Thurston: "I'm sure you will. All right."

So matters rest. This sparring for legal advantage has been not so much translated as it has been summarized and interpreted for Mrs. Sanchez, who understands little except that her son's trial has been again postponed. . . .

Angel Sanchez's probable cause hearing convenes a little after 11 A.M. on July 7. . . .

Curtis, this morning, is dressed in his most conservative style: white shirt, dark tie, blue pinstripe suit, his hair slicked back forcibly against his head. "It's not an afro today," Schwartzstein observes. "He looks like a prosecutor now. Kinky hair is for law guardians." Immediately the hearing begins, Curtis moves for a conference at the bench—much of what happens in Family Court happens off the record—and Doran invites counsel to his chambers. There Curtis explains to the judge what his motions are going to be and the order in which he will present them. "I have a tendency to talk very fast," Curtis observes later, "but I don't want to antagonize the judge. What good would *that* do? I get more of my clients out on the street than those who irritate judges do. So I was trying to keep the atmosphere very courtly. The scene in court had to be orderly. After all, it's what's on the record that counts, and the stenographers have trouble when three people talk all at once. Sometimes the record is a mess. I want to be sure this one is clear."

Forty-five minutes later, the hearing resumes. As the courtroom settles down, Detective Joyce, who is unruffled by Curtis's intention to suppress his confession ("I've got the murder weapon. I've got three witnesses. It won't matter if they throw the confession out"), sticks a needle into Tom: "Ah, you're the enemy."

This is not to Curtis's taste. "I'm *not* the enemy. I'm a good guy."

"Aren't you the law guardian?"

"Yes."

"The enemy."

Annoyed, Curtis shakes his head. "I've just spent two weeks in the National Guard protecting you."

"I've been doing that all my life."

Curtis is interested. "Where?"

"The police."

On the record, two minutes later, Curtis asks Judge Doran for a suppression hearing on what he calls Angel's "statement to the police." He argues that the suppression hearing—in legal terms, a voir dire, or a Huntley hearing—be heard *before* the probable cause hearing. Curtis hopes to prove either that Angel's confession was given involuntarily, or that it was extracted from him in flagrant violation of his rights. If he can bring this off, and if the confession is found inadmissible, he hopes to persuade Doran to disqualify himself from any further hearings on the grounds that he has been exposed to the illegal evidence. . . .

Larry Schwartzstein, no stranger to technicalities himself, opposes Curtis's motion: "It has been my understanding that in Family Court when we are dealing with a Court absent a jury that all matters are before the same tryer of fact. As a matter of fact, the Court of Appeals in the matter of *People* v. *Brown* cited at 24 New York 2d 168 299 New York Supp. 2d 199 concluded as follows: 'Since a jury trial is not constitutionally required referring to Family Court proceedings, respondent's claim to the right of a separate hearing is without merit absent a jury trial. All questions of fact, including those dealing with the voluntariness of any statement, are determinable by the same judge who presides at the trial.'" Schwartzstein goes on to argue that the validity of Angel's statement is not a question to be determined before the fact-finding stage of the proceedings, that the existence of a statement, whether admissible or not, is sufficient to establish probable cause.

Judge Doran agrees: there will be no separate hearing for suppression. Curtis immediately asks that the case be sent back to Intake A "so the probable cause hearing could be heard by another judge." He reminds Doran that because inadmissible evidence may be heard in the probable cause hearing, it is essential that the judge who will preside over the fact-finding hearing—in this case, Doran—remain uncontaminated by it.

Schwartzstein opposes this motion as well. Judge Thurston, in Intake A, has already denied this motion. "I don't think that once we have a ruling by an Intake judge that we have to send it back to another Intake judge for another ruling." In fact, with the elapse of time, another judge now presides in Intake A.

Doran agrees again. The rotation of judges among the Parts is a matter so arbitrary that it alarms most people who have anything to do with Family Court, so Doran may well not, after all the delays, hear the fact-finding part of this case himself. "But apart from that," he says, "since the motion is that I refer this matter back to Intake A, I am not disposed to do that. I question my authority to do it. I may add I don't see any substantial merit that would require the Court to take such action." The only merit, from Curtis's point of view, is not one of law, but of defense strategy: the new Intake judge might well rule differently from Thurston. "Accordingly, Mr. Curtis, the motion to refer back to Intake A is denied."

Curtis: "Note my objection."

Doran: "Certainly. Are there any further applications at this time?"

Curtis has one. He wants to change the phrase in the petition that reads "and such death was caused" to read "and/or such death was caused." The emendation makes some legal sense.

Doran: "So this will be an and/or pleading?"

Curtis: "Yes."

Doran: "Grammatical purists would be horrified by that pleading. I don't want to take any responsibility for whatever legal complications may arise from grammatical improprieties." But he allows it. "Are we ready to proceed, gentlemen?"

They are. Schwartzstein introduces a certificate of death, an identification of the body by the police and another by a relative of the deceased. Curtis continues to object: "I would note that I think no proper foundation for their admission has been laid. . . . I would submit that further perusal of Section 190.30 of the Criminal Procedures Law makes me object to the submission of the third document," and so on.

Schwartzstein: "I will take it back. I merely offered it. It is my position and my position always has been to give the Legal Aid Society as much information as I have." The very image of the prosecutor anxious to cooperate with the defense: this is Schwartzstein's style, and Curtis shrugs; he knows what will be withheld.

Curtis: "I withdraw my objection."

Doran: "I would think you would."

Detective Joyce is then sworn in. He testifies that he "responded to Bellevue about 11:15 P.M. June 29th at the emergency ward. One male identified as José Rodriguez was being operated on, emergency operation. He expired a couple of minutes later." Ten minutes later, he took five men, friends of the deceased, to his office in the 13th Precinct. At 12:30 A.M. he went to the park where Rodriguez was stabbed. "A group of Spanish people flagged me down. Amongst them was Angel Sanchez and his mother." He identifies Angel and Mrs. Sanchez as being present in court. "Angel spoke to me and said, 'I stabbed José.' I took Angel into custody. A second police car had turned the corner and I borrowed handcuffs from one of the officers." Joyce drove Angel and his mother to the 13th Precinct. While in the car, Angel told Joyce that he was fifteen, which alerted Joyce to the special problems he faced in dealing with a juvenile. At the precinct, he took Angel to the "designated area for juveniles"—a room that must be of a certain size, on the ground floor, with a window. He offered Angel and Mrs. Sanchez coffee and sodas, which were declined, and then, because Mrs. Sanchez speaks little English, he had to cast about for an interpreter, finally coming up with a bilingual policeman at 2:00 A.M. "I proceeded to advise Angel and his mother in English of their rights under the Miranda warnings. As I did that, Officer Alicea did it in Spanish." He then gave Angel pencil and paper. The confession was written and signed, then read aloud twice, once in English and again in Spanish.

Schwartzstein: "Did the respondent indicate any participation in a crime?"

Curtis: "Objection. It is not established my client's rights were afforded him. I would note at this time my request for a voir dire on the admissibility of the statement at the probable cause hearing."

Doran: "It hasn't been offered yet."

Curtis: "He's been asked if my client indicated his involvement in a crime. I would submit the answer would be the fruits of inquiry which has not been established."

Schwartzstein protests: "I am attempting to give the Legal Aid Society as much of an outline as they can have so they can prepare for trial." He is, he says, only "indicating" that a statement exists, its admissibility to be determined later.

Doran: "Objection overruled, Mr. Curtis."

Curtis: "Note my exception."

Doran: "Surely."

Further questions from Schwartzstein elicit the information that Angel stabbed José Rodriguez once with his knife, that Joyce informed Angel that Rodriguez had died and that Joyce had interviewed three witnesses to the killing, who referred to Angel as "Shorty."

Schwartzstein: "Did they indicate that they observed what transpired that evening in the park?"

Curtis: "I'm going to object to this line of inquiry on the grounds that it is hearsay. Hearsay is excludable under the rules of evidence set forth in Section 193."

Schwartzstein: "If we were on trial, there is no question that the information which is being elicited from the detective would be hearsay. It being probable cause, I'm trying to gain for Legal Aid as much information as I can," and so on. Curtis's objection is again overruled, and Schwartzstein introduces the confession in evidence. Curtis objects again and is again overruled.

On cross-examination, Curtis runs over Joyce's testimony again until Schwartzstein objects: "The information being elicited at this time is not material for a probable cause hearing."

Doran: "Objection sustained. Exception noted." He seems faintly amused. Throughout all of this, Doran, who appears hard of hearing, has screwed up his face and cupped his hand behind his ear. Seeing this, Curtis raises his voice, but then allows it to fade away again. "All judges here," Curtis says later, "see themselves as part of the law enforcement process—and that's not so. All judges pay too much attention to what the police say—as if that were fact. It isn't, necessarily." Now, Curtis protests that "180.60 of the Criminal Procedures Law says I have a right to cross-examine this witness."

Schwartzstein: "I would take exception to the comment that Mr. Curtis has made. I think Mr. Curtis is being given the opportunity to cross-examine this witness."

Curtis loses again. Doran says, "I have already made a ruling." In a probable cause hearing, as opposed to a fact-finding hearing, the judge has the discretion of limiting cross-examination. He must allow some, but he will never allow as much as the law guardian, who is trying to discover as much as he can of the prosecution's case, would like. "They play games," Doran says, "but I can play games, too."

Curtis makes a final stab: "Officer, you said you interviewed three individuals. Who were those three individuals?"

He doesn't have a chance. Schwartzstein is on his feet. "I would at this point object to the identity of these three individuals for the following reasons: one, for their own protection, and two, because I want to be sure they will come forth at the date of the trial without being harassed or being bothered by investigators or anyone of the Legal Aid Society."

Doran: "Well, counselor, probable cause hearing is not a substitute for discovery. Objection sustained."

Curtis: "I would submit that we have a right to interview those witnesses if they wish to be interviewed. We can't force anybody to be interviewed if they don't wish to be." Doran is impervious to such pleas. "I would note my strong objection," Curtis says. He believes he has a right to know who the opposition's witnesses are. "With research," he says later, "you can often prove that they couldn't have seen what they'll swear they saw." But if after talking to them, Curtis sees his case is weak, he may persuade Angel to plead to Murder 3, manslaughter, and get him sent away for a year and a half insted of five. On this matter, Curtis is mistaken: unlike federal law, New York State law does not require the disclosure of witnesses.

Having lost these skirmishes, Curtis declines to call his own witnesses. He tells the court that probable cause has not been proved at this hearing because the disputable confession "indicates that my client *accidentally* caused the death of this individual." Schwartzstein replies that it is for the fact-finding hearing to determine whether death was "accidental." Doran agrees, finds probable cause has been established and sets a trial date for July 22. Firing his last bullet, Curtis asks Doran to disqualify himself from hearing the trial on the grounds that he has heard evidence that might be suppressed later on. Doran brushes the idea aside. . . .

On July 22, the confusion in Part IV is worse than ever. Tom Curtis received the autopsy report and the transcript of the probable cause hearing only the night before, and the toxicological report—a test for the presence of alcohol and drugs in the deceased's blood and kidneys—only minutes before the court convened. "The autopsy," Curtis says, "always has an effect on judges that is detrimental to my clients. The description of the wounds, the fractures, the contusions, the *defensive* wounds on the victim's hands—that has a strong effect." In Judge Doran's chambers, Curtis says that he must ask for an adjournment of the trial. The autopsy shows that José Rodriguez was killed by a single blow, which may help Angel's claim that the death was "accidental." The toxicology report shows the presence of morphine and quinine, a compound used to cut morphine in the manufacture of heroin. "I need time to consider this."

"It takes twenty seconds to read," Larry Schwartzstein says in an aside. "We should proceed. This shows the stupidity of this Part. Nothing's going to be done. Why shouldn't it be tried? I brought in six people. This is the day it's *supposed* to be tried!"

But Curtis cannot be rushed. What was the effect of the morphine? he wonders. What did it make him do? "My kid is confronted in a park by a drug abuser who's been to prison. It may be self-defense." Curtis wants the "yellow sheet"—the Police Department's arrest record—on Rodriguez; this can be subpoenaed, but it will take time to get.

Time is the problem: Detective Joyce is about to start his vacation; when he returns, Schwartzstein begins his. The scheduling mess is impossible. "Let's do it the easy way," Schwartzstein says to Curtis. "Take a plea." He offers Curtis Manslaughter 1, which will result in a five-year term: one year in restricted placement, two years in a less restricted facility, two more years elsewhere. Self-defense, however, is Manslaughter 2, worth only a year and a half.

Back in the courtroom, Curtis requests his adjournment.

Doran: "I grant your application. This is a serious matter." Curtis suspects that Doran, who will return to the Bronx in ten days, would just as soon not get tangled in a case that might bring him back to Manhattan, or be reversed on appeal.

Doran calendars the case for September 6 and continues Angel's remand. Curtis objects. Doran gives him a wintry smile. . . .

Afterward, Curtis is very upset. In a corridor behind the courtroom, he paces nervously back and forth, his hands clasped tightly behind him. "I'm feeling very defensive about this," he says. In fact, he knows he has not prepared his record well for a writ of habeas corpus that he wants to file in the state Supreme Court to have Angel tried as soon as medical records can be obtained. For an hour in the judge's chambers they argued the question of adjournment. Curtis had wanted the trial to proceed the following week and had said so, but there was no court reporter present and his arguments were consequently all off the record. He should immediately have made the same argument on the record when they went back into the courtroom, but he forgot. He could, too, have asked the judge to substitute Angel's pressing case for another on his calendar that involved a boy at home on parole, but he did not. If all this were not damaging enough, Curtis is in the awkward position of reversing himself: during the probable cause hearing, he had argued that Doran should *not* hear the trial, and now he wants to file a writ arguing that Doran *must* hear the trial. These omissions and contradictions may very well sink his writ, because the Supreme Court justice who hears it will be guided by what the record shows. Allowances will not be made for Curtis's legal lapses. "I've made a bad record," he says. . . .

Curtis sits on his briefcase and begins writing notes for his writ. He is tempted to move for a jury trial. Never mind that the U.S. Supreme Court has ruled that juveniles are not entitled to jury trials. Never mind that the Family Court has no facilities for a jury trial. "That's not my problem," Curtis snaps. There's a statute which says that any person who may be incarcerated for a year or more is entitled to a jury trial, and under this new Designated Felony Act such incarceration is what Angel faces. . . .

The writ fails. . . . In the interim, Angel has been convicted in one of his other cases, the knifing case, and he has been remanded for a statutory twenty days pending his other trials. Curtis had applied in his writ either for a speedy trial in the matter of Angel's alleged homicide, or parole until the September 6 date. He thought he might be ordered to go to trial the next day, unprepared, but instead the Supreme Court justice ruled that since Angel was legally remanded until the middle of August, the writ would be adjourned. Curtis had not expected that. By mid-August, Angel has been found guilty again: in the rifle case, the charge of menacing is dropped because Angel cooperated in returning the rifle, but he is found guilty of petty larceny, for taking a packet of plaster from the store.

A few weeks later, Angel is tried for the attempted murder in the movie theater. The trial takes two days. The victim is present. He hasn't seen Angel since the incident, but very coolly he points his finger at him and says, "He stabbed me."

Curtis is surprised. He still thought Angel innocent of this one. "I don't like being surprised in the courtroom," Curtis says; he doesn't approve of a complainant's coming into court, looking over at the defendant's chair and saying: "You." He thinks the complainant was lying; he thinks there should have been a proper lineup, but with Angel's runty figure, what good can a lineup do? "It would have been a futile gesture. But then, that's what the law's about: futile gestures."

This case is heard before Judge Stanley Gartenstein, who presides in Part IV in September. On September 6, a few days later, Curtis makes pro forma gestures to persuade Gartenstein to disqualify himself from hearing the Rodriguez case. Gartenstein declines. What's the use? Curtis asks. He's heard the other case, he knows Angel's record. Curtis confers with Schwartzstein and accepts a plea: Manslaughter 2 in the Rodriguez case, combined with an Assault 1 finding in the movie theater case. The two admissions together should result in no more than a three-year sentence: a year "inside," Curtis estimates, followed by two years in a residential facility. No question, of course, of consecutive sentences being imposed. "He who commits more crimes gets punished less," Larry Schwartzstein observes.

So now, after all of Curtis's legal maneuverings, there will be no trial in the Rodriguez killing, but only a formality to be observed. Curtis rises to address Judge Gartenstein, motioning for Angel to rise with him.

Source: From *The Child Savers: Juvenile Justice Observed* by Peter S. Prescott.

REFERENCES

BAY AREA SOCIAL COUNCIL

1968 The juvenile hall. Chapter 6 in *Background Information on the San Francisco Juvenile Court.* San Francisco: Bay Area Social Council.

BEST, JUDAH, AND PAUL I. BIRZON

1963 Conditions of probation: An analysis. *Georgetown Law Journal* 51:809–836.

BLACK, DONALD J., AND ALBERT J. REISS, JR.

1970 Police control of juveniles. *American Sociological Review* 35:63–77.

BLACK, T. EDWIN, AND CHARLES P. SMITH

1981 *A Preliminary Assessment of the Numbers and Characteristics of Juveniles Processed in the Juvenile Justice System.* Washington, D.C.: U.S. Government Printing Office.

CHILDREN'S DEFENSE FUND

1976 *Children in Adult Jails.* Washington, D.C.: Washington Research Project, Inc.

COMMUNITY RESEARCH FORUM
1980 *Removing Children from Adult Jails.* Urbana-Champaign, Ill.: University of Illinois.

FELD, BARRY C.
1978 Reference of juvenile offenders for adult prosecution: The legislative alternative to asking unanswerable questions. *Minnesota Law Review* 62:515–618.

FERSTER, ELYCE Z., ET AL.
1969 Juvenile detention: Protection, prevention, or punishment. *Fordham Law Review* 38:161–196.

GOLDFARB, RONALD
1975 *Jails: The Ultimate Ghetto of the Criminal Justice System.* Garden City, N.Y.: Anchor.

HOWARD, DAVID C., ET AL.
1977 Publicity and juvenile court proceedings. *Clearinghouse Review* 11:203–211.

HUSSEY, FREDERICK A.
1976 Perspectives on parole decision-making with juveniles. *Criminology* 13:449–469.

INSTITUTE OF JUDICIAL ADMINISTRATION/AMERICAN BAR ASSOCIATION JOINT COMMISSION ON JUVENILE JUSTICE STANDARDS
1977a *Standards Relating to Dispositions.* Cambridge, Mass.: Ballinger.
1977b *Standards Relating to Interim Status: The Relapse, Control, and Detention of Accused Juvenile Offenders Between Arrest and Disposition.* Cambridge, Mass.: Ballinger.

JOHN HOWARD ASSOCIATION
1974 *Michigan Juvenile Justice Services: Appraisal of Local Services, Recommendations for Change.* Chicago: John Howard Association.

KITTRIE, NICHOLAS N.
1969 Can the right to treatment remedy the ills of the juvenile process? *Georgetown Law Journal* 57:848–885.

LEVIN, MARK M., AND ROSEMARY C. SARRI
1974 *Juvenile Delinquency: A Comparative Analysis of Legal Codes in the United States.* Ann Arbor, Mich.: University of Michigan, National Assessment of Juvenile Corrections.

MILLER, FRANK W., ET AL.
1976 *The Juvenile Justice Process.* Mineola, N.Y.: Foundation Press.

NATIONAL CENTER FOR JUVENILE JUSTICE
1977 *Respondents Panel, State Profile Questionnaire.* Pittsburgh, Pa.: National Center for Juvenile Justice, Research Division of the National Council of Juvenile Court Judges.

NATIONAL COUNCIL ON CRIME AND DELINQUENCY
1967 Corrections in the United States: Juvenile institutions. *Crime and Delinquency* 13:73–96.
1959 Standard Juvenile Court Act. *National Probation and Parole Association Journal* 5:323–391.

NATIONAL CRIMINAL JUSTICE INFORMATION AND STATISTICS SERVICE
1975 *The Nation's Jails: A Report on the Census of Jails from the 1972 Survey of Inmates of Local Jails.* Washington, D.C.: U.S. Government Printing Office.

PAPPENFORT, DONNELL M., AND THOMAS M. YOUNG
1980 *Use of Secure Detention for Juveniles and Alternatives to Its Use.* Washington, D.C.: U.S. Government Printing Office.

PERKINS, ROBERT F.

1968 Your detention program: Is it focused on the needs of the children detained? *Juvenile Court Judges Journal* 19:55–60.

PIERSMA, PAUL, ET AL.

1975 The juvenile court: Current problems, legislative proposals, and a model act. *St. Louis University Law Journal* 20:1–99.

PRESIDENT'S COMMISSION ON LAW ENFORCEMENT AND ADMINISTRATION OF JUSTICE

1967a *Challenge of Crime in a Free Society*. Washington, D.C.: U.S. Government Printing Office.

1967b *Task Force Report: Corrections*. Washington, D.C.: U.S. Government Printing Office.

RUBIN, SOL

1970 *Crime and Juvenile Delinquency*. Dobbs Ferry, N.Y.: Oceana.

SALEEBEY, GEORGE

1975 *Hidden Closets: A Study of Detention Practices in California*. Sacramento, Calif.: California Department of Youth Authority.

SARRI, ROSEMARY C.

1974 *Under Lock and Key: Juveniles in Jails and Detention*. Ann Arbor, Mich.: University of Michigan, National Assessment of Juvenile Corrections.

SCHWARTZ, IRA M.

1979 Juvenile detention and alternatives, Scott County, Iowa. Technical assistance report prepared for the National Juvenile Law Center, St. Louis, Missouri.

SCHWARZENBERGER, GEORG

1971 Juvenile probation: Restrictions, rights, and rehabilitation. *St. Louis University Law Journal* 16:276–339.

STAMM, MORTIMER J.

1973 Transfer of jurisdiction in juvenile court: An analysis of the proceeding, its role in the administration of justice, and a proposal for the reform of Kentucky law. *Kentucky Law Journal* 62:122–199.

STREIB, VICTOR L.

1978 *Juvenile Justice in America*. Port Washington, N.Y.: Kennikat Press.

TERRY, ROBERT M.

1967 Discrimination in the handling of juvenile offenders by social control agencies. *Journal of Research in Crime and Delinquency* 4:218–230.

VINTER, ROBERT D., ET AL.

1975 *Juvenile Corrections in the States: Residential Programs and Deinstitutionalization*. Ann Arbor, Mich.: University of Michigan, National Assessment of Juvenile Corrections.

VITIELLO, MICHAEL

1976 Constitutional safeguards for juvenile transfer procedure: The ten years since *Kent* v. *United States*. *DePaul Law Review* 26:23–53.

VOLENIK, ADRIENNE

1975 Juvenile court and arrest records. *Clearinghouse Review* 9:169–174.

WISCONSIN HEALTH AND SOCIAL SERVICES DEPARTMENT

1976 *Juvenile Detention in Wisconsin 1976: Final Report*. Madison, Wis.: Wisconsin Health and Social Services Department.

CASES

Davis v. *Alaska*, 415 U.S. 308 (1974)
Gagnon v. *Scarpelli*, 411 U.S. 778 (1973)

In re Gault, 387 U.S. 1 (1967)
Kent v. *U.S.*, 383 U.S. 541 (1966)
Lake v. *Cameron*, 364 F.2d 657 (D.C. Cir. 1966)
Miranda v. *Arizona*, 384 U.S. 436 (1966)
Morrissey v. *Brewer*, 408 U.S. 471 (1972)
Oklahoma Publishing Co. v. *District Court*, 430 U.S. 308 (1976)
Rouse v. *Cameron*, 373 F.2d 451 (D.C. Cir. 1966)
Schall v. *Martin*,—U.S.—(1984)
Shelton v. *Tucker*, 364 U.S. 479 (1960)
Smith v. *Daily Mail Publishing Co.*, 443 U.S. 97 (1979)

STATUTES AND CODES

Alabama Code 12–15–71 (c)(2) (1979)
District of Columbia Code 16–2307 (1973)
Maryland Courts and Judicial Proceedings Code Ann. 3–810 (1978)
Neb. Rev. Stat. 43–202(3)(b), 43–202.01 (1978)

Juvenile Diversion 11

Recent observers of the juvenile court system argue that we have expected too much of it, overloading it with cases and calling on it to deal with difficult and complex behavioral and social problems without equipping it with resources for achieving those goals. Then, too, others note that there are limits to the extent to which courts can be transformed entirely into therapeutic organizations. For example, courts often tag juveniles as delinquents in spite of their best efforts to avoid doing so. Consequently, many scholars contend that courts should restrict their efforts to "hard core" offenders (Schur, 1973; Lemert, 1971). These same commentators say that new agencies, outside the official juvenile justice system, should be created to divert less serious cases away from the courts and to provide services that will address many of the individual and collective problems of youth in contemporary society.

QUESTIONS ABOUT JUVENILE DIVERSION

Many ideas about the notion of diversion have sprung up in the United States in the past decade. "Judicious nonintervention," "benign neglect," "decriminalization," "diversion," "youth-services bureaus," "release on own recognizance," and other proposals are all part of a basic drive to reduce the number of offenders in the criminal and juvenile justice systems. The need to minimize the number of youths admitted into the juvenile justice system is clear enough. But we must address several basic questions concerning youth diverson before we can assess diversion programs.

1. What *is* diversion? (Are there differing conceptions of diversion? Are different forms of diversion practiced?)
2. Who should be diverted? (Relatively minor offenders? Relatively serious offenders? If the latter, how are "serious offenders" to be identified?)
3. When should diversion take place? (Prior to police arrest? At the station house? At court intake?)
4. Where should youth be diverted? (To no program? To an alternative program? If so, what kind? Should diversion programs be part of the juvenile justice system or not?)

What Is Diversion?

Diversion has carried several different, and sometimes conflicting, meanings. The term is often used to describe disposition prior to involving the juvenile justice system, but it is also commonly used to describe the process whereby cases are removed from the juvenile justice system after they have been admitted to it. The President's Commission noted that diversion was a process of referring youth to an existing community treatment program in lieu of further juvenile justice processing at any point between apprehension and adjudication (President's Commission, 1967). Diversion was "designed to suspend or terminate juvenile justice processing of youth in favor of release or referral to alternate services" (Office of Juvenile Justice and Delinquency Prevention, 1977:141). Another view is that diversion is simply a means of informal processing. For Kenney and Pursuit (1975:199), it is "an exercise in discretionary authority to substitute an informal disposition prior to a formal hearing on an alleged violation." Haggard (1976) sees diversion as the decision not to take legal action—in other words, a means of noncriminal processing for certain offenders. Its goal is to provide rehabilitation by substituting human services for punitive ones.

Perhaps the dominant view is expressed by Cressey and McDermott (1973): diversion is any action that keeps an offender from going into the courtroom. Similarly, Sundeen (1974:333) argues that diversion "is the return of the offender by the police to the community (the family or a referral agency) rather than referral to an official sanctioning agency, such as the probation department and juvenile court."

There is a wide spectrum of opinions concerning the ingredients of diversion. Diversion, to most persons, involves *doing something* with the offender. At the same time, some would extend the meaning of diversion to include policies of "benign neglect" or "judicious nonintervention," that is, doing nothing further to cases.

To many persons, diversion means referral to programs *outside* the justice system. Sarri (1975:2) likens diversion to "those activities by public officials such as police, intake and probation officers, and so forth that result in direct referral of the juvenile to agencies and persons who are capable of handling the problem outside the jurisdiction of the juvenile justice system." Elliott (1974:14) concurs: "Diversion represents a referral to a community-based program or agency which is independent of the justice system." The National Advisory Commission on Criminal Justice Standards and Goals (1973:27), on the other hand, includes as diversion programs "run by agencies of the criminal justice system."

Who Should Be Diverted?

A number of suggestions have been made regarding candidates for diversion. Sarri (1975:12) argues that diversion should be automatic for youth who are "first offenders charged with status offenses or minor misdemeanors, repeated status offenders, or youth known to be receiving service [treatment] in community agencies." It has also been suggested that youths who are referred to the court because of problems at school, or because social service agencies do not wish to handle them, be diverted to programs that can deal with them more appropriately.

One major recurrent fear is that diversion programs will end up "widening the net" of the juvenile justice apparatus, rather than narrowing it. That is, many people have suggested the possibility that diversion might come to be used primarily as a disposition for youths who would be screened out of the system if a diversion program did not exist (Klein et al., 1976; Lerman, 1975).

Who is to be screened out, diverted, or sent on to court referral will most probably differ across communities. The nature of the delinquency problem varies widely from community to community, both in terms of levels of community concern and the patterns of juvenile misconduct. But one thing is clear in all of this: however juvenile justice system administrators define the pool of youths eligible for diversion in a particular community, great care must be taken to ensure that juveniles are diverted out of official system processing in increased numbers, so as to avoid "widening the net."

When Should Youth Be Diverted?

Arguments have been proposed for diverting youngsters at several points in the juvenile justice system. Most definitions of diversion allow it to take place at any point between apprehension and adjudication. If the goal of diversion is to minimize the penetration, then youngsters probably ought to be diverted at every possible opportunity. Youth can be diverted (1) after initial police apprehension or (2) at court intake or (3) prior to adjudication.

Diversion at different points will involve differentiating youths in terms of seriousness of offense and related factors: those diverted from the system at initial police contact are likely to be less serious offenders than those diverted at court intake. Similarly, programs to which divertees are sent at these various diversion points will also differ. For example, court-intake divertees may well require a more detailed, complex program than those diverted at initial contact.

Where Should Youth Be Diverted?

Most observers have argued that diverted youths should receive positive life experiences that will open up legitimate roles for them in American society. Polk and Kobrin (1972:21–22), for example, have enumerated five conditions that must be met by any responsible diversion program:

> First, [the program] starts from the assumption that young people, including the troublesome, have positive resources to contribute to the community. This assumption is quite different than the classical rehabilitation programs, which begin with the premise that the youth has a problem which must be identified and corrected.
>
> Second, the program proceeds immediately to place the young person in an active role where something valuable is contributed, rather than in a passive role where some service is provided.
>
> Third, it is located within a legitimate institution, i.e., the school, a crucial factor in the formation of legitimate identities.
>
> Fourth, the experience can be organized quite easily so that a mix of "good" and "bad" youth is possible.
>
> Fifth, the activity constitutes diversion, both in the sense that it is not connected with the court process and in that legal coercion is not present, i.e., the program is purely voluntary.

The possibilities for creating structures within individual communities to address the needs of youth probably differ somewhat from place to place, so that there can be no single formula for creating a diversion organization. Still, some broad goals for diversion programs can be identified, paralleling the model put forth by Polk and Kobrin, among others. Diversion programs should stress youth involvement and participation; they should endeavor to include youth in various aspects of decision making; and, most important, they should regard youths as an integral part of the program, not merely as clients.

Diversion programs must offer an innovative approach to treatment and rehabilitation. Time after time, traditional treatment models—intensive counseling, therapy, and other "change the offender" types of programs—have been shown to be ineffective. In assessing delinquency-prevention programs, the President's Commission on Law Enforcement and Administration of Justice (1967) noted that such intervention strategies as individual and group counseling, social casework, and the use of detached workers have consistently failed to either prevent or reduce juvenile delinquency.

However, there is still no convincing evidence that intervention into the lives of delinquent youngsters, even by means of programs based on a highly sophisticated theoretical rationale, will actually be more effective than policies of minimal interference. For example, the problems of implementing theoretically sound diversion programs may turn out to be massive ones, frustrating the development or effectiveness of innovative programs. As a result, it is crucial that programs be tested against both conventional justice system processing and minimal interference with juveniles.

THE ROLE OF THE POLICE IN DIVERSION

Most state juvenile codes are so broad in scope that almost every youth could be arrested at some point. Moreover, children are generally accountable to the adult world for virtually everything they do, so the range of the surveillance exceeds even the broad limits of what is prohibited juvenile conduct by law (for example, alcohol consumption or truancy). While most misconduct goes unnoticed by the authorities, when it is detected, it is most often the police who serve as the major source of diversion away from the application of the juvenile code. Thus, we now will examine the major issues concerning the role of police in diverting youth.

Police Discretion

Since police forces were first organized, they have exercised a screening function by deciding which offenders will be handled formally and which will be handled informally. In this very basic sense, the police have always "diverted" certain offenders from the justice system. Historically, this screening function of the police has been called *discretion*—the freedom or authority to choose among alternative forms of disposition. The police use a number of alternatives to dispose of the large and diverse volume of juvenile cases they must handle. These options include ignoring the situation, handling the matter in the field (for example, warn, counsel, and release), detaining a suspect, deferring action pending further investigation, turning the juvenile over to a special youth-assistance bureau within the department, directing the child to a community service agency, or referring the offender to another police agency, juvenile court, or adult court. Obviously, an officer's decision can have a major impact upon the life of the youth involved. The consequences of these discretionary decisions become clearer when we consider that somewhere between 2 and 3 million juveniles will have police contacts during a given year. However, less than 15 percent of these police-juvenile encounters are likely to result in an arrest. And of all children taken into police custody, more than one-third are informally handled (for example, warned or reprimanded) in the department and released. Police diversion is the most far-reaching attempt to handle youthful offenders outside the juvenile justice system. The following sections examine the concept of police diversion, explore the various forms it takes, identify the issues surrounding its use, and assess its impact on juvenile justice processing.

Rationales for Police Diversion

Diversion programs have developed out of attempts to cope with the increasing spectrum of tasks that police officers are expected to perform; traditional methods of case handling and disposition have proven inadequate. Diversion procedures (once informal) are now becoming more formalized because of a sense that officers lack the education and training to handle a wide range of cases; a desire to hold police accountable for actions that have occurred unofficially for years; development of progressive police administrations; public pressure, especially from minority groups; and a growing disenchantment with the juvenile court's ability to provide needed services.

The push toward police diversion of juvenile offenders is generally premised on the following arguments:

Needed Services: Police uncover many frustrating situations in the routine investigation of complaints involving youths where the officer perceives that the child simply needs help in coping with his or her environment. In most cases, short of individual involvement, the officer has no alternative but to refer the child to juvenile court for processing. However, when the police use diversion, an alternative to court intake is available. The officer can determine the child's need and refer that child directly to a service agency that will address that need rather than the offense that was committed.

Police Control over Dispositions: Over the years, police have become cynical about the fact that after they investigate a case and turn it over to the prosecutor, the offender is released or put on probation without ever going to court. Even when the offender does go to court, the disposition is usually probation. The use of diversion allows the police to investigate a case and, in a sense, to determine the nature of its disposition. Diversion thus provides the police sufficient control to ensure that the offender is provided a disposition deemed appropriate by the individual officer.

JAPAN AS NUMBER ONE

Police discretion in the United States is common; youths are set free by the police, often because the case is not deemed serious. In Japan, the police use discretion less. Instead, they pursue cases relentlessly and offenders expect no mercy from them.

Observers uniformly note that people walk anywhere in Japan at all hours of the night, fully confident of their personal safety. To an extent that would shock Americans, the Japanese carry a great deal of cash with them because they pay large bills with cash rather than checks. Taxicab drivers give no indication of worrying about their personal safety. These subjective judgments are supported by the data available. Americans studying Japanese crime records, which are more complete than American records, indicate that around 1960 the rates for major crimes such as homicide, assault, theft, and rape were several times higher in America than in Japan. From 1960 to 1973 American crime rates rose 110 percent and other modern countries' crime rates went up also, except for Japan, where they declined further. . . .

Why have the Japanese police recently been so successful in controlling crime? Part of the answer lies in the readiness of citizens to call police . . . the speed of response to calls, and the thoroughness of pursuit. In 1976 the average time it took police to respond to a call throughout the country was three minutes and twenty-three seconds. . . .

Second, Japanese police have great advantages in pursuing complaints. Police in mini stations are in close touch with the local community and know about household composition and household valuables. Residents acknowledge the need for police to ask questions in order to gather information and are prepared to be cooperative. When polled as to how they would advise a relative who commits a crime, the Japanese respond overwhelmingly that they would tell the relative to turn himself in to the police. In the United States the suspect is advised that he has the right to seek counsel and not to cooperate in giving information to the police. Japanese find it puzzling that American suspects are not urged to help the police find out about the crime. In Japan the suspect knows that it is prudent to assist the policemen in gathering information. Nor are Japanese offenders likely to receive leniency because they are considered to have psychological difficulties or to be victims of a society. . . . Japanese punishments are generally mild . . . but Japanese officials are relentless and systematic in pursuing all cases.

Source: Ezra F. Vogel, *Japan as Number One* (Cambridge, Mass.: Harvard University Press, 1979), pp. 17, 18, 205, 206. Reprinted by permission.

Immediacy of Response: When a youth is petitioned to juvenile court, the case waits its turn to be brought to trial—often a long and drawn-out process. After the youth is released by the police, he or she may wait weeks before being asked to appear at the juvenile court for an interview with the intake worker or for a preliminary hearing. Unless the case is disposed of informally at that stage, the child waits again before the case is tried. By the time the case is heard and a disposition is determined, the child is likely to see little relationship between the offense he or she committed and the disposition of the case. A potential advantage of diversion is that it can result in a more immediate or timely response to the needs of the child.

More Appropriate Response: The juvenile justice system is a large, overwhelming process composed of the police, prosecutor, courts, and corrections system. An accused child thus receives thorough exposure to the bureaucratic proceedings of the individual parts of the system. In this process, the child is likely to lose sight of the reason he or she is there and is also likely to be exposed to the case-hardened attitudes of the members of the system and of other juvenile offenders who may be more mature criminally. It is felt that diversion of the youth at the earliest possible point—but yet with provision of needed services—increases the chance that the child will avoid the negative effects of the court process. Of course, there are cases for which the court is an appropriate vehicle. In fact, the diversion of lesser offenses will allow the court to focus its full attention on those cases that need it.

Lower Cost: The juvenile justice system is expensive. A great many bureaucrats are involved in the operation and support of the prosecutor, courts, and correctional components of the system. If more youthful offenders can be handled outside the system, then the size of the juvenile justice bureaucracy can be reduced. Moreover, if the offender can be identified by the police and diverted at that point, costs are reduced, and some would say the child has a lesser chance of repeating the offense, therefore resulting in secondary cost savings. Diversion also keeps out those children for whom formal processing is not appropriate, thereby saving money.

Community Involvement: Diversion is a local responsibility, so diverted youths are usually treated in a way the local community supports (and has resources to handle). Diversion forces the community to recognize and deal with its delinquency problem. For too long people have ignored this problem, assuming that the juvenile justice system could handle it. Community involvement in the juvenile diversion process often draws attention to the performance of schools, social-service agencies, and parents in their response to local juveniles' needs and problems.

Formalized Police Discretion: An advantage to juvenile diversion by the police is that the largely informal handling of juveniles becomes formalized. If the diversion process is handled properly, the criteria for selecting candidates for diversion will be drawn up by a community-based board and incorporated into the written policy of the police department. Such a procedure helps to ensure that the selection process is more equitable and based on more than the intuitive feelings of one officer.

Types of Police Diversion

Diversion Without Referral The most basic form of juvenile diversion by the police is *diversion without referral.* Typically, this involves an "informal adjustment" (for example, warn, counsel, and release), whereby the offender is immediately diverted from the system without further significant action. This is the most common police diversion practice. This option, especially if it is exercised in the field, is the purest form of diversion because the youth's exposure to the juvenile justice system is kept to a bare minimum.

Internal Referral Programs A second type of diversion is to send or refer the youth to some program. This referral may be internal or external. An *internal referral* (in-house diversion) involves referral of a case from one branch of the police department to another branch that is better equipped to handle it. An *external referral* involves turning over the case to a community-service agency or, at times, an individual. Diversion with referral is generally dictated by departmental policy or by written agreement between police and community agencies. It involves filing reports and sometimes official transfer of jurisdiction from police to another agency.

Juvenile diversion programs that are operated totally within a police department are referred to as *in-house programs.* Such programs can take several different forms. Many departments use an officer to administer the program and supervise a team of full-time professional counselors (usually civilian personnel). A variation of this approach involves an officer who serves as an administrator and directs the efforts of a team of volunteer counselors. The degree to which specialized counseling skills are required depends on the assessed needs of the youths who are being targeted, as well as the overall program goals.

Community Volunteer Type: The goal of this program is to identify and recruit interested individuals from within the community to assist problem youth. Potential candidates contribute by serving as "big brothers/big sisters" or as educational tutors or by providing employment opportunities. The police officer is responsible for identifying and developing liaisons with the appropriate community members. One example of this volunteer approach is the firefighter-counselor program. Based on the premise that the firefighter often projects a positive, nonthreatening image to many youths, some police departments (including Dallas's and Los Angeles's) have organized interested volunteers from the local fire department to serve as "big brothers/big sisters" and part-time counselors to troubled youths. The volunteers are trained mainly in the objectives of the diversion program (for example, counseling about drugs, alcohol, and sex) with some additional training in adolescent development and crisis intervention techniques. The value of this type of program is that it increases the number of available resources at minimal cost and can provide long-range follow-up to initial counseling and work with a youth.

Recreation Type: Through the use of athletic activities, especially team sports, this program attempts to channel the energy of delinquent youths into socially constructive activities. It is based on the assumption that exposure to the benefits of good sportsmanship, playing by the rules, and healthy competition will inculcate these behaviors in a delinquent youth and enable him or her to apply them to other spheres of life. Also associated with this type of program is the belief that health and attitude, which can contribute to a modification in behavior, will improve as well. Since police personnel are directly involved with this program, it is further thought that there will be a resulting positive influence on attitudes toward police officers among individual youths and the community in general.

Probation Type: This type of program, which is based on informal police probation, makes it clear that the youth is to stay out of trouble and that the police officer is there to see that he or she does so. This approach is authoritarian and intentionally coercive in nature and intent. If the youth is involved in subsequent misconduct, he or she is threatened with removal from the diversion program and referral to the juvenile court. The program explicitly incorporates a negotiation process whereby the officer and youth work out a deal that "gives the kid a break" this time, but not the next. Generally, police departments require youths to report to an officer at the police station or elsewhere on a regular basis. The juvenile reports on his or her activities since the last visit was made and receives encouragement, warning, or advice (as warranted) from the officer.

External Diversion Programs External referral involves the diversion of youths to available outside community resources for assistance. These resources can range from general family services to specific drug-treatment programs. External diversion programs focus on the organization and cultivation of local community agency resources to meet the needs of troubled youths in lieu of traditional processing through the juvenile justice system. In a more formalized type of external referral, a police department may contract with professional service agents (for example, a child psychologist or drug therapist) when a service is unavailable through public agencies or is deemed especially critical in addressing the needs of a particular youth.

Police departments face four problems when referring youths to community service agencies. They are acceptability, suitability, availability, and accountability (Klein, 1976).

Acceptability: Police officers have a tendency to stereotype certain service agencies as soft, lenient, coddling, and permissive. Free clinics, runaway shelters, and crisis centers are examples of such endeavors that are often successful in helping troubled youths but are viewed with suspicion by the police. The police tend to see these programs as catering to the vices of youths rather than controlling or preventing them.

Suitability: Many community service agencies are unsuitable for use by the police as potential referral sources; an agency may accept only certain cases, or its policies and practices may conflict in some way with the police's. Other practical considerations that affect suitability are restrictive fee schedules, long waiting lists, and insufficient personnel. Furthermore, many service agencies are open only between 9 A.M. and 5 P.M. and thus are not conducive to police referral needs. Police officials can adapt to this situation, or they can begin to work with the agencies in question to iron out whatever problems stand between their cooperation.

Police should be careful to select a referral agency whose resources will match the needs of the individual youth. Referral agencies sometimes tend to begin accepting a wide variety of clients based on past successes in one particular area. For example, an agency that has been effective in treating juveniles with drug or alcohol problems may expand its services to include counseling runaways and incorrigible youths. Such expansion may be inappropriate and detrimental to the youths and the agencies; the quality of services may decline and, if so, the credibility of the agency will probably follow.

Availability: Over the years, various recommendations have been made in an attempt to provide community resources where none now exist. But, there are two problems that may arise regarding such resources. First, mere availability of resources is no guarantee of quality. This problem must be dealt with on a community-by-community basis; where weaknesses are known and acknowledged, the police may have a responsibility to demand higher-quality services.

Second, there is a low level of awareness of resources among the police; this is a problem that both police and community agencies must address. Klein (1976) interviewed officers in six California cities concerning the availability of community resources; he found an almost total lack of knowledge on the subject. Reasons included the fact that juvenile officers are not required to seek out referral services as a normal part of their job, officers often do not live in the communities they serve, and private agencies often do not make their services available to the police. Police and resource people must actively and regularly meet to discuss youth needs in order to ensure that there are available resources.

Accountability: The appropriateness of a referral can never be known without some formal procedures for following up on it. By actively soliciting comments from referral agencies, police are better equipped to make future referrals and improve communication with service agencies. Better communication, in turn, serves to improve coordination and the ability of agencies to respond to police needs. MacIver (1966) suggests that the selection of an agency should be rigorous and systematic. There should always be a follow-up to find out what, if anything, has been done. He further suggests that the trained juvenile officer is best qualified to undertake this task.

Some Warnings

The main attraction of diversion is that it will minimize youths' experience with the juvenile justice system. But some people fear that as diversion becomes more routine, police may find that they get "credit" for diversions, much as they may for arrests. This whole concern is with "widening the net" and sweeping in more youths than otherwise would have been brought in.

Some police departments have attempted to minimize this possibility by restricting their diversion efforts to those offenders who have been formally arrested. But some observers are concerned that more youths will end up with arrest records. Another problem is that the police may use diversion as a dumping ground for weak cases. When a case against a youth has not been sufficiently established, the police can offer the child the "choice" between participation in a diversion program or referral to juvenile court (Maron, 1976; Bullington et al., 1978).

One of the key aspects of the diversion process is directing the youth to a referral program that actually corresponds to his or her needs; it is of little value to refer the youth to a program or activity simply because it is available. Such diversion may actually be counterproductive because of a lack of responsiveness to the problems of the youth on the part of the referral.

COURT DIVERSION ALTERNATIVES

Informal Adjustment

It is now quite common for juvenile code provisions to request that the formal juvenile court process be halted or suspended prior to filing a petition or adjudication to allow a juvenile to be handled informally by community agencies—a process called informal adjustment. Most states now have statutory provisions that allow diversion through informal adjustment. A typical example is the Iowa provision, which requires an admission by the child to a delinquent act; voluntary, intelligent consent by the child with advice of his or her attorney; terms of the adjustment clearly stated and signed to by all parties; a six-month limit on the duration of the adjustment; and the right of the child to terminate the agreement. Petitions can be filed only within the six-month period and are dismissed if the child has complied with the terms of the agreement; some of the "informal" adjustment provisions are actually very formal.

An increasing number of states have adopted provisions that allow for intake screening by community agencies. For example, in Pennsylvania, if the probation officer deems it in the best interest of the child and public, the officer refers the child and his or her parent to any willing public or private agency that reports to the officer. The child and parent must voluntarily consent to this referral, and a six-month limit is put on the screening process. The agency can send the case back to the juvenile court for further informal adjustment at any time, but no petition can be filed.

Mediation

Many cases that come before the juvenile court are not well suited for the more formal adversarial proceedings that have developed as a result of Supreme Court rulings in *Kent, Gault,* and *Winship,* requiring adherence to basic due-process requirements. Cases involving continuing personal conflicts between disputants, for example, may be inappropriate for a court whose primary concern is the specific complaint at hand. One emerging alternative for the resolution of such conflicts is mediation. Mediation programs schedule meetings among the complainant, the respondent (the accused juvenile), and a neutral hearing officer who facilitates communication between the disputants and helps them to reach a mutually acceptable resolution to their conflict. Mediation can involve varying degrees of intervention, ranging from merely providing the disputing parties with a place to meet and ground rules for discussion to actively recommending possible solutions.

The claimed advantages of mediation are that disputants have far more time in a mediation session than they would before a judge; they are more relaxed; and they are able to explore more thoroughly all the aspects of their dispute, not just the particular complaint at issue. Thus, the parties become actively engaged in resolving their dispute and are led by a skilled hearing officer to negotiate a mutually acceptable settlement. Advocates of these programs often suggest that mediation is most effective when disputants are involved in a valued, ongoing relationship (Fuller, 1971). In such cases, the parties are more likely to consider compromises and to uphold the terms of any settlement reached.

Cases may be referred to a mediation program at three different points in case processing: (1) noncourt referral (by police, social service agencies, and so on) prior to the filing of a petition; (2) court intake referral by an intake officer, either before or after filing a petition; and (3) court referral following a hearing by a judge. While mediation programs vary in their formats and procedures, the following description of a session is fairly typical of the basic operation.

Hearing officers begin a mediation session with a brief opening statement that describes the nature of the proceedings. Complainants speak first and present their evidence and witnesses; then respondents are given the same opportunity. After these initial presentations, the disputants may question each other and any witnesses who are present. The mediator helps to pinpoint relevant facts, tries to identify possible areas of agreement, and helps to compensate for unequal bargaining abilities that the parties may have. If the mediator discovers that the parties' disagreement goes beyond the specific complaint at hand, the discussion can be broadened into an attempt to resolve the full dispute. If a settlement is reached, the mediator writes out the specific terms of the agreement and asks both parties to sign it. If the parites cannot agree on the appropriate settlement, the mediator informs them of their remaining options for resolving the dispute (such as initiation of formal court proceedings). When a dispute has been referred to mediation following the filing of a petition, the settlement is typically reviewed by a judge before it is converted to an order of the court. Cases referred to mediation prior to formal court intake are not subject to judicial review or enforcement.

Two important and related issues surround the use of mediation in juvenile court: (1) the type of information given to parties about the referral to mediation; and (2) the degree of choice afforded parties in determining whether or not they will use it. Parties cannot make an informed choice unless they understand the differences between court adjudication and case resolution through mediation. At a minimum, disputants need the following questions answered:

1. How quickly can the hearing be scheduled?
2. Can the respondent be forced to attend, or is participation voluntary?
3. Do the parties waive any legal rights by accepting the alternative forum?
4. What is the format of the hearing?
5. What is the role of the hearing officer?
6. What options are available if the attempt at mediation fails?
7. Is the mediated settlement enforceable by the court?

To guarantee that disputants are properly informed about the mediation process, the program should prepare a written description that addresses these questions, either for the parties to read or to guide intake officers or judges in their representations of the program to potential clients. The disputants should then be allowed to decide for themselves whether a mediation session or a court hearing will best serve their interests (Vorenberg, 1982).

Youth-Service Bureaus

One of the more specific diversion recommendations of the President's Commission on Law Enforcement and Administration of Justice (1967) was the establishment of youth-service bureaus (YSBs) as community diversion agencies. These bureaus typically refer children to existing agencies and themselves provide individual counseling, family and group counseling, drug treatment, help with jobs, education, recreation, medical services, and legal services. Unfortunately, almost any type of youth program can call itself a youth-service bureau. In fact, many of these programs are clearly mere extensions of the juvenile justice system, adopting similar service patterns, relationships to other official agencies, and most important, coercive practices.

Another serious problem concerns the coordination of community services available to young people. In recent years, policymakers have recognized the vast number of existing organizations that have significant untapped service capacities. They could be much more effective if properly organized and coordinated. The youth-service bureau has been publicized as fulfilling this need for coordination.

In reality, little apparent coordination has been accomplished by youth-service bureaus. They have had to spend considerable energy and resources in attempting to establish themselves as legitimate and viable service organizations in their communities. Even though their announced goals may agree with those of other community agencies, they are often cast in a competitive position. Thus, few youth-service bureaus have even attempted to work with other organizations in setting overall policy, assigning priorities, or adopting uniform procedures for the referral of young people (Polk, 1971).

Community Youth Boards

An *involuntary* system of diversion from the traditional juvenile court process uses community youth boards. These agencies are informal hearing boards to determine what, if any, services should be provided to children referred by schools, the police, the juvenile court, parents, or the children themselves. Their ideals are the same as those of the first juvenile courts—to help children in trouble to become useful and healthy citizens, not to determine fault. While some boards only accept status-offender referrals, others allow referral of all juvenile offenders. Children must obey the board's orders for receiving services unless they choose to ask for a juvenile court review, in which case the court has the power to revoke the board's orders.

ISSUES IN PROGRAM EVALUATION

Many questions about diversion remain unanswered. Few agree on who should be diverted (preoffenders, first-time offenders, repeat offenders); on what types of behavior diversion should apply to (delinquent tendencies, minor offenses, felonies); or on the point at which diversion should be made (prearrest, postarrest, prior to filing a petition, after filing a petition).

Diversion programs seem to be serving several different goals; any comprehensive evaluation must determine whether each of these goals is attained. Among the many rationales underlying current interest in, and support for, diversion programs are six reported by Klein and his colleagues (1976:105–107):

1. Increasing diversion overrides system biases in releasing and detaining suspects, stressing more equitable and universal criteria.
2. Increased diversion will decrease the volume of cases inserted into the criminal justice system.
3. Diversion processing is less expensive than system processing.
4. Diversion avoids stigmatization.
5. Diversion effectively prevents youthful offenders from coming into contact with more hardened offenders.
6. Diversion provides better and more humane treatment.

Unfortunately, the assumptions underlying these rationales are still largely taken for granted. Systematic assessments of the validity of such program contentions are rare. It has taken scholars, program planners, and funding agencies an extremely long time to realize that answers to many of their questions about diversion require organized evaluative research.

Vorenberg and Vorenberg (1973) described police diversion programs in Boston and Brockton, Massachusetts, Sacramento, California, and New York City. They concluded that there was no way of knowing how many departments were engaged in diversion programs since many practices were unidentifiable and unacknowledged. The Vorenbergs note that police diversion programs have grown rapidly; yet there are few data analyzing their effects on crime or delinquency, justice system operations, or quality of treatment:

> What is far more disturbing is that so little groundwork is being laid that would permit judgments about the worth of various programs three, five, and ten years from now. The two principal reasons are (1) lack of research funds and (2) chronic reluctance of operating agencies to subject themselves to intensive and possibly critical evaluation . . . (1973:182).

Klein and Teilmann (1976) report that in most of the California police diversion programs they examined, evaluations were minimal, poorly formulated, and often conducted by in-house evaluators and thus not designed to reveal negative results. Nejelski (1976) also criticized the lack of evaluation by outside reviewers. He argued that motion should not be mistaken for progress, and that unless a diversion project is adequately tested and verified:

> . . . it may be merely a placebo that helps the system struggle through another decade. . . . If the project is coercive, it must show success; if it is voluntary, it can justify public expenditure merely by presenting itself as not a failure (Nejelski, 1976:406).

Cressey and McDermott (1973) advocate qualitative, longitudinal studies of diverted individuals, focusing on each individual's reactions to diversion. There are very few systematic evaluations of the consequences of police diversion for juveniles. Most evaluative research has compared recidivism rates and has paid scant attention to other potential effects. In fact, a major objective of diversion programs—increasing police effectiveness in dealing with juveniles' problems—is almost a nonexistent topic in the literature.

> The faddist nature of diversion has produced a proliferation of diversion units and programs without generating a close look at whether the individuals subject to all this attention are receiving a better deal (Cressey and McDermott, 1973:59).

In many programs, readily available statistics on diversion apply only to the number of juveniles processed. These figures may or may not be grouped by sex, age, race, seriousness of offense, or other factors. There is never an indication of the number of diversion opportunities ignored or of the number of informal diversions, especially those occurring in the field. Often a social history or "face sheet" is compiled only for cases in which petitions are filed. This means that for many diversions, information is likely to be nonexistent or incomplete. Given demands on officers' time, referrals are often handled without any paperwork. Recidivism statistics cited in program evaluations are suspect.

The first step in any program evaluation is to define the problem the program is supposed to solve. But many program administrators are often confused about exactly what their programs were designed to accomplish. Three types of program evaluation should be considered: *effectiveness evaluation,* concerned with whether the program was in fact directed at the target population for which it was intended; *efficiency evaluation,* which examines the frequency and quality of service and the extent to which referral strategies were actually implemented; and *impact,* or *outcome, evaluation,* which concentrates on the intended consequences of referral. Most referral program evaluations have not considered all of these evaluative criteria. Effectiveness, generally measured by recidivism rates, receives the most attention; efficiency, usually measured by estimates of cost savings, is typically discussed but not measured.

The California Youth Authority (CYA) tried a simultaneous evaluation of eight diversion projects. CYA reviewed program objectives and developed nine evaluative categories, three of which were selected: the extent that clients were diverted, program costs, and the extent that client delinquency was reduced. In other words, CYA looked at impact, efficiency, and effectiveness of the programs. More than one-half (55 percent) of all cases referred to the projects came from police agencies. Juveniles referred by police were termed "diversion clients" and would otherwise have been placed on probation after initial police screening. The percentage of diversion clients ranged from 11 percent to 55 percent across the eight projects. CYA then calculated a cost-per-client figure by dividing total project expenditures by number of diversion clients served. The average cost was $195 per client—no less than the estimated cost of processing a person through the justice system.

Finally, CYA examined the extent to which projects reduced subsequent client delinquency. CYA compared subsequent justice system contacts of diversion clients with those of matched cases not referred to a diversion project. In six projects, both clients and comparison cases had approximately the same rearrest rates; in the other two, clients had fewer subsequent arrests. Thus, diversion clients did no worse, and sometimes fared better, than individuals processed in the traditional manner (California Youth Authority, 1976).

As with other evaluations, the CYA study suffers from methodological problems. It could not conduct a true comparison of the eight projects since each was structured differently. Some were run by police departments; others were not. It occasionally reported summary measures whose interpretation is suspect because of variations in program operation, structure, and objectives. Second, the evaluation may have been conducted prematurely, before the effects of the project could be determined. Third, the evaluation did not attempt to determine what characteristics of each project were efficient or effective. Fourth, CYA had problems collecting necessary data; some projects refused to cooperate, while others did not keep track of particular statistics. Fifth, calculation of project costs was not wholly dependable. Had each project budget been itemized by function, then divided by number of clients of particular types, more accurate conclusions might have been drawn. Sixth, the evaluation claimed that two projects significantly reduced delinquency but failed to explain why, or why the other six did not. Nonetheless, the CYA evaluation is a promising model for future evaluations of police referral programs.

Until in-depth analysis of departmental diversion practices is conducted and conclusions are supported by sound empirical data, diversion will remain an overlooked and misunderstood method of on-scene police case disposition. As Vorenberg and Vorengerg (1973:182) suggest:

> the sad fact [is] that almost everything we do in the criminal justice field is on the basis of faith . . . There is generally no more empirical support for continuing what is being done than there is for changing.

THE IMPACT OF DIVERSION ON THE JUVENILE JUSTICE SYSTEM

Increased Efficiency

It has been suggested that police diversion increases overall efficiency of the juvenile justice system. Efficiency is usually thought of as the difference between costs and benefits, but it is rarely possible in the public sector to measure costs (or inputs) and benefits (or outputs) in the same units. Conclusions about efficiency often depend on the value assigned by the analyst. Partly because there is no consistent definition of efficiency, diversion's impact on efficiency is more often attributed than demonstrated empirically. Contentions about diversion's efficiency involve two claims: that it reduces court caseloads and police agency costs; and that it reduces the time officers spend in case processing. Literature presents both supporting and contradictory evidence.

Many argue that diversion lowers court caseloads by removing from the juvenile justice system individuals who would normally have been processed through it. Binder et al. (1973:255) assert that:

> caseload volume alone provides ample justification for experiments with the prejudicial disposition of juvenile offenders using practices such as police discretion, station adjustment, planned diversion, and informal handling by probation officers and court staffs.

Cole (1976) notes that diverting juveniles could take many forms, including in-house police treatment or treatment by public or private community agencies; any alternative method of disposition is appropriate, given the overwhelming need to reduce court crowding. Di Vito (1975:14) pleads for increased police disposition of juveniles:

> Visualize for a moment the added strain on the juvenile court if every juvenile who is apprehended by police is routinely sent through the courts much the same as an adult. Visualize also some of the typical very minor offenses of the young going into court while the more serious offenses must wait for the dockets to clear. With this vision of chaos in mind, you will better appreciate the policy of station adjustment utilized by police departments with the blessing of the juvenile court.

In one of the few empirical studies of the relationship between referral and court caseload, Schregardus (1974) described a federally funded drug-abuse counseling project in Yolo County, California. Police referred young offenders to the project and, although details of an individual's progress were not regularly reported, police were notified when the juvenile had completed the program. Not only were police and court caseloads reduced over time, but the program significantly lightened the work loads of other community agencies.

Thomson and Treger (1973) noticed a reduction in the number of cases sent to court after the introduction of the Social Service Project in the Wheaton, Illinois, Police Department in 1969. The Social Service Project offered a number of services including juvenile counseling, crisis intervention, and referral to community agencies. Statistics showed a sharp decrease in cases sent to juvenile court in Wheaton, while sixteen other communities in the same county that did not participate in the project showed increases. Controlling for juvenile population and number of police-juvenile contacts, the authors concluded that the Social Service Project accounted for at least 35 percent of the decline in Wheaton's juvenile court caseload. Cases were either adjusted by the project or referred to community agencies for handling.

While it may seem that, by definition, diversion will reduce court caseloads, this is not necessarily true. Some research indicates that because police diversion programs handle some individuals who would not otherwise come in contact with police, diversion may increase the number of cases sent to court. Klein (1976) and Gibbons and Blake (1976) have suggested that diverted youngsters are drawn from a group traditionally released without further police action. That is, officers may contact juveniles who would have been ignored if no diversion program existed. Some programs contain active delinquency prevention components whose efforts increase the contact population (California Youth Authority, 1976).

Lincoln (1976), in a study of two matched groups of juveniles, found that the diverted group committed more repeat offenses than the nondiverted group. Diverted youths committed offenses so minor that, without the project, they would have been counseled and released:

> One can infer that the referred [diverted] counterparts to these matched juveniles would have been released rather than inserted into the juvenile justice system if there had been no referral program. This is interesting in view of the fact that diversion has been advertised by its proponents as an alternative to insertion into the juvenile justice system, not as an alternative to release (Lincoln, 1976:327).

Morris and Hawkins (1970) and Pink and White (1976) agree that the presence of referral programs increases the number of police-juvenile contacts and the number of cases handled by official police action.

The second contention regarding diversion and efficiency—that diversion reduces the amount of time officers must spend counseling citizens, making arrests, or appearing in court, thereby freeing them for other duties and ultimately reducing agency costs—is neither supported nor refuted by empirical data. Nejelski (1976) and Klein et al. (1976) argue that diversion decreases the costs of processing individuals through the criminal justice system. Pitchess (1974) reports, without supporting data, that a diversion program operated by the Los Angeles County Sheriff's Department has reduced agency costs.

Stratton (1975) studied a diversion program operated by the San Fernando (California) Police Department. Status offenders and first-time misdemeanor offenders were randomly assigned to two groups: one diverted, the other admitted into the justice system. Stratton found some evidence that expenditures for the processed group were higher than those for the diverted group, although his sample size was very small. As discussed on page 322, the California Youth Authority (1976) found that project costs per client were no less than estimated costs of processing through the justice system.

Increased Effectiveness

Whether diversion is considered effective depends upon the goals of the juvenile justice system and community agencies. Effectiveness is a measure of what an agency achieves, but agency goals are rarely defined or are so general that they are difficult to measure. Juvenile justice experts and program planners usually list reduction in delinquency and improved treatment for juveniles as primary goals of police diversion. While recidivism rates are one measure of the former, the latter is determined by subjective evaluation.

Most literature on effectiveness of juvenile diversion is speculative. In his review and assessment of police diversion programs, Klein (1976) argued that diversion would reduce recidivism because community service agencies could establish better rapport with clients than police agencies could. Empey and Lubeck (1973) postulate that delinquency prevention and rehabilitation will be more attainable if diversion is clearly understood as an alternative to traditional means of case disposition. External referral can be effective if police are knowledgeable about community agencies and can explain to parents and juveniles the purposes and goals of the agency prior to diversion (Kobetz and Bosarge, 1973). Other authors indicate that effectiveness depends almost entirely upon the quality of the diversion agency and the extent of its interaction with police (MacIver, 1966; Kenney and Pursuit, 1975; Pink and White, 1976).

Some experts believe internal referral is crucial in ensuring effective reduction of juvenile delinquency. Cohen (1969) argued that juvenile cases should be referred first to specialized units within the police department for handling; these units contain more highly trained personnel with greater experience and better sources of information than regular patrol officers or community agencies. Binder et al. (1973) proposed a project that would allow officers to refer juvenile cases to civilian staff within the department. Under the supervision of these civilians, a juvenile would no longer be considered in police custody. These writers argued that internal referral would be more effective than conventional juvenile justice processing, but they offered no empirical support for their claims.

Studies of recidivism rates lend some support to the claim that diversion is effective. Several studies have speculated about reduced recidivism rates (*Yale Law Journal,* 1974; Pitchess, 1974); others have presented supporting data. A study of a Wayne County, Michigan, program for screening juvenile offenders examined two samples—one of youths handled through a decentralized referral system, the other of youths handled through the central juvenile court intake system. Findings indicated that admission into the juvenile court system was positively related to recidivism; the farther an individual was conventionally processed, the more likely he or she was to break the law in the future. Also, the more often the juvenile was contacted by a justice system agent, the more likely he or she was to recidivate (Kelley et al., 1976).

Baron and Feeney (1976) reported that the Sacramento County (California) Probation Department diversion program reduced recidivism for both status and minor criminal offenders. Since referrals were not made by police and involved only minor offenders, it was not clear that police diversion would also reduce recidivism in cases involving more serious crimes. Duxbury (1971) noted that frequency of police referral to youth-service bureaus decreased the probability that a case would subsequently be sent either to the probation department or to court. While recidivism rates were slightly lower for juveniles referred by police than for nonreferred youths, Duxbury asserted that YSBs were not used often enough by police to produce the substantial reduction originally expected (Duxbury, 1973).

Klein (1974) reported diversion rates for thirteen police agencies in California. He found that departments that relied on diversion more often than traditional processing showed lower recidivism rates for first offenders. In contrast, departments with high diversion rates had higher recidivism rates for repeat offenders than did departments with lower diversion rates. Klein's conclusions about first offenders are consistent across a number of studies. Kobetz and Bosarge (1973), in their review of juvenile diversion programs, concluded that diversion is effective in reducing recidivism for first offenders, minor violators, and drug abusers. Stratton's (1975) study of status and first offenders referred by the San Fernando, California, Police Department showed that juveniles who received crisis counseling and follow-up assistance were less likely to be arrested again than were youths admitted normally into the justice system.

Empirical evidence about diversion's effect on recidivism rates is not unanimous. In a study of a large West Coast police department, Lincoln (1976) compared a group of 30 youths referred by police to community agencies with a control group of 250 youths apprehended, but not referred, during the same period. She found that the diverted group committed *more* repeat offenses than the nonreferred group. Referral "widened the nets." Apparently, referred youths committed offenses so minor that without diversion projects, they would have been counseled and released.

Sorensen (1974) agreed with Lincoln; his study of referrals to a youth-services system indicated that diversion was positively related to recidivism among first offenders but was unrelated to repeat arrest among multiple offenders. Sorensen argued that informal case handling by police, not diversion, reduced recidivism.

SUMMARY

Like many other technical terms, the word *diversion* has been applied very loosely and sometimes indiscriminately to so many procedures and programs that it may be futile to try to define it in any useful way. Nevertheless, the increasingly eager support for the *principle* of diverting youths from the juvenile justice system results from several widely held notions: (1) traditional strategies for dealing with juvenile offenders have not worked; (2) informal diversion is used both widely and effectively now; and (3) the most humane treatment of troubled youths is based on the *parens patriae* philosophy of justice.

The most conspicuous fact about the diversion movement in juvenile justice has been the magnitude of its growth in the face of relatively little objective data that it will remedy deficiencies of the juvenile court. Moreover, diversion may be seen as potentially dangerous and harmful. Three major criticisms of diversion programs are: (1) the concept's ambiguity allows many people to promote expansion of the juvenile justice system in the form of diversion *to* other programs, while true diversion *from* the system is nonexistent; (2) the goals of diversion programs—such as the elimination of stigmatizing labels and formal duplication of existing informal processes—are unattainable; and (3) formal diversion is incompatible with due-process ideals.

Although the principle of diversion indicates that it should be used to redirect cases that otherwise would be processed through the juvenile justice system, it often has worked otherwise. Cases selected for diversion have included many that formerly would have been screened out or dismissed after brief contact with police. Also an important, unintended consequence of the diversion movement has been its substantial adoption by police and probation departments. In many areas, they have set up in-house programs, hired their own personnel, and programmed cases in terms of their agencies' special goals and circumstances. This development is diametrically opposed to the main idea of diversion--that is, to shift cases away from the juvenile justice system. These procedures are not new, but their increased use may be.

Diversion from juvenile justice processing also raises fundamental issues of fairness. Selection for diversion may be arbitrary or biased; procedural rights may be overlooked or ignored; eligibility requirements may violate due process; long-term effects may hinder the juvenile's return to society. It is important for those lawmakers, policymakers, and citizens who are involved in the field of juvenile justice to be aware of both the protections that are needed in diversion and how these can be made available.

The impression is widely fostered that diversion should be evaluated according to its success in reducing recidivism or in terms of balancing costs and benefits. But it is more plausible that its future will hinge on sociopolitical developments in various branches of the juvenile justice system. The co-opting of the diversion movement by juvenile justice officials may lead one to conclude that the purposes of diversion have been perverted. What began as an effort to establish alternative methods for handling problem youths became a warrant to increase discretion and extend control where there was none before. To many, diversion represents yet another coercive social control system with low visibility and accountability. If we learn nothing else from the current state of diversion, at least we know something of the extent of the de facto power of police and court officials in the scheme of the American juvenile justice system.

DISCUSSION QUESTIONS

1. What various views of diversion have been advanced in recent years?
2. How may the use of diversion result in "widening the net" of juvenile justice processing?
3. What are the conditions Polk and Kobrin argue diversion programs must meet?
4. What are the rationales on which police diversion of juveniles is based?
5. What are the major types of police diversion programs?
6. What are the problems police face when referring youths to community service agencies?
7. What are two important and related issues surrounding the use of mediation in juvenile court?
8. What are some of the key problems involved in evaluations of diversion programs?
9. What impact has diversion had on the efficiency of case processing in the juvenile justice system? Explain your answer.
10. What evidence exists to suggest that diversion programs are effective in reducing juvenile recidivism? What findings contradict this evidence?

REFERENCES

BARON, ROGER, AND FLOYD FEENEY
1976 *Juvenile Diversion Through Family Counseling.* Washington, D.C.: U.S. Government Printing Office.

BINDER, ARNOLD, ET AL.
1973 University-police cooperative approach to juvenile diversion: Evaluating its applicability and effectiveness. *Journal of Criminal Justice* 1:255–264.

BULLINGTON, BRUCE, ET AL.
1978 A critique of diversionary juvenile justice. *Crime and Delinquency* 24:59–71.

CALIFORNIA YOUTH AUTHORITY
1976 *The Evaluation of Juvenile Diversion Programs: Second Annual Report.* Sacramento, Calif.: Health and Welfare Agency, Department of Youth Authority.

COHEN, BERNARD
1969 The delinquency of gangs and spontaneous groups. Pp. 61–111 in Thorsten Sellin and Marvin E. Wolfgang (eds.), *Delinquency: Selected Studies.* New York: Wiley.

COLE, PHILLIP Z.
1976 Diversion and the juvenile court: Competition or cooperation? *Juvenile Justice* 27:33–37.

CRESSEY, DONALD R., AND ROBERT A. McDERMOTT
1973 *Diversion from the Juvenile Justice System.* Ann Arbor, Mich.: University of Michigan, National Assessment of Juvenile Corrections.

Di VITO, ETTORE R.
1975 Station house adjustments in juvenile cases. *Police Law Quarterly* 4:13–20.

DUXBURY, ELAINE
1973 *Evaluation of Youth Service Bureaus.* Sacramento, Calif.: Health and Welfare Agency, Department of Youth Authority.
1971 *Youth Service Bureau in California: A Progress Report.* Sacramento Calif.: Health and Welfare Agency, Department of Youth Authority.

ELLIOTT, DELBERT S.
1974 *Diversion: A Study of Alternative Processing Practices.* Washington, D.C.: U.S. Government Printing Office.

EMPEY, LAMAR T., AND STEVEN G. LUBECK
1973 Delinquency prevention strategies. Pp. 274–295 in Gary B. Adams et al. (eds.), *Juvenile Justice Management.* Springfield, Ill.: Charles C Thomas.

FULLER, LON L.
1971 Mediation: Its form and functions. *Southern California Law Review* 44:305–314.

GIBBONS, DON C., AND GERALD F. BLAKE
1976 Evaluating the impact of juvenile diversion programs. *Crime and Delinquency* 22:411–420.

HAGGARD, LENORE
1976 Effect of the Myers Act on the criminal justice system in Alachua County. Unpublished manuscript, Department of Political Science, University of Florida.

KELLEY, THOMAS M., ET AL.
1976 Decentralized intake and diversion: The juvenile court's link to the youth service bureau. *Juvenile Justice* 27:3–11.

KENNEY, JOHN P., AND DAN G. PURSUIT
1975 *Police Work with Juveniles and the Administration of Juvenile Justice,* 5th ed. Springfield, Ill.: Charles C Thomas.

KLEIN, MALCOLM W.
1976 Issues and realities in police diversion programs. *Crime and Delinquency* 22:421–427.
1974 Labeling, deterrence, and recidivism: A study of police dispositions of juvenile offenders. *Social Problems* 22:292–303.

KLEIN, MALCOLM W., AND KATHIE S. TEILMANN
1976 *Pivotal Ingredients of Police Juvenile Diversion Programs.* Washington, D.C.: U.S. Government Printing Office.

KLEIN, MALCOLM W., ET AL.
1976 The explosion in police diversion programs: Evaluating the structural dimensions of a social fad. Pp. 101–119 in Malcolm W. Klein (ed.), *The Juvenile Justice System.* Beverly Hills, Calif.: Sage.

KOBETZ, RICHARD W., AND BETTY B. BOSARGE
1973 *Juvenile Justice Administration.* Gaithersburg, Md.: International Association of Chiefs of Police.

LEMERT, EDWIN M.
1971 *Instead of Court: Diversion in Juvenile Justice.* Chevy Chase, Md.: National Institute of Mental Health, Center for Studies of Crime and Delinquency.

LERMAN, PAUL
1975 *Community Treatment and Social Control: A Critical Analysis of Juvenile Correctional Policy.* Chicago: University of Chicago Press.

LINCOLN, SUZANNE B.
1976 Juvenile referral and recidivism. Pp. 321–328 in Robert M. Carter and Malcolm W. Klein (eds.), *Back on the Street: The Diversion of Juvenile Offenders.* Englewood Cliffs, N.J.: Prentice-Hall.

MacIVER, ROBERT M.
1966 *The Prevention and Control of Delinquency.* New York: Atherton.

MARON, ANDREW W.
1976 The juvenile diversion system in action: Some recommendations for change. *Crime and Delinquency* 22:461–469.

MORRIS, NORVAL, AND GORDON HAWKINS
1970 *The Honest Politician's Guide to Crime Control.* Chicago: University of Chicago Press.

NATIONAL ADVISORY COMMISSION ON CRIMINAL JUSTICE STANDARDS AND GOALS
1973 *Courts.* Washington, D.C.: U.S. Government Printing Office.

NEJELSKI, PAUL
1976 Diversion: The promise and the danger. *Crime and Delinquency* 22:393–410.

OFFICE OF JUVENILE JUSTICE AND DELINQUENCY PREVENTION
1977 *Federal Juvenile Delinquency Programs: Second Analysis and Evaluation.* Washington, D.C.: U.S. Government Printing Office.

PINK, WILLIAM T., AND MERVIN F. WHITE
1976 Delinquency prevention: The state of the art. Pp. 5–26 in Malcolm W. Klein (ed.), *The Juvenile Justice System.* Beverly Hills, Calif.: Sage.

PITCHESS, PETER J.
1974 Law enforcement screening for diversion. *California Youth Authority Quarterly* 27:49–64.

POLK, KENNETH
1971 Delinquency prevention and the youth services bureau. *Criminal Law Bulletin* 7:490–511.

POLK, KENNETH, AND SOLOMON KOBRIN
1972 *Delinquency Prevention Through Youth Development.* Washington, D.C.: U.S. Government Printing Office.

PRESIDENT'S COMMISSION ON LAW ENFORCEMENT AND ADMINISTRATION OF JUSTICE
1967 *Task Force Report: Juvenile Delinquency and Youth Crime.* Washington, D.C.: U.S. Government Printing Office.

SARRI, ROSEMARY C.
1975 Diversion: Within or without the juvenile justice system. Pp. 11–12 in *Sounding on Youth.* Tucson, Ariz.: National Council on Crime and Delinquency.

SCHREGARDUS, D. J.
1974 Youth diversion and the myth of parental influence. *Police Chief* 41:48–51.

SCHUR, EDWIN M.
1973 *Radical Nonintervention: Rethinking the Delinquency Problem.* Englewood Cliffs, N.J.: Prentice-Hall.

SORENSEN, JAMES L.
1974 The Effect of a Juvenile Referral System on Prevention of Recidivism with Early Offenders. Doctoral dissertation, University of Rochester.

STRATTON, JOHN G.
1975 Effects of crisis intervention counseling on predelinquent and misdemeanor juvenile offenders. *Juvenile Justice* 26:7–18.

SUNDEEN, RICHARD A., JR.
1974 A four-dimensional perspective on police typologies. *Criminology* 12:328–337.

THOMSON, DOUG, AND HARVEY TREGER
1973 Police–social work cooperation and the overburden of the juvenile court. *Police Law Quarterly* 3:28–39.

VORENBERG, ELIZABETH
1982 *A State of the Art Survey of Dispute Resolution Programs Involving Juveniles.* Washington, D.C.: American Bar Association.

VORENBERG, ELIZABETH, AND JAMES VORENBERG
1973 Early diversion from the criminal justice system: Practice in search of a theory. Pp. 151–183 in Lloyd E. Ohlin (ed.), *Prisoners in America.* Englewood Cliffs, N.J.: Prentice-Hall.

YALE LAW JOURNAL
1974 Pretrial diversion from the criminal process. 83:827–860.

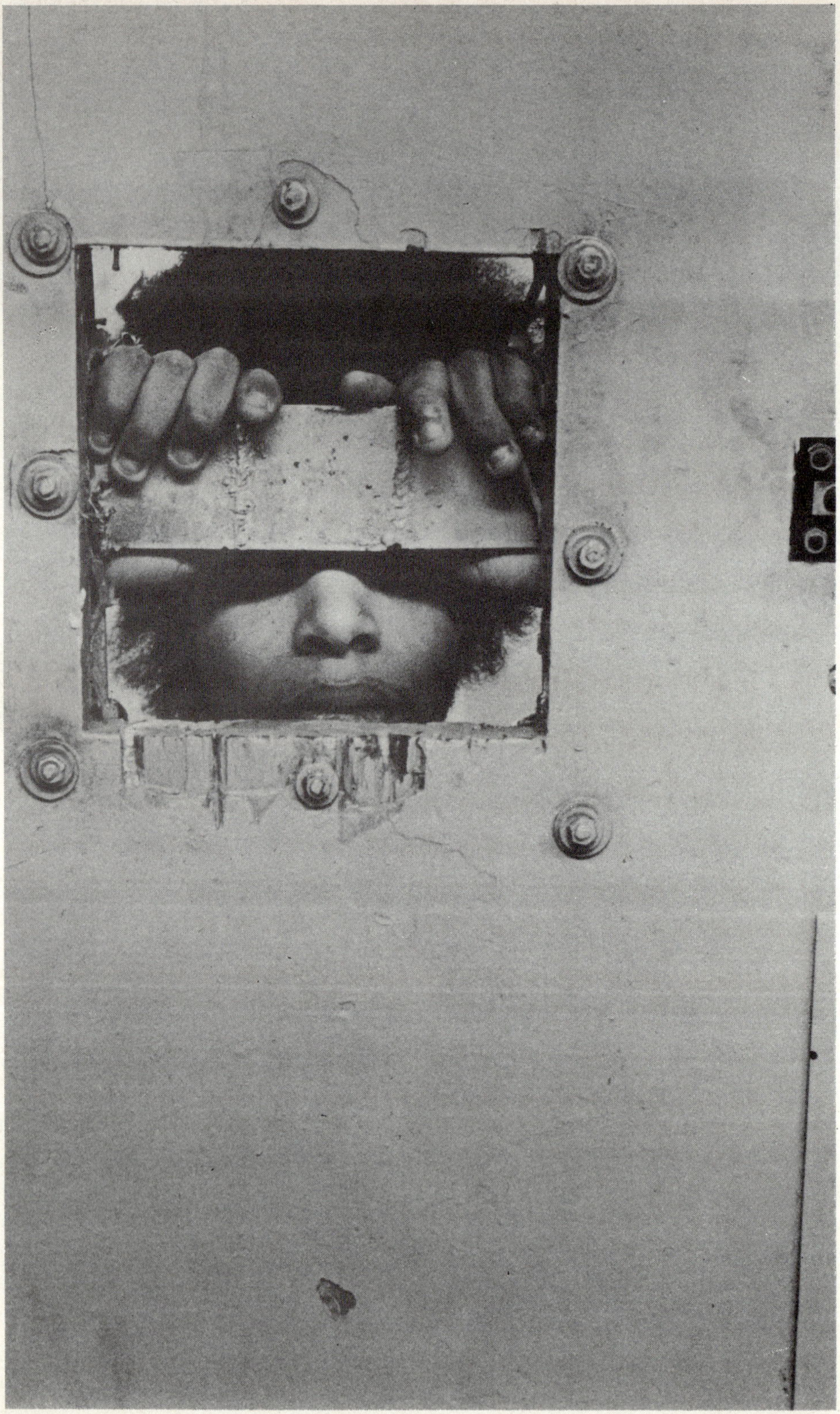

Juvenile Corrections 12

INTRODUCTION

Imprisonment is one of the most frequently criticized mechanisms for dealing with our social problems. The range of complaints reflects inconsistent public expectations concerning correctional institutions: they should reform offenders but fail to do so; they should punish lawbreakers but coddle them; they should be secure and orderly but there are many escapes and disturbances; they should operate with minimal cost to the taxpayer but are expensive. A review of the corrections system reveals a fundamental flaw in it: it was developed under certain sociocultural circumstances that made it germane to the goals sought at the time. But, although the circumstances and goals have changed drastically, the system has not and is now an obstacle to significant correctional reform.

The development of correctional facilities for juveniles was grounded in the historical connection between poverty and social control. Starting in the 1820s, several independent institutions for the care of juveniles were constructed, most under private charitable auspices. Among the first and the most notable of these institutions was the New York House of Refuge, opened in 1825 for vagrant, dependent, and delinquent children. It was sponsored by a philanthropic association of merchants calling itself the Society for the

Prevention of Pauperism. In principle and program, Houses of Refuge anticipated the juvenile court movement that emerged at the end of the nineteenth century. They were subsequently placed under state jurisdiction.

When juvenile institutions first began to appear on the American scene in the early nineteenth century, it was commonly supposed that youngsters who became delinquent had no proper respect for such societal values as hard work, obedience, honesty, thrift, self-sufficiency, and cleanliness. It was the purpose of the juvenile institution, therefore, to instill these values, and it took the approach of "learning by doing," with harsh penalties for failure to comply. Total conformity with institutional rules and regulations was demanded, and youngsters were expected to contribute to their reformation through physical labor. Common in this era was the practice of *indenture*, the assignment of youngsters to employers in the community for work training, which was a forerunner of both parole and foster-home care. By the late nineteenth century, training delinquents for work came to be closely associated with the emerging concept of vocational training, which in turn led to the rise of the boys' industrial school.

At the turn of the century, fundamental changes in society were profoundly affecting the status of children. Compulsory school attendance and child-labor laws gave societal sanction to the belief that the proper place for the child was the classroom, not the factory or the shop. Moreover, bolstered by fresh theories and ideologies regarding human nature, popular thinking came to regard childhood as an extended period during which the child's growth was to be zealously nurtured. Juvenile institutions were affected by these changes and soon adopted new goals and methods. Academic education gained prominence, and organized programs of recreation appeared. Furthermore, juvenile-institution authorities, in the wake of the Progressive movement, came to repudiate the goal of conformity and began instead to speak about individual differences among juveniles and their need for self-realization. The emerging fields of psychology, psychiatry, and social work also altered juvenile-institution planning and practices, fostering efforts to handle youngsters through means other than regimentation and punishment.

One notable innovation at this time was the *cottage system*, which helped to break down the impersonal bureaucratic nature of the institution. Under this arrangement, small groups of youngsters are assigned to cottage living units where, under the protective eye of "cottage parents," a family identification can be fostered. Needless to say, the intended objective often is not realized, but the introduction of the cottage system signified a major departure from adult prison design.

In the face of the many pressures toward change, reform has been easier to achieve in juvenile than in adult institutions because their smaller scale makes the introduction of new programs and approaches more feasible. Furthermore, since the public is generally more tolerant of juvenile than of adult offenders, these institutions have been able to worry less about preventing escapes and place more emphasis on new programs. Consequently, developments in juvenile institutions have generally been more striking and innovative than they have in adult facilities.

CONCEPTUAL MODELS

In recent years, a number of divergent conceptual models have influenced the development of juvenile institutions. Some are deeply rooted in the past, while others represent major directions for the future. All, however, have affected juvenile institutions today.

1. *The discipline-oriented model.* This model advocates a secure work-oriented institution with less emphasis on work than on conformity to institutional rules and regulations. The limited programs for offenders consist primarily of farm and institutional maintenance work and an often primitive academic school program. The overriding concern of staff is in maintaining the integrity of the institution through prevention of escapes, disorders, insubordination, and violation of rules. Order is maintained through regimentation of offenders and the use of a punishment-reward system, with particular emphasis on punishment.

   A great many training schools have gone through a discipline-oriented phase. While this orientation seems to describe the early nineteenth century facilities discussed above, a number of present-day training schools are also grounded in it; and even in those which have progressed beyond it, substantial vestiges of this model often remain.
2. *The public school model.* In this case, the focus is on simulating for the confined offender the formal educational experience of the free community. Much of the curriculum, philosophy, and technology of the public school is transposed to the institution, and educational purposes and concepts tend to predominate with many staff members. In some instances, there is even an emphasis on "varsity" athletics.

   Among institutions that subscribe to this model, the educational program frequently operates more or less separately from other aspects of a youth's experience: cottage life, contact with family and the outside world generally, and institutional work assignment, if any. Teachers operate the school, the child-care staff attends to cottage life, case workers focus on the community, and the maintenance staff has charge of youths while they are assigned to work duties. As a result, a youngster may be exposed to a series of poorly coordinated and at times contradictory influences.
3. *The individual treatment model.* The objective, in this case, is personality change or "personal growth," and the method is the relationship between

the offender as client and the therapist, who is preferably a highly trained professional such as a psychiatrist, clinical psychologist, psychiatric social worker, or clinically trained chaplain. Ideally, the therapist has frequent and probing interviews with the youth in order to help the delinquent gain greater objectivity about himself or herself and other people. Such insight is seen as essential to maturation and to the effective planning and restyling of the offender's life.

Advocates of this model have sought to extend its application through three devices: (1) substitution of group therapy for individual therapy or counseling; (2) use of various staff members such as cottage officers and teachers as individual or group counselors; and (3) consultation with other staff regarding the day-to-day decisions affecting youth.

The individual treatment model frequently generates resistance among nonclinical members of the staff. The cottage officers, teachers, and maintenance workers often have difficulty in understanding the methods and purposes of the clinicians, or they may find themselves in strong disagreement with what is taking place. Therefore, even though the clinicians usually have administrative support, many clinicians become disgruntled and leave for less hostile settings.

4. *The "homespun" model.* The ideal of this type is a small camp, staffed with mature, well-adjusted individuals who are firmly committed to working with youths and imbued with a good balance of personal concern, firmness, and patience. Educational qualifications are secondary, but staff are often expected to have a specialized work skill or general "handiness," since supervision of youths in various work projects may be involved. Staff may also be expected to lead youths in organized sports, handicraft projects, and other leisure activities.

An underlying assumption of this model is that delinquent youngsters are alienated from the adult world, or at least that part of the adult world that is law-abiding and self-maintaining. To some extent, this alienation is seen as attributable to a lack of a dependable parent figure at home and to a failure to develop a satisfactory substitute in a teacher or some other respectable citizen. It is reasoned, therefore, that if the youth can come to trust and respect his or her camp counselor, he or she might be able to develop into a law-abiding adult. This goal is thought to be enhanced by a "wholesome" rural or semirural environment in which barriers to communication and understanding are broken down by cooperative work and play.

A weakness of this approach, as with most of the models discussed, is that insufficient attention is given to the poor social environment from which confined delinquents tend to come. Camp staff often are rather unfamiliar with "street youths," and vice versa. Moreover, the positive effects of reorienting a child in an isolated forestry camp for a few months tend to be quickly undone when he or she is returned to his or her usual environment.

5. *The "therapeutic community" model.* This model stresses the primacy of full and candid communication between staff and confined offenders and has an objective approach to decision making in the institution. Both staff and youths are encouraged to act and to perceive each other "as people" rather than as performers of stereotyped roles. The assumption is that in an open, collaborative setting youths will gain in self-control and judgment and will be better able to behave in nondelinquent ways. A secondary gain is seen in the ability of youths to participate more fully as citizens.

   The "therapeutic community" model represents a comprehensive and sophisticated approach to the management of coercive institutions. It serves to reduce the social distance between the various factions of the institution and fosters a cooperative atmosphere. It has the added advantage of being almost equally applicable to large institutions and small facilities. Its relevance for individual rehabilitation, however, remains unproved.

6. *The community-oriented model.* The essence of this model is the recognition of the extent to which an individual is a product of the social environment of which he or she is a part. In view of the fact that almost three-fourths of the boys and girls committed to training schools return to delinquency after release, this model makes the assumption that taking a youngster from his or her community and treating him or her in a new environment has proved to be an almost total failure. If rehabilitation is to occur, not only must the offender be changed but so must various elements of his or her community situation—family, peer groups, neighbors, schools, places of employment, police, church, and other agencies and groups. When delinquents are confined, a continual effort is required to work with the communities and social institutions to remove or alleviate the forces that contributed to the delinquency.

These six models reflect ways of theoretically defining and organizing the central task of the juvenile institution. In reality, few institutions represent clear-cut applications of any one model. Programs in juvenile institutions tend to grow by bits and pieces, rather than being designed as a whole and faithfully implemented. As a result the total program at a given institution may reflect greater influence of one model over another, but most have been influenced by a variety of conceptual orientations as to organizational goals and means.

The above discussion represents a typical organizational perspective of juvenile institutions and correctional programs. But what about the juvenile who must live in these facilities? How do inmates adjust to being incarcerated? What determines the nature of their adaptations? To answer these questions, we now take a look at the correctional institution from the inmate's perspective.

INMATE ADAPTATIONS

Studies of correctional institutions have viewed inmate behavior either as a response to the conditions of imprisonment or merely as an extension of previously held values and motivations. These two alternative, though complementary, explanations are generally known as the *deprivation* and *importation* perspectives, respectively. The *deprivation perspective* views inmate behavior as a response to problems of adjustment posed by the deprivations, or pains and degradation of imprisonment. The institutional setting is seen as shaping the nature of inmate adaptations. On the other hand, the *importation perspective* attributes inmates' behavior to their preprison attitudes, values, and experiences. It is thus assumed that those "imported" characteristics of the inmate population determine their responses to incarceration. Since both perspectives emphasize the adaptive character of inmate behavior, we will briefly examine how each approach accounts for the nature and development of institutional adjustments.

The Deprivation Perspective

Incarcerated youths share at least two things in common. First, the juvenile court has decided that they must be confined for a period of time in a juvenile correctional facility. Second, they must all undergo processes that involve varying degrees of degradation and deprivation. Usually, admission includes a series of degrading ceremonies, during which personal property is removed, personal debasement is practiced, and self-effacement is promoted (Goffman, 1961). In addition, inmates are deprived of autonomy, physical comforts, and heterosexual contacts (Sykes, 1958; Sykes and Messinger, 1960). Although the degradation ceremonies are usually discontinued after the intake process, they, along with the ongoing deprivations, contribute to the "pains of imprisonment" (Sykes, 1958).

Advocates of the deprivation perspective have suggested that an inmate subculture emerges as a collective response to the pains and pressures of imprisonment (Sykes, 1958; Sykes and Messinger, 1960). In discussing the development of delinquent subcultures in free society, Cohen (1955) noted that culture is continually being created and modified wherever individuals sense similar needs in others. The group standards that result from mutual interchanges signal the advent of a new culture. The juvenile correctional community maintains a confined, limited environment in which inmates, faced with a sense of powerlessness to change their situation, are exposed to others with similar problems. Furthermore, the institution keeps them in a continuous state of interaction. According to the tenets of the deprivation approach, the inmate subculture is a collective attempt to reduce the effects of the institutional degradation and deprivation. Devoted in part to obtaining and distributing scarce licit and illicit goods, this subculture response provides a personal identity, independence from official sanctions, and legitimation of opposition to staff (Sykes, 1958; McCleery, 1961). In summary, the inmate subculture, especially in custody-oriented institutions, enables the inmate to reject his or her rejectors rather than himself or herself (McCorkle and Korn, 1954).

The deprivation approach initially appears to predict that group opposition will arise in response to the pains of imprisonment. Yet this approach actually does little to predict how individual inmates within the same institution will react to the same pressures. That is, why does the degree of assimilation vary within the institution? Do all inmates receive the same amount of deprivation? Would not conformity to the rules produce fewer "pains" than opposition does? While the deprivation approach fails to answer these questions, the organizational structure does appear to cause problems for the individual inmates, to different degrees. These problems, however, are even more tangible when the inmate is unfavorably predisposed toward aspects of his or her present situation.

The Importation Perspective

The proponents of the importation approach contend that there are similarities in the preinstitutional experiences of inmates that are brought into the prison or other facility (Thomas and Peterson, 1977). This claim is supported by studies that have investigated the discretionary decision making of police and juvenile court officials and by research examining similarities in the socioeconomic status, race, age, and previous correctional placements of inmates. In the final analysis, the incarcerated juvenile is not a social blank, and to conceptualize him or her in such a way is a great error. In fact, many inmates enter correctional facilities with a well-developed set of attitudes, values, and beliefs originating in their preprison experiences (Thomas, 1977).

In addition to a well-developed set of attitudes and values, many inmates also enter prison with a "deep reservoir of hostility to authority which may lead them to view staff attitudes and opinions as highly opposed to their own" (Wheeler, 1961:250). The conflict that often emerges from such hostility could conceivably endanger the ability of the institution to change the inmates. According to Wheeler (1961:250):

> The degree of conflict between inmates and staff found in most of our penal institutions could easily lead to a negative stereotyping process which may account for a greater perceived than actual conflict in attitudes and opinions between staff and inmates.

This is a crucial point since institutional programs, at the operational level, are largely a reflection of staff attitudes and opinions (Wheeler, 1961; Sarri and Vinter, 1965). In conclusion, it is doubtful that an inmate who perceives that the staff is in conflict with his or her basic attitudes and opinions will be a likely candidate for rehabilitation.

Reflecting on the strength and unity of the potential culture of a group, Becker and Geer (1960:305–308) have noted that:

> If recruitment is restricted to persons coming from similar backgrounds, latent culture will be strong and consistent.... [To] the degree that members have different latent identities, a latent culture will not be possible. Thus, one of the conditions for the existence of latent culture is some degree of exclusiveness of recruitment.

The selective recruitment of inmates for correctional institutions is therefore a potentially decisive factor in the quality of the inmate subculture and inmate identification with that subculture. The inmate who has had previous police and court contacts, engaged in gang activities on the outside, or lived in similar total institutions appears more inclined to associate with and be assimilated into the inmate subculture. And the norms of the inmate subculture seem to be extensions of the focal concerns of the lower class, who are disproportionately represented in prisons (Miller, 1958; Irwin, 1970). Therefore, the inmate subculture, which may stress negative norms and perspectives toward the law and society that some inmates may already hold, provides the inmates with a familiar value system in an otherwise strange and disruptive environment.

The Contextual Perspective

The final model of inmate adaptations closely parallels the institutional focus of the deprivation model. This *contextual* perspective differentiates institutions on the basis of their goals and orientations, and relates these differences to differences in inmate behavior. Illustrative of this emphasis is the classic study by Cressey (1960), in which he distinguishes treatment-oriented and custody-oriented institutions. The work of Zald (1962), Berk (1966), Sarri and Vinter (1965), and Street et al. (1966) has shown that many institutions mix treatment and custody orientations. Treatment, mixed, and custody orientations have been treated as points on a continuum. However, the picture is not really so simple. The treatment-oriented institution may officially promote the rehabilitation of its clients, but this goal can be complicated by control or security considerations. Similarly, custodial institutions generally offer some minimal training or rehabilitation programs, though their prime concern is custody. And since the mixed-goal institution is an attempt to combine elements of both polar types in more or less equal amounts, the result is, in terms of organizational effectiveness, often as mixed as the goals. However, using this simplified continuum of orientational types, comparative studies have demonstrated that the formal structure of the institution affects inmate responses to the institution as a whole, staff, and programs, as well as assimilation into an inmate subculture. And related research has generally shown that as the organizational orientation shifts from custody to treatment, the negative influences of confinement are either reduced or become positive ones.

In his study of a cross-section of organizational types, Berk (1966) examined both juvenile detention centers and minimum security prisons. He not only found that inmate attitudes toward the institution were more positive in treatment-oriented than in custody-oriented institutions, but he also discovered that inmate attitudes, regardless of institutional orientation, were shaped significantly by the prison experience. Specifically, inmates who had spent long periods of time in custody-oriented institutions were more likely to hold negative attitudes than those who had been in one only a few months, whereas the reverse was true at treatment-oriented prisons. Furthermore, Berk demonstrated that the difference in the informal social organization of the inmates in the two types of institutions was the result of the different functions performed by the subcultures in response to the organizational goals of each type. The informal inmate structure in treatment-oriented institutions was based less on coercive sanctions, and its power was less likely to be centralized than in custody-oriented institutions.

Street et al. (1966), dealing specifically with five juvenile institutions that differed in goal orientation, found support for the hypothesis that juveniles in treatment-oriented institutions are more cooperative and positive than those in custody-oriented facilities. Testing one of the basic assumptions of the deprivation model, Street and his colleagues investigated the claim that identification with the criminal subculture is a response to the deprivations of imprisonment. Regardless of institutional orientation, little support was found for the group-opposition model of the inmates. Rather, the type and severity of the inmate response reflected the institutional orientation.

Sarri and Vinter (1965) used the same sample of five juvenile institutions that Street and his colleagues did. They found that in the custody-oriented institutions, the inmates tended to view the institution negatively, remained socially distant from the staff, and did not believe that the staff were attempting to solve their problems. The opposite was found in the treatment-oriented juvenile institutions. Sarri and Vinter acknowledged the possibility that many juveniles enter the institution with attitudes and beliefs based on information obtained from peers, representatives of social agencies, or officials in the juvenile justice system (Sarri and Vinter, 1965). Since inmates are especially aware of the general tone set by the staff, experience with particular staff members, as well as predetermined attitudes, may lead not only to specific positive or negative attitudes toward the institution but also to generalizations about the entire staff. These studies suggest that different organizational structures and orientations affect inmates in different ways.

While many scholars have examined the problems of confinement in juvenile institutions, two studies stand out in terms of their extensive (Feld, 1977) and intensive (Bartollas et al., 1976) analyses of the nature of inmate adaptations. In a comparative study of ten facilities in Massachusetts, Feld (1977) identified four types of institutional treatment settings in terms of correctional goals, programs, and social control techniques. Differences in organizational structure had a major impact on the inmates' informal social systems. In the oppressive custody-oriented settings, staff roles were structured in an authoritarian, hierarchical fashion. Staff members were strictly custodial, minimizing their contacts with inmates and attempting to maintain a high level of surveillance and control. Such practices, coupled with a high degree of institutional deprivation, provided inmates with a variety of incentives to engage in covert deviance. In this setting, there emerged a group of tough inmates who exploited weaker inmates and used violence to reinforce their own status. The use of violence by inmates, paralleling staff practices of social control, resulted in a rigidly structured, authoritarian subculture in which the social distance between high- and low-status inmates was comparable to the gulf between inmates and staff. On the other hand, in the treatment-oriented facilities, which used a cottage system, substantially less hostility and aggression among inmates was observed. This greater harmony was largely due to the introduction of formal collaboration between staff and inmates, which increased the social solidarity of the entire institution and diminished the incentives for violent solutions.

Perhaps the most detailed account of the brutalizing conditions in the more custody-oriented institutions is provided by Bartollas et al. (1976) in their study of an Ohio facility for boys. Upon their arrival at the institution, boys are subjected to a testing process by the inmate leaders who want to know whether they will defend themselves when attacked and whether they have a history of sexual exploitation. The staff or other inmates offer no help to the new boys. The less able they are to defend themselves, the farther down the exploitation scale they are pushed. The exploitive acts on this scale, ordered in terms of increasing severity, are taking a victim's dessert and favorite foods at meals, his canteen pop and candy, pop and candy given to him by his parents, his institutional clothing, his toilet articles, his cigarettes, his personal clothing, his radio, and physically beating him, forcing him to masturbate others, to play the passive role in anal sodomy, and to be the receptor in fellatio. To inmates, being the "girl" in fellatio is the most degrading of all victimization experiences. His commission of this act is publicized via an informal grapevine throughout the institution, representing a status-degradation ceremony. He is then viewed a social outcast and is avoided by self-respecting inmates, except when they choose to victimize him. Some of these victims gradually accept their low social standing and internalize the negative perceptions attached to themselves. They come to display little outward emotion, keeping their guilt, shame, and indignation to themselves. Their personal habits begin to deteriorate, and they may no longer brush their teeth or take regular showers. Many of the boys in this situation end up mutilating themselves in their despair.

Unfortunately, such patterns of exploitation and victimization in juvenile institutions are scarcely unique to the facilities studied by Feld and Bartollas and his colleagues. Rather, they have been well documented in a variety of settings across the country over the past twenty-five years or so (Ward, 1958; Fisher, 1961; Polsky, 1962; Allen, 1969; Johnson, 1978; Poole and Regoli, 1983).

CORRECTIONAL EVALUATION

Perhaps many of the problems in juvenile corrections could be tolerated if the system as a whole produced positive results—that is, if it successfully reintegrated juvenile offenders into the mainstream of society. But does the system work? To answer this, the area of evaluative research has attracted increasing attention over the past twenty years.

In this section we review some of the issues in the evaluation of juvenile institutions, emphasizing how organizational goals affect the evaluation of processes and outcomes. As in other human service organizations today, evaluation is now a popular activity in corrections. Consequently, resources are now focused on thorough evaluation of correctional programs so that well-informed decisions can be made about the probability of achieving a given outcome from a specified program of intervention. Any review of the evaluation research literature in corrections, however, would draw essentially the same conclusions as those drawn by Rossi and Williams (1972) in their assessment of the evaluation of poverty, education, and other social action programs: there are few sufficiently powerful research designs among these studies to permit unequivocal statements that could be used to formulate policy.

The Focus of Evaluation Research

What should be evaluated when assessing juvenile corrections? At least three types of phenomena are important in any evaluation that has explanatory, as well as policy, implications:

1. The personal and social characteristics of the target population that the organization seeks to change.

2. The structures and practices within the organization that must be implemented if an offender is to be changed from one condition to another.
3. The exchange among units within or linked to the juvenile justice system that influences the careers of juvenile offenders.

Most evaluative research to date has addressed the personal and social characteristics of the individual offender—personality, behavior, values, attitudes, and capabilities. Insufficient attention has been directed toward overall organizational goal implementation, stability and adaptability, technological feasibility, referral rates, and organizational structures required for quality performance. Programs typically are judged as effective or ineffective with respect only to results at the individual level. Moreover, evaluation at even this level often fails to consider sufficiently the differential selection and assignment of offenders to particular types of treatment programs. When such differences in program assignment occur, as they do in most correctional classification, they must be somehow taken into consideration before there can be comparative evaluation across programs or organizations.

A related problem involving the differential selection of offenders for treatment is "tracking." This process is observed when individual characteristics are used as a basis for assignment to a given program that has a certain probability for successful outcome, independent of those individual characteristics. For example, a juvenile assigned to probation has greater opportunities for education and employment than do most youths assigned to institutions. Yet the criteria for assignment may be race, sex, family composition, and so forth—characteristics unrelated to ability to take advantage of education or employment. Such organizational processes need to be considered in evaluation; too often they are ignored or explained away as "random" effects.

Standards of performance at the organizational level have been almost nonexistent in corrections; those that have been found are based largely on the collective, subjective opinions of administrators. Objective criteria and ongoing program evaluation are only now being developed. At least five categories of criteria can be devised for organizational evaluation and then linked with outcome evaluation. These include: (1) effort (including cost, time, and types of personnel needed to achieve goals); (2) level of performance (for example, the number of individuals of those who enroll who complete Program X); (3) adequacy of performance (for example, value of the program to offenders); (4) efficiency (relative cost of Program X and similar factors); and (5) organizational processes (such as program attributes that relate to success or failure).

Mott (1972) and others have proposed that organizational evaluation be based simply on the extent to which program goals are attained. Difficulties arise because of the ambiguity of the goals of correctional agencies; some goals may be covert, and there may also be actual or potential contradictions among multiple goals. For example, rehabilitation of offenders is a typical goal of a correctional agency, but an agency is also concerned about releasing an offender who may pose a threat to society.

The researcher, in any effort to measure organizational goals, must distinguish between ultimate long-range goals and intermediate shorter-range goals. These objectives must then be linked to each other and measured in relation to the behavioral outcomes for juvenile offenders. Involved in any such effort is the definition of the problem that is or will be the target for change. The way in which a problem is defined influences the means of intervention for resolving it. Thus, if delinquency is defined primarily in terms of the individual person rather than in terms of the peer group, neighborhood, or other social situation, the goals, targets, and technologies should relate to individual-level phenomena. On the other hand, if the problem is viewed as situational, the physical, social, or economic environments would be the targets for change.

The use of goals in evaluation is complicated by unclear definitions and measurement techniques. Objective procedures for measurement of organizational goal attainment are presently not available in human service organizations. Research, therefore, must examine both official, executive-level mandates, objectives, and priorities and staff perceptions of what the desired goals of the organization should be. For example, the National Advisory Commission on Criminal Justice Standards and Goals (1973) proposed that the primary function of juvenile corrections should be the rapid reintegration of the offender into his or her usual social roles, with the least possible severing of ties with the external environment during the period of incarceration. While there is widespread consensus among the experts that the primary mandate of juvenile corrections is reintegration, correctional staff members typically assert that the goals of custody and security should not be compromised. Thus, evaluative procedures must include multiple measures and variable weighting of goal priorities if they are to be used appropriately.

Recidivism as an Evaluative Criterion

When one thinks of effectiveness and outcomes in corrections, the concept of *recidivism* is inevitably considered. Most often the term is used to refer to some absolute measurement of postprogram illegal or morally disapproved activity or behavior. In the case of juvenile offenders, data about recidivism reinforce the "criminal" label. However, a large proportion of juvenile offenders in many programs are guilty of only status offenses—truancy, running away, promiscuity, incorrigibility, and so on. None of these behaviors are crimes for adults, but juvenile "recidivists" are labeled as lawbreakers along with adults who commit felonies.

Another problem associated with the use of recidivism in absolute rather than in relative terms is that positive results may be obscured. Thus, using abolute measures, a single arrest or violation is enough to classify the person as a "recidivist" and an outcome failure. If recidivism is conceived in relative terms, though, one merely expects that the program will result in fewer and less serious offenses by participants. The addition of other outcome measures reduces reliance on recidivism as an absolute criterion. Thus, positive changes in education, employment, family life, and so forth may be linked to program experiences.

The results of the Provo and Silverlake experiments (Empey and Erickson, 1972; Empey and Lubeck, 1971) indicate very clearly a relative reduction in the seriousness and frequency of law-violative behavior. Their findings are similar to those obtained by Miller (1962) in a study of a community delinquency-prevention program. Both investigations observed that program results varied according to the age of the youth at the time of entrance and exit from the program. These patterns could be linked to general patterns of criminal behavior for all youths at different ages. Thus, youths who entered the program at younger ages would be expected to demonstrate a slower reduction of criminal behavior than those who entered and left at older ages, because criminal behavior peaks in the late teens and then tapers off sharply. It is also possible that other general developmental patterns of youth may affect outcomes in similar program experiences. When known, these patterns can be considered in the program design and in the development of basic criteria for classifying populations according to the probability of success or failure in the community. Moberg and Ericson (1972) argue that if recidivism is to be used meaningfully as an outcome criterion, it must be envisioned as a continuum, with variable probabilities of occurrence for different programs and individuals. These writers also assert that it is wholly unrealistic to expect "total conversion," as we apparently now do when measuring change from criminal to noncriminal behavior. For purposes of program planning, knowledge about the length of time and phases of change are as important as ultimate outcomes.

Recidivism is also a problematic evaluative criterion because it obscures differentiation between short- and long-run consequences for the society. An intervention that may protect society from a youth in the short run (say, incarceration in a closed institution) may have long-run negative consequences, and vice versa. The effectiveness of any intervention should be assessed on the basis of its ability to reintegrate juveniles into meaningful social roles, not merely to reduce immediate illegal behavior. Furthermore, far too few studies ever measure negative impacts of correctional experiences other than recidivism, despite general awareness of the inevitability of this outcome in many programs. Were such data to be made routinely available as recidivist data are, opportunities for change in custodial programs might be vastly increased. Only recently, in the wave of legal actions against correctional agencies, has there been any substantial effort to measure negative impact.

Ward and Kassebaum (1972) contend that the lack of concern about the overwhelming evidence of the negative results of correctional intervention occurs because departments of corrections are concerned more with surveillance and control than with rehabilitation; it makes little sense to measure present outcomes in terms of rehabilitated individuals, because rehabilitation is not the primary goal. Much evaluation has failed to address this phenomenon.

The unreliability of crime statistics and the manipulation of data by administrative boards, police, and other agencies is another reason for caution in the use of recidivism data to evaluate correctional programs. Police, courts, parole boards, and other agencies may seek to improve or lessen the public status of a particular program, and in order to do so, data may be covertly manipulated. One aspect of the unreliability of crime statistics was revealed in an analysis by Seidman and Couzens (1972), who analyzed police reports in several metropolitan communities. They observed that reports of selected types of crime decreased, corresponding to political pressures to reduce such crime. Thus, they conclude, "crime statistics . . . are highly misleading indicators of what they are used to measure, at least in part, simply because they are 'used as measures'" (Seidman and Couzens, 1972:29).

A View from the Inside

Our discussion of issues in evaluating juvenile corrections would be incomplete if we did not refer to direct involvement of the offender population in the assessment of the program. Much corrections evaluation is completed without any direct participation from the offenders; when they do participate, they are asked only to comment positively or negatively about the program as it is presented to them. They are not asked to formulate goals or suggest means for achieving them, despite research findings that suggest that one's expectations and assessments are critically linked to one's behavior. Certainly, the youth who views his experience negatively and is pessimistic about the future is not likely to succeed in postprogram situations (Thomas and Zingraff, 1976). Youths are committed to correctional programs for vastly different behaviors and attitudes—yet much evaluation rests on the assumption that all offenders will respond similarly to a standardized program experience.

Reviews of Evaluation Research

Where does correctional evaluation stand at present? In particular, what are the results of evaluation? For twenty years, evaluative research has been carried on steadily in corrections facilities. Numerous reports and papers have been produced, detailing methods and findings in many varied aspects of corrections. At times, the volume of material has grown so large that special efforts have been made to assemble, organize, and distribute it. Although a comprehensive review of all the literature has not yet been attempted, several efforts to pull together and assess portions of it have been made. These "evaluations of evaluations" contain some important lessons, and the best known will be summarized below.

Robison and Smith (1971) examined ten quasi-experimental studies that related to five major choices in offender processing in California corrections: (1) imprisonment versus probation, (2) length of imprisonment, (3) kind of treatment program in prison, (4) intensity of supervision on probation or parole, and (5) direct discharge from prison versus release on parole. The authors reported that differences in recidivism rates between experimentals and controls were often difficult to interpret because measurement procedures were confounded by the reporting methods of the correctional systems. Those variations in rates that could be satisfactorily determined apparently resulted from initial differences among the types of offenders that were processed. The remaining variation was judged to be the result of differences in the way agency staff interpreted or defined behavior of offenders. The authors concluded that there was no evidence to support any program's claim to superior rehabilitative efficacy.

Shireman et al. (1972) reported on twelve experimental studies of treatment of juvenile and adult offenders in state and local institutions in the 1960s. The treatments included milieu therapy, group counseling, and plastic surgery. Follow-ups into the community twelve months later showed that in five of the twelve studies, the experimental subjects performed better than the controls. In the remaining seven studies, there was no difference in performance between the two groups. And subsequent follow-up data, at twenty-four and thirty-six months, revealed that recidivism rates of experimentals and controls were about the same; and in one case (plastic surgery) the experimental rate was even higher.

Perhaps the best and most comprehensive review of rehabilitation efforts in corrections was assembled by Martinson (1974). His study provided a critical summary of all studies published since 1945 that *rigorously* assessed the effects of any kind of treatment applied to convicted juvenile and adult offenders, including educational and vocational training, individual and group counseling, milieu therapy, medical treatment, sentencing, community treatment, and probation and parole. The survey found 231 studies that met the methodological and empirical criteria for inclusion in the analysis. The author's main conclusion was that pitifully little evidence existed that any prevailing mode of correctional treatment had an appreciable effect on recidivism.

Most recently, Romig (1978) reviewed more than 825 books and articles on the effectiveness of various types of treatment applied to juvenile offenders. He restricted his assessment to 170 programs that had both measurable outcomes and matched or randomly assigned control groups. Projects ranged from rehabilitation approaches based on individual psychotherapy, behavior modification, and group counseling to system-wide intervention strategies based on diversion, probation, and parole. Romig characterized the programs as overwhelming failures. Typically, doing nothing to an offender produced about the same results as "treatment," regardless of the treatment approach.

AN ALTERNATIVE CORRECTIONS STRATEGY

Based on these reviews of evaluation research, it would appear that to try to reduce the problem of delinquency by expanding conventional correctional programs is absurd. The inability of agencies to handle the problem is reflected in (1) the generally high levels of recidivism and (2) the maintenance of high levels of recidivism even among those who have been exposed to apparently competent, well-operated correctional programs.

Some tentative leads can be suggested from these experiences. First, we must remember that since all juvenile offenders return to society, correction or rehabilitation ultimately must be determined in natural settings of the community and by community standards (Empey and Erickson, 1972). In the commonsense everyday terms, we expect correctional activity to treat the traditional type of offender so that he or she will be able to reenter the community and behave. Behaving, in this sense means, first, that the individual will not violate the law and, second and more positively, that the person will assume some of the attributes of a legitimate identity, choosing one of the many acceptable educational, occupational, family, political, and cultural roles that our society offers.

With these thoughts in mind, we begin to see some of the problems with correctional activities as they are presently constituted. First, most so-called correctional activities isolate and segregate the offender from the community. This is true not only of incarceration, but also of many community-based correctional efforts as well. In the case of a community-based program, resident offenders often encounter the resistance and hostile response of the public, such rejection possibly leading to the further locking of these juveniles into a troublesome role (McGee, 1981).

Second, the forces that generate and shape deviation careers often lie within community institutions, especially in the areas of education and work. When the reformative effort is segregated from community and its activities, the individual correctional worker will frequently have little systematic or meaningful access to educational, occupational, recreational, or other community agencies. While the individual worker may have individual contacts, his or her ability to influence the policy of other organizations to benefit his or her client-offenders is negligible.

But these organizations could well provide the most meaningful resource for reintegration, and the specific settings that give some constructive meaning to this term. Central to the identity of most people who function in legitimate roles are the character of their work (and their feelings of competence and self-worth that flow from work), how they stand in school, and the extent to which they feel some power to determine their own lives. The importance of work, education, recreation, and participation in politics or other community activities for persons in legitimate roles suggests that these experiences might play a critical role in reintegrative procedures.

If correction requires adjustment to community standards, if many of the factors that create the problem of youthful deviance lie inside various community institutions, and if potentially more effective corrective experiences lie in community settings, then the inescapable conclusion is that there must be more aggressive development of community-situated corrections efforts. These efforts will involve more than creating ways for offenders to remain in the community and work through their difficulties with counselors and probation or parole officers. Rather, alternative institutional arrangements will be required—structural changes, in other words—that offer new options for educational, work, recreational, and political involvement. The central task is to provide delinquents with meaningful opportunities to succeed in normal social and economic roles. Our next task, then, is to specify the location, rationale, and shape of such changes and to determine how to bolster community resources so that delinquents can truly be reintegrated.

Of course, it remains even more desirable to prevent delinquency than to cure it. But to combat the major forces that contribute to delinquency—such as unemployment, poverty, racism, and inadequate educational systems—we would have to undertake difficult and massive legislative programs that many voters would not accept—programs aimed to transform our society fundamentally. For example, the grim employment situation facing most delinquents can be altered significantly only if an equal-opportunity structure is established, accompanied by new patterns of occupational and educational training for the deprived. Such integrating mechanisms, linking the worlds of work and education, would be a basic component of any such employment strategy (Johnson et al., 1979). In addition to far-reaching programs aimed at the large-scale social forces that help to create delinquency, we can suggest a series of more specific, limited steps aimed at delinquency itself that can be undertaken in individual neighborhoods.

Community Involvement

There seems to be a clear need to encourage and facilitate the assumption of responsibility for correctional tasks at the local community level. The correctional process used in the United States suffers from its isolation and segregation from society at large and its institutions. Nelson (1961:1) has noted:

> There is general consensus in both professional and academic circles that American communities are relatively impotent in developing indigenous programs for the prevention of crime and delinquency. Community leadership appears all too willing to delegate (or default) its responsibility for dealing with antisocial behavior. Eventually that responsibility is assumed by large public agencies which take jurisdiction over the offender only after he has been defined as a lawbreaker by judicial action. Although extremely expensive, these services (probation, institutions, and parole) never seem to catch up with the need. They come too late to be "preventive" in the most desirable sense of the word. Moreover, the policies are controlled from political and administrative centers far removed from the "grassroots" of city and neighborhood where delinquency and crime originate through obscure and complex processes.

One problem identified by Nelson is the tendency for correctional programs to be withdrawn from the community. Kobrin (1959:28) observes that correctional programs:

> . . . whatever their initial intention or resolve, understandably tend to move away from direct contact with the delinquent and his milieu. Distance is achieved by interposing institutional forms between workers and delinquents, as in programs of formal and official treatment, or by dealing with the delinquent as a person arbitrarily abstracted from his social environment, as in programs based on individual therapy. This kind of evolution is comprehensible in the former type of retreat because the delinquent arouses anger and resentment in the law-abiding person, who consequently is hard put to form a sympathetic identification with him. Retreat from the milieu of the delinquent is even more understandable, for nothing would seem more unrewarding than to attempt to put aright the social disorder of the delinquency area.

In the past, then, it has proven expedient, for both the correctional system and the community, to isolate the offender from the community. In consequence, correctional agencies are not responsive to neighborhood and community social organizations and are unable to communicate effectively with such organizations. It is precisely these neighborhood organizations, however, that can play such a key role in reintegration and correction programs. Kobrin argues that effective correctional activities must somehow become the province of the residents who constitute the natural social world of the offender. He notes, further, that effective community action will require substantial involvement by local residents:

> Here another commonplace of sociological observation suggested that people support and participate only in those activities in which they have a meaningful role. The organized activity of people everywhere flows in the channels of institutions and organizations indigenous to their cultural traditions and to the system of social relationships which defines their social groups. Consequently, one could

> not expect people to devote their energies to enterprises which form part of the social systems in which they have no membership (Kobrin, 1959:23).

Kobrin observed that effective involvement of the community in the Chicago Area Project, a program aimed at preventing delinquency, was achieved through active participation of community residents. He felt that this program offered the following advantages:

> It became quickly evident . . . that, for cogent reasons, the employment of qualified local residents offered advantages in the establishment of such programs. In the first place the indigenous worker usually possessed a natural knowledge of the local society. Second, he was hampered by none of the barriers to communications with residents for whom the nonresidents, especially those identified with "welfare" enterprise, tended to be an object of suspicion and hostility. Third, his employment was a demonstration of sincere confidence in the capability of the area resident for work of this sort. Fourth, he was more likely than the nonresident to have access to the neighborhood's delinquent boys and therefore to be more effective in redirecting their conduct. Fifth, his employment represented a prime means of initiating the education of the local population in the mysteries of conducting the welfare enterprise (Kobrin, 1959:24).

To date, however, such programs have had only a minimal capacity to integrate delinquent youth into the larger society's institutions of education and work. As with official correctional agencies themselves, these programs lack sufficient "clout" to alter the broader institutional arrangements that continue to shut out vast numbers of deprived youths (McGee, 1981).

Yet the several advantages of this kind of program should not be ignored or interpreted narrowly as pertaining only to lower-class inner-city communities. Delinquency can be found in rich, poor, urban, suburban, and rural areas. Whatever the setting, individuals in the community are likely to have more "natural" access to offenders than workers attached to the correctional system. Moreover, the involvement of local residents in the corrections enterprise serves equally well to orient the community to the problems facing their youths and the juvenile justice system.

The Integration of Youth

A second goal of improved correctional strategies is to develop mechanisms within the community to integrate youth into the mainstream of activities and decision making affecting both their own lives and, ideally, the wider community as well. The need for such mechanisms arises from the changing role of young persons in modern society and how these changes have served to isolate the young.

America has gone through a rapid transition from a relatively underdeveloped country to a highly urbanized and technologically advanced one.

One important result of this development is that more young persons are staying in school for much longer periods of time.

But we pay some prices for the specific ways we have chosen to educate our young. Our model of education makes two fundamental problematic assumptions: (1) youths should be segregated from the rest of the community in order to be educated (for an increasingly long period of time), and (2) youths, while they are being educated, should play a passive role, in which they should have no responsibility or authority either in school or in the community. One might defend these assumptions when discussing students who are very young children, but the extension of these ideas to youths who have reached physical and social maturity is less defensible, especially in light of what now appear to be the resultant costs (Bird et al., 1978). Quite simply, many youths do not feel that they belong to, or make any difference to, the communities where they live. And persons who behave irresponsibly may do so, in part, because they have few opportunities to be responsible.

While youths in general have few opportunities for responsible and meaningful participation in their communities and local institutions, those youngsters identified as "problems" suffer especially acutely. Our existing correctional techniques, such as "special adjustment" classes (or schools), court referral, or institutionalization, as they are presently constituted, isolate offenders, make them exceptionally vulnerable to the power of the community, and remove any chance for them to influence decisions affecting themselves or anyone else. The resultant feelings of isolation and lack of belongingness can be viewed as one of the fundamental aspects in the low stake in conformity that characterizes problem youths. The situation is thus a vicious circle where the individual's isolation and alienation contribute to a low stake in conformity and then problematic behavior, which is dealt with by the individual's enforced segregation, which confirms and heightens his or her sense of isolation and alienation.

This issue is not easy to resolve. On the one hand, we cannot tolerate flagrant and persistent violations of the law. Thus, we can anticipate the continued operation of the juvenile justice process, which carries with it the threat that where other corrective techniques fail, institutionalization will be used. In short, youths will and should be accountable for their actions. On the other hand, if reintegration of juvenile offenders is also accepted as a correctional goal, then it would seem reasonable to develop supportive community mechanisms to heighten youths' sense of belongingness.

SUMMARY

The need to preserve an orderly society has been a pervasive concern throughout American history. The creation of Houses of Refuge in the early nineteenth century, the removal of children from cities to country farms, and the creation of the juvenile court were all designed to control dependent and delinquent children who were considered actual or potential threats to society's well-being. As originally conceived, these reforms were viewed by both the reformers and the public as benevolent—designed not just to protect society but to transform neglected children into model citizens of the future. In cases where institutional control was to be the mode of reform, segregation from society was to be accompanied by reformation and then reintegration into the community. Beginning in the late nineteenth century, the family, either one's own or a form of foster care, was viewed as an alternative to institutional upbringing. Finally, with the spreading dominion of the juvenile court, the whole family (usually poor or immigrant) was to be transformed under the watchful eye of the court into respectable, responsible citizens. In theory, these efforts were designed to promote the interests of both the dependent and delinquent children and the community.

In practice, however, these formulations took a different course. From the beginning, institutions were quickly filled to overcrowding; staffs were largely untrained, poorly paid, and not up to the task of caring for sizable numbers of children. The institutions themselves were often inadequately built and financed. The incontrovertible evidence of institutional shortcomings and of neglect and often actual physical abuse of institutionalized children stands in stark contrast to the good will, enthusiasm, and energy of the reformers who conceived the new programs. The tremendous disparity between barren custodial care and the assurance of rehabilitation raises important questions: Who should be held accountable for the woefully inadequate attention to the needs of these children? Why have courts continued to commit children to such institutions? Why have legislatures continued to fund these facilities? And why have professional staffs accepted the myth of rehabilitation when they offer primarily custodial care?

As observers of the juvenile justice system have pointed out, both from historical and contemporary perspectives, we have not sought out the knowledge that would enable us to design effective methods of reforming individuals. In addition to the absence of knowledge and of agreement on how to transform recalcitrant children, there has been an abysmal lack of experience and information that would allow reformers to construct institutions to house large populations adequately.

One prime factor in the perpetuation of existing programs has been the fear of alternatives. If difficult children were not institutionalized or placed under the wing of the juvenile court, where would they go? Many fear that such youths would be free to disrupt and damage the lives and homes of proper citizens. While the public has perhaps been overly concerned about protecting its own interests at the expense of the liberty and welfare of problem children, they have also tended to believe that the services they have helped provide as taxpayers have been far superior to the abuses of the past.

American society and individual communities must bear a large share of the blame for having failed to insist that all individuals are provided sufficient income, conditions, and services to allow them to participate meaningfully in structuring their lives. We lack neither the vision nor the energy to provide for our children—all of them. But beyond the preservation of the ideal and the dynamics of reform, we must rigorously work to understand the realities and the complexities of the challenges that face us.

DISCUSSION QUESTIONS

1. The development of correctional facilities for juveniles was grounded on what assumptions about delinquency?
2. What fundamental changes in society at the turn of the twentieth century affected the status of children, as well as the nature of juvenile institutions?
3. What are the six major models of juvenile institutions and the distinguishing features of each?
4. What are the major assumptions of the deprivation and importation perspectives?
5. How do organizational structure and goals affect inmate adaptations to confinement?
6. What factors should be considered in evaluating juvenile corrections programs?
7. What problems are involved in using recidivism as an indicator of correctional effectiveness?
8. What have been the major conclusions drawn from evaluative research in corrections?
9. What are the basic difficulties faced by correctional activities as they are presently constituted?
10. What assumptions underlie proposals for increased community involvement in correctional responses to youth?

MANCHILD IN THE PROMISED LAND

In a delinquent career, the experience of being locked up in an institution can be significant. There one makes new enemies and meets old friends. It is crucial to know which is which, because fights often break out, sometimes because of tensions among races or ethnic groups. Fighting is a prime factor in determining an inmate's prestige or "rep."

When you went to Warwick, you had to spend time in a reception center. They didn't put you with the other cats right away. They gave you all kinds of tests. You saw a psychologist. You got shots for smallpox, diphtheria, and anything else that you might catch. Then they showed you the procedures.

You learned how to get your clothes. You learned how to clean up the cottage that they were going to assign you. You learned most of the ropes that you could learn before you got into a cottage. But you never really learned the ropes until you got with the cats who were up there and really knew the whole thing. The people who trained you tried to show you how to get along in the cottage and get out in a hurry. But nobody ever made it. I never heard of anybody coming out the way they showed you to at Warwick.

The reception center was a different setup altogether. You were kind of isolated. Usually there were only about twenty-eight boys in a reception center at the same time. While I was there for my two weeks, any time they took us out they would have some runners with us, some of the older cats from the D section. The cottages were divided into alphabetical sections—A1, A2, and on down to D1, D2, D3, D4—and in the D section they had the older and the bigger cats.

One of the runners was a guy who lived in Brooklyn, but who used to live in Harlem. We were in the Youth House together before I went to Wiltwyck. It was good to see a familiar face. I remembered his name was Bishop. I knew he didn't remember me, so I didn't try to make him recall.

Bishop came in and said, "Man, who is Claude Brown?" Everybody stood aside. We were outside doing our exercises, and there was nobody there but him and another cat from the D group to watch us. I guess they all figured he was going to job me. Nobody said anything, but cats started moving away from me. I got kind of scared too. Bishop was a big cat. He wasn't so tall, not much taller than I was, but he was stocky, and I remembered him from the Youth House. People didn't mess with him. He was real good with his hands. They said he had knocked a few cats out.

I stepped forward. He said, "Man, you Claude Brown?"

"Yeah, man, like, I'm the one."

He said, "A whole lotta cats up here have got it in for you, man."

"Yeah, I guess so."

He said, "It looks like I know you from somewhere."

"Yeah, man, we were in the Youth House together, about four years ago."

"Are you the little cat who I told to punch Bullock in his mouth that time and you did?"

I said, "Yeah, man, like, I'm the one."

He said, "Damn, man, like, if you got the heart that you had back in the Youth House in those days, like, you gotta make it. You just go out there when those niggers start comin' down on you—you just run out there as soon as somebody call your name and say, 'Who is Claude Brown?' Like, you say, 'I am,' and run up and hit the biggest nigger first. Hit him first, and hit him as hard as you can."

I said, "Yeah," and I was listening. I was listening hard, but Bishop didn't know that I wasn't sure I could fight. I didn't know what would happen if I got punched in the stomach. I didn't know if I should hit anybody first or just try to stay away.

After I thought about it, it sounded like some damn good advice, because I knew they were going to kick my ass anyway. I knew it. I'd heard about the copper knives that the cats made in the sheet-metal shop. I could almost feel it. I knew somebody was going to try to knife me. I wouldn't mind getting shot again so much, but I was scared of knives. I didn't mind getting stomped. That shit was nothing new. I'd had my ass kicked good a lot of times, and I'd been hit in the head by just about everything. I'd even been thrown out of a window. Just about everything had been done to me but stabbing. I guess it was always that scar on Dad's neck that made me fear getting stabbed so much.

I made up my mind. When they came down on me, I was just going to hit the biggest cat and pray.

Warwick seemed to be a real nice place. April had something to do with it. It was a nice time of the year to be in the country. The place looked like it was maybe a farm or a summer resort.

I didn't get tight with anybody in the reception center. Mumbles and Charlie Tucker and the cats I had known in the nutbox started pulling away after they heard that a whole lot of bad cats were waiting to get me. They'd talk. They'd say, "Hi, man," and, "How you doin'?" but they wouldn't hang out.

The funny thing was that this Italian cat, Minetti, seemed determined to get tight with me. Every time smoking session came around after the meals, he'd come and sit down and want to talk to me. He would tell me about his girl. He would tell me about "that no-good fuckin' Joe." Just about everything that came out of Minetti's mouth was "fuckin' " or "mother-fucker." He was a funny sort of guy. It was almost like watching somebody out of a comic book, and he used to talk with that funny kind of talk, like Louie, the iceman.

I couldn't seem to stop this guy from getting tight. A lot of times I would catch myself and try to pull away from this cat. I thought, I know I can't be tight with this paddy boy when I get outta here; I'm gon have to find me some strong cats to get tight with, cats with reps. I knew that Minetti wasn't going to be any help. But if it hadn't been for him, I wouldn't have had anybody to talk to. Out of all the cats I knew at the reception center, he was the only one who wasn't scared that there were a whole lot of niggers waiting to get next to my head when I came out. So it just had to be that way. Everybody threw us together.

Sometimes this cat used to make me forget that I'd been shot only three or four months before. We'd start messing around, just joking and clowning. But somebody was always coming up and screaming on him. Minetti was good with his hands, so cats would say, "Man, why don' you stop messin' with so-and-so?" They'd try to talk up a whole lot of ill feeling against him. I usually stayed out of it. I wasn't in too good fighting shape, at least I didn't think so. I just didn't know.

But one day Minetti started arguing with a boy named Freddie Bemar. Freddie was a loudmouthed guy. He was harmless, but he was a loudmouth. He was always messing with people, but everybody knew he couldn't do anything with his hands, so most people paid no attention to him. But this day, Minetti and I were sitting and talking at a table in the recreation room at the reception center. Freddie came in and started screaming at Minetti and saying, "Man, you took my cigarettes off the table."

Minetti just joked it off and started screaming at him playfully. Freddie came over and snatched a cigarette out of Minetti's mouth. When he did that, Minetti was kind of frozen. He didn't know what to do. He said, "Like, Freddie, what you doin', man? What's it all about? What's the matter?" This is the way he used to talk, with just a tiny bit of an Italian accent. When he got excited, he used to go real fast, and you couldn't understand whether he was saying "What's the matter?" or "What's-a what's-a what's-a?"

Nobody understood Minetti as well as I did. It seemed as though he was going to cry in a minute, as though he wanted to say, "Well, Freddie, I don't bother you, and I wouldn't want to bother you; so, like, why, why would you come over here and snatch my cigarette outta my mouth like that and make me look bad?"

I started rising and I started feeling scared. I could almost feel a punch in the stomach already. But I saw all these cats crowding around Minetti, and I didn't dig it, because there were no other paddy boys in there with any heart, and this cat was all right with me. I wasn't going to see him stand alone, so I got up.

Before I realized what I was doing, I said, "Minetti, don't explain yourself to that mother-fucker. Just go on and git your cigarette. That's all. Just go on and git your cigarette and tell that nigger not to do it no more 'cause you ain't playin' with him. That's all you gotta do."

Tucker looked at me and said, "Brown, damn, man, you shouldn't have said that."

It was real wrong to call somebody a nigger in front of a paddy boy. That's the way they felt. It made me feel a little bit bad myself. This sort of cooled everything down. But saying "nigger" wasn't the main thing to me. The main thing was that these cats were trying to fuck over this paddy boy. And this paddy boy was more man than any of those cats there. I didn't care. Between us, there was no nigger thing. There was no white, no color thing. To me, he was a beautiful cat; and if you dug people and if people had something that was beautiful about them, they were raceless. And that was the only fucking thing that mattered.

I told those cats, "Don't try to tell me how to carry myself. I been through twice the shit all you niggers been through. And as far as I'm concerned, that paddy boy is twice the nigger any of you cats might think you are or might ever try to be."

After that, nobody ever said anything to me about it.

I came out of the reception center on a Friday afternoon. They put me in cottage C2. There were mostly Puerto Rican fellows in there, a few Negroes, and a sprinkling of white cats. The cottage parents were Puerto Rican. I remember it well.

When they were bringing us all up the walk of the cottage area, a lot of cats started bowing their heads and saying, "Bye, Brown," in a whisper, as if they thought I was going to my funeral or something.

Minetti went to cottage A3. But he didn't stay there long, because he kept fucking up, right and left.

When I got into my cottage, there was nobody in there looking for me. There was nobody in there I knew. But I made out and I sat and I waited. A lot of cats in there had heard about me, and they'd heard that cats were out to get me, so they stayed away.

Warwick was a funny kind of place. It was a jail in disguise. The windows in the cottage and in most of the buildings were divided into very small sections, and they had steel dividers that were painted to look like wood. The panes between the dividers were only about six square inches, and the windows were usually down from the top and up from the bottom. It would look like a normal house to anybody from the outside. But if any of the cats had tried to push a window up more from the bottom or pull it down more from the top, they would have found out that it had slats on the side, long wooden slats that wouldn't allow the window to go up or down any more than a couple of inches farther.

It was a pretty place. They had people walking around and looking like they were free, but you had to have a pass to go anywhere; and if you were gone too long, they had somebody out looking for you. They had what they called "area men," and the area men were like detectives up at Warwick. Anytime something happened—if something had been stolen or if someone had gotten stabbed—these were the cats who came around and investigated and found out who had done it. They were usually big cats, strong-arm boys. And they usually found out what it was they wanted to know.

The area men would come for you if you were gone from a place too long, and they would bring runners. Runners were like trustees. They would run after guys in the woods if they ran away, and they'd bring them back. The runners usually came from cottage A4 or one in the D group, where most of the big cats were. A4 was a crazy cottage. They had the nuts in there; they had the rapists, murderers, and perverts in there. These were the most brutal cats up there, and everybody knew it. A lot of times when people ran away, if they saw these cats behind them they would stop, because they knew they didn't have much chance of getting away. And if they gave the A4 guys a hard time, they'd catch hell when they were caught.

To someone passing by, Warwick looked just like a boy's camp. But everybody was under guard, all the time, and everybody had a job to do. You worked in the bakery or in an office or on the work gangs, and so on. Work gangs were a lot like chain gangs, minus the chains. In the summer, work gangs just busted rock and threw sledgehammers and picked onions and stuff like that. In the winter, the work gangs shoveled coal and shoveled snow. If you were a decent guy or if you could be trusted, you could get a job in one of the offices or in one of the buildings. That's where most of the younger guys worked if they weren't hell raisers. Most of the older guys were runners. They'd take people back from offices, take them around whenever they had to go see their sponsors or social workers. That sort of business. Everybody had a place to fit into, so it seemed.

On Monday, I went out, and they told me I was going to be assigned to a job working in the halls with some woman named Mrs. Washington. She was an elderly lady, about fifty-five, I guess, and she had a gang of boys who used to mop the halls and sweep up in the detail building. Next thing I know I'm down on my knees scrubbing away when I hear something funny. I look up and all these cats are standing about ten feet away. One rugged-looking cat had on a cap and a ragged vest, and he said, "Man, is your name Claude Brown?" I didn't say anything, so he said, "Punk, don't you hear me talkin' to you?" I still didn't say anything. He and all the other cats kept coming closer.

Quick as a flash, this cat was in my collar. He said, "Git up, little punk!"

I said, "I'm gon give you two seconds, man, to git a hold-a yourself and git your hand outta my collar."

All these other cats moved back; I guess I figured it was time for action.

He said, "You gon what?"

Before I could answer, another voice came from in back of the crowd, and the voice said, "I'll give you one second to git your hand outta his collar, or I'm gon bust your mother-fuckin' ass."

The rugged guy let my collar go and turned around real quick.

I recognized the voice. I couldn't see anybody, but I recognized the voice. It was the most beautiful voice I'd ever heard in all my life. It was K.B.

K.B. pushed his way on through the crowd. This first guy was a Spanish cat named Black Joe. I hadn't done anything to him or any of his relatives, but he'd heard a lot of guys were out to get me, so he was going to be the first one and make a rep on me. K.B. came to the front of the crowd, snatched him, pushed him up against the wall, and told him to throw up his hands. He wouldn't throw up his hands, so K.B. gutted him and dropped him.

Then he turned around and faced the crowd. Everybody was looking. The next thing I knew, cats started moving away. K.B. said, "Look, don't nobody move. Don't a nigger move, 'cause I got somethin' to say, and I want all-a y'all—I want every livin' ass here—to hear it, because if you don't, you liable to make the same mistake Black Joe made, and you'll end up right down there wit him. Look, this is my main nigger, my number one nigger, and anybody who fucks wit him, it's just as well as if they'd came and fucked wit me. If you got anything to say to him, against him, or about him, say it to me, because when you fuck wit him, you fuckin' wit me."

Everybody looked and said, "Yeah, man." They started mumbling to themselves. One cat said, "Damn, K.B., I thought this cat was from Harlem, man; like, we didn't know he was tight wit you."

He said, "There's a whole lotta things you cats don't know. But, like, if you fuck wit him, you gon find out all you need to know in a hurry." So everybody moved on.

Then a big cat with one arm came up to me and said, "Hey, Claude, how you doin'?" I didn't know who he was, not for a while anyway. He said, "You don't remember me, huh?"

K.B. knew him, so he smiled at me, and he said, "You don't remember this cat, Claude? You don't remember Gus Jackson?"

Then I recognized him, but the cat had gotten twice as big as he was when he was at Wiltwyck. Gus was one of my first partners when I was at Wiltwyck. He was a big cat, and I used to bully him when I first went up there. But then he started fighting, and we got tight and became partners. Gus had lost one of his arms bebopping in Brooklyn. It didn't matter too much, because all the cats up at Warwick had a whole lot of respect for him. They had more respect for him than they did for the average half-dozen cats up there with two arms. I was so glad to see them; I was so glad to see K.B. and Gus. When I saw them, I relaxed. I felt right at home. I wasn't scared of anything any more. I had a feeling that it wouldn't be long before I'd be running things up there.

After this, I met a lot of cats I'd known at Wiltwyck, in Youth House, in the streets; cats from Brooklyn, cats K.B. had cut me into; and cats I had only seen passing by. But it seemed there were more people up here waiting to get to know me, who'd heard about me and wanted to know me even before I got there, than there were enemies looking to do me in. There were so many people in my corner and people I had been tight with at some time or other, nobody would fuck with me. So I just took my time. I suppose I was the first guy in a long time, or maybe in the history of Warwick, to come up there and stay for four months without getting in a fight. That was probably a record.

One of the first guys I met up at Warwick was a guy I'd read about in the paper. Just about everybody had read about him, I suppose. He had been blamed for shooting somebody in the Polo Grounds in the summer of 1950. It was a jive tip, but there were a whole lot of cats up there on humbles. He was a damn nice guy, but they had him in A4, the crazy cottage. Just about all the guys under sixteen who were up there for murder were in A4.

This guy was on Mrs. Washington's gang with me, and he was telling me one day how they sent him up there on a humble. He said when this guy had gotten shot in the Polo Grounds, they started looking in all the houses on Edgecombe Avenue, and that's where he lived. They started looking for guns and stuff. They had a house-to-house search for guns. And they found a .22 rifle in his house. The man had been shot with a .45, but they blamed it on him.

He turned out to be a real nice cat. It was a funny thing, but all the cats I met up there and all the cats I knew on the streets who had been accused of murder or who had actually killed somebody always seemed to be the nicest cats.

After I'd gotten out of reception, Minetti and I started palling around, and we got tight. A lot of guys used to say, "Oh, man, like stay away from that cat. You know, like, those paddy boys, they all for themselves," and that sort of thing. But I liked him a lot. He was one of the first cats I'd gotten close to up there. In the reception center, if it hadn't been for this paddy boy, I would have been alone. So I didn't give a damn what anybody said.

After a while, Minetti was moved into A4, the crazy cottage. He kept breezing and getting caught and brought back into the detail building. He would have to wait outside the office sometimes. I was usually out there cleaning the halls when they brought him back.

One afternoon, they brought Minetti in, and I was talking to him. He sat on a bench outside the detail office and waited for an area man to come and take him someplace. I asked him what had happened, how he'd gotten caught. He told me he'd stolen a car and it conked out on him. He was running through the woods, and then Skylo, one of the area men, saw him. The cats from A4 ran him down and caught him.

I said that was weak stuff and went on down the hall, mopping. Then I saw some guys coming up to him. I paid it no attention, but he got up, and I heard his voice raised. I turned around. Some cats had him up in a corner and were punching him. There were three of them, and they were runners from A4. It sounded like they were kicking his ass for giving them such a hard time catching him. I thought that was crazy. If a guy is running away, the reason he's running away is to get away, and why should he stop just because somebody is coming for him?

He started going down, and they started kicking him. I knew that in a little while they were going to stomp him. So I ran up there with the mop in my hand. I guess I just didn't do too much thinking. The first thing I knew, I was lashing into those cats with that mop handle, and everybody was hollering and going on. We were raising hell out there in that hall. Skylo, the area man, came out, and said, "What are you doing, Brown? What's wrong with you?"

Then Mrs. Washington came down the hall, all excited, hollering, "Good God, what is going on here?"

So I told them that the cats had been jumping on this one boy and that I was trying to help him.

Skylo looked at me, and he said, "He's a friend of yours, isn't he?"

"Yeah, in a way."

"Well, take some advice from me, Brown. You stay away from him, because this guy is heading for trouble, and he's not gonna be around here long, and I wouldn't want to see you get yourself into any trouble on account of him."

I pretended to appreciate his advice, then I walked away. But the main thing was that I'd gotten those cats off Minetti. At the same time, I had made them enemies of mine. But that was all right, because I didn't like those cats anyway. I thought they were all jive. The way I saw it, those niggers weren't so crazy. They were just acting like they were crazy. And they'd only act like that with cats who didn't know any better. Now I knew that if I was to breeze and they came after me, one of us would get hurt—me or whoever it was. But I just couldn't get too scared of them. I'd seen cats like that just about all my life.

There were a lot of hip young criminals at Warwick. It wasn't like Wiltwyck. For one thing, Wiltwyck only had about a hundred guys, and Warwick had five hundred. And Warwick had guys from all over New York City. They had cats from Brooklyn, the Bronx, Manhattan, Queens, and Richmond—everywhere. There were even cats from small towns upstate and from suburban areas of New York City. And Warwick had real criminals. Nobody at Wiltwyck was there for murder, and they didn't have any cats up there who knew how to steal a car without the keys. But it seemed like just about everybody at Warwick not only knew how to pick locks but knew how to cross wires in cars and get them started without keys. Just about everybody knew how to pick pockets and roll reefers, and a lot of cats knew how to cut drugs. They knew how much sugar to put with heroin to make a cap or a bag. There was so much to learn.

You learned something new from everybody you met. It seemed like just about all the Puerto Rican guys were up there for using drugs. They had a lot of colored cats up there for using drugs, but most of them were jive. Most of these guys were just using drugs to be down and to have a rep as a junkie. You could tell that these cats were jive by the way they went around saying, "Yeah, man, do you shoot stuff?" and all this sort of nonsense, as though they were bragging about it. They would start talking about how much stuff they used a day. I'd look at them and say, "Yeah, like, that's real nice," but they could never make me feel bad or anything, because all I had to do was say my name was Claude Brown. I didn't have to use drugs. I already had a reputation. I'd been other places. I knew people from here, I knew people from there.

Cats had heard about me when I was in Brooklyn gang fighting with K.B. and the Robins. And when I got shot, it was something that everybody seemed to respect me for. I'd only gotten shot with a .32, but the word was out that I'd gotten shot in the stomach with a .38. Cats didn't believe it. They'd come up to me and say, "Man, did you really git shot wit a .38?" and I'd either joke it off or act like they were being silly. I'd say, "Shit, people have gotten shot with .45's, so what?" They would go away marveling.

When we were in the dormitory getting ready to take a shower, the cool guys would say, "Hey, Brown, could I see your scar?" or they would just say, "Man, is that your scar?" I'd say, "Yeah, that's it." If they were hip cats, they might just say something like, "Yeah, man, those bullets can really fuck you up." And I'd say something like, "Yeah, but you can keep gittin' up behind 'em."

Cats used to come up and offer me ins or reefers or horse or anything I wanted. I had two or three flunkies after I'd been there for a month. It was no sweat for me; I was ready to stay there for a long time and live real good. I knew how to get along there. I'd had a place waiting for me long before I came. If I'd known that Warwick was going to be as good as it turned out to be, I would never have been so afraid. As a matter of fact, I might have gotten there a whole lot sooner.

At Warwick, it all depended on you when you went home for a visit. The first time, you had to stay there twelve weeks before you could go home. After that, you could go home for a three-day visit, from Friday to Monday, every eight weeks. That's if you didn't lose any days for fucking up or fighting. This was pretty good, because some people were always going home, and they would see your fellows and bring messages back, and your fellows were always coming up every Friday. A new batch of guys would come up and drugs would come up. When you came back from a weekend home visit, you were searched everywhere. They'd even search in the crack of your ass. You had to go to the doctor and let him look for a dose of clap. But cats would always manage to bring back at least a cap of horse or least one reefer. Everybody could always manage to smuggle in a little bit of something.

By the time Dunny came up to Warwick, I had a place for him. I was there and ready, sitting pretty. I'd already established myself and was waiting for some of the fellows to come up. I'd been up there about eight weeks when Dunny came. He told me Turk was in the Youth House. They'd gotten busted robbing a hardware store on 145th Street, and for some reason—I guess because he had a worse record than Turk—they sent Dunny right on up, but Turk was still in the Youth House waiting to go to court.

When Dunny came up, I saw him passing by the reception crowd, and I stopped and said something to him before Mr. Jenkins, the cat in charge, told me to go on. Dunny said, "Damn, Sonny, we gon live up here, man; like we gon really run the place!" And I sort of had the feeling it was true, because Dunny was a crazy cat, and he had a whole lot of heart. But I wanted to get a chance to pull his coat about the place called the Annex.

The cats who had a little bit of sense but who were just general fuck-ups were sent to the Annex. At the Annex, you didn't get any visits home, and you could only have a visitor once a month. At Warwick, you could have a visitor every Sunday, if your folks wanted to come and see you. Not too many people actually came up there every Sunday, though. At the Annex, you had to do two years. For all that time, you weren't going to be back on the street, see any girls, go to the places you liked to go, or do the things you liked to do. They said the work was harder too.

Up at Warwick, the cats had never really served any time before. They might have been someplace like Wiltwyck, where you went home only every six months, but they could go home for a visit or could go someplace eventually. In places like Warwick, you find a lot of guys who never had any home to go to, so they didn't mind. One place was just as good as another. For them, Warwick was just one more place until the next stop, which would probably be Coxsackie or Elmira or someplace like that. But to the average cat who hadn't ever served any time, the thought of going to the Annex was something frightening. I hadn't served any time, and I wasn't about to serve any time. I wanted to get back on the streets.

My folks didn't come up too much. Dad would never come any place to see me, and Mama couldn't come often because she didn't have that much money. Dad wouldn't give her any money to come up and see me. The way he felt about it was "Shit, he got his damn self in that trouble, so let him worry about it himself."

We all came out of Warwick better criminals. Other guys were better for the things that I could teach them, and I was better for the things that they could teach me. Before I went to Warwick, I used to be real slow at rolling reefers and at dummying reefers, but when I came back from Warwick, I was a real pro at that, and I knew how to boost weak pot with embalming fluid. I even knew how to cut drugs, I had it told to me so many times, I learned a lot of things at Warwick. The good thing about Warwick was that when you went home on visits, you could do stuff, go back up to Warwick, and kind of hide out. If the cops were looking for you in the city, you'd be at Warwick.

One of the most interesting things I learned was about faggots. Before I went to Warwick, I used to look down on faggots like they were something dirty. But while I was up there, I met some faggots who were pretty nice guys. We didn't play around or anything like that, but I didn't look down on them any more.

These guys were young cats my age. It was the first time I'd been around guys who weren't afraid of being faggots. They were faggots because they wanted to be. Some cats were rape artists because they wanted to be, some cats were flunkies, some cats were thieves, and some cats were junkies. These guys were faggots because they wanted to be. And some of the faggots up there were pretty good with their hands. As a matter of fact, some of them were so good with their hands, they had the man they wanted just because he couldn't beat them.

At Warwick, there was even a cottage just for faggots. If a cat came up there acting girlish, they'd put him right in there. They had a lot of guys in there—Puerto Ricans, white, colored, everything—young cats, sixteen and under, who had made up their minds that they liked guys, and that's all there was to it.

When I first came up there, I had to go to school for half a day. They put me in a class, and there was a faggot in the class. The cat was about a year older than I was, a real nice-looking guy. As a matter of fact, he was so handsome, I guess it would have been hard for him not to be a faggot. He said that he just liked guys, and that's why he was a faggot. This was the first faggot I had ever talked to, except for Earl, Bucky's brother. His name was Baxter.

He used to give me things and offer me cigarettes. These were things you weren't supposed to have outside of the cottages—cigarettes and candies, stuff like that. One day, I had to talk to him. I said, "Like, look, man, I been talkin' to you, and we been all right, and I like you, but I don't want you givin' me things, 'cause that could be misunderstood. And I suppose sooner or later, you'd be wantin' me to give you somethin' or do somethin' for you, and it's, like, that's just not my way, man. Like, the way I hear it, cats who mess around wit faggots usually come out wit claps or somethin' like that sooner or later."

He looked at me and laughed and said, "No, I don't want anything from you, Brown. I know how you are, but there aren't many guys around here who think they are down who would . . . you know, who I could talk to and who would treat me like I'm somebody or somethin'. It's like, I just like you, and I know we couldn't have anything goin' in the love vein, but, well, I just like you."

I said, "Yeah, well, I like you too, man. And as long as we both understand how things are, there's no reason why we can't go on bein' friends. But, like, it's gotta be friends like this, man, everybody understandin' where he is."

The cats up there I really disliked as a group weren't the faggots but the guys who were afraid somebody might think they were. Warwick made everybody very conscious of his masculinity, and there were a lot of cute guys up there, guys who were real handsome. They were so handsome that if they weren't good with their hands, somebody was liable to try to make a girl out of them. So these guys used to be brutal, dirty. They used to do a whole lot of wicked stuff to cats. They would stab somebody in a minute or hit a cat in his head with something while he was sleeping, all that kind of stuff, because they were afraid guys would think they weren't mean.

Source: Reprinted with permission of Macmillan Publishing Co. from *Manchild in the Promised Land* by Claude Brown, pp. 133–148.

REFERENCES

ALLEN, THOMAS E.
1969 Psychiatric observations on an adolescent inmate social system and culture. *Psychiatry* 32:246.

BARTOLLAS, CLEMENS, ET AL.
1976 *Juvenile Victimization: The Institutional Paradox.* New York: Halsted Press.

BECKER, HOWARD S., AND BLANCHE B. GEER
1960 Latent culture: A note on the theory of latent social roles. *Administrative Science Quarterly* 5:305–308.

BERK, BERNARD B.
1966 Organizational goals and inmate organization. *American Journal of Sociology* 71:522–534.

BIRD, TOM, ET AL.
1978 *A Design for Youth Development Policy.* Washington, D.C.: U.S. Government Printing Office.

COHEN, ALBERT K.
1955 *Delinquent Boys: The Culture of the Gang.* Glencoe, Ill.: Free Press.

CRESSEY, DONALD R.
1960 Limitations on organization of treatment in the modern prison. Pp. 78–110 in George H. Grosser (ed.), *Theoretical Studies in Social Organization of the Prison.* New York: Social Science Research Council.

EMPEY, LAMAR, AND MAYNARD T. ERICKSON
1972 *The Provo Experiment: Evaluating Community Control of Delinquency.* Lexington, Mass.: Heath.

EMPEY, LAMAR, AND STEVEN LUBECK
1971 *The Silverlake Experiment.* Chicago: Aldine.

FELD, BARRY C.
1977 *Neutralizing Inmate Violence: Juvenile Offenders in Institutions.* Cambridge, Mass.: Ballinger.

FISHER, SETHARD
1961 Social organization in a correctional residence. *Pacific Sociological Review* 4:87–93.

GOFFMAN, ERVING R.
1961 *Asylums.* Garden City, N.Y.: Anchor.

IRWIN, JOHN
1970 *The Felon.* Englewood Cliffs, N.J.: Prentice-Hall.

JOHNSON, GRANT, ET AL.
1979 *Delinquency Prevention: Theories and Strategies.* Washington, D.C.: U.S. Government Printing Office.

JOHNSON, ROBERT
1978 Youth in crisis: Dimensions of self-destructive conduct among adolescent prisoners. *Adolescent* 13:461–482.

KOBRIN, SOLOMON
1959 The Chicago area project: A 25-year assessment. *Annals of the American Academy of Political and Social Science* 322:20–29.

MARTINSON, ROBERT M.
1974 What works?—Questions and answers about prison reform. *Public Interest* 35:22–54.

McCLEERY, RICHARD H.
1961 Authoritarianism and the belief system of incorrigibles. Pp. 260–306 in Donald R. Cressey (ed.), *The Prison: Studies in Institutional Organization and Change.* New York: Holt, Rinehart & Winston.

McCORKLE, LLOYD W., AND RICHARD KORN
1954 Resocialization within walls. *Annals of the American Academy of Political and Social Science* 293:88–98.

McGEE, RICHARD A.
1981 *Prisons and Politics,* Lexington, Mass.: Lexington.

MILLER, WALTER B.
1962 The impact of a total-community delinquency control project. *Social Problems* 10:168–191.
1958 Lower-class culture as a generating milieu of gang delinquency. *Journal of Social Issues* 14:5–19.

MOBERG, DAVID O., AND RICHARD ERICSON
1972 A new recidivism outcome index. *Federal Probation* 36:50–56.

MOTT, PAUL
1972 *The Characteristics of Effective Organizations.* New York: Harper & Row.

NATIONAL ADVISORY COMMISSION ON CRIMINAL JUSTICE STANDARDS AND GOALS
1973 *Corrections.* Washington, D.C.: U.S. Government Printing Office.

NELSON, E. KIM
1961 Community approaches to the prevention of crime and delinquency. Los Angeles: Youth Studies Center, University of Southern California.

POLSKY, NED
1962 *Cottage Six.* New York: Wiley.

POOLE, ERIC D., AND ROBERT M. REGOLI
1983 Violence in juvenile institutions. *Criminology* 21:213–232.

ROBISON, JAMES, AND GERALD SMITH
1971 The effectiveness of correctional programs. *Crime and Delinquency* 17:67–80.

ROMIG, DENNIS A.
1978 *Justice for Our Children.* Lexington, Mass.: Lexington.

ROSSI, PETER H., AND WALTER WILLIAMS
1972 *Evaluating Social Programs: Theory, Practice, and Politics.* New York: Seminar Press.

SARRI, ROSEMARY C., AND ROBERT D. VINTER
1965 Group treatment strategies in juvenile correctional institutions. *Crime and Delinquency* 11:326–340.

SEIDMAN, DAVID, AND MICHAEL COUZENS
1972 Crime, crime statistics, and the great American anti-crime crusade: Police misreports of crime and political pressures. Paper presented at the 1972 Annual Meeting of the American Political Science Association, Washington, D.C.

SHIREMAN, CHARLES H., ET AL.
1972 Findings from experiments in treatment in the correctional institution. *Social Service Review* 46:38–59.

STREET, DAVID, ET AL.
1966 *Organization for Treatment.* New York: Free Press.

SYKES, GRESHAM M.
1958 *The Society of Captives.* Princeton, N.J.: Princeton University Press.

SYKES, GRESHAM M., AND SHELDON L. MESSINGER
1960 The inmate social system. Pp. 5–19 in George H. Grosser (ed.), *Theoretical Studies in Social Organization of the Prison.* New York: Social Science Research Council.

THOMAS, CHARLES W.
1977 Theoretical perspectives on prisonization: A comparison of the importation and deprivation models. *Journal of Criminal Law and Criminology* 68:134–145.

THOMAS, CHARLES W., AND DAVID M. PETERSON
1977 *Prison Organization and Inmate Subcultures.* Indianapolis: Bobbs-Merrill.

THOMAS, CHARLES W., AND MATTHEW T. ZINGRAFF
1976 Organizational structure as a determinant of prisonization: An analysis of the consequences of alienation. *Pacific Sociological Review* 19:98–116.

WARD, DAVID, AND GENE KASSEBAUM
1972 On biting the hand that feeds: Some implications of sociological evaluations of correctional effectiveness. Pp. 300–310 in Carol H. Weiss (ed.), *Evaluating Action Programs: Readings in Social Action and Education.* Boston: Allyn & Bacon.

WARD, JACK L.
1958 Homosexual behavior of the institutionalized delinquent. *Psychiatric Quarterly Supplement* 3:301–314.

WHEELER, STANTON B.
1961 Socialization in correctional communities. *American Sociological Review* 26:697–712.

ZALD, MAYER N.
1962 Organizational control structures in five correctional communities. *American Journal of Sociology* 68:335–345.

Critical Issues in Juvenile Justice 13

A LEGACY OF FAILURE

The failure of juvenile justice in America has been announced by many criminologists, the news media (*Time,* 1977), and a U.S. Senate subcommittee that commented,". . . our present system of juvenile justice is failing miserably" (Krisberg and Schwartz, 1982:24). Nearly everyone agrees that our juvenile justice system has not delivered on its promise, made more than eighty years ago, to rid society of troublesome youths.

Since its inception, the juvenile justice system has implemented many programs designed to reform or control delinquent children. These have ranged from farming out children to work as indentured servants under the guise of Charles Brace's Children's Aid Society, to community-based facilities, to imprisonment alongside adults. Early programs were designed to curb delinquency, rehabilitate wayward youths, and save society from destruction by providing youths with moral and religious training (Platt, 1969). Unfortunately, however, no program since 1820 has achieved these goals (Liazos, 1974).

Long before the juvenile court officially emerged, wealthy philanthropists feared that if something were not done to deter children, especially working-class youths, from misbehaving, society would be undermined and ultimately destroyed. Something was done. A juvenile justice system was created for working-class children. As one judge wrote of the children most likely to need help:

> In many cases the parents are foreigners, frequently unable to speak English, and without an understanding of American methods and views. What they need, more than anything else, is kindly assistance; and the aim of the court . . . is to help them to train the child right (Mack, 1909:106).

Even today, juvenile institutions are filled predominantly with working-class children, whom the court has determined need training.

> . . . in Massachusetts the inmates of the reform schools were the children of the poor. Research indicated that 95 percent of all children who appeared in court were not committed. Of those who were committed, 88 percent came from families at, or near, the poverty level. . . . [C]hildren in poor and black neighborhoods have an almost even chance of being taken to juvenile court (Liazos, 1974:7).

Such statistics do not result from chance. They are a function of institutionalized social inequalities. Today, as in the past, not a single remedy has addressed the actual needs of those children they intend to help. Not a single program, for instance, has focused on root causes of existing disparities such as poverty or discrimination; these conditions are considered "beyond the scope of the program." Rather, since 1820, delinquency prevention and control programs have tried "to integrate children of the poor, working class, and minority groups into the bottom of the social and occupational worlds" (Liazos, 1974:8). A case in point is the Mobilization for Youth program, an attempt by the federal government in the 1960s to provide working-class children legitimate work opportunities. The program received massive funding to train poor children for jobs. It simulated ten work situations, such as a gasoline station, an auto-repair shop, a shoe factory, and a luncheonette. Youths were to learn punctuality, neatness, proper demeanor, and how to approach a prospective employer. But when the program ended, few of the youths got jobs in the area in which they had been trained. Of the forty-six gas-station trainees, only one got a gas-station-related job. And for the more than 1,700 adolescents in the program during 1962–1963, jobs were found for only 25 percent, and nearly always in marginal occupations at low wages (Marris and Rein, 1973). Such failures prompted the President's Commission on Law Enforcement and Administration of Justice (1967) to recommend that future delinquency prevention programs be aimed at changing social conditions and not individual offenders. But apparently this suggestion, like other allegedly radical ones, fell on deaf ears. As in the past, the overwhelming majority of contemporary programs focus on bringing about individual and not social change. Thus, lower-class children remain socialized to accept positions that permanently keep them at the "bottom of the barrel." Many of those who resist placement in dead-end, menial jobs at minimal wages find themselves housed in juvenile reformatories.

Ideology and Policy

The current controversies surrounding the juvenile justice system can be more fully comprehended by considering the underlying economic, political, and social factors that affected the formulation of its present structures and institutions. The periodic movements for reform of the system have continually asserted the role of the family as the primary instrument for cultural transmission and socialization (although at times they have inadvertently led to a supplanting rather than a supplementing of the family). But as the American economy became increasingly industrialized, growing pressures on family structures, particularly those of the lower socioeconomic classes, have reduced the power of the family to act as a stable socializing force. The state, seeking to protect both the broad-ranging interests of society as a whole and the interests of the individual child, has attempted to fill this vacuum by assuming the role of surrogate parent. This development gave rise to the dual role of the juvenile justice system that in many regards has been counterproductive to the interests of both society and the juvenile. On the one hand, in order to meet its mandate to protect the community and control youths (perhaps for their own protection), the system must exert a certain level of coercive control. At the same time, the system is expected to supplement family authority by serving a nurturing and rehabilitative function. It therefore embraces ideologically conflicting roles.

This situation raises the question of whether the juvenile justice system can realistically serve these two contradictory ends. The basic issue that juvenile justice policymakers must now address is how and to what extent can societal institutions in general and the juvenile court in particular be expected to act as both an agent of social control and a protector of juvenile rights. This issue has broad implications that question the assumptions on which the juvenile justice system operates. Furthermore, despite the trend toward treating delinquents more like adult offenders, juvenile offenders remain victims of the inconsistencies and contradictions inherent in the system.

A traditional argument in support of the juvenile court has been that treatment or rehabilitation of the nonconforming child by the court can guide the child toward a law-abiding and productive role in society. Given the contradictory roles of the juvenile justice system, however, the court's ability to serve this function has become a matter of doubt. For example, because the system is mandated to protect the security and safety of the community, it is seen as incapable of diagnosing and treating troubled youths objectively.

While the combination of coercive and noncoercive approaches to treatment might be feasible in some therapeutic environments that seek to deal with deviant behavior, it is not compatible with the alleged rehabilitative approach of the juvenile court. For example, most of the specific treatment methods available in the present juvenile justice system—for example, individual counseling, group therapy, academic and vocational training, and family crisis-intervention counseling—require some measure of voluntary cooperation. Yet the system's requiring juveniles to participate in treatment programs essentially precludes allowing its "clients" the option of voluntary cooperation.

When the United States Supreme Court took cognizance of the contradictions in the juvenile justice system in the 1960s, it seriously questioned the effectiveness of the *parens patriae* doctrine of the juvenile justice system. By so doing, the court acknowledged that the juvenile justice system, despite its good intentions, was serving primarily as an agent of social control and that the system's ability to protect the rights and best interests of its clients was wholly inadequate. To counteract this problem and reduce the inequities that had been created by the long-term institutionalization of the *parens patriae* doctrine, the Court introduced a series of due-process protections for children within the juvenile justice system. Today, a different agenda of reforms has emerged. Juvenile justice policymakers now face the imperative task of defining institutional limitations and reeducating society as to what can pragmatically be expected from government in solving juvenile offender problems, as well as defining what responsibilities communities must assume.

The contradictory roles of the juvenile justice system have far-reaching implications when policymakers try to coordinate the widely divergent agencies that constitute the juvenile justice system. Police, courts, probation and social welfare departments, state correctional agencies, and community programs for youths each have somewhat different roles, goals, and objectives in relation to their handling of juvenile offenders. There are often conflicts among them, since one may be pursuing ends which are seen as contravening the interest of another.

For example, in states, such as Massachusetts, that have sought to divert or deinstitutionalize juvenile offenders on a large scale, law-enforcement agencies and juvenile courts have often reacted with skepticism, if not adamant opposition. The response of these institutions seems natural when such a policy is perceived as potentially threatening their status quo, diluting their jurisdictional authority, and eliminating staff jobs. On the other hand, human resource/child welfare–type agencies and community-treatment agencies may view such a policy more favorably since it generally reinforces their own philosophical position, while at the same time increasing their client population, budgets, and staffs.

As a result of these underlying competing philosophical, economic, and political interests, legislators often find themselves making allocations to various parts of the juvenile justice system based more on political pragmatism than on sound policy considerations. Legislators rely to a great extent on information provided by various interest groups and constituents; therefore, their decisions are in many instances unduly influenced by a particular group within the juvenile justice system without realizing that they are dealing with only part of a much larger entity. Since there is generally no well-organized or well-funded constituency for children's (especially working-class youngsters') interests in most states, legislative programs in this area often are based primarily upon perceptions of justice system personnel.

Since it is unrealistic to expect to reverse the tendency of institutions to look out for their own interests, the most reasonable alternative for policymakers is to build in checks and balances. They should carefully consider and analyze the interests underlying a particular proposed program and ascertain the implications of the proposed course of action for juveniles and the juvenile justice system alike. Furthermore, it seems wise for policymakers to encourage and support the loose-knit grass-roots efforts that presently advocate the interests of juveniles in order to ensure the presentation of a more balanced picture to decision makers and the public alike. It is necessary that the community be aware of delinquency policies so that institutions can receive the necessary support and direction they need to carry out their legislative mandates.

The fact that juvenile justice institutions can become so independent of public policy that they can focus primarily on serving their own purposes indicates the seriousness of maintaining control over enacted policy. The juvenile justice system may react to legislation it disapproves of by using bureaucratic inefficiency to hamper it or even using bureaucratic procedure to sabotage it. Because many legislative approaches have lacked adequate monitoring and enforcement provisions to cope with this reality, even innovative advances that become law may never actually be implemented. Worse yet, the programs are often deemed failures for reasons unrelated to their conceptual or practical value (for example, they cost too much).

Our comments here rest on a very obvious and basic assumption—that the *intent* of juvenile justice is to help youths. We should note that even though none of the proposals reviewed above challenges the existing social arrangements that perpetuate discrimination, ignorance, and inequality, these conditions should not be allowed to continue.

CONTEMPORARY CONCERNS AND POINTS OF DEPARTURE

The problem is a grave one. While many instant remedies are being put forward, most current juvenile justice reform tactics are grounded in alarmist thinking. Alarmists like Wilson (1975) and van den Haag (1975) believe that citizens in democratic societies willingly sacrifice certain rights in return for protection of their personal and private interests. The implied contract forces the state to punish offenders; otherwise nonviolators will feel cheated:

> . . . few of us will reinsert the coin into a public phone when it is accidently returned after a call is completed. . . . Most passengers buy tickets for a train ride; only a few try to cheat. However, if it became known that there were no conductors on trains anymore, the habit of paying would soon disappear. . . . Ultimately, those who pay might be as few as those who now cheat (van den Haag, 1975:23).

This passage sums up the alarmist position and, by extension, the juvenile justice reform measures being proposed. Alarmists see people as rational and intelligent and thus capable of making sound decisions and living in an orderly manner. Furthermore, they believe people choose to commit crimes; they are not compelled or motivated by strain and frustration.

Alarmists also assume that deterrence from delinquency or crime can be achieved only through legal penalties. In fact, though, fear of legal punishment probably has little to do with behavior and thus does not induce 99 percent of children to conform 99 percent of the time. Rather, conformity is common because youths fear losing the respect of those whose opinions they value most (Hirschi, 1969; Kornhauser, 1978; Gottfredson, 1982). After all, adolescents who engage in delinquency seldom define their behavior as illegal and even more rarely know the penalty for the offense or the probability of being apprehended and punished. But it is likely that youngsters do consider what their parents and peers will think when they commit a particular act.

Even though the alarmist position has many advocates, most data addressing the subject do not support the proposition that toughness (measured by sentence severity) deters crime (Erickson and Gibbs, 1980). Nevertheless, the public believes that the alarmists are correct. In July 1978, for instance, New York state passed a "get tough" juvenile statute that stated that children as young as 13 years old who are accused of certain heinous crimes are to be tried as adults. While awaiting trial these alleged criminals are housed in adult prisons like Rikers Island. Alarmists' reforms are not concerned with kindly care for children, but with making justice equal for all offenders and making sure that swift and certain punishment is administered.

Age of Accountability

Consistent with their retributive philosophy, alarmists want the age of accountability lowered. They argue that society must stop coddling criminals and that delinquents must be treated as would any other criminal offender. This view is popularly accepted despite evidence that juvenile courts react more harshly to children than would an adult court if the child were waived to that jurisdiction (Snyder and Hutzler, 1981). Still, several states have rewritten their juvenile statutes consistent with alarmist concerns.

Alarmists also want juvenile courts to administer sanctions based only on the seriousness of the offense. All other factors—including criteria such as the court's view of the child or his or her background—should be ignored. The alarmists' argument is straightforward. It makes no difference whether an offender is 12 or 16 or 33 years old. The result is the same—a bloodied nose, a burgled house, a dead body, and so on.

Support for this position is found in many circles. The state of Washington recently redrafted its entire juvenile code to be consistent with this sort of mechanized justice: ". . . the further intent of the legislation is that the young, in turn, be held accountable for their offenses" (Washington Revised Code Ann. 13.04 et seq. [1979]). This philosophy also pervades the twenty-four volumes of material analyzing the juvenile justice system prepared jointly by the Institute of Judicial Administration and the American Bar Association (IJA/ABA). The publication of the IJA/ABA standards, however, reflects nothing more than an abandonment of the belief that causes of delinquency can be found and treatment programs successfully implemented. Those who drafted the IJA/ABA volumes presumed the causes of delinquency are already known; they are poverty, discrimination, and broken homes. But because these are firmly rooted in the social structure, they are, in effect, unalterable. Alarmists argue that society is wasting its time and resources trying to eliminate the causes of delinquency. Instead, juvenile justice should only concern itself with *doing justice,* not with social reform projects (Paulsen, 1979). However, by doing so, it ignores the needs of children who enter the juvenile justice system. Eight-year-old Stephen illustrates certain characteristics of children who typically come before the juvenile court:

> Stephen is tiny, desperate, unwell. Sometimes he talks to himself. He moves his mouth as if he were talking. He is also an indescribably mild and unmalicious child. He cannot do any of his school work very well. His math and reading are poor. . . . Stephen . . . does not have any mother or father. Stephen is a ward of the state of Massachusetts and . . . he has been placed in the home of some very poor people who do not want him now that he is not a baby anymore. . . . Stephen often comes to school badly beaten (Kozol, 1967:1).

The thousands of children like Stephen are the ones who are candidates for America's juvenile reformatories. These children's lives are already filled with ignorance, despair, shame, and abuse; simply punishing them for their offenses is likely only to aggravate their problems and, in turn, pose additional problems for society in handling them.

Something else must—and can—be done. Children must acquire a "stake in conformity" (Toby, 1957). A stake in conformity could be realized if social programs were designed to strengthen youths' bonds to school and parents, to create educational programs providing access to legitimate work opportunities, and to instill a belief in adolescents that they (and not fate) can affect their destiny through legitimate avenues. Programs of this type will be difficult to construct and will require more than money. Their successful implementation means a shift in society's thinking about childhood and justice.

One way of possibly meeting these goals is community-control programs initiated and operated by local residents (Krisberg and Austin, 1978). Unlike the community-based strategies discussed in Chapter 12, community-control programs require no involvement by state or federal officials. Resources and decision making are the responsibilities of community members. On the surface, community-control programs make sense since they require neighborhood adults and children to work together in dealing with problems. But there is no guarantee that community-control programs would effectively combat and control delinquency. Indeed, such programs may prove problematic. After all,

1. Is it realistic to expect communities to take over social service programs?
2. What of disorganized communities that need community-control programs, but do not have the resources to bolster and sustain adequate community organization?
3. What mechanisms would insure equity of treatment and uniformity of rules?

However, answers to these questions will come only through research and experimentation, not from idle speculation. It is much easier to criticize a set of proposals than to offer concrete recommendations for change. We have called for changes in existing social arrangements as only one possible solution, but we have intentionally been vague about what such changes would involve because before the social system can change, society's attitudes toward adolescents must be radically revised. Americans must come to recognize and accept the fact that children are people, too.

The Status Offense Controversy

There are a vast number of studies and arguments on the status offense issue. Although difficult to categorize, three major positions can be identified:

1. Juvenile court jurisdiction over status offenders should be retained.
2. Juvenile court jurisdiction over status offenders should be retained, but the focus of court intervention should be directed toward the family unit rather than the child, and/or juvenile court jurisdiction should be assumed only as a last resort.
3. Juvenile court jurisdiction over status offenses should be eliminated.

Several reassuring arguments are cited to support the position that juvenile courts should retain jurisdiction over status offenders. These are premised on the rehabilitative nature of the juvenile justice process. Although they concede that status offense charges reflect complex family and school problems, they argue that intervention is necessary to provide meaningful treatment to troubled children and families; that juvenile courts do divert every possible status offense case to appropriate community agencies but that such services are scarce (and even if available, many troubled children will refuse to accept treatment voluntarily); and that status offenders, unless identified and treated through the juvenile court, are likely to become juvenile delinquents (Arthur, 1977a,1977b).

Some commentators support retention of juvenile court jurisdiction over status offenders but seek to change the focus of the court in such cases from the child to the family and/or to prohibit judicial intervention unless all community treatment alternatives have been exhausted. A task force report by the National Advisory Committee on Criminal Justice Standards and Goals, *Juvenile Justice and Delinquency Prevention* (1976), for example, acknowledged that noncriminal misbehaviors require an exploration of family relationships and that all nonjudicial and voluntary resources should be exhausted prior to court intervention. The task force recommended, however, that certain specifically defined behaviors (habitual truancy, repeated disregard for or misuse of lawful parental authority, repeated running away, repeated use of intoxicating beverages, and delinquent acts committed by a juvenile younger than 10 years of age) be subject to family court jurisdiction and that the clients be designated "Families with Service Needs." The dispositional alternatives available to the court under this scheme would prohibit institutional confinement for any child under this jurisdiction (National Advisory Committee on Criminal Justice Standards and Goals, 1976). Yet, proposals to alter but maintain juvenile court jurisdiction over status offenses fail to address issues of vagueness, fairness, and effectiveness. These concerns form the foundation of a growing movement, supported by alarmists and reassurers alike, aimed at the elimination of juvenile court jurisdiction over status offenses.

Other commentators argue for elimination of status offense jurisdiction on the basis of both legal and practical considerations. First, statutes that confer status offense jurisdiction are often extremely vague. Language such as "habitual," "beyond control," and "endanger the morals of himself/herself or others" delegates to police officers, social workers, and the courts the decision as to whether particular conduct is unlawful. But generally, courts have been reluctant to declare such language void for vagueness (Katz and Teitelbaum, 1977). Second, status offense jurisdiction sanctions judicial intervention in the absence of any criminal act. Such intervention is seen as totally unwarranted. While the judicial system can decide whether or not a person has committed a given act, "it is incapable of managing, except in a very gross sense, so delicate a relationship as that between parent and child" (IJA/ABA, 1977c:11). As a consequence, and "although some juvenile court judges . . . question the wisdom of certain parents, the rule is 'the parents right or wrong,' and the child is treated as the one with the problem" (Ketcham, 1977:648–649).

Although accurate data are difficult to retrieve, one national study estimated that 20 percent of the cases referred to juvenile courts in 1977 were status offenses (Black and Smith, 1981). As indicated earlier, reclassifying children from one jurisdictional category to another has no meaning if more appropriate dispositional alternatives are not applied or created to care for these children. While many status offenders are jurisdictionally separated from delinquents, they are regularly subjected to the same preadjudication detention and postadjudication custody as alleged and adjudicated delinquent children. In 1977, it was estimated that 22 percent of the juveniles awaiting a court hearing and 16 percent of those committed to correctional facilities were status offenders (Black and Smith, 1981). The fact that about one-fifth of all juvenile court cases are status offenses is a clear indication that such jurisdiction is costly because it diverts the attention of court personnel, judges, and probation officers from those cases where intervention is truly warranted. The expense of detaining and institutionalizing status offenders must also be added to the costs of court processing (Kobrin and Klein, 1982).

Some writers have also attempted to base the argument for eliminating the status offense jurisdiction on whether status offenders really differ from delinquents (Clarke, 1975; Thomas, 1976; Weis, 1979). In short, if status offenders and delinquents are both involved in illegal activities, then separate jurisdiction is unnecessary. Weis (1979) has provided the best study of this issue to date. Weis found that while status offenders and less serious offenders were not behaviorally distinguishable, both groups differed from youths involved in serious delinquency. He therefore suggested that this observed difference in behavior justifies the restriction or removal of jurisdiction for both status offenses and less serious delinquent acts. But even if, for example, two juveniles have identical behavioral histories, should one who has been referred to court for "incorrigibility" be processed under the same jurisdiction as one who has been referred for aggravated assault? To view the present referral offenses as the same because past behaviors are similar seems illogical and unjustified.

Nevertheless, it is important to note that several studies have demonstrated that the behavior encompassed by status offense statutes is not likely to escalate to criminal activity (Clarke, 1975; Weis, 1979). As Weis (1979:96) observed, "the findings do not support the notion that early involvement in status offenses leads to later involvement in delinquency—for some it does and for others it does not." Moreover, these studies contend (Andrews and

Cohn, 1977:85) that the goal of preventing status offenders from embarking on a criminal career rests on the faulty assumptions that a court can

1. understand accurately a youth's past behavior;
2. predict accurately how a youth will develop in the future without court intervention; and
3. predict accurately that with court ordered "treatment" a youth's development will follow a different, more "desirable" path.

They argue that, while status offense conduct is usually symptomatic of an unhealthy family dynamic, there is no consensus as to what constitutes a "healthy" family. Indeed, even the "healthy" adult has escaped definition. It is now well recognized, though, that "treatments" that focus on the child and not the family further worsen, rather than improve, family relationships (Ketcham, 1977). Even if the focus of status offense jurisdiction can be shifted from the child to the family, it is doubtful that court intervention at this level could have any significant effect on complex family interactions—an area ill suited to legal analysis and coercive treatment (Mahoney, 1977).

In addition to arguments that focus on the inability of juvenile courts to treat status offenders effectively, some observers condemn the pervasive sexual discrimination in the application of status offense jurisdiction. A 1972–1973 study in New York state concluded that most juvenile girls who appeared in court were charged with noncriminal misbehavior, while only one-fifth of the boys referred to family court were charged with status offenses (Sussman, 1977)—a finding corroborated by a report that in 1971, 75 percent of the girls in detention centers in this country were charged with noncriminal offenses as compared to 20–30 percent of the boys so detained (Chesney-Lind, 1977). The New York study also concluded that girls adjudicated for noncriminal misconduct were disproportionately represented in state training schools and reformatories (Sussman, 1977). This phenomenon is largely attributable to the vague standards of conduct that characterize PINS statutes. "Their breadth (ungovernability, incorrigibility, beyond control) invites discretionary application and allows parents, police, and juvenile authorities, who ordinarily decide whether PINS proceedings should be initiated, to hold girls accountable for behavior—often sexual or in some way related to sex—that they would not consider serious if committed by boys" (Sussman, 1977:179).

Little justification exists for treating a truant, runaway, or other status offender as harshly as a criminal-law violator. In apparent recognition of this point of view, most states have removed status offense behavior from the delinquency category. Furthermore, some states authorize adjudication and subsequent treatment as a status offender on a finding that the child not only has committed an act such as running away but also is in need of court-administered care and rehabilitation. These developments signal recognition of the fact that responsibility for status offense behavior often lies with the entire family unit and with the child's natural growth process (Goldstein et al., 1979). Moreover, several states have shifted some status offense activities into the dependency category and totally eliminated court jurisdiction over others, apparently in recognition of the fact that a status offense is seldom, if ever, solely the fault of the child and/or that the juvenile court system is poorly suited to deal with this kind of problem (Ketcham, 1977). Similarly, many states have determined that a juvenile criminal-law violator should not be treated as or labeled delinquent if he or she is especially young, if the offending conduct has been precipitated by improper or inadequate parental guidance, or if the child is otherwise not in need of care and rehabilitation (IJA/ABA,1977a).

A final reassuring argument set forth in support of eliminating status offense jurisdiction is that the development of nonjudicial services for troubled children and families does not rationalize the retention of juvenile court jurisdiction. Indeed, passage of the Juvenile Justice and Delinquency Prevention Act, which contains (as Title II) the Runaway Youth Act, has prompted state and local governments, as well as private agencies, to initiate numerous alternative services including family crisis-intervention centers, runaway shelters, and alternative educational programs. It is argued that the growth of such programs will be hampered as long as juvenile courts encourage parents and schools to abdicate their functions and roles. Instead, removal of status offense jurisdiction will stimulate the creation and extension of a wider range of voluntary services than is presently available (IJA/ABA, 1977c).

It cannot be denied that status offense jurisdiction as it now exists and is exercised in most states is in need of immediate reform. The ultimate issue is whether any legal or moral justification exists for subjecting children to judicial intervention in the absence of any criminal conduct.

CHILDREN'S RIGHTS

> The child's subjugated status (is) rooted in the same benevolent despotism that kings, husbands and slave masters claimed as their moral right. According to Blackstone, the architect of English law, parents had a legal duty to provide maintenance, protection and education for their children in return for obedience. The social philosophers of the 19th century [sic]—Hobbes, Locke, Mill—never considered children parties to the social contract; they owed absolute obedience to their sovereign parents whose duty was to educate them to the degree of competence necessary to participate as adults in the social contract or the utilitarian society. For the child, said Hobbes, "like the imbecile, the crazed and the beasts . . . there is no law." Even the ultimate libertarian, John Mill, complacently announced that "the existing generation is master of . . . the entire circumstances

> of the generation to come." To economic determinists, on the other hand, the inferior status of children was an essential counterpoint to parental control if parents were to support and protect children—as society wished them to do—and to the value of the child's labor as a contribution to the family's economic survival (Wald, 1974:15).

The search for legally enforceable rights and obligations for children proceeds against a legal background that includes the notion, expressed by numerous courts in a variety of contexts, of "family privacy" or "family autonomy" (IJA/ABA, 1977d). As articulated by the courts, the principle of "family autonomy" assumes that judges have no more expertise in making intrafamilial judgments than parents do. Courts, therefore, should refrain to the maximum extent possible from interfering with family decision making unless the parents' behavior falls below the legislatively mandated minimum standards of parental care as established in the juvenile court's nonoffender jurisdiction (neglect, abuse, and dependency cases). The principle of "family autonomy" further implies that as long as the minimum standard of parental care is maintained, children have no legal basis from which to make claims against their parents. Children are generally recognized as having rights under the law only through default of parental legal authority (Baumrind, 1978; Boli-Bennett and Meyer, 1978).

To establish rights for children independent of parental authority, some commentators have proposed legislative adoption by the states of a comprehensive "bill of rights" for juveniles (e.g., Foster and Freed, 1972; Katz et al., 1973.) One formulation of a children's bill of rights contains the following tenets (Foster and Freed, 1972:343):

A child has a moral right and should have a legal right

1. To receive parental love and affection, discipline and guidance, and to grow to maturity in a home environment which enables him to develop into a mature and responsible adult;
2. To be supported, maintained, and educated to the best of parental ability, in return for which he has the moral duty to honor his father and mother;
3. To be regarded as a *person*, within the family, at school, and before the law;
4. To receive fair treatment from all in authority;
5. To be heard and listened to;
6. To earn and keep his own earnings;
7. To seek and obtain medical care and treatment and counseling;
8. To seek emancipation from the parent-child relationship when that relationship has broken down and the child has left home due to abuse, neglect, serious family conflict, or other sufficient cause, and his best interests would be served by the termination of parental authority;

9. To be free of legal disabilities for incapacities save where such are convincingly shown to be necessasry and protective of the actual best interest of the child; and
10. To receive special care, consideration, and protection in the administration of law or justice so that his best interests always are a paramount factor.

Support for a legislative affirmation of the basic rights of juveniles through a comprehensive bill of rights has been premised upon not only philosophical justifications as implied in the preceding proposal (see also Worsfold, 1974), but also on sociological grounds. Holt (1974), for instance, has argued that a primary source of many individuals' problems is the modern nuclear family. Wald (1974:23) concurs and further suggests that:

> . . . the fundamental reason why children's rights has emerged as a serious topic at all is the erosion in confidence in the family reliability to meet all the needs of the child. Our technological society has isolated the nuclear family and subordinated its welfare to the demands of great economic entities for mobile labor; others point to the escalation of child abuse and to the incidence of mental illness, alcoholism, and suicide among both parents and children. Intact families whose members love and respect each other would not be likely to disintegrate if there were to be a different allocation of rights and privileges within the family. I would wager that most strong family units already allow their children the freedom we are talking about. It is the borderline, shaky or unstable family structures that might split open when the lines of authority become more blurred. These are also the high risk families in which abuse and exploitation of children are most likely to occur, and where children most need an affirmation of their basic rights.

Finally, advocates of juvenile rights argue that contemporary concepts of fairness support the presumption that children should be allowed the same rights and freedoms as adults. This presumption could be rebutted only by either a clear showing of irreversible damage—physical, psychological, or emotional—from the exercise of such rights or by evidence indicating the inability to exercise those rights.

Children represent our poorest, least organized, and most vulnerable group of citizens. As such, they have traditionally comprised a powerless and unrepresented class within the legislative process. Social policy pertaining to children has largely been left to such special-interest groups as juvenile court judges and administrators, police and state welfare agencies, lawyers, and social workers. State welfare and juvenile justice systems, while based on the rhetoric of "helping" children, often subject them to the arbitrary and excessive authority of parents, custodians, and the state. As a result of the glaring absence of effective child advocacy, many children—whether labeled as abused, neglected, dependent, incorrigible, or delinquent—are denied their basic human rights (Short, 1979).

CONCLUSION

Juvenile delinquency continues to be one of the social problems about which large numbers of people think we can and should do something. Toward that end, the structure and function of the juvenile justice system have been the subject of much theory, research, and criticism. A substantial fraction of the criticism, and more than a little of the theory and research, appear to stem from the realization that almost a century of work designed to create a viable, effective system of dealing with delinquency has failed.

Yet no single system can be expected to counter the forces that affect juvenile delinquency. Indeed, most observers would agree that, at best, the various elements of the juvenile justice system can do little more than react to delinquent behavior when it occurs. Stated somewhat differently, there are a variety of psychological, social psychological, and structural factors that can either push juveniles toward involvement in delinquency or make such involvement more attractive than conventional options. Viewed in this fashion, delinquency is, in effect, a symptom of those other factors, many of which cannot be corrected by those responsible for the operation of the juvenile justice system. For example, there is ample reason to believe that delinquency is related to such factors as parent-child relationships, peer-group pressures, academic performance, and access to legitimate work opportunities, over which the juvenile justice officials have little or no control.

One option, of course, is simply to deny or to ignore these influences. Instead, the system can and does contend that it can somehow identify and respond to the individual needs of a particular child. In other words, while paying some lip service to the relevance of broader causal factors over which the juvenile justice system has no meaningful influence, the daily operation of the system can be designed in a way that reflects the belief that the system can respond to the unique requirements of individual children. Should attempts to do this fail, the implication is that better results could be obtained if we were in a better position to individualize our responses. Thus, we hear demands for more staff, more money, more research, more time, and so on, if the goals of the system are to be fully realized. More important, such contentions encourage us to look at virtually anything other than the viability of the basic premise that individualized efforts are potentially effective.

To begin with, the notion of individualized justice and treatment is questionable for at least two important reasons: (1) it ignores broad causal factors that are not unique to the special circumstances or personality structure of an individual juvenile; (2) the operation of the juvenile justice system only infrequently reflects the actual application of an individualized treatment model. As observers have noted repeatedly, the real (as opposed to the professed) activities of the system are far less individualized and far more bureaucratic simply in order to process large numbers of juveniles as rapidly as possible given limited resources. Thus, the loosely connected set of agencies that we call the juvenile justice system claims to have adopted a treatment philosophy that (1) often ignores more factors related to delinquency than it emphasizes and (2) is seldom translated into tangible courses of action or programs geared to individual needs and problems.

Several remedies seem in order. First, the goals of the system should better reflect what the system can reasonably expect to attain. While there is certainly nothing negative about a very general statement of ideals, it is imperative that the system devise precise operational goals if it is to be able to monitor the extent to which its activities are either efficient or effective. Only then will it ever be possible to become accountable; to determine which programs, policies, and decisions serve agreed-upon goals; and to identify potential changes in organizational arrangements that might prove useful. Such precise statements of goals, careful evaluation research, and thoughtful restructuring of organizational arrangements to better serve the purposes of various elements of the juvenile justice system are only infrequently encountered anywhere in the juvenile justice system. Consequently, administrative officials often have little or no quantitative information about the impact of their efforts, and policymaking necessarily remains based more on speculation and intuition than on hard empirical evidence. This type of situation is seldom found in other kinds of organizations, and most would find it impossible to continue were it not for a careful and systematic monitoring of exactly what kinds of organizational efforts have what kinds of effects on the success or failure of the organization.

Second, many delinquents and delinquent acts are either ignored or informally disposed of by juvenile justice officials. Cases are screened by police, by specialized juvenile divisions of larger police departments, by those responsible for various diversion programs, by juvenile court intake personnel, and so on. Often, no records of contact are made. When they are, much of the so-called system remains uninformed about contacts initiated by other divisions. The police, for example, often make a determination of whether to intervene and of how to dispose of a case. Much previous research shows that they exercise unusually broad discretionary powers in their determination of whether the case merits intervention, the creation of a formal record of police contact, and any further processing. Equally important, such determinations are commonly based on the judgment of individual officers rather than any one official departmental or system policy. The consequences of such individualized discretionary powers include blatant forms of discrimination and abuse. Such problems are subject to correction through explicit rules and policies that can be made and enforced by administrative officials.

Third, many of the negative consequences of formal intervention and processing are as much a reflection of the method of processing as of processing per se. Specifically, juveniles who find themselves processed by officials—not only police but also judges and probation officers—whose decisions reflect little more than personal preferences are likely to view those officials and the system they represent as arbitrary, capricious, and unfair. This, in turn, can easily foster the feeling that one is the victim of the system rather than the realization that one has violated a rule and is being justly handled for having done so. Thus, our third general recommendation is that immediate attention be given to the negative impact that ill-conceived efforts at "individualized justice" can have on the subsequent attitudes, values, and behavior of those processed through the system.

Ironically, these general remedies have more to do with changing the system than with changing offenders. The system, after all, is a system in name only. A real system would include rationally interrelated and interdependent parts structured and restructured in the service of agreed-on system goals. A real organizational system, when applied to the processing of people, must have carefully articulated goals, a systematic means of determining which policies and programs serve those goals, official regulations that ensure that those being processed will be treated equitably and fairly, and so on.

There is some validity to the philosophical view that one should change what can be changed, accept what cannot, and hope for the wisdom to know the difference between the two. For progress toward a "system of justice" to be made, the juvenile justice system requires hope, desires wisdom, and demands change.

DISCUSSION QUESTIONS

1. How has the state become more powerful and the family less powerful as a socializing force?
2. What is the major contradiction in the juvenile justice system?
3. Why is legislation regarding juvenile justice usually one-sided?
4. What do alarmists feel about deterrence?
5. Why do authorities focus on the status offenses of girls?
6. How do alarmists feel about the age of accountability?
7. What are some merits and drawbacks of community-control programs?
8. How has the principle of "family autonomy" affected the position of youths in society?
9. What are the social policy implications for implementing a "bill of rights" for children?
10. What are the three general remedies proposed by the authors?

REFERENCES

ANDREWS, R. HALE, AND ANDREW H. COHN

1977 PINS processing in New York: An evaluation. Pp. 45–113 in Lee E. Teitelbaum and Aidan R. Gough (eds.), *Beyond Control: Status Offenders in the Juvenile Court.* Cambridge, Mass.: Ballinger.

ARTHUR, LINDSAY

1977a Status offenders need a court of last resort. *Boston University Law Review* 57:631–644.

1977b Should status offenders go to court? Pp. 235–247 in Lee E. Teitelbaum and Aidan R. Gough (eds.), *Beyond Control: Status Offenders in Juvenile Court.* Cambridge, Mass.: Ballinger.

BAUMRIND, DIANA

1978 Reciprocal rights and responsibilities in parent-child relations. *Journal of Social Issues* 34:179–196.

BLACK, T. EDWIN, AND CHARLES P. SMITH

1981 *A Preliminary Assessment of the Numbers and Characteristics of Juveniles Processed in the Juvenile Justice System.* Washington, D.C.: U.S. Government Printing Office.

BOLI-BENNETT, JOHN, AND JOHN W. MEYER

1978 The ideology of childhood and the state: Rules distinguishing children in national constitutions, 1870–1979. *American Sociological Review* 43:797–812.

CHESNEY-LIND, MEDA

1977 Judicial paternalism and the female status offender: Training women to know their place. *Crime and Delinquency* 23:121–130.

CLARKE, STEVENS H.

1975 Some implications for North Carolina of recent research in juvenile delinquency. *Journal of Research in Crime and Delinquency* 12:51–60.

ERICKSON, MAYNARD L., AND JACK P. GIBBS

1980 Punishment, deterrence, and juvenile justice. Pp. 183–202 in David Shichor and Delos H. Kelly (eds.), *Critical Issues in Juvenile Delinquency.* Lexington, Mass.: Lexington.

FOSTER, HENRY H., JR., AND DORIS J. FREED

1972 A bill of rights for children. *Family Law Quarterly* 6:343–375.

GOLDSTEIN, JOSEPH, ET AL.

1979 *Beyond the Best Interests of the Child.* New York: Free Press.

GOTTFREDSON, MICHAEL R.

1982 The social scientist and rehabilitative crime policy. *Criminology* 20:29–42.

HIRSCHI, TRAVIS

1969 *Causes of Delinquency.* Berkeley: University of California Press.

HOLT, JOHN

1974 *Escape from Childhood: The Needs and Rights of Children.* New York: Dutton.

INSTITUTE OF JUDICIAL ADMINISTRATION/AMERICAN BAR ASSOCIATION JOINT COMMISSION ON JUVENILE JUSTICE STANDARDS

1977a *Standards Relating to Abuse and Neglect.* Cambridge, Mass.: Ballinger.

1977b *Standards Relating to Dispositions.* Cambridge, Mass.: Ballinger.

1977c *Standards Relating to Noncriminal Misbehavior.* Cambridge, Mass.: Ballinger.

1977d *Standards Relating to the Rights of Minors.* Cambridge, Mass.: Ballinger.

KATZ, AL, AND LEE E. TEITELBAUM
1977 PINS jurisdiction, the vagueness doctrine, and the rule of law. Pp. 201–234 in Lee E. Teitelbaum and Aidan R. Gough (eds.), *Beyond Control: Status Offenders in the Juvenile Court*. Cambridge, Mass.: Ballinger.

KATZ, SANFORD N., ET AL.
1973 Emancipating our children: Coming of legal age in America. *Family Law Quarterly* 7:211–241.

KETCHAM, ORAM W.
1977 Why jurisdiction over status offenders should be eliminated from juvenile courts. *Boston University Law Review* 57:645–662.

KORBRIN, SOLOMON, AND MALCOLM W. KLEIN
1982 *National Evaluation of the De-institutionalization of Status Offender Programs—Executive Summary*. Los Angeles: University of Southern California, Social Science Research Institute.

KORNHAUSER, RUTH
1978 *Social Sources of Delinquency*. Chicago: University of Chicago Press.

KOZOL, JONATHAN
1967 *Death at an Early Age*. New York: Bantam.

KRISBERG, BARRY, AND JAMES AUSTIN
1978 *The Children of Ishmael: Critical Perspectives on Juvenile Justice*. Palo Alto, Calif.: Mayfield.

KRISBERG, BARRY, AND IRA SCHWARTZ
1982 Rethinking juvenile justice. Paper prepared for the Hubert H. Humphrey Institute of Public Affairs, University of Minnesota.

LIAZOS, ALEXANDER
1974 Class oppression: The functions of juvenile justice. *Insurgent Sociologist* 5:2–24.

MACK, JULIAN W.
1909 The juvenile court. *Harvard Law Review* 23:104–122.

MAHONEY, ANNE R.
1977 PINS and parents. Pp. 161–177 in Lee E. Teitelbaum and Aidan R. Gough (eds.), *Beyond Control: Status Offenders in the Juvenile Court*. Cambridge, Mass.: Ballinger.

MARRIS, PETER, AND MARTIN REIN
1973 *Dilemmas of Social Reform*, 2nd ed. New York: Aldine.

NATIONAL ADVISORY COMMISSION ON CRIMINAL JUSTICE STANDARDS AND GOALS
1976 *Juvenile Justice and Delinquency Prevention: A Report of the Task Force on Juvenile Justice and Delinquency Prevention*. Washington, D.C.: U.S. Government Printing Office.

PAULSEN, MONRAD G.
1979 Current reforms and the legal status of children. Pp. 211–233 in LaMar T. Empey (ed.), *The Future of Childhood and Juvenile Justice*. Charlottesville, Va.: University of Virginia Press.

PLATT, ANTHONY
1969 *The Child Savers*. Chicago: University of Chicago Press.

PRESIDENT'S COMMISSION ON LAW ENFORCEMENT AND ADMINISTRATION OF JUSTICE
1967 *Task Force Report: Juvenile Delinquency and Youth Crime*. Washington, D.C.: U.S. Government Printing Office.

SHORT, JAMES F., JR.
1979 Social contexts of child rights and delinquency. Pp. 175–210 in LaMar T. Empey (ed.), *The Future of Childhood and Juvenile Justice*. Charlottesville, Va.: University of Virginia Press.

SNYDER, HOWARD N., AND JOHN L. HUTZLER

1981 *The Serious Juvenile Offender: The Scope of the Problem and the Response of Juvenile Courts.* Pittsburgh, Pa.: National Center for Juvenile Justice.

SUSSMAN, ALAN

1977 Sex-based discrimination and PINS jurisdiction. Pp. 179–199 in Lee E. Teitelbaum and Aidan R. Gough (eds.), *Beyond Control: Status Offenders in the Juvenile Court.* Cambridge, Mass.: Ballinger.

THOMAS, CHARLES W.

1976 Are status offenders really so different?: A comparative and longitudinal assessment. *Crime and Delinquency* 22:438–455.

TIME

1977 The youth crime plague (July 11):18–28.

TOBY, JACKSON

1957 Social disorganization and stake in conformity. *Journal of Criminal Law, Criminology, and Police Science* 48:12–17.

VAN DEN HAAG, ERNEST

1975 *Punishing Criminals.* New York: Basic.

WALD, PATRICIA M.

1974 Making sense out of the rights of youth. *Human Rights* 4:13–29.

WEIS, JOSEPH G.

1979 *Jurisdiction and the Elusive Status Offender: A Comparison of Involvement in Delinquent Behavior and Status Offenses.* Washington, D.C.: U.S. Government Printing Office.

WILSON, JAMES Q.

1975 *Thinking About Crime.* New York: Basic.

WORSFOLD, VICTOR L.

1974 A philosophical justification of children's rights. *Harvard Educational Review* 44:142–157.

STATUTES AND CODES

Washington Revised Code Ann. 13.04 et seq. (1979)

Glossary

abandonment leaving infants alone to die or selling them into slavery or prostitution
adjudication hearing a fact-finding hearing to determine whether the child has committed the offense he or she is accused of
adversary system court system featuring a fight or contest between opposing sides, the defense and the prosecution
aftercare (juvenile parole) release from training school accompanied by periodic supervision by the juvenile court
alienation feeling that one is an isolated outsider, not a part of the group or community
anomie a breakdown of societal rules caused by an imbalance between cultural goals and socially accepted means of attaining these goals
atavism regression to an earlier stage of evolution
attachment the extent to which a person cares about other people
authoritarianism psychological term referring to an uncritical attitude toward authority, a tendency to condemn people who violate conventional norms, and an exaggerated emphasis on toughness

baby boom rapid upswing in the U.S. birth rate that occurred between 1946 and 1964
burglary breaking and entering a structure to commit a theft or other crime

chromosomes small structures found in all cell nuclei that contain DNA and transmit genes
citizen mobilization police intervention in a situation only after having been called by a citizen
classical school philosophical school of thought that sees people as rational and intelligent and sees delinquency as a choice based on free will

clique a small group of intimate friends
coercion domination and control by force
cohort a group of people who have gone through the same experience at the same time (for example, a birth cohort)
commitment a person's dedication to conventional types of activity (such as work or education)
community-based corrections place where inmates are housed part of the time, otherwise being allowed to leave for school or work
concern about crime belief that crime is more serious than other problems
concordance phenomenon in twins where both display the same behavior (for example, delinquency); opposite of *discordance*
concrete fear worry that one will be the victim of a particular kind of crime, such as rape
conflict subculture delinquent subculture that offers neither legitimate nor illegitimate opportunities to succeed; emphasis is on gaining a reputation through violence
corrections prisons, penitentiaries, training schools, reformatories, and the personnel and policies connected with them
correlation extent to which two variables are related
court intake screening cases to determine if they ought to be taken before the juvenile court for a hearing
crime behavior that violates the criminal law and is punishable by the state
crime index offenses homicide, forcible rape, aggravated assault, robbery, burglary, motor vehicle theft, larceny-theft, and arson
crime peaks offenses that are notably common among people of a particular age
crime rate number of offenses committed per 100,000 people per year
criminal justice system police, courts and correctional system
criminal subculture delinquent subculture that offers illegitimate opportunities to succeed; the emphasis is on money-making activities
culture conflict disagreement among people in the same society on which norms, values, and beliefs are important and correct
cultural transmission older people passing on their values, beliefs, and practices (some of which may be illegal) to younger people in the same neighborhood
cult of domesticity a mid-nineteenth-century sex-role doctrine that proclaimed home as the woman's sphere and the outside work world as the man's
custodial approach warehousing inmates and emphasizing security rather than rehabilitation
custody under arrest; in this condition, one may be taken to juvenile hall for processing

dark figure of crime gap between the number of offenses that occur and the number that end up in official records
decriminalization taking an offense off the books and making it no longer illegal
deinstitutionalization removing juveniles from jails and reformatories
delinquency behavior that violates laws pertaining to minors; many but not all of these behaviors are also crimes
delinquent a person who commits delinquent acts (whether caught or not)
demonological theory early theory that tried to blame crime and other events on invisible spirits
dependency situation in which, because of some handicap, parents cannot take care of their children properly
desensitization being exposed to a phenomenon, such as violence, long enough to dull one's senses and feelings about it

detention center place where youths are held temporarily, pending a hearing by the court

determinism belief that people, instead of having free will, are subject to the influence of various social forces over which they have little or no control

deviant behavior crime, suicide, mental disorder, and other behaviors that violate important social norms

differential association theory that delinquency is learned from associating with close friends and family who generally endorse lawbreaking

discretion making decisions without regard for written rules or procedures

disposition hearing hearing in which the child is sentenced

distancing belief belief that allows people living in a high-crime area to feel safe and unthreatened

diversion keeping a juvenile away from the juvenile court and its formal processing

drift a condition in which a youngster feels no commitment either to conventional rules or to delinquency

driving under the influence driving while drunk or under the influence of drugs

due process basic rights of the accused such as notice of charges, right to confront accusers, privilege against self-incrimination, and so on

ecological studies studies that map out the rates of a phenomenon such as delinquency to show how it is distributed throughout a city or region

ectomorph lean and fragile body type

ego Freud's term for the rational part of the personality, the part that must deal with the conflicting demands of id and superego

endomorph round, fat body with short arms and legs

ethnic group a group with the same language, religion, food and music tastes, and so on, such as Haitians

ethnocentrism judging people in other cultures by the standards of our own

evaluative research research designed to find out whether a program has reached the appropriate population, whether it delivered the needed services, and whether it had the intended impact

feeblemindedness mentality far below average; as a rule, this is indicated by an IQ score consistently below 70

forcible rape sexual intercourse with a woman against her will, using force

formless fear a feeling that one is somehow not safe in one's environment

functional illiterate person unable to handle simple tasks such as counting change or reading a want ad

functionalism a way of thinking that emphasizes the interrelation of parts and how each part contributes to the smooth functioning of the whole

general deterrence a justification for punishment; one person is punished in order to strike fear in the hearts of others so that they will not commit the same offense

grand jury a group of persons who must decide whether a suspect should be indicted and held over for trial

hedonism pursuit of pleasure

hyperactivity a condition including short attention span, fidgeting, restlessness, and impulsiveness

id Freud's term for the innate part of the personality dominated by the drive for pleasure and by inborn sexual and aggressive impulses

ignorance not knowing that an offense took place and someone in one's family was the victim
incapacitation a justification for punishment that argues that while a person is locked up, he or she cannot commit any crimes against the society outside
incarceration locking someone up in prison
incorrigibility condition in which the child is beyond the parents' control; also known as *ungovernability*
indeterminate sentence confinement for an unspecified period of time; the decision when to release the person is made after the person has served part of the sentence
infanticide the practice of killing infants at birth or shortly thereafter
informal adjustment handling a juvenile case without ever bringing it to the attention of the court
inmate subculture norms, values, and beliefs that unite inmates against the corrections' staff and policies
innovation striving to reach the cultural goals while not caring if one breaks the rules in doing so

jurisdiction the authority of the court to deal with a particular case
juvenile justice system police, courts, and corrections that deal with juveniles
juvenile status offense behavior for which a minor can be arrested but an adult cannot; examples include running away from home, truancy, and incorrigibility

larceny theft without force, fraud, or violence
latent function contribution of a part to the smooth functioning of the overall system, though it was never planned or intended to work this way
limbic system part of the lower brain that plays an important role in emotional and aggressive behavior
liquor laws liquor violations other than drunkenness and driving under the influence

malice spite or meanness
matriarchy family in which the power belongs to women
memory decay knowing that an offense took place but forgetting about it when asked during a survey
mesomorph muscular, athletic body type
"monster myth" the belief that 5 to 10 percent of youths are repeatedly committing especially violent and vicious offenses
moral entrepreneurs people who seek to have laws passed to outlaw behaviors that they find heinous and repulsive
mugging assault with intent to rob

negativistic a term used to describe the delinquent subculture, because people in this subculture define as right whatever the "straight" culture says is wrong
neglect condition in which parents are able to take care of their children but fail to
nonutilitarian useless, not producing a direct benefit
norm rule that may be written or unwritten

offenses against family offenses that include violations such as nonsupport, neglect, abuse and desertion
official data data collected by officials such as police or courts
omnibus clause part of the early delinquency laws that served as a "catch-all" phrase to include any remotely delinquent behaviors that the more specific wording may have omitted

open classroom school setting in which children are encouraged to move around freely and study whatever interests them
opportunity costs curtailing one's normal activities due to one's fear of crime

parens patriae doctrine giving the state broad parentlike powers over the life of a child
paternalism governing people (perhaps benignly) without giving them a chance to make decisions regarding their own interests
petition a statement of the offense the child is accused of committing
plea bargaining bargaining in which defense and prosecution agree on a trade: defendant pleads guilty in return for (usually) a lesser sentence
police mobilization police intervene in a situation without any citizen first calling for them
positivist relying on scientific methods such as observation and experimentation
primary deviance deviance that a person engages in now and then and that others generally tolerate or overlook
probation sentence in which the person is not locked up but instead remains in the community with the obligation to report to a probation officer periodically
Progressives turn-of-the-century reformers who gave special attention to children; they urged the creation of child-labor laws, compulsory education, and the juvenile court
psychoanalysis a theory of personality and a method of therapy that focus on repressed desires and bringing them out of the unconscious
psychopath a person who is calm, unpredictable, impulsive, and capable of acting warm, friendly, and genuine; psychopaths are prone to committing impulsive crimes where the risks are high and the gains are small
public opinion prevailing attitudes of the citizenry on an issue of wide interest
punishment institutionalized cruelty; painful treatment approved of by society for people who are said to have violated important rules

recidivism repeated participation in crime or delinquency
referral sending a youth to an agency in the community
rehabilitation a justification for punishment that implies that therapy will restore the person to a useful and healthy life
reliability in research methodology, the extent to which different studies produce the same results
replication repeating a research study to see if the same results will emerge a second time
restitution compensating the victim for the damages or losses one has caused
retreatist subculture subculture in which youths abandon cultural goals and withdraw from society; they tend to turn to drugs
retribution justification for punishment according to which punishment should be given to the offender simply because he or she deserves it
retrospective interpretation giving a person a label, then viewing him or her in a new light because of the label
revocation removing a person from parole or probation because of some violation, then giving the person a more severe punishment
robbery using force or threats to take money or valuables away from someone

scapegoating blaming some problem on an innocent person or group
secondary deviance deviance that becomes part of a deviant role; one way a person may react when society reacts negatively to his or her primary deviance

self-report study study that asks a general sample of the population what offenses they have committed and how often

sexual adventurer a nonvirgin who seeks many different sex partners and who has no interest in a continuing relationship with only one person

situation-compliant choosing what to do in a particular situation on the basis of whether one likes the activity, not whether friends or parents approve or disapprove of it

social disorganization confusion resulting from the concentration (in one part of the city) of people with different languages, work experiences, and expectations

socialization lifelong process of learning who one is, how to fit into the culture and various subgroups, and what is expected as one moves from one role to another

social problem social condition that is regarded as undesirable and in need of correcting

social promotion school promotion to the next grade in order to remain with one's friends and agemates although one has not earned the promotion academically

solidarity extent to which members of a group know, like, and support each other

special deterrence justification for punishment according to which a person should be punished in order to strike fear in that person's heart so he or she will not commit the offense again

stereotyping taking a single cue and basing a sweeping generalization on it, perhaps to characterize an entire group

stigmatize to brand or label in a very negative way

subculture language, values, beliefs, and norms that are different from and opposed to those of the larger culture

survey research questionnaire or interview

technique of neutralization a way to justify behavior that is delinquent while still holding on to nondelinquent norms and values

therapeutic approach generally, counseling by a trained psychologist; opposite of the *custodial approach*

total institution an organization where batches of inmates are herded together and closely regulated by a central authority

tracking assigning students to a particular level of difficulty in school; the highest level or track is usually called college-preparatory

turf gang a gang that identifies strongly with a particular territory or neighborhood and may use violence to defend it

Uniform Crime Reports annual summaries of offense and arrest data compiled from reports filed with the FBI by local police departments

unobtrusive observation research method in which the people being studied are unaware of the fact

unresponsive bystander citizen who sees or hears an apparent crime in progress but does nothing about it

validity accuracy of measurement

vandalism malicious destruction of property

variable a trait or characteristic that takes on different values; for example, the variable *age* has values such as teenage, young adulthood, and middle age

vice deviant behavior (such as use of marijuana) regarded by some people as immoral and by others as enjoyable

victimization survey survey of the general population to determine how many have experienced various crimes recently

Name Index

Abbott, Edith, 64
Abramson, Jacob, 91
Adler, Freda, 37, 137–138
Ageton, Suzanne S., 75, 77
Albrecht, Gary, 208
Allen, Francis, 241
Aries, Philippe, 233
Aronson, Elliot, 215

Baker, Harvey H., 235
Baron, Roger, 326
Bartollas, Clemens, 342–343
Beccaria, Cesare, 150
Becker, Howard S., 198, 212–213, 218, 340
Belden, Evelina, 238
Bell, Daniel, 10
Bengston, Vern L., 130
Berk, Bernard B., 340, 341
Berk, Richard A., 38
Berkowitz, Leonard, 160–161, 164
Berlage, Gai Ingham, 138
Biderman, Albert D., 44
Binder, Arnold, 323, 325
Black, Donald J., 34, 254
Blackmun, Harry, 244, 245
Blake, Gerald F., 324
Blau, Peter, 148
Blyth, Dale A., 129
Bohannon, Paul, 36
Boland, Barbara, 25
Bosarge, Betty B., 326
Bowerman, Charles E., 128
Brace, Charles Loring, 72, 233
Breckenridge, Sophonisba P., 64
Brennan, William, 244
Brittain, Clay V., 128
Bronfenbrenner, Urie, 65, 124
Bronner, Augusta J., 131
Brown, B. Bradford, 129
Brown, Lawrence, 239–240
Brown, Peewee, 57–58
Brown, S.W., 66
Brown, Waln K., 133
Bundy, Ted, 158, 164
Burgess, Ernest, 171–172

Canter, Rachelle J., 136, 205
Caplow, Theodore, 58
Capone, Al, 159
Carpenter, Mary, 233
Cernkovich, Stephen A., 137
Cicourel, Aaron V., 100
Cleckley, Harvey, 157, 164
Cloward, Richard, 186–189, 190
Cohen, Albert, 183–186, 190, 338
Cohen, Bernard, 325
Cohen, Jere, 128
Cohen, Stanley, 48
Cole, Phillip Z., 323
Coleman, James S., 104, 107, 124–126, 130, 139
Coleman, John C., 127
Conger, Rand D., 206
Conklin, John, 16–17
Conrad, John P., 21
Copperman, Paul, 96, 97, 98, 103
Couzens, Michael, 347
Covinginton, Jeanette, 126–127
Cressey, Donald R., 150, 177, 306, 321, 340
Crouse, Mary Ann, 231–232

Dalgard, Odd S., 153
Dalton, Katharina, 155
Darwin, Charles, 151
Datesman, Susan K., 136
Davis, F. James, 48
DeCiantis, 245
Demara, Ferdinand Waldo, 157–158
DeMause, Lloyd, 6
Dinitz, Simon, 21
DiVito, Ettore R., 323
Dollard, John, 160
Douglas, William, 245
Durkheim, Emile, 10, 16, 36
Duxbury, Elaine, 326

Eliot, Thomas, 237
Elliott, Delbert S., 75, 77, 307
Empey, Lamar T., 123, 325
Ennis, Philip H., 12
Erickson, Maynard L., 131
Ericson, Richard, 346
Estrick, Susan, 43
Eve, Raymond, 136

Feeney, Floyd, 326
Feld, Barry C., 342
Ferster, Elyce Z., 266
Fogelman, K.R., 128
Fortas, Abe, 241, 242, 243, 244, 261
Fox, Sanford, 232, 238
Freud, Anna, 129
Friedan, Betty, 59
Friedberg, Ardy, 40, 51
Furstenberg, Frank F., Jr., 39, 40, 51

Gault, Gerald, 242, 243
Geer, Blanche B., 340
Genovese, Kitty, 16
Gerbner, George, 49
Gibbons, Don C., 178, 324
Giordano, Peggy C., 137
Glueck, Eleanor, 66, 152
Glueck, Sheldon, 66, 152
Goddard, Henry, 156, 163
Gold, Martin, 136
Goodlad, John I., 94
Goring, Charles, 151
Graber, Doris A., 49, 51
Greenberg, David, 98–99, 105, 108
Gross, M.B., 159–160

Hacker, Andrew, 59
Hackler, James C., 206
Hall, G. Stanley, 120, 139
Harper, William Rainey, 169–170
Hart, John L., 230
Hawkins, Gordon, 324
Healy, William, 64, 131
Hechinger, Fred M., 89
Hechinger, Grace, 89
Hetherington, E. Mavis, 63
Higgins, Paul C., 208
Hill, C. Russell, 66, 67
Hill, John P., 128
Hill, Robert, 67
Hindelang, Michael J., 40, 74, 77, 131, 136, 205
Hirschi, Travis, 66, 103, 106, 108, 203–205, 206, 207, 208, 217
Hollingshead, August B., 122
Holt, John, 96, 384
Hoover, J. Edgar, 11
Hughes, Michael, 49
Hurley, Timothy, 235

Jacklin, Carol, 154
Jackson, Bruce, 176
James, Jennifer, 138
Jenkins, Richard, 160, 164
Jennings, M. Kent, 130
Jensen, Gary F., 131, 136
Johnson, Lyndon, 7, 62, 89
Johnstone, John W.C., 134
Jurow, George L., 46

Kandel, Denise B., 128, 129, 179
Karman, Andrew, 48
Kassebaum, Gene, 347
Kelly, Delos, 100, 101, 105
Kelly, Joan Berlin, 63, 64
Kenney, John P., 306
Kent, Morris A., Jr., 261
Kinch, John W., 128
Kitsuse, John I., 100
Kittrie, Nicholas N., 277
Klein, Malcolm W., 133, 135, 320, 324, 325, 326
Kobetz, Richard W., 326
Kobrin, Solomon, 308, 351–352
Konopka, Gisela, 135–137, 140
Korn, Richard R., 131
Kozol, Jonathan, 96
Kringlen, Einar, 153

Landy, David, 215
Larson, Lyle E., 129
Lemert, Edwin, 210–211, 217
Lerman, Paul, 130, 240
Lesser, Gerald R., 129
Levin, Mark M., 266
Lincoln, Suzanne B., 324, 326
Lindsey, Edward, 239
Lombroso, Cesare, 150–151, 163
Lotz, Roy, 35, 46
Lubeck, Steven G., 325
Lykken, David T., 158–159, 164

Mack, Julian, 238
Maccoby, Eleanor, 154
Maeroff, Gene I., 91, 95
Martinson, Robert M., 24, 45, 348
Marx, Karl, 201
Matza, David, 202–203, 217
McCorkle, Lloyd W., 131
McDermott, Robert A., 306, 321
McDonough, Josefina Figueira, 136
McKay, Henry D., 72, 170–177, 198
Mead, George Herbert, 170
Mead, Margaret, 120–121
Merton, Robert K., 182–183, 189
Miller, Walter, 8, 131, 132, 138, 179–181, 189, 346
Moberg, David O., 346
Morris, Norval, 324
Mott, Paul, 344
Moynihan, Daniel Patrick, 62, 66, 67
Murphy, Suzanne, 135

Neill, A.S., 96
Nejelski, Paul, 321, 325
Nelson, E. Kim, 350–351
Niemi, Richard G., 130
Nye, F. Ivan, 73, 77, 200–201, 205, 208, 217

Offer, Daniel, 127–128
Ohlin, Lloyd, 186–189, 190

Pappenfort, Donnel M., 272
Park, Robert, 170
Patterson, Gerald R., 68, 69, 76
Pink, William T., 324
Pitchess, Peter J., 325
Polier, Justine Wise, 240, 241
Polk, Kenneth, 106, 308

Poole, Eric D., 216
Pursuit, Dan G., 306

Rainwater, Lee, 186
Redl, Fritz, 161–162, 164
Regoli, Robert M., 46, 216
Reiss, Albert J., Jr., 34, 254
Rice, F. Philip, 7
Riege, Mary Gray, 66
Riesman, David, 123–124, 129
Rivers, William L., 50
Robinson, James, 348
Rockefeller, John D., 169–170
Rodman, Hyman, 18, 186
Romig, Dennis A., 348, 349
Roosevelt, Theodore, 48
Rose, Vicki, 45
Roshier, Bob, 48
Rossi, Peter H., 38, 343
Roth, Loren H., 155
Rothman, David, 235
Roy, Prodipto, 66
Rutter, Michael, 128
Ryder, Norman B., 122
Ryerson, Ellen, 236

Sacco, Vincent F., 49
Sarri, Rosemary C., 266, 307, 340, 341
Scarpitti, Frank R., 136
Schafer, Walter, 100, 101
Schregardus, D.J., 323
Schur, Edwin, 213–215, 218
Schwartz, Richard, 215
Seidman, David, 347
Shah, Saleem A., 155
Shaw, Clifford R., 72, 170–177, 198
Sheldon, William, 152, 163
Sheley, Joseph F., 18
Shireman, Charles H., 348
Shoemaker, Donald J., 156
Short, James F., Jr., 130, 132, 133, 181, 188, 207
Silberman, Charles E., 18, 96
Simon, Rita, 138
Simons, Ronald L., 136
Skolnick, Jerome H., 43, 215
Smith, Gerald, 348
Sorensen, James L., 327
Sorenson, Robert, 71, 72, 76, 136
Speck, Richard, 154
Spock, Benjamin, 6, 123
Stafford, Frank P., 66
Stark, Rodney, L., 208
Steffens, Lincoln, 47
Stratton, John G., 325, 326
Street, David, 340, 341
Streib, Victor L., 254
Strodtbeck, Fred L., 133, 181, 207
Sumner, William Graham, 36
Sundeen, Richard A., Jr., 306
Sutherland, Edwin, 102, 150, 157, 177–179, 189, 198, 207

Tannenbaum, Frank, 208–210, 217
Teilmann, Kathie S., 320
Teresa, Vincent, 176
Terry, Robert M., 254
Thomson, Doug, 324
Thornton, William, 138
Thrasher, Frederic M., 133, 135
Tittle, Charles R., 74, 77
Toby, Jackson, 105, 107, 198–200, 216
Treger, Harvey, 324
Tuthill, (Judge) Richard, 23, 235

van den Haag, Ernest, 36, 375
Vinter, Robert D., 340, 341
Vorenberg, Elizabeth, 320, 322–323
Vorenberg, James, 320, 322–323

Wald, Patricia M., 384
Wallerstein, Judith S., 63, 64
Ward, David, 347
Wattenberg, William W., 160
Weaver, Timothy, 94
Weis, Joseph, 136, 380
Wheeler, Stanton B., 339
White, Mervin F., 324
Wiatrowski, Michael D., 106
Wilkinson, Karen, 64, 76
Williams, Walter, 343
Wilson, James Q., 9, 25, 148, 375
Wilson, W.E., 159–160
Wineman, David, 161–162, 164
Witkin, Herman A., 154
Wolfgang, Marvin, 106, 150
Wright, Erik Olin, 15, 16

Yablonsky, Lewis, 132
Yankelovich, Daniel, 61
Young, Jock, 48
Young, Thomas M., 272

Zald, Mayer N., 340

Subject Index

Adjudication hearing, 256–257
Adolescence, 119–121
  anomie in, 126–127
  biological, 119
  freedom of, 201
  historical, 121
  psychological, 120
  sociocultural, 120–121
Adolescent Society, The (Coleman), 124
Adolescent subculture, 130
Adoption studies, 153, 163
Adventurers, 70, 136
Aftercare, 281
Age mates, 123
Age of accountability, 376–378
Age segregation, 122–123, 124
Aggression
  definition of, 160–161
  theories of, 160–162, 164
Alarmist view
  of crime and delinquency, 7–28
  of juvenile justice reform, 375–376
Alienation, 186
Ambition, 204, 207
Anger, aggression and, 161
Anomie
  definition of, 126, 182
  theories of, 181–189, 204, 207
Arrest(s), 11, 134, 137
Arrestees, age of, 19–21
Arrest records, public access to, 283
Assailants, symbolic, 43
"Assault with a Deadly Weapon," 78–83
Atavism, theory of, 151
Attachment, as bond to society, 204, 205–207, 217
Autonomy
  group, 184
  in lower-class culture, 181
  peer group weakening of, 124
Avoidance techniques, 17

Baby-boom generation, 121–122, 123
Belief, as bond to society, 204, 205, 207, 217
Benign neglect, 305, 307
Biological theories, 150–155
  adoption studies, 153
  blood chemistry, 154–155
  body type, 152
  chromosomal abnormalities, 154
  positivism, 150–151
  twin studies, 152–153
Birth rate, decline in, 60–61
Black families, 62–63, 66–67
Blood chemistry, and deviance, 154–155
Body type, delinquency and, 152
Bonds to society, 203–205
  attachment, 204
  belief, 204, 205

Bonds to society (*cont.*)
commitment, 204
involvement, 204–205
Borderland of Criminal Justice, The (Allen), 241
Breed v. *Jones* (1975), 245, 248
Brothers in Crime, 171

California Youth Authority (CYA), 322, 325
Capital punishment, 36, 45–46
Career in delinquency, 78–83, 175, 191–193
Case-screening process, 255–256
Causes of Delinquency (Hirschi), 203
Certification as an adult, 259
Challenge of Crime in a Free Society, The, 240
Chicago Area Project, 352
Chicago School, 169–181
anomie perspective, 181–186, 189–190
cultural perspectives, 170–181, 189
origins of, 169–170, 179
"Chic Conwell," 177
Child abandonment, 70
Child abuse, 69
Children's Defense Fund, 271, 276
Children's rights, 382–384
Children Who Hate (Redl and Wineman), 161
"Child Savers, The," 287–299
Child-welfare institutions, 231–239
China, 187
CHINS (Children in Need of Supervision), 4
Chromosomal abnormalities, 154, 163
Classical school, 149–150, 163
Commitment, as bond to society, 204, 207, 217
Commonwealth v. *Fisher* (1905), 238–239
Community-control programs, 378
Community delinquency-prevention program, 346
Community involvement, 312, 351–352
Community-oriented correctional model, 337
Community youth boards, 319
Concordance, 153
Conditioning, 69
Confessions, 256
Conflict delinquent subculture, 188
Conflict theorists, 36
Conformity, 124, 128, 182
Consensus theorists, 36
Contextual perspective, 340–343
Control theory, 198–208, 216–217
bonds to society and, 203–205, 217, 219–225
drifting into delinquency and, 201–203
education and, 199
family and, 200–201, 217
focus of, 198
limitations of, 198
methodology of, 198
research on, 205–208
social disorganization and, 198–200
stake in conformity, 198–200, 377–378
subcultural theorists and, 201–203, 217
Correctional evaluation research, 343–349
focus of, 343–345
offender participation in, 347
organizational goals and, 344–345
organizational variables in, 344
recidivism, 345–347
reviews of, 347–349
tracking and, 344
Correctional facilities, 333–368. *See also* Correctional evaluation research; Detention; Institutionalization; Jail
alternatives to conventional, 349–353
community-oriented model of, 337
community participation with, 351–352
conceptual models of, 335–338
cottage system, 334
discipline-oriented model of, 335
"homespun" model of, 336–337
individual treatment model of, 335–336
inmate adaptation to, theories on, 338–343
isolation of, from community, 350–351
origins of, 333–334
primary function of, 345
problems with, 349–350
public school model of, 335
therapeutic community model of, 337
treatment vs. custody orientation of, 340–341
Counsel, right to, 243–244, 248, 256, 280–281
Court intake screening procedures, 255–256
Court records, public access to, 282
Courts. *See* Juvenile court dispositions; Juvenile court judges; Juvenile court jurisdiction; Juvenile court proceedings; Juvenile justice system
Crime. *See also* Fear of crime
age of arrestees, 19–21
causes of, 42–44, 49
definition of, 4
economic costs of, 15, 16
fear of, 38–42
illegal service, 75
mass media reporting on, 47–50
mobilizations against, 17
moral reasons for, 42
opportunity costs of, 14
positive function of, 16
predatory, 75
public disorder, 75
responsibility for, 17–22
solutions to, 22–26
status, 75
Crime and Community (Tannenbaum), 208
Crime Index offenses, 11
Crime rates

Crime rates (*cont.*)
public perception of, 38–42
research on, 10–17
views of, 7–10
Criminal class, 72
Criminal courts, 22–23, 24–25. *See also* Juvenile justice system; Waiver of jurisdiction
Criminal delinquent subculture, 186, 188
Crouse decision (1938), 238
Cuba, social control and deviance in, 174–175
Cultural conflicts, 173–175
Cultural transmission, 175
Custody decision, 264–265

Dangerous classes, 72, 233
Davis v. *Alaska* (1974), 284
Death penalty, 36
Decriminalization, 305
Delinquency
careers in, 78–83, 191–193
definition of, 4, 257
national interest in, 5–7
Delinquency rates
research on, 10–17
view of, 7–10
Delinquent Boys (Cohen), 183, 190
Delinquent subcultures, types of, 186, 188
Demonological view, 149, 163
Dependent child, 234
Deprivation perspective, 338–339
Descent of Man (Darwin), 151
Detention, 264–272. *See also* Institutionalization; Juvenile court dispositions
criteria, 265–267
definition of, 264
incidence of, 268
pretrial, 266–267
screening procedures, 264–265
time limitation, 267–268
Detention hearing, 266, 267
Determination of fitness, 259
Deterrence, 376
general vs. special, 24
Deviance, 212–213, 217–218
forces shaping, 349, 350
primary vs. secondary, 210–211
types of, 3–4
Differential association theory
criticism of, 178–179
peer attachment and, 206
principles of, 177–178
Discipline-oriented correctional model, 335
Discordance, 153
Discretion, definition of, 309. *See also* Police, discretionary power of
Dispositional hearing, 257
Dispositions. *See* Juvenile court dispositions; Police, discretionary power of
Distancing beliefs, 41–42
District of Columbia Court Reform and Criminal Procedure Act of 1970, 263
Diversion programs, 274, 305–331
candidates for, 307
cautions about, 316
conditions for, 308–309
court, alternatives, 316–319
and court effectiveness, 325–327
and court efficiency, 323–325
evaluation of, 320–323
meaning of, 306–307
police role in, 309–316
purpose of, 306, 307, 320
rationales for, 320
results of, 323–327
timing of, 307–308
Divorce, 63–68
Double jeopardy, right against, 245–246, 248
Drifting into delinquency, 201–203
Dropouts, school, 91, 98, 135
Drug use, 37, 42, 75, 129
Dualistic fallacy, 208
Due process and fairness standards, 241–244, 248, 261–263, 266

Ecological approaches, 170, 171
Ectomorphs, 152
Education. *See also* Schools
House of Refuge movement view on, 233
social control by, 199, 216
Ego development, 124, 162, 164
Endomorphs, 152
Enlightenment, 149, 163
"Europe's Dead-End Kids," 14–15
Ex parte Sharpe (1908), 239

Families with Service Needs, 379
Family arguments, characteristics of, 127–128
Family autonomy, principle of, 383
Family life, 57–87. *See also* Parent(s)
adolescent anomie and, 126–127
aggression and, 161
declining birth rate, 60–61
differential association theory and, 177
discipline and punishment in, 68–69
divorce and separation, 63–65, 67
hedonism and, 61–62
parental attachment, 71–72
peer group influence on, 123–124, 139
role changes in, 59–60
runaways, 160, 164
sacrifice and self-denial in, 61
single mothers, 63–65
social control by, 200–201, 217
in transition, 58–67
working mothers, 62–65
Fate, in lower-class culture, 180–181
Fearlessness, 158–159, 164
Fear of crime, 38–42
concrete, 41
formless, 40–41
psychological defenses against, 41–42
youth groups, 43
Feeblemindedness, 156–157, 163

Feeblemindedness: Its Causes and Consequences (Goddard), 156
Felonies, designated, 24
Female delinquency
  Adler's theory on, 137–138, 140
  broken homes and, 65
  incidence of, 136, 138–139
  Konopka's theory on, 135–137, 140
  offense patterns in, 136, 139
  peers and, 135–139
  Simon's theory on, 138, 140
Field research, 198
Fines, 279
Fortress mentality, 41
Frustration/aggression theory, 160–161, 164

Gangs, 127, 179–181
  cohesiveness of, 133
  conditions giving rise to, 134–135
  female, 135–139
  leadership in, 132
  meaning of, 131
  as near-group, 132
  opportunities for success and, 188
  organization in, 131–132
  peer groups and, 130–131
  purpose of, 133–134
  traits of, 131–134
  turf of, 132–133
In re Gault (1967), 4, 242–244, 246, 248, 261, 275
Generation gap, 127, 129, 130
Genetics, and crime, 152–153, 163
Gratification, deferral of, 61
"Great imposter, The," 157–158
Group autonomy, 184
Group delinquency. *See* Gangs

Hedonism, 61–62, 126, 129, 184
"Hellfire and Delinquency" (Hirschi and Stark), 208
Homemaking, 59–60
Homespun correctional model, 336–337
House of Refuge movement, 7, 231–233, 238, 281, 333
Hyperactivity, 159–160, 164

IJA/ABA Joint Commission on Juvenile Justice Standards, 246, 248
  on age of accountability, 377
  on detention, 265, 267–268
  on duration of dispositional orders, 275–276
Illiteracy, functional, 93
Importation perspective, 338–339
Imprisonment, pains of, 338, 339. *See also* Correctional facilities; Detention; Institutionalization; Jail
Impulsiveness, 158
Incapacitation, 24
Indenture, 334
Individual treatment correctional model, 335–336
Informal adjustment, 316–317
Inmate behavior adaptations, 338–343
  contextual perspective, 340–343
  deprivation perspective, 338–339
  importation perspective, 339–340
  research analyses on, 342–343
Inmate subcultures, 338–339, 341, 356–365
Innovators, 182
Institutionalization, 276–278. *See also* Detention; Jail
  alternatives to, 257, 271–272, 316–319
  costs of, 277
  harmful effects of, 276
  ineffective rehabilitation and, 276–277
  lack of guidelines, 276
  recidivism and, 277
  rights to treatment and, 277–278
Intake screening procedures, 255–256, 273–274
Intelligence, low, 156–157, 163
Intelligence quotient (IQ), 102–104, 156–157, 164, 204
Involvement, as bond to society, 204–205, 207, 217

Jack Roller, The, 171, 176
Jail, 268–272. *See also* Detention; Institutionalization; Juvenile court dispositions
  age considerations, 268–269
  alternatives to, 271–272, 316–319
  harmful effects of, on youth, 269–271, 278
  medical and other basic necessities in, 271
  misuses of, 271, 272
  physical and sexual assaults in, 269–270
  psychological effects of, 270
  public opinion of, 36, 37–38, 46
  reform of, 37–38
  separation requirements, 269, 270
  statutory approaches to, 268–269
"Japan as Number One," 311
Judges. *See* Juvenile court judges
Judicious nonintervention, 305, 307
Jury trial, right to, 244–245, 248, 257, 281, 282
Juvenile court dispositions, 274–281. *See also* Detention; Institutionalization; Jails; Probation
  aftercare/parole, 281
  diversion alternatives, 316–319
  duration limitations, 280
  fines and restitution, 279

Juvenile court dispositions (*cont.*)
hearing, 257, 286
indeterminate sentencing, 242–246
lack of guidelines, 276
least restrictive alternative principle, 277–278
limitation on authority for, 275–276
number of, 275
revocation of, 280–281
Juvenile court judges, 235–236, 237
abuse of authority of, 283–284
Juvenile court jurisdiction, 257–264. *See also* Waiver of jurisdiction
definitions of, 258–259
limits of, 258
reform and rehabilitation, 257
Juvenile court proceedings
adjudication hearing, 256–257, 286
as adversary process, 287–289
constitutional rights of young people, 238–239, 241–247
dispositional decisions, 274–281
dispositional hearing, 257, 286
diversion alternatives, 316–319
indeterminate sentencing by, 242–246
informal adjustment, 316–317
intake screening procedures, 255–256, 273–274
media involvement in, 283–284
mediation, 316–319
petition filing, 255–256, 273–274
public access to, 282–285
waiver of jurisdiction, 238–239, 241–242, 259–264
Juvenile court records
confidentiality of, 283
destruction of, 284–285
sealing of, 284
Juvenile delinquent, definition of, 240
Juvenile justice system, 229–251, 253–302
access to court proceedings and records, 282–285, 286
bias in, 214, 215
as civil forum, 159, 234, 238, 247
community protection by, 241
contemporary history of, 239–246
contradictory roles of, 373–375
court hearings, 256–257, 286
court intake, 255–256, 273–274
detention, 264–272, 285
dispositions, 274–281, 286
diversion programs' impact on, 323–327
early history of, 231–239
failure of, 371–373
goal of, 243
jurisdiction, 257–264, 285
lack of centralized management of, 254
origins of, 23, 371–372
parens patriae doctrine, 231–233, 235, 238, 239, 241–242, 243, 246, 247–248
paternalism of, 235
philosophy of, 23–24, 373–375
police in, 254–255, 264–265, 285
probation officers, 234, 235–236, 237–238, 240
public opinion of, 35–36, 44, 47
reform of, 375–384
rehabilitation vs. institutionalization in, 236, 238–241, 247
structure and process of, 258–259

Kent v. *United States* (1966), 241–242, 246, 247
developments after, 263–264
impact of, 261–263
Klinefelter's syndrome, 154
Labeling theories, 208–216, 217–218
deviation, primary and secondary, 210–211
dramatization of evil, 208–210, 217
effects of, 215–216
focus of, 198
limitations of, 198
methodology of, 198
by moral entrepreneurs, 211–213, 218
negotiation, 214, 218
research on, 215–216
retrospective interpretation, 214, 218
school tracking and, 100–101
stereotyping and, 212, 213–214, 218
Latchkey children, 65
Law Enforcement and Administration of Justice, President's Commission on, 269–270, 276, 309, 319
Laws, delinquency, 4
Law violations
differential association theory of, 178
in lower-class culture, 181
Least restrictive alternative principle, 277–278
Legislative method of transfer, 263–264
Liberation-causes-crime hypotheses, 137–138
Lower-class
alienation in, 186
culture, 179–181, 189
in anomie theory, 182, 185
law violations in, 181
legitimate opportunities available to, 186, 188–190
middle-class values and, 186

Male delinquency, 131–135
Malicious behaviors, 184
"Manchild in the Promised Land," 356–365
Marriage, 59. *See also* Family life
Martinson report, 45

Mask of Sanity, The (Cleckley), 157
Mass media
  coverage of court proceedings, 283–284
  influence on public opinion on crime, 47–50
Maturational reform, 20, 202
In re McCloud (1971), 245
McKeiver v. *Pennsylvania* (1971), 244–245, 248
Mediation programs, 317–319
  advantages of, 317–319
  procedures, 318–319
  timing of, 317–318
Mesomorphy/delinquency relationship, 152, 163
"Middle-class measuring rod," 184–185, 190
Middle-class standards, 185
Minority(ies):
  black families, 62–63, 66–67
  as gang members, 134
MINS (Minors in Need of Supervision), 4
Miranda v. *Arizona* (1966), 256
Miranda warning, 256–257
Mobilizations
  collective vs. individual, 17
Monster myth, 14–15, 18
Moynihan Report, 62–63, 66–67
Moral entrepreneurs, 211–213
Moronity, 156
Motivational theories. *See* Chicago School

National Advisory Committee on Criminal Justice Standards and Goals, 307, 345, 379
National Assessment of Juvenile Corrections study, 270–271, 276
Natural History of a Delinquent Career, The, 171
Near-group, 132
Negativistic behavior, 184
Neglected child, 234
Negotiation, 214, 218
New York Juvenile Justice Reform Act of 1976, 24
Nonutilitarian behavior, 184

Oklahoma Publishing Co. v. *District Court* (1969), 284
Omnibus clause, 4
Oregon Social Learning Center, 68–69
Other Side, The (Becker), 212
Outsiders (Becker), 212

Parens patriae doctrine, 231–233, 235, 239, 241–242, 243, 246, 247–248, 258, 274, 276, 374
Parent(s). *See also* Family life
  adolescents' view of, 127–128, 139
  influence of, 128–129
  lower-class, 211
  social control by, 200–201
Parental attachment, 71–72
  social control and, 204, 205–206
Parental supervision
  control theory and, 204, 205
  measures of, 205
  and self-reported delinquency, 205, 206
Parenting skills, 68–69
Parole, 281
Peer(s), definition of, 123
Peer attachment
  differential association theory and, 206
  self-reported delinquency and, 206–207
Peer groups, 121–139
  adolescent subcultures and, 130
  age segregation in schools and, 122–123
  baby boom and, 121–122, 123
  differential association theory and, 177, 179
  drifting into delinquency and, 202–203
  drug use and, 129
  family life and, 123–124
  female delinquency and, 135–139, 140
  gangs and, 130–131
  girls and, 129
  influence of, vs. parental influence, 128–129
  lower-class youth and, 180
  male delinquency and, 131–135, 139–140
  rise in importance of, 121
Permissiveness, 42
Petition filing procedures, 255–256, 273–274
PINS (Persons in Need of Supervision), 4, 240, 256
Plea bargaining, 214
Police
  citizen cooperation with, 34–35
  discretionary powers of, 11, 254–255, 264–265, 309, 312–313. *See also* Police diversion programs
  juvenile justice system, role of, 254–255
  public opinion of, 35, 44
Police diversion programs, 309–316, 320–321
  alternatives for, 309
  community involvement with, 312
  community volunteers, 313–314
  cost of, 312, 324–325
  dispositional control and, 310, 312
  diversion without referral, 313
  evaluation of, 320–321
  external referral, 314–316
  internal referral (in-house), 313–314, 325–326
  probation, 314
  rationales for, 310–313, 321
  recidivism rates in, 324, 325–327
  recreation, 314
  response appropriateness and, 312
  response immediacy and, 312

Police diversion programs (*cont.*)
results of, 323–327
special needs of youth and, 310
types of, 313–316
Positivism, 150–151, 163
Poverty, equation of, with crime, 232, 334
Premenstrual syndrome, 155
Preponderance of evidence, 256
Pretrial detention, 266–267
Prevention techniques
in Cuba, 174–175
Prisons. *See* Jails
Probation, 23, 25, 278–279, 314
definition of, 278
goal of, 278
informal, 274
rationale behind, 278
restrictions on, 279
revocation of, 280–281
Probation hearing, right to, 280–281
Probation officers, 234–238
caseload volume of, 240–241, 278
petition filing by, 255–256
lack of training, 278
Progressive reformers, 6, 7, 22, 89, 233–234, 335
Prosecutor, authority of, 263–264
Prostitution, 136
Protective reaction hypothesis, 41
Provo experiment, 346
Psychological theories, 156–162
aggression, 160–162
fearlessness, 158–159
hyperactivity, 159–160
low intelligence, 156–157
psychopathy, 157–158
runaways, 160
Psychopathy, 157–158
Public opinion, 33–35
arousing, 36–37
on capital punishment, 45–46
of courts, 35–36, 44, 47
of crime rates, 39–42. *See also* Fear of crime
importance of, 34–39
laws and, 36
media influence on, 47–50
of police, 35, 44
of prisons, 36, 37–38, 46
on rehabilitation, 45
on responsibility for crime and delinquency, 42–44
on retribution, 45
and tolerance of deviance, 37
Public school correctional model, 335
Punishment
forms of, 25
justification of, 24
negative vs. positive, 69

Ragged Schools, 233
Reaction formation, 148, 185–186
Reasonable doubt vs. preponderance of evidence, 244, 248, 256
Reassuring view, 7–28
Rebellion, 183
Recidivism, 24, 26, 277
absolute vs. relative, 345–347
in diversion programs, 321, 324, 326–327
as evaluative criterion, 345–347
Referral problems, 315–316
acceptability, 315
accountability, 316
availability, 315–316
suitability, 315
Referral programs. *See* Diversion programs; Police diversion programs
Reformatory experience
nineteenth century, 233
school of crime, 209
Reformatory Schools for the Children of the Perishing and Dangerous Classes, and for Juvenile Offenders (Carpenter), 233
Rehabilitation, 22
goal of, 349
public opinion on, 45
vs. institutionalization, 236, 238–241, 247, 276–277
review of efforts, 348–349
Release on own recognizance, 305
Religion, 217
social control by, 201
Restitution, 279
Retreatism, 183, 188
Retribution, 24, 25, 45, 376
Retrospective interpretation, 214, 218
Ritualism, 182–183
Role changes, 201
Runaways, 64–65, 136, 160, 164

Schall v. *Martin* (1984), 266
School(s), 89–117
academic performance, 91–94, 104
age segregation by, 122–123, 353
attachment to society and, 204
decline in quality of, 90–95
flexible scheduling, 97
grade inflation in, 93
malpractice suits against, 93
open classrooms, 96–97
parental support of, 96
problematic assumptions about, 353
racial/ethnic factors in, 99
social promotion in, 93–94
student misbehavior and fear in, 90–91
teacher inadequacies in, 94–95
truancy and dropouts from, 91, 98
urban, 95
violence in, 90–91, 97, 98, 100, 104, 105
white flight from, 95
School dropouts, 91, 98, 135
Schools and delinquency, 96–103
IQ and, 102–103, 106–107
loss of teacher authority and, 96–98, 103–104
regimentation and revenge, 98, 105
research on, 103–107
tracking, 100–101, 105–106
Self-incrimination, right against, 242–243, 248, 256

Self-reported delinquency, 73, 136
 frequency of, 183
 parental supervision and, 205–206
 peer attachment and, 206–207
Self-report questionnaires, 198
Sentencing, 246
 determinate, 36
 indeterminate, 242, 281
Sex delinquency, 136, 140
Sexual behaviors, 71–72, 73
Short-term intervention, 274
Silverlake experiment, 346
"Situation compliant" individuals, 129
Social class, 72–75, 103
 elements of, 179–180
Social control
 direct, 200, 217
 family and, 200–201
 indirect 200–201, 217
 informal, 37
 internal, 200
 religion and, 201
Social disorganization, 173, 175
Social files, disclosure of, 283
Socialization, primary agents of, 204
Social-psychological approaches, 170, 171–172
"Social structure and anomie" (Merton), 182
Social Theory and Social Structure (Merton), 182
Society for the Prevention of Pauperism, 334
Soviet Union, 125–126
Spatial mobility, 201
Stake in conformity, 198–200, 377–378
Status offenses
 controversy over, 378–382
 definition of, 4
 incidence of, 380
Stereotyping, 212, 213–214, 218
Stigmatization, 238, 239–240, 243, 247, 283
Street crimes, 16
Subcultural theory, 202, 217
Subcultures:
 adolescent, 124–126, 130
 delinquent, 186, 188
 inmate, 338–339, 341
Suburbs, migration to, 123

Temperament, 152, 158–159
Theories
 characteristics of, 147–148
 criticism of, 148–149
Therapeutic community correctional model, 337
Toughness, in lower-class culture, 180
Tracking, 100–101, 344
Transfer of jurisdiction. *See* Waiver of jurisdiction
Treatment, right to, 278–279
Trial, right to, 244–245, 248, 257, 281, 282
Truancy, 64–65, 75, 91
Turf gangs, 132–133
Turner's syndrome, 154
Twin studies, 152–153, 163

Uniform Crime Reports (UCR), 10–13, 20, 126
Unobtrusive observation, 179
Urban schools, 95

Versatility, 184
Victimization surveys, 12, 13
View from the Bench, A (Polier), 241
Violent Schools—Safe Schools, 91, 104
Vulnerability hypothesis, 41

Waiver of jurisdiction, 22–23, 24–25, 259–264
 age of young person and, 262
 community protection and, 263
 District of Columbia Code guidelines, 261–262
 due process concerns of, 261–263
 effects of, on young people, 260
 impact of *Kent* v. *United States* on, 262–264
 legislative method of, 263–264
 limitation of juvenile facilities and, 263–264
 seriousness of alleged offense and, 262–263
White-collar crimes, 13, 15
"Why Freddy Got His Gun," 219–225
In re Winship (1970), 244
Women. *See also* Female delinquency
 lower-class families, 180
 single mothers, 63
 working, 62, 65–66
Working class, 75

Youth ghettos, schools as, 123
Youth-Service Bureaus (YSBs), 319

Zonal hypothesis, 171–175, 189

About the Authors

Roy Lotz is an associate professor of sociology at John Jay College of Criminal Justice in New York City. Born and raised in Illinois, he received his bachelor's degree from Carleton College (Minnesota) and his doctorate from the University of Washington. He has written primarily in the fields of crime and delinquency, but also in the sociology of sport, collective behavior, the sociology of religion, and research methods.

Eric D. Poole is an associate professor of sociology at Auburn University. Since receiving his Ph.D. from Washington State University in 1976, he has done studies of both the juvenile and criminal justice systems. Professor Poole currently serves as a consultant and affiliate to many professional associations and is a frequent contributor to scholarly journals.

Robert M. Regoli is an associate professor of sociology at the University of Colorado. He has written extensively on criminology and criminal justice and is presently an editor of the *Social Science Journal.* Professor Regoli is actively involved in the professional associations and will become the president of the Academy of Criminal Justice Sciences in 1986. Among the books he has authored or coauthored are *Police Administrative Issues, Criminal Justice in America: The Past Twenty-five Years, Research Methods and Statistics,* and *Police in America: A Study of Cynicism.* His current research continues to assess work relations and discretion among a variety of the participants in the criminal justice system.